THE MATHEMATICAL QUESTIONS PROPOSED IN DIARY AND THEIR ORIGINAL ANSWERS • VOLU LEYBOURN

Publisher's Note

The book descriptions we ask booksellers to display prominently warn that this is an historic book with numerous typos or missing text; it is not indexed or illustrated.

The book was created using optical character recognition software. The software is 99 percent accurate if the book is in good condition. However, we do understand that even one percent can be an annoying number of typos! And sometimes all or part of a page may be missing from our copy of the book. Or the paper may be so discolored from age that it is difficult to read. We apologize and gratefully acknowledge Google's assistance.

After we re-typeset and design a book, the page numbers change so the old index and table of contents no longer work. Therefore, we often remove them; otherwise, please ignore them.

Our books sell so few copies that you would have to pay hundreds of dollars to cover the cost of our proof reading and fixing the typos, missing text and index. Instead we let most customers download a free copy of the original typo-free scanned book. Simply enter the barcode number from the back cover of the paperback in the Free Book form at www.RareBooksClub.com. You may also qualify for a free trial membership in our book club to download up to four books for free. Simply enter the barcode number from the back cover onto the membership form on our home page. The book club entitles you to select from more than a million books at no additional charge. Simply enter the title or subject onto the search form to find the books.

If you have any questions, could you please be so kind as to consult our Frequently Asked Questions page at www.RareBooksClub.com/faqs.cfm? You are also welcome to contact us there. General Books LLC™, Memphis, USA, 2012.

❧ ❧ ❧ ❧ ❧ ❧ ❧ ❧

OA *Hi* MATHEMATICAL QUESTIONS, PROPOSED IN THE
LADIES' DIARY,
AND THEIR ORIGINAL ANSWERS,
TOGETHER WITH SOME NEW SOLUTIONS,
FROM ITS COMMENCEMENT IN THE TEA 1704 TO 1816.
IN FOUR VOLUMES.
BY THOMAS LEYBOURN,
OF THE ROYAL MILITARY COLLEGE.
VOL. I.
lUmtian:
PRINTED BY W. GLENDINNING, HATTON GARDEN;
AND
PUBLISHED BY J. MAWMAN, LUDGATE STREET
f. DEIGHTONAND SON, CAMBRIDGE; AND J. PARKER, OXFORD.
PREFACE.

The Ladies' Diary having been published annually, in the form of an Almanack, for more than a century past; it must, at all times, have been difficult, and, indeed, during the latter part of that period, next to impossible, to obtain a complete copy of the work. This circumstance induced the ingenious and learned gentleman that has superintended it for the last fortyfour years (Dr. Charles Hutton, Emeritus Professor of the Mathematics in the Royal Military Academy at Woolwich) to re-publish every thing either curious or valuable, that had appeared in it from its commencement to the year *1773,* at which period he became the Editor. Dr. Hutton's edition of the Diaries has, however, been out of print for many years, and is now seldom to be procured; and even if if could be had, forty-four more *Diaries* are now required to complete the work, so that the difficulty of obtaining a perfect set is as great as ever. .

On this account, and with a view to gratify such as are anxious to possess what may be considered as a curious, and valuable monument, of the Mathematical genius of the English nation, the Mathematical questions and their answers are here republished, but the a

Enigmas, Rebuses, and such other parts of the work, as have no reference to Mathematics are omitted.

In accomplishing this object, the Editor has availed himself of the labours of Dr. Hutton, by adopting, with his permission, the numerous valuable additions and improvements with which that gentleman had enriched his edition; and as to the sequel of the work, comprehending the questions and answers since the year 1773, he hopes that, with the aid of some ingenious friends, who have, for a number of years past, contributed to the *Mathematical Repository,* he has been able to render it, in some measure, not altogether unworthy of being incorporated with the labours of his learned predecessor....

Two changes have been made in the disposition of the work, which it is hoped will render it more Commodious to the reader. In the first place, each question is now immediately followed by its answer, instead of the questions and answers being separated from one another, as is the case in the original Work, as well as in Dr. Hutton's republication; and in the next place, such questions as had been proposed in the original Diaries in verse, which in almost every case was bad, and often hardly intelligible, are, generally speaking, changed into plain but perspicuous prose.

The importance of the work, as a collection of Practical Exercises in almost every branch of Mathematical learning, must be obvious, if we consider that it is the result of the joint labour of almost all the Mathematicians of eminence, that have appeared. 4n England in the course of the last century Of these, passing over such as are yet living, we shall only mention the names of Emerson, Landen, and Simpson, whose writings, and more especially those of the two last, have considerably extended the science, both of pure and mixt Mathematics, and are justly regarded as' among the most elegant examples of analytical investigation . The work may also be considered as exhibiting a view of the state of Mathematics in this country, and, on this account, must be valuable, as illustrative of the progress of the science in England, during the last century.

The beneficial influence which the Ladies' Diary, has exerted upon the state of Mathematical science in this country, has been long felt, and acknowledged, and has been particularly noticed by the writer of the very valuable analysis of the *Mecanique Celeste,* given in the *Edinburgh Review.* Speaking of the comparative state of Mathematical knowledge in England and on the Continent, he says: —" A certain degree of Mathe"matical science, and indeed no inconsiderable degree, "is perhaps more widely diffused in England than in "any other country in the world. The Ladies' Diary, w with several other periodical and popular publica"tions of the same kind, are the best proofs of this assertion. In these, many curious problems, not of "the highest order indeed, but still having a con"siderable degree of difficulty, and far beyond the "mere elements of science, are often to be met with: Dr. Maskelyne, the late Astronomer Royal, *h* known to have contributed occasionally, under feigned names, to the Diary.

tc And the great number of ingenious men who take a "share in proposing, and answering these questions, whom one has never heard of any where else, is not V a little surprising. Nothing of the same kind, we Llf believe, is to be found in any other country." Again— "The geometrical part has always been conducted in a "superior style; the Problems proposed have tended "to awaken curiosity, and the Solutions to convey "instruction, in a much better manner than is always "to be found in more splendid publications."—(See Edinburgh Rev. vol. xi. p. 282.),

The Diary was projected and begun in the year 1704 by Mr. John Tipper, who conducted it until 1713. It does not appear that the improvement of Mathematical Science, was a particular object with the ingenious projector: indeed the law, which the first contributors imposed on themselves, of not only proposing, but also of answering all questions in rhyme, was not favourable to the developement of Mathematical genius.

The superintendence of the work devolved in 1714, on Mr. Henry Beighton, F. R. S. who, as we learn from Dr. Hutton's valuable Mathematical Dictionary, was a respectable mathematician, and mechanist, and the most eminent civil engineer of his time. He conducted the work until his death, which happened in 1743 or 1744, and gave such satisfaction to the company of stationers, the proprietors of the work, that they permitted his widow to continue it, employing a deputy in the compilation.

The next Editor was Robert Heath, who managed the Diary from 1745 to 1753: He was a half-pay Captain of Invalids, and the editor of a similar periodical work, called the Palladium, as well as some other works now entirely forgot. He published several schemes for finding the longitude, and abused the Astronomer Royal, and Board of Longitude, because they did not think his productions worthy of notice. He unfortunately made the Diary a vehicle for low scurrility; and abused, under various signatures, and in different publications, all the Mathematical writers of that day, except Emerson, who is supposed to have assisted him in his speculations. In particular, he was virulent beyond all bounds against Mr. Thomas Simpson, towards whom, he appears to have entertained great rancour. He, however, in the end, had the worst of the controversy, for he was expelled from the editorship with disgrace, and succeeded by his rival.

Simpson conducted the work from 1754 to 170, and gave it that degree of respectability which it has ever since maintained. He wrote in it himself, under various signatures, such as *Hurlothrumbo, Kuhernetes, Patrick O'Cavanah, Anthony Shallow,* Esq. *Timothy Doodle, Marmaduke Hodgson,* and probably several others. During this period, his friend, Mr. Landen, occasionally contributed to the work. Simpson died in 1761, and in the same year, Mr. Edward Rollinson became the Editor, and continued until his death, in 1773. It has ever since been ertirely under the able direction of Dr. Charles Hutton.

Besides the nominal editors, others have, at different times, superintended this useful publication. In particular, it has been said, that in the latter years of Mr. Beighton's life, his friend, Mr. Ant. Thacker, who was more skilled in "Mathematics, relieved him from the labour of that department. bc X Ba expresses half the area of the rectangle Abcd, and Bh (bc+Ha) expresses the area of the space occupied by the walk; therefore the walk is half the garden, L.

The Editor would gladly have given some account, of the more distinguished contributors to the Diaries, and have ascribed to the real authors, the solutions they have contributed under feigned names; the information he has gleaned, however, has been so scanty, as to afford but little satisfaction on either of these points. As to biographical notices of English Mathematicians, he believes that all that can possibly be collected of any interest, has found a place in Dr. Hutton's Mathematical Dictionary. There are some writers alive, whose real names would have added dignity to the work, but these, without their consent, he could not take the liberty to insert. The names of such Authors as are dead, and have come to his knowledge, he has inserted in the general Index.

Of the Additional Solutions, which the Editor owes to the kindness of friends, the names of the contributors are put to a part, but not to the whole. He owes, in particular, to his colleagues, the following:

To Dr. Henry Clarke, the additional solution to quest, 206 (vol. i.), marked

M.

To Mr. John Lowry, the solutions to which the letters J. L. are annexed.

To Mr. James Cunliffe, those having the letter c.

To Mr. William Wallace, those having the letter w.

To Mr. Mark Noble, those having the letter N, also the first additional solution to question 51 (vol. i, page 52).

To questions which appeared to be interesting, he has given solutions at considerable length, from academical memoirs, also from the writings of foreign Mathematicians, with a view to the accommodation of mere English readers. Upon the whole, it has been his wish, to provide the Mathematical student with a valuable collection of examples, in every department of the science, to bring together and preserve the labours of many ingenious men, who, during the" period of a century, have rendered much service to society, by the practical application of the science in the circumscribed spheres, to which they have been confined, and lastly, to exhibit to the public a picture of the taste of the British nation, for the study of Mathematics, which has certainly more cultivators in this country, than is com-, monly supposed.

Royal Military College,
November 1817.

MATHEMATICAL QUESTIONS PROPOSED IN THE LADIES' Diary, AND THEIR ANSWERS. *Questions proposed in the Diaries for* i707-8, *and answered in those of* 1708-9.

It QUESTION 1.

In how long time would a million of millions of money be in counting, supposing one hundred pounds to be counted every minute without intermission, and the yearto consist of 365 days, 5 hours, 45 minutes?

Answer. 19013 years, 144 days, 5 hours, 55 minutes.
Solution.

The solution of this question is evidently thus: As 100 1.: 1 minute:: 10000000000 1.: 10000000000 minutes = 19013 years 144 days 5 hours 55 minutes, the true time required, H. 11.

Question 2.
If to my age there added be
One half, one third, and three times three;
Six score and ten the sum you'ld see,
Pray find out what my age may be.

Answer. 66 years.
Solution.
The meaning of the problem is, that the number 9 added to once his age, together with one half and one third of his age, the sum shall be 130; or since the sum of the parts 1, and f, and j is ", that V- of his age is $(130 - 9 =) 121$; consequently $11:6::121:66$ = his age. 11.

Algebraic Solution. Let 6a; represent the required age; then, by the question, $6x + 3x + 2x + 9$, that is $11x + 9 = 130$; therefore $x = 11$; consequently $6x = 66$, as before, L. All the solutions marked with the signature H, are by Dr. Hutton, and taken, with permission, from his edition of the Ladies' Diaries. VOL. J. A lit, QUESTION 3.

If thirteen tuns of claret cost nineteen pounds, how many pinti can be had for a thousand crowns?

Answer. 344842 T pints.
Solution.
As 19 1.: 26208 pints = 13 tuns:: 250 1. = 1000 crowns: 344842-rV pints, H. IV.

QUESTION 4.
If thirteen marks with fourteen groats will buy fifteen loads of hay, how many pounds together with sixteen crowns will pay for ninety loads?

Answer. 49 1. 8s.
Solution.
As 15 loads: 90 loads:: 1: 6:: 178s. 2= 13 marks +.14 groats: 1068s. r: the value of 90 loa'ds. From which deducting 80s. = 16 crowns, leaves 988s. = 49 1. 8s. or 49 1. for the number required, H. ' v. Question 5.

A person remarked that upon his wedding day the proportion of his own age to that of his wife was as three to 1; but 15 years afterwards the proportion of their ages was as 2 to 1. What were their ages upon the day of marriage?

Answer. The husband's age was 45, and the wife's 15 years.
.. Solution.
Put z and 3; for the two ages, and $a -$ 15; then $2:1::3s + a: z+a$, or $3z+a$ 3= $2z+2a$; hence $z=a=:15$, and $3z=45$.

But perhaps the more masterly way of solving this problem is thus: since 2: 1:: $3z + a: z +$ «, subtract each consequent from its antecedent, and we have $1:1::2z: z + a$: but $1:1::z: z$, hence, by subtracting, $1:1::z,: a;$ or $z - a$ the number added universally, H. *Questions proposed in* 1709, *and answered in* 1710.

1. Question 6.

A rich Indian merchant brought sixty-four diamond? of an ex. traordinary value and great beauty to sell to a King of Persia, and upon being asked the price of some said, that he would sell them all together upon the following conditions, viz. for the first stone lie would have a grain of wheat, for the second stone two grains, for the third stone four grains, &c. doubling the number of grains for each succeeding stone. The King thinking it an advantageous bargain, readily agreed to the proposal, imagining that a few sacks of wheat, at the most, would pay for the whole. But how great was bis astonishment, when informed that all the corn in his kingdom would be far short of satisfying the merchant's demand. Now suppose a pint of corn to contain 1001)0 grains, and a bushel to weigh half a *act.*; what would the whole quantity of wheat be worth at 5s. per bushel, and how many horses carrying 1000 1. each would it take to remove the same: also how many ships of 100 tons burden, would it load?

Solution by a Lady.
Suppose (saith she) navigation to have begun with Adam, and 67279 ships of 100 tons each to have been built every year since the creation of the world (which she supposes to be about 5655 years); and so to build the "same number continually to the end of the world, and the world to last 5000 years longer, and all those ships to be in being at once; all of them together, according to the tenor of the question, would not be sufficient to transport the wheat, so prodigious is the quantity. She adds,

For there would be 7205759403 horse loads, (besides 7921. 15s. lOd. odd money) and the same number of ship loads.

s *Additional Solution.*
The number of terms being 64, the ratio 2, and the first term 1; $2^{64} — 1$ the sum of all the terms of the series will be — X 1 —i64 — 1 2 — 1 — 18446744073709551615 for the number of grains of wheat; which being divided by 10000 X 64 = 640000 the number of grains in a bushel, we have 28823037615171-1743984375 for the number of bushels; the value of which at 5s. each is 7205759403792-79, &c. I. and the double of this number will be the weight in *acts,* then the value divided by 1000) and the weight by 2000, give each 7205759403 79 &c. for the number of horse or ship loads required. H.

II. Question 7.
Two persons, of the same age, discoursing together, says one to the other, my eldest son is just half as old as I am, and if *340* is added to the continual product of our three ages, the sum will amount to 30000; required the ages of all three.

Answer. The age of the son is 19 years and a half, and that of each of the two persons 39 years.

Solution.
This question is to find three numbers, of which two shall be equal to each other, and each double of the third, and whose continual product shall be (29659-5) 340 5 less than 30000: or, to find two numbers, the one double the other, and the less multiplied by the square of the greater shall produce 296595: or, to find a number, the half of whose cube shall be 296595,: or its whole cube 59319; and consequently that number must be $59319=39$—the age of each of the elder; and consequently 19 is that of the youngest, H. *Algebraical Solution.*

Let x represent the age of the son, then $1x$ will represent the age of each of the elder. By the question $2x \times 2ar \times + 340\ 5 = 30000$; therefore $4\text{-}c^3 = 296595$; $=7414875$, and $\#=195$ the age of the son; and $1x — 39$ years the age of each of the elder persons, L. III. Question 8.

A Vintner has wines of 8, 5 and 4 groats per quart, and wants to make a mixture of 56 quarts, worth 22 pence a quart; how many different ways can this be done in whole numbers?

Answer.
Best 10, U, 12,13, 14,15,16,17, 18,19, 20 quarts, at 32d. each. Mean 44, 40, 36, 32, 28, 24, 20, 16, 12, 8, 4 quarts, at 20d. each. Worst 2, 5, 8, 11, 14, 17, 20, 23, 26, 29, 32 quarts at 16d. each. Being eleven answers in whole numbers, which are all that can be found to sell 55 quarts, at 22d. a quart.

Solution.
Putting x, y, and z for the number of quarts of the best, middle, and worst sort, respectively; then $x + y + z — 56$, and $32x + 20y + 16z = 22 \times 56 = 1232$; hence $z = 8x — 28$, and $y = 84 — 4x$. Now must be such a whole number as will make both $3x — 28$ and $(84 — 4x$ or) $21 — x$ whole numbers; from the latter of these two equations, it appears that the greatest value of x is 20; and from the former, that its least value is 10; so that x may be any number from 10 to 20 inclusive; and by substituting every number from 10 to 20 for x, in the two equations $z — 3x — 28$, $y = 84 — 4x$, we obtain these eleven answers in whole numbers, viz. $x = 10, 11, 12, 13, 14, 15, 16, 17, 18, 19, 20$ quarts, at 32d. each. $y\ zz\ 44, 40, 36, 32, 28, 24, 20, 16, 12, 8, 4$ quarts, at 20d. each. $z = 2, 5, 8, 11, 14, 17, 20, 23, 26, 29, 32$ quarts, at 16d. each.

IT. QUESTION 9.
Seven men bought a grinding stone, the diameter of which was 5 feet, and they agreed that each should use it till he had ground away his share. What part of the diameter must each grind away?

Answer. The first must grind 44508 inches.
Second.. 4-8400
Third 5-3535
Fourth.... 6-0765.''
Fifth 7-5079
Sixth 9-3935
Seventh 22-6778 60 inches.

Solution.
This question is to divide a circle, of 60 inches diameter, into 7 equal parts, or rings, bounded by concentric circles; of which the solution "will be thus:—The whole circle, and each inner circle, after the several preceding rings are ground off, must be to each other, by the question, as the numbers 7, 6, 5, *4*, 3, 2, 1; but circles are as the square of their diameters; therefore the diameters of those circles will be to one another as $/7$, $/6$,-5, $/4$, $Z3$, $/\%\ fl$; but the greatest diameter is 60 or 60;therefore, by proportioning, all the other diameters will come out thus, $60\$\text{-}60y\#$, $60Vf$, COy, sOy, fiOy'f. Now the last of these is the diameter of the last person's' share, and the difference between every two adjacent terms being taken, will give the double breadth of the rings, or the parts of thewhole diameter to be ground off by the other persons, viz.

gQy „. 601 — 77" X 60 = 4-450794 the 1st person's
'" share.
the sum of them all is 60 000000 the whole diameter. *The Construction* will be thus: Divide the radius Ab of the given circle into 7 equal parts; and at the points of division erect perpendiculars meeting the circle, described on the diameter, Ab, in », r, H, K, M, o, then with the To, /, / / v oeutrc A, and radiuse Ao, Am, «*dulTJJti*
Ak, &c. circles being described, the thing is done. For, By the nat&re of the circle, the squares of the chords or radiuses AO, Am, Ak, &c. are as the versed sines An, Al, Ai, &c.

Scholium. It is evident that the above method of calculation and construction will both hold true also when the shares are unequal in any proportion; by using the respective proportional numbers in the former, and dividing the radius Ab in the same proportion in the latter, H.

The above solution lias been inserted by Dr. Huttony at the end of a valuable work which he has just published, entitled "Tracts on Mathematical and Philosophical Subjects; comprising, among other important articles, the Theory of Bridges, with several plans of recent improvement. Also the results of numerous experiments on the force of Gunpowder, with applications to the modern practice of Artillery;" in 3 vols. 8vo. There is a short history of the Problem and some anecdotes connected with it, prefixed to the solution, which we shall here insert, with the author's permission, believing that they will not fail to prove interesting to the reader.

"A particular case of the present problem was first of air, "as far as I know, proposed in that useful and valuable little "annual work, the Ladies' Diary, for the year 1709. In the "year following an answer was *so* far given only, as merely to "specify the numbers denoting the parts of the diameter to be "ground down, or cut off, without any mode of solution whalevor, "either arithmetical or geometrical. Many years after, a geomc-i "trical construction was given by a Mr. Hawney, in his little book "on Mensuration, but so clumsy in its manner, as to require the "description of a separate circle to ascertain the point through:' "which each of the dividing concentric circles was to pass. And' in *u* this state it remained till about the year 1770, when Mr. James "Ferguson, the ingenious lecturer on astronomy and mechanics, in "his peregrinations came to Newcastle, where I then resided, to ' give the usual course of his public lectures; on which occasion, "with the assistance of my friends, I not only procured him a-nu"merous and respectable audience, but also accommodated1 him (' with the free use of the new schoolrooms, which I had lately,c built, to deliver his lectures in. As Mr. F. commonly amused my *u* family and friends at evenings, with showing his ingenious me chanical contrivances and drawings, on one of these occasions he *u* produced a very neat and correct drawing, on a large scale, being "a construction of this problem, in the very prolix way as before "given by Hawney; but which he exhibited as a great curiosity. "I ventured to remark to him that I thought a much simpler couJ' struition might be found out, for this problem, which was then f new to me. As Mr. F. expressed a wish to see such a thing as "a simpler construction, which however he seemed to have his "doubts of procuring, I was indured: to Consider it that evening, before "going to rest, and discovered the construction as given above.

"The. next morning I showed him the new and very simple con"struction, with its demonstration, which he seemed much pleased "with, on account of the apparent simplicity, but doubted very "much that it might not be correctly true. On referring him to the *u* accompanying demonstration, to satisfy himself of its geometrical £ truth, I was much surprised by his reply, that he could not un"derstand that, but he would make the drawing correctly on a large "scale which was always his way to try if such things were true. *u* In my surprise I asked where he had learned geometry, and "by what Euclid or other book; to which he frankly replied he £ had never learned any geometry, nor could ever understand the "demonstration of any one of Euclid's propositions. Accordingly "the next morning, with a joyful countenance, he brought me the "construction, neatly drawn out on a large sheet of paste-board, "saying he esteemed it a treasure, having found it quite right, as every point and line agreed to a hair's breadth, by measurement *u* on the scale. This problem and the construction he afterwards "inserted, with the proper acknowledgment, as a curiosity, in his "Select Mechanical Exercises, page 123. Printed in 1773.

"Very soon after the first publication of the solution of the Diary *u* question as above, it was seized by a shameful plagiary, in the "person of a Mr. Samuel Clark, who had commenced, after mine, a "re-publication of the Diary questions, under the title of ' The c Diarian Repository.' When this editor arrived at the question above referred to, he copied my solution, and very inconsistently *u* ascribed it to Mr. Hawney before mentioned, though it was mani"fest to every geometrician that no two constructions could be more ' unlike one another, as the one employed seven different circles, and (' as many separate constructions, in effecting what the other ac"complished by only one single circle and construction. From the "many gross errors, and the numerous omissions and absurdities in that ' Repository of Errors,' as it was commonly called, it soon "fell under the necessity of coming to a sudden and premature end." v. Question 10.

What is the length of the pendulum which will make as many vibrations in a minute as it is inches in length f

Answer. 52 063039916251851082, being the cube root to 20 decimals.
Solution.
Since the lengths of different pendulums are to each other reciprocally as the squares of their vibrations made in the same time; we shall have, putting x for the length required, x: 39-2:: 60s = J600: xx; hence $x3$ — 3600 X 39-2, and x 3600 X 39'2 = $1/141120$ = 52-06304 inches, nearly, u.

Questions proposed in 1710, *and answered in* 1711.
I. Question 11.

A man being asked what money he possessed, replied (hat he had three sorts of coin, namely, half crowns, shillings, and sixpences; the shillings and sixpences together, amounted to 409 pieces; the shillings and half-crowns to 1254 pieces; but if 42 was subtracted from the sum of the half-crowns and sixpences, there would remain 1103 pieces. What sum did the man possess in all?

Answered by Mr. Thomas Gosling. 995 half-crowns, 259 shillings, 150 sixpences; in all 1411. Is. 6d. *Solution.*
The meaning of this question is, that the sum of the shillings and sixpences is 409, the sum of the shillings and half-crowns is 1254, and the sum of the sixpences and half-crowns 1145; to find the number of each. That is, having given the sums of every two of three numbers, to find the numbers.

Put x = the number of sixpences, y — the shillings, and z — the half-crowns. Then, by the question, $x + y$ — 409, y + s, — 1254, and i + 145. The sum of the first and third, is $lx + y + z$ — 1554, from which taking the second, we have lx — 300; hence x — hO,y — 409 — x — 259, and z = 1145 — x = 995. And the sum of these all together amounts to 1411 Is. 6d. H.

Otherwise.' Put a = 409, b — 1254, and c— 1145. Then by the question, $x + y$ — $a, x + z$ — $b, y + z$ = c. The sum of the three equations is $2x + ly + 2s = a + b + c$,
$a + b + c$
or $x + y + z$ —

From this equation, take each of the given ones; then

In this manner the problem may be resolved, whatever be the number of equations. Thus, suppose it were required to find four numbers having given the sum of every three.

And in general if there were n unknown quantities, of which the sum of every $(n-1)$ was givenr then the quantities might be found in a similar manner by subtracting each/ of the given sums from the aggregate of all the sums, divided by »— 1. %. II. Question 12.

A gentleman has to pay a thousand pounds, and has only two sorts of coin, guineas valued at 21s. 6d. each, and louis-d'ors at 17s. each; how many diiferent ways may the payment be made with these coins.

Answered by Mr. John Boswel.
Guineas—32, 66, 100, 134, &c. by adding always 34. Louis-d'ors—1136, 1093, 1050, 1007, &c. by subtracting always 43 will give 27 answers, each two sums making 10001.
Solution.
Put for the number of guineas, and y for that of the louis-d'ors.

Then will $43a; + 34y$ be $= (1000 \times 40 =) 40c00$; hence $y - 40000 - 43$. ..... Ste $-16 - =$ (by dividing) $1176 - x -$ —j consequently $9x-16$,. „,. . $36a:-64$ — a whole number, as also 4 times the same, viz. —— 34 *l* 34

—..., =: (by dividing) £—2 4. ——; hence—j—a whole number $=p$ then a; $= 17p - 2$. This written for it in the ex $40000 - 43x$.,,,,,,,.., prcssion y — —, gives $y - 1179 - 21 p$; consequently p — any even number = (suppose) *In*; then $y = 1179 - 43/1$, and $\_ 34« - 2$; where n is any integer number.

Taking successively the numbers 1, 2, 3, 4, &c. for n, we have a: $= 32, 66, 100, 134, 168, 202, 236, 270, 304,$ &c. $y - 1136, 1083, 1050, 1007, 964, 921, 878, 835, 792,$ &c. H.

IIf. QUESTION 13.

A farmer hired a servant 30 days, upon the condition, that for every day he worked he was to receive sixteenpeuce, and for every day he was idle or absented himself he should forfeit twenty. pence; now upon coming to settle their account it was discovered that the farmer had nothing to pay, and the servant nothing to receive; how many days did the servaut work, and how many was he idle?

Answer. He worked 16 days 8 hours, and idled 13 days 4 hours.
Solution.
Since the two products of each number of days by their respecrtve prices are equal to each other, it follows that the said number of days will be reciprocally as the prices; but the prices are as 20 to 16, or as 5 to 4, whose sum is 9, and the whole number of days is 30; whence 9: 30, or as 3 MO:: J g JjJ J" , *Algebraic Solution.*

Let $x =:$ the number of days he worked, and y zr those he was idle. Then by the question $x y = 3.0$, and $16 - 20//.$
20m $5u$
The first equation gives x 30—y, and the second gives $xzz - - -i$.

Iv. Question 14.

How long must the tether of a horse be to allow him just to graze an acre?
Answered by Mr. Nath. Browne. The length of the tether is 39-2507375 yards. *Solution*
The number of square yards in an acre being 4840, and a circle being equal to 314159 &c. drawn into the square of the radius; therefore--f — c—— the square of the radius, and conse314159 &c. ' quently the radius itself or length of the cord will be v

"3-14159 &c.
= 39-25073 yards, H.

V. QUESTION 15.

A lady being asked her age by an impertinent spark, made the following reply; if my age be multiplied by three, and two-sevenths of that product trebled, the square root of two-ninths of that will be four. Now tell my age or never see me more?
Answered by Mr. John Ford. The Lady's age was twenty-eight years. *Solution.*
Put x for the lady's age. Then, by the question, (3 X f X 3 X *0 36x*, . 16X63 16 x 7 *t* ,, ao

—— = 4; hence = —— = ——— = 4 x 7 =28. H. *V* TI. PRIZE QUESTION 16.

Walking through Cheapside, London, on the first day of May, 1709, the sun shining brightly, I was desirous to know the height of Bow steeple. I accordingly measured its shadow just as the clock was striking twelve, and found its length *to* be 253 feet; it is re. quired from thence to find the steeple's height.
Anszeercd by Mrs. Mary Wright.
May 1, 1709.,, ,,

Sun's longitude, from its ingress into aries 51 28 0

Oblique angle of the ecliptic and equator 23 29 0

Thence the declination tliat day 18 9 45

Consequently its merid. altitude in lat. 51 32' 56 37 45

The complement thereof to 90 is 33 22 15

Then as the sine of the angle 33 22' 15".

To the base 253-125 feet.

So is the sine of the angle 56 37' 45".

To the perpendicular 384-307 feet the height of the steeple. Note. The true height of Bow steeple is 225 feet, for which at first I had proportioned the length of the shadow, but upon second thoughts I altered it, for fear some, who had read its height in history, should claim the reward, without having art enough to investigate it by trigonometry.
Solution.
This solution, at length-will be thus:

The sun's longitude being supposed 51 28', and the angle made by the equator and ecliptic 23" 29'; by right-angled spherical triangles, as radius: sine of 51 28':: sine 23 *W*: sine 18. 9' 45" the declination for the time; to which adding 38 28' the complement of the latitude, there results 56 37' 45" for the meridian-Altitude that day. Then, by right-angled plane triangles, the height of the steeple will be found by Mrs. Wright's proportion above, or rather thus, as radius: 56 37' 45"::: 253J: 384-31 the steeple' height, a.

Questions proposed in 1711, *and anszeered in* 1712.
I. QUESTION 17.

I happen'd one ev'ning with a tinker to sit,

Whose tongue ran a great deal too fast

for his wit:
He talk'd of his art with abundance of mettle.
So I ask'd him to make me a flat-bottom kettle,
That the top and the bottom diameters be
In just such proportion as five is to three.
Twelve inches the depth I would have and no more,
And to hold in ale gallons seven less than a score.
He promis'd to do't, and to work he strait went;
But when he had done it, he found it too scant.
He alter'd it then, and too big he had made it,
And when it held right, the diameters fail'd it:
So that making't so often, too big, or too little,
The tinker at last had quite spoH'd the kettle:
Yet he vows he will bring his said purpose to pass,
Or he'll utterly spoil ev'ry ounce of his brass.
To prevent him from ruin, I pray help liim out,
The diameter's length else he'll never find out

Anszeered by Mr. Richard Parker.
Lesser diameter 14 6390238; greater diameter 24-398373 inches.

First Solution.

Putting 5s and $3z$ for the top and bottom diameters, by page 525 Mensuration, we shall have (3 X 64zs + $4zz$ or) *196zz* X 12 X-00023209 = 13: hence z = /196 x H'' = 4-880057; consequently 3:: = 14-640171, and bz = 24-400285, the two diameters required, H. *Second Solution.*

Find the content of the frustum of a cone, whose altitude is the same as that of the given one, and the diameters of the top and bottom 5 and 3. This content will (by prob. 6. vol. ii. page 48. of the course) be = j X (52 4-32 + 5 X 3) X-7854 X i2 = 153-982 cubic inches. The content of the given frustum is =13X 282=3666 cubic inches. Because the frustums have the same altitude, they are to one another in the same ratio as the areas of their ends, or as the squares of the diameters of their ends. Hence 153-982: 3666:: 5:: 595-3687, the square of the diameter of the greater end; the square root of which is 24-4002, the greater diameter: and as 5: 3:: 244002 the greater diameter: 14-6401, the less diameter. lu *Tldrd Solution.*

Let the given frustum be completed into a cone. Then the part added will be a cone similar to the whole cone. Let D and d denote the diameters of the greater and less ends of the given frustum respectively; p and p the perpendiculars of the whole cone and the part added, the contents of these cones being denoted by c and c. Then by the question 5: 3:: D: d, but by similar triangles D: d :: p :p; therefore 5: 3:: P : p, and therefore 5 — 3:3:: p—-p (or 12 the height of the frustum):p, the height of the part added =18; hence P = 18 + 12 = 30 inches, the height of the whole cone. Because similar solids are to one another in the same ratio as the cubes of their altitudes, we have as p3:$p3$ :: c: c, therefore »a — $p3$: $v3$ :: c — c, (the given frustum): c; that is, as 27000 — 5832 or 21168: 27000:: 3666: 3666 — = c = 4676-02, the con 21168 tent of the whole cone. Hence, because-7854 X n' Xf = c, / c. / 4676 02 D = V X-7854 X P = V, x-7854 X 30 = 24'4002' the greater diameter. And 5:3:: 24-4002: 14-6401, the less diameter, L.

The ingenious Mrs. Babara Sidway, in her answer to this question, proposed another very pretty QUESTION.

If the frustum of the cone was to hold as much again: what would be the length of the part added to the greater end?

First Solution to Mrs. Sidway's *Question.*

Tf *ba* and *3a* be the diameters of the first or given frustum,-whose altitude is 12, and z the altitude of the frustum to be added: Then by similar triangles. &c. %az + ba — the greater diameter of the part added; and since the two contents are equal, we shall have *((iaz+ 5a)2* + (£flz+5a) x5a+25a) X s=(25aa+ *15aa* +9aa) X 12, or ((is + 5)» + (s + 5) X 5 + 25) X 2=49 X 12 = 588, or z + 90 s2 4-2700s = 21168. Hence = 6-3847619 = the height of the part to be added, H. *Second Solution to Mrs.* Sidway's *Question.*

Let the given frustum be completed. Let the height and content of the whole cone be found as in the last solution to the original question: The height is 30 inches, and the content of the whole cone is 4676-02 cubic inches. To this add 3666 cubic inches, the content of the given frustum; the sum is 8342-02 cubic inches, which is the content of the cone, including the lengtheued frustum. Then since similar solids are to one another as the cubes of their altitudes, we have as 4676-02: 8342-02:: 30': X 303, the cube of 4676-02' the altitude of the last mentioned cone; the cube root is 30 X 3 /8342-02 V — = 36-382 nearly, from which taking 30, (the altitude 4o7o"02 of the cone, including the given frustum), there remains 6-382 for the length of the frustum to be added to the greater end of the given frustum, *so that it may hold twice the quantity as at first*, L.

Ii. Question 18, *by Mrs.* Lydia Fisher.
What two numbers are those whose sum is 16J, and the greater divided by the less gives the quotient 27.
51 33
Answer. The numbers are 15—and —.
56 56 *First Solution.*
Put 2 for the less number: then, by the question, either 16f — x or 27s will expressthe greater: hence 272 = 16 — 2, or 28s — 33 33 33
—: then z — — = the less number, and consequently *161* — 2 56 ' '2 56 — 15f £ — the greater, H.
I *Second Solution.*
Let x — the less number; then 27x — the greater, and 28a? 33 16- = —; hence the rest will be as above, H. *Third Solution.*
Since, as above, the numbers are in proportion as 27 to 1, and 33 their sum = 16: hence as 28: 18:: 5 1: 56 = the less m,mber' 127: 15=the greater, H. *Fourth Solution.*
Let x be the greater number, y the less: s:z 16 and q — 27.
iv. Question 20, *by Mr.* William Hawney.

A General who had served the King successfully in his wars, asked as a reward for his services, a farthing for every different file of ten men each, which he could make with a body of 100 men. The King thinking the request a very moderate one readily assented. Pray what sum would it amount to?

Answered by Mrs. Barbara Sidway. 17310309456440 farthings = 180315723501. 9s. 2d. *Solution.*

The number of variations of 10 in 100 are X X 7 X 2 X f X ƒ X £ X f x « x £ = 17310309456440 = the number of farthings = 180315723501. 9s. 2d. = the sum demanded. H.

The following Theorem will answer all.questions of this nature:

Theorem. The number of combinations of m given things, all different from each other, taken by a given number n at a time, is equal to $m \; m — 1 \; m — 2 \; m — 3$ „

— x——— X ——— X -,— X &c. to n terms, L. 12 3 4 v. Question 21, *by Mr.* Gideon Cosier.

A gentleman riding by a common where a number of shepherdesses were tending their flock, after saluting them he asked the number ofj their sheep, when one of them answered, that if the flock was to bq equally divided amongst the shepherdesses, the share of each would be twice as many sheep as there were shepherdesses: but if to one he gave one sheep, to another two, to the third four, &c. doubling the number to each succeeding shepherdess, then the last would have for her share as many sheep as there were in all. How many sheep were there?

Answered by Mr. Alexander Weedon, *and Mrs.* Barbara Sidway. The number of sheep was 128. *Solution.*

If 2 be put to denote the number of maids; then, by the question X 22 — 222 will denote the number of the sheep, and 2zs = 2l; hence, multiplying by 2; we have 4«z.= 2 and, by extracting the VOL. I. B root, 2z 2z; From this equation, by trials, we easily find Z— % the number of maids; and then Izz — 128 the number of sheep.

When the value of z is an integer number, it is best found by trials as above. But if it be some infinite decimal, put the above equation into logarithms, and we have ±z X log. 2 — log. 2 + log. s, or 1-505153 —z =-301030, putting z =: log. of:; then find the value of z by double position or the method of trial-and-error. H.

Vi. Question 22, *by Mr.* Amos Fish.

A ship sails north, from a certain port; after running some days, in this direction she alters her course and steers due west till her difference of longitude was a degree more than the difference of latitude made upon the first course. And it was also observed that a perpendicular from the point where the ship altered her course, to the right line joining the ship and the, port sailed from, was 150 miles. Required the distance run in all, and the direct distance from the ship to the port sailed from.

Answered by Mrs. Babara Sidway. Sailed North 188-256 miles.
Sailed West 248-256
Distance run 436-512
From the port sailed from to the ship's place 311-555 . *Solution.*

From the right angle B let fall the perpendicular 7,5

Bd: If Ab represent the distance sailed north, and Bc / the distance west; then will Ac represent the distance x/ between the place sailed from and the place arrived-'vn at, and Bd 150 miles.

Now by right-angled triangles we have Ac = Cb + BA% and 2ac X Bd — 2cb X Ba; hence, subtracting the second equation from the first, we have AC8 — 2ac X Bd = Cb2 — 2cb X Ba + Ab2 = (cb — Ba)4, and AC = Bd + /(bd2 + (cb — Ba)2) = 150 +./(1502 + 6O2) = 150+ 30/29 = 311-554944214 = the distance from the place sailed from.

And, by adding the second equation to the first, we have Ac2 -2ac X Bd= Cb2 + 2cb x Ba + Ab2 = (cb + Ba)2, and cu+ Ba — ((ac + 2bd) X Ac) = V(6H-5549 &c. X 311-5549 &c.) = 436-50082 &c.) = the whole distance run.

Also, by adding and subtracting the difference and sum, we have Cb and »A = = 248-25041 and 188-25041.

The *Construction* is evident from the above process, *viz.*

Make Ac = (bd + (bd + (cb — Ba)2)) — the sum of Bd and the hypothenuse of a right-angled triangle whose two legs are Bd and Cb — Ba: then the sum of the legs (cb + Ba) being equal to (./((ac + 2bd) x Ac)) the mean proportional betwenn Ac and Ac + 2bd, the legs Cb, Ba themselves will be = the half sum and difference of Cb — Ba and the said mean proportional. 11.

Another solution to this question, on the principles of Mercator's sailing.

Let a — Bd — 150; b — the latitude, in minutes, of A the place sailed from; m — 3437 the reciprocal of the length of an arc of 1 min. to the radius l;c = «ix: b + %b3 + i bs+ bi + &c. = the meridional parts in the latitude b, or c might be taken from a tabic of mcrid. parts; d — 60, the difference between the difference of latitude and longitude, also put x — the latitude of c, the place arrived at.

Then m X:x + £ ar + xs + x7 + &c. = the merid. parts in the Iat. x., Hence x — h — Ab, the proper difference of latitude; and — c + m X:x + £ x3 + x! + x1 — merid. difference of latitude.

Now Ad = — b)2 — a2): Db:: (ab: Bc::) merid. diff.
of latitude: difference of longitude =z — Ttz + V((x—) —a —r--tt r X:x + ix3 + iii &c. But the difference of Y((x — by — a2) longitude is — Ab + 60 — x — b + d. Then this value being equated to the other, there will result an equation from which the value of x may be found, and thence every thing else. H.

THE PRIZE QUESTION FOR 1711.

In a level garden there are two lofty firs having their tops ornamented with gilt balls, one is 100 feet high, the other 80, and they are 120 feet distant at the bottom: now the owner wants to place a fountain in a right line between the trees, to be equally distant from the top of each; and to make a walk or path, from the fountain, in every point of which he shall be equally distant from each of the balls: also at the end of the walk he would fix a pleasure house, so that a couch placed therein should be at the same distance from each ball, as the two balls are from each other. How must this be done?

Another construction is given at ques-

tion 252. L. *Answered by Mr.* Henry Beighton, *Mrs.* Anna Wright, *and Mr.* Ford, *Sult.Ojficer of Middlezeich, and several others.*
From ball to ball.. 121-65525
From each ball to the pleasure house 121-6552S
From the lower-tree bottom to the house 91-65151
From the taller-tree bottom to the house..... 69-28203
From the house to the fountain 5267827
From the lower-tree bottom to the fount 75
From the higher-tree bottom to the fount 45 *Solution.*

Let Ad be the one tree, and Bc the other. Draw Cd the distance of the two balls. On the middle of which and perpendicular to it draw Ge, and E will be the fountain. For then De will be — Ec by *Eucl.* I. 4.

Also the required path, at the end of which stands the pleasure house, will be a right line Ih perpendicular to Ab, and — one leg of a tight-angled triangle whose other leg is Ea, and its hypothenuse Ah — the base of another right-angled triangle ADH whose perpendicular is Ad and hypothenuse nil — Dc.—For,.because of the path's continual equal distances from the balls, it will be the intersection of the horizontal plane and another plane perpendicular both to the line Dc and the vertical plane Abcd, and this, intersection is perpendicular to Ab by *Eucl.* XI. 19.

Vie Calculation. Since (ed'z:) Da2 + Ae2=.(ec2 =) Cb2 + Be; therefore, by equal subtraction Bc2—Da = Ae2 — Eb2 = Ab K .,, Bc2—"da2 1002 —802 (ae — Eb); and hence Ae— Eb = = — —— = 30: v Ab 120 n .. . Ab ± 30 120 ±30 mc , Consequently Ae and Eb = = —— — 75 and 45, the distances of the fountain from the bottoms of the two trees, And De = Ec =./(cb2 + Be2) = /(1002 + 452) = 5/481 = 109-65856099 the distance of each ball from the fountain. Also Dh = Hc = Cd — Vdf2 + Fc2) = + 20) = 20-y/37 — 121-6552506. Hence Bh =./(nx2 — Cb2) = X 37 — 1002) == 20/12 = 69-2820323 = the distance of the pleasure house from the foot of the taller tree. Ah = /(hd2—Da2)=./(202 X 37—803) = 20 /21 = 91-651513899 = the distance of the same from the lower tree. And Eh = (hb2 — Be2) = /(202 X 12 — 452) = 5/111 = 52-67826876 = the length of the walk, or the distance of the pleasure house from the fountain, u. Questions proposed in 1712, *and anszcered in* 1713. i. Question 23, *by Mr.* Lewis Evan.

A person at his death left his wife with child, and bequeathed his property, which was,£7000, as follows, *viz.* if it was a son, the mother was to have one-third, and the son the rest of the property; but if a daughter, then the mother was to have two-thirds, and the daughter the rest. Now it happened that she had twins, a son arid a daughter. This being a case not provided for in the will, the executors are perplexed how to divide the property equitably between the mother and the children. Required the share of each.

Answered by Mrs. Anna Wright.
The daughter's share is £1000, the mother's.£2000, and the son's.£4000.
Solution.

By the *will,* the mother's share was to be the double of the daughter's, and the son's double of the mother's; wherefore they will be in proportion as the numbers 1, 2, and 4; and the sum of these numbers being 7, it appears that the share will be , £, and-f of the whole estate: *viz.* of 7000/. = 1000/. =: the daughter's share.

I-of 70002. = 2000/. = the mother's share.
i of 7000/. = 4000/. = the son's share, H, *Algebraic Solution.*

Let x represent the daughter's share; then $1x$ will represent the mother's share, and $4x$ the son's.

Then by the question $x + 1x + 4x$ or $7x - 7000$: Hence $x - 1000$.

Therefore the three shares are 1000, 2000, and 4000 as before, L.

Ii. Question 24, *by Mr.* Amos Fish.

A merchant had Holland, Muslin, Scotch linen, and Cambric, in all 30,009 ells, and he remarked, that if the number of ells of Holland was multiplied by those of Cambric, the product would be equal to that of the number of ells of Muslin multiplied by those of Scotch linen: And the sum of the squares of the number of ells of Holland and Cambric is 160,000,000. He also remarked that the number of ells of Holland was much greater than any of the others. How many *ells* were there of each?

Answered by Mr. John Newbold.
Holland 12000, Muslin 8000, Scotch cloth 6000, and Cambric 4000.
Solution.

This question is unlimited, for there are four unknown quantities, and only three conditions. And, to determine the rest, one of them must be assumed.

Put z, y, x, v for the four quantities; then
$z+y+x+v= 30,000 =?$ O,
$zv = yx,$
$zz + vv — 160,000,000 = b$. To and from the third adding and subtracting the double of the first, we have $zz ± Izv + vv = b ± \%xy;$ hence $z ± v — /(b ± Ixy),$ then by substitution in the first, we gety $+ x$ 4-$fb + 2xy) — a$; from this is obtained $\# — a — A/(b + 'iax — xx)$: by assuming $x — 600O$, this expression gives $y — 8000$. And then s and $u — «b + 2xy)± S(b-2xy) U0QQ$ ' 400a H 2 in. Que&tion 25, il/r. Alexander Weeden.

There is a piece of timber in the form of the frustum of a square pyramid, its length is 12 feet, the side of the square of the greater end is 21 inches, and that of the less end 3 inches, what is the content in cubic feet; and supposing the timber divided into pieces of a cubic foot each, by cuts parallel to the ends, what is the thickness, of each, beginning at the greater end?

Ansisered by Francius,
The first solid foot's length is 4 0136, the second is 4-2208, the 3d is 4-4552, the 4th is 4-7272, the 5th is 5-0448, the 6th is 5-42, the 7th is 5-876, the 8th is 6-4408,. the 9th is 7-1656, the 10th is 8-1352, the 11th is 9-5208, the 12th is 11-7096, the 13th is 15-8776, the 14th is 29-4824, and the 15th is 21-9104, *Solution.*

By page 159 Mensuration, the solidity of the whole piece will be tl X 21 +81 X 3 + 3X3 x 12 x n _ 24g24 jnches _ M, feeti o

And if the frustum be supposed to be

compleated to a pyramid; then, by similar triangles, as 21 — 3 is to 21, or as 18 to 21, or as 6 to 7, so is 12 to 14 feet its altitude; and hence 21 21 × 14 × 12 = 24696 inches =: 14-291 feet = the content of the whole pyramid. Whence, as similar solids are as the cubes of their like dimensions, we shaH

V 1-2916 —V 0-2916: X 69-228 = 29-4827 = 14th the sum 122-0896 being taken from 12 feet or 144-0000 inches, we have 21-9104 = alt. of the if. H.

iv. Question 26, *by Mr.* John Burnet.

The depth of a standard bushel measure is 8 inches, and its diameter 18 inches: what must be the diameter of another bushel of th« same capacity whose depth is 7 inches?

Answered by Mr. Thomas Shepheard. The diameter is 19-1067 inches. *Solution.*

Since equal cylinders have their altitudes reciprocally proportional to the squares of their diameters, we shall have, As *J7: n/i* :; i«I 181%/--lsiv/-74 £L8 = 19-10671784 inches = the diameter required. H.

v. Question 27, 6 *Mr.* John Wilson.

A person being asked his age replied, if to the months of my age you add (heir one half and one eighth, the sum will be 442: What was his age?

Answered by Mrs. Mary Nelson. Twenty-two years and 8 months. *Solution.*

This question being to find a number which being added to its one-half and one-eighth shall make 442; or, since the sum of 1, , and is y, to find a number which multiplied by V3 shall produce 442 X 8 *y* 442; wherefore as 13: 8:: 412: —— — 34 X 8 = 272 months = 22 years 8 months =: his age. H.

Algebraic Solution.

Let x =i his age: then by the question x + + — 442, or $9x + 4x + x$ — 3536. Hence $13x$ = 3536, and x = 272 months — 22 years and 8 months, L.. y_ vi. Question 28, *by Mr.* Henry Bcighton.

A person hired a horse in London at the rate of *3d.* a mile, and proceeded to Bristol, lying west from London 94 miles; from Bristol he went to West Chester, lying due north, and from Chester he returned towards London till he arrived at Coventry, 66 miles from Chester. From Coventry he went again to Bristol, where having dispatched his affairs, he returned to Coventry and went thence directly to London. Now he is at a loss how to settle for the hire of the horse, not knowing the distances of Bristol and Chester, Coventry and Bristol, and Coventry and London. However he recollected that at Coventry the direct road to Bristol was at right angles to the London road. From the preceding data it is required, to find the turn due?

This question is in effect the same as the following: In a right angled triangle, there are given one of the legs and the segment of the hypothenuse, adjacent to the other leg, made by a perpendicular from the right angle to determine the triangle.

Then the distance which the traveller rode will be equal to "the sura of the perimeter of this triangle, and twice the perpendicular from the right angle upon the hypothenuse.

Answered by Mrs. Mary Nelson.

JE5 13s. 2rf. is the sum due for the hire of the horse.

First Solution.

Construction. Make Ab, Ac perpendicular to each other, the former z: 94 the distance between London and Bristol, and the latter =: 66 the distance between Chester and Coventry. Bisect Ac in D, and with centre D and radius Db describe a circle meeting Ac produced in E and F; then draw Cg perpendicular to Ae, and with the hypothenuse Ae construct the right-angled triangle Age, by describing a semicircle on Ae to meet Cg in *a;* so shall E represent London, G Bristol, A Chester, and c Coventry.

For by similar triangles, Ge2 — Ea × Ec — (by the construction) EA × Ae-Ab2, or Ge = AB.

Calculation. The radius Ed — Db = = *A/(bas* + Ad2) =-x/(942 + 332) — A/9925 = 5/397 =: 99-62429. Hence Ce = Ed — DC 6662429 — the distance from Coventry to London; Ga = V(AE'2 — Eg2) = ((ad + De)2 — Eg2) = (226-62429 X 38-62429) = 93-55855; and Gc = ,.GA or = (ge2 — Ec2) = 66-31141. Then Ga + Ae + Eg-f 2gc — 452 80566 miles =: the whole distance travelled; which at *3d* a mile will produce *5l.* 13s.

2d. 1-66792?. H. *Second Solution.*

If E represent London, G Bristol, A Chester, and c Coventry; then in the right-angled triangle Age we have given the side Ge, and the segment Ac of the hypothenuse made by the perpendicular from the right-angle to construct it. Make Ge of the given length and F draw Agh perpendicular to Ge making Gh half the given segment Ac; with the centre H and radius Hg describe a circle, and draw Eh to meet it in D and F.; make Ea — Ef, and the triangle will be constructed.

For Ge being a tangent to the circle, Eg-— Ed-ef (36. in.), also Kg2 = Ce-ea (8. vi.); therefore Ed-ef = Ce-ea: but Ea = Ef by construction; therefore Ce is *zz* Ed, and consequently Ac *zz,* Df *Zz* 2hg — the given segment.

Prize Question, *by Mr.* Peter Hingeston, *junior, a scholar in Ipswich Grammar School.*

A dodecaedron is a solid composed of twelve regular pentagonal pyramids, whose vertices meet in the centre of the circumscribing sphere, and the bases of the pyramids form the superficies of the dodecaedron. Now suppose a dodecaedron having the side of each pentagon composing the superficies thereof 8 inches, and supposing every two of its composing pyramids to be hollowed out in the form of the greatest hemisphere, cylinder, cube, cone, triangular pyramid, and square pyramid: What will the remainder of the dodecaedron weigh after having been hollowed or scooped out as above described, supposing each cubic foot of the matter of which it is composed to weigh 60lb?

Anszcered by Mrs. Barbara Sidway *and Mr.* Beighton.

The dodecaedron weighs, after all the twelve cavities are cut out, 60-6527 pounds.

Solution.

Let Abefgh be one of the twelve pyramids constituting the dodecaedron, and c the centre of its base: draw Cd perpendicular to Be, and the rest of the lines as in the figure.

Putting A — 8 =: Be one side of the pentagon or base, by page 410 Mensuration,

$S + vft$

Again, $Da = ./(ac^2 + Cd') Zz$ —— $A = 1\text{-}309071 A$, and by similar triangles $Ad: Dc:: Ca: AC\ c'' zz\ 5 + 3/5a = 5854102A\ DA\ JiO$ — the radius of the inscribed hemisphere; and consequently its solidity is $(-5854102a)3 \times 1 \times 3\text{-}14159$, &c. $= -4201837a^3$.

Also, a square may be inscribed in a pentagon by placing one of its sides parallel to a side of the pentagon; and, by calculation, it appears that if 2 be the side of the square, z -J-1-0604974 will be the side of the pentagon; hence, if this square be one face of the cube, and the pentagon the section of the pentagonal pyramid parallel to the base and distant from it the height of the cube, we shall have, by similar figures, $Ac: Be:: Ac - z: z$ -r 1-0604974; hence $z - 2',64,974c \times A = -5431802A =$ the side of the cube: And con1.0604974a-J-Ac sequently the cube of this, or- 1C02626A the content of it.

Collecting now these three sums together, and multiplying by 2, we have 4-2516646A3 for the contents of the twelve cavities.

But, by p. 408 Mensuration, 5A3 y47- — = 7-6631189A3 = the content of the dodecaedron.

Consequently the difference of these two = 341 14543a' — 1746-6646016 inches = 1-0108013 feet — solidity remaining; which at 601b. a foot, weighs 60-648077lb.

N. B. *False numbers (but no method of solution) are given to this question in* The Diarian Repository.

A false solution is also given to question 25 in that book, dissimilar solids being used as similar ones. u. *Questions proposed in* 1713 *and answered in* 1714. i. Question 29, *by Mrs.* Sarah Brown.

A lady being warmly importuned by her lover to consent to their union, answered, that she thought herself then too young: the lover desired to be informed when she would think herself old enough to make him happy; she replied when the square of her age diminished by £ and then increased by 4-of the same was 891: What would then be her age *I I Answered by Mr.* Lingen, *from* Ireland. Twenty-seven years.

Solution.

Since taken from 1 leaves f, and this increased by J-or f becomes y; hence the question is to find a number whose square multiplied by y may produce 891.

Consequently, 11: 9:: 891:the square of the number,

„ 891 x 9

Or, /ll : /9:: /891:V n ' = (81 X 9) = 27 = the number sought. H.

Algebraical Solution. Let .= her age: then by the question xx — . + = 891; reduced xx — 729 J therefore x — 27. L. ii. Question 30, 6y A. W.

In London, on the morning of the 10th of May, happening to hold my walking-cane upright upon level ground, the sun shining brightly, I observed that the lengths of the cane and its shadow were exactly equal: What was the time of the day when this happened?

Aastcered by Mrs. Adway.

Thirteen minutes and sixteen second past nine o'clock.

Solution,

Supposing the sun's, declination May 10th, 1712, to be 20 6' 32"; we shall have given the three sides of a spherical triangle, to find an angle: viz. the complement of the declination — 69 43' the complement of the latitude 38 28', and the complement of the altitude — 45, to find the hour angle, or angle between the two former; and which by calculation comes out 41 41' 4" — in time to 2h. 46m. 44s. which being taken from 12h. we have 9h. 13m. 16s. for the time required. H.

in. Question 31, *by Mr.* Rob. Wilson.

Suppose a ladder 100 feet long, placed against a perpendicular wall *100* feet high, how far would the top of the ladder move down the wall, by pulling out the bottom thereof 10 feet?

Answered by Mr. John Boswell *and Mr.* T. Busey. 0012G feet = 6-01512 inches. *Solution.*

By right-angled triangles,./(loo2—102) = 3011 =99-4987437

In like manner, if the first equation be multiplied by b', and the second by b, and the latter product subtracted from the first, we have $(ab' - a'b) x = cb' - c'b cb' - Cb$ or x — -rj r,. $ab - ab$

In this case, where there are only two unknown quantities, it is evident what factors will render the co-efficients of x and y, in the two equations equal to one another, as above; but when there are more unknown quantities than two, it is not so obvious what factors will answer; therefore in what follows I shall make use of a method for determining them, which is applicable to all cases, whatever may be the number of equations.

In the preceding example if we multiply by the indeterminate factors m and w, the equations become $a»ix + bmy - cm\ u'nx + b'ny - t/tt$ and subtracting the second equation from the first, we have $(am - afn)x + (bin - b'n)y - cm - c'n$. Now in order that y may disappear from this equation, $bm - b'n\ fjjn\ (j\ ft$ must be $= 0$, then x — -r 'am — an

But $bm - b'n$ will be =: 0, when $m - b'$ and $n - b$; and these values being substituted for m and n in the expression for x, we havo $cb1 - c'b X - ab' - db'$

Again, to make x disappear from the equation, $am - u'n$ must be — 0, then y — — rA But $am - a'n - 0$, when $m - a!$ and $n\ a$, therefore substituting for m and n their values, we have y or changing the signs in the numerator and denominator, $bal - b'a'\ acl - a'c V - 7 ab' - ab$

When one of the unknown quantities has been determined by this method, the other may be found, without repeating the process, by only changing the coefficients; or writing a in place of b, and a' in place of b', or the contrary. Thus, if in the value for x we write a for b, and a' for V, it becomes " the value of y. And if in the va '$ba - ba$ lue for y we write b for a and b' for a', we have —'ci for the value $ah - a'b$

Of X. 2nd. Let there be three equations $ax + by + cz - d a'x + b'y + dz - df a''x + V'y + d'z = df'$ to find the values of x g and z. miles-r 1142 feet = 36960 feet-4-1142 = 32= 32-36427 seconds — the time of the ascent of the sound.

Again since the times of descent are as the roots of the spaces, and 16TV feet is the space fallen in the 1st second, wherefore-v/l6T'T: 36960:: 1 second: =

47-03778 seconds = the time of the body's descent. H.

Mrs. Sidway also answered this question, and at the same time proposed the following one.

From what height must a heavy body fall so that the time of descent to the earth's surface may be equal to the tune in which sound would move the same height; and with what velocity would the body strike the ground?

Mrs. Sidway's Question solved.

Putting $a = 16T'Tj$ $b = 1142$, and $x =$ the height of the castle in feet. Then, as in the last solution, T will express the time of the $x \times$ sound's ascent, and — the time of the body's descent; hence — /-, and $x = -- = 81087jU$ feet = 15 miles 1887U? feet = $y\ a\ a\ 9\ J$ » the height of the castle.

And since the velocity is as the root of the space descended, and *la* the velocity acquired by falling through a, we shall have $/a: fx :: 2«: 1fux - \%/bb\ zz\%bzz$ double the velocity of sound, or 2284 feet per second, H.

Vi. Question 34, *by Mr.* Josiah Clayton.

Suppose an army consisting of 60,000 soldiers drawn up in the form of an oblong or rectangle upon a vast plain; how many acres will they cover, allowing 2 yards from man to man; the sides of the rectangle having the proportion of 3 to 2?

Answered by Mr. J. Lewes *and Mr.* Jos. Boydall. Ninety-two acres, 3 roods, 35 perches. *Solution.*

As the sides must be in proportion to each other as 2 to 3, and their product 60,000, it is evident that they must be 200 and 300. Then the ground upon which they stand will be = 299 X 2 X 199

X 2£ = yards = 92 acres, 3 roods, 35 perches, H.

Prize Question, *by Mrs.* Anna Wright.

What star of the second magnitude was nearest to the north pole at the creation, supposing it to have happened 5716 years since; also what was its distance from the pole at that time?

Answered by Mr. John Edens.

The third star in Draco, reckoned from the tip of the tail was the nearest to the north pole at the creation, and its distance from the pole was 6 48' as appears from the following calculation: o I II

The longitude of the first in T 1712 29 11 14 v

The star in Draco from *T* ad. 124 33 30

Longitude of that star, 1712 153 44 44

Moved in 5716 years sub. 80 52 53

Remains the long, at the creation 72 51 51

Lat. according to Tycho, 66 36' north. Then As the cotang. 23 3C/:is to the radius::

So is the sine"72 51': to the tang. 22 33', which subtract from the compl. of the star's lat. leaves 50/12". Then

As the cosine 22 33' To the cosine 50/12"

So is the cosine 23 30 To the cosine 6 48

Six degrees forty-eight minutes the distance of that star from the pole at the creation.

Additional Solution.

The annual precession of the stars being 50-336 seconds of a degree, the precession from the creation to the year 1760 will be r (5716 + 48) X 50-336 — 5761 X 50-336 = 290136 seconds = 80 35' 36". To this precession add 3 signs or 90, the longitude of the north pole of the equator, and we shall have 5s. 20' 35' 36" for the present longitude of the star required; and the star of the second magnitude, whose longitude is nearest to that, and latitude 66 nearly, was the pole star required; which appears to be the third star in Draco, reckoned from the tip of the tail, which is the star marked, by Bayer, *a. Now to Jind the distance of this star from the pole at the creation.* By the catalogue of stars at the end of the Nautical Almanac for the year 1773, the latitude of « DracQnis is 65 21' 15A", (its complement 23 38' 44£"), and its longitude in the year 1760 was 154 2' 46"; from this subtract (80 35'36") the precession since the creation, and we have *73 17'* 10" for the longitude of this star at the creation, whose complement is 16 32' 50": Also, since the diminu.. tion of the inclination of the earth's axis is 47" in 100 years, in 5764 years its change will be 45'9", which being added to 23 28' 17" the inclination in the year 1760, we shall have 24 13' 26" for the angle made bv the axss of the ecliptic and equator at the creation,-. Hence in an oblique spherical triangle, we have given two sides and the included angle, to find the third side; *vie.* given one side 24 *is'* 26" the distance of the pole of the equator from that of the ecliptic, the other side = 23 38' 44-j" (he distance of the star from the pole of the ecliptic, and the included Z — 1C 32' *bo"* the complement of the star's longitude: Thon, by trigonometry, is found the 3d side = 6 43' 10" the required distance of the star from the pole of the equator at the creation, H. *Questions proposed in* 1711, *and answered in* 1715.

i. Question 35, *by Mr.* John Wilson.

A father informed his daughter's lover that the cube of the number f pounds in his estate was 352947 X 64 X 9; and that he designed to give three-sevenths of it as her marriage portion; and being an odd kind of fellow, refuses to give his consent to the match till the lover has discovered what the portion is. The young gentleman has puzzled himself a great deal to no purpose, and is almost distracted for fear of losing both the moRey and his mistress; pray set him at ease by informing him what the portion is?

Answered by Mr. Peter Walter, *Mr.* James Cale, *of Portsmouth, and Mr.* William Vorley, *Writing-master, at Holbech, Lincolnshire.*

The father's estate, 588/. The daughter's portion, 252/.

Solution.

Since the cube of the number of pounds in the whole estate is equal to 352947 X 64 X 9 = 203297472, the number itself must be equal to the cube root of this number, which is 588/. = the whole estate. Consequently f of 588 = 252/. is the lady's portion, H.

Ii. Question 36, *by Mrs.* Barbara Sidway. From a given cone to cut the greatest cylinder possible.

Answered by Mr. Bcriff, *Mr.* Hall, *Mr.* Wylde, *and Mr.* Clayton. The cone must be cut at *one-third* of its altitude. *Solution.*

Let Acd be the given cone, De the diameter, and Pq the altitude of the greatest inscribed cylinder; then the solidity of the cylinder is $= De^2 \times .7854 \times pp.$, therefore $De^2 \times Pq$ must be a maximum. But De has to Ap a given ratio, namely that which the diameter of the base has to the altitude, and therefore when $De^2 \times Pq$ is the greatest, $Ap^2 \times Pq$ will also be the greatest; and this is the case when Ap is double of Pq (Theo. xxiv. page 44, vol. 3, of the course;) hence the cone must be cut at a third of its altitude from the base. L. OTHERWISE, by FLUXIONS.

Put $Aq = a$, $Bc = b$, and $x = Ap$; then by similar triangles $a : b :: x : x - = De$: whence $De^2 \times Pq = \times x^3 \times (a-x)$; a $a1$ $ft2$ therefore, leaving out the constant factor —, $x(\ll - x)$ must be a maximum. Taking fluxions $2arr - 2x - i = 0$, and reducing, $x = a$, whence $a - x = Vq.$ — as before, L.

Hi. Question 37, *by Mr. John Hodge, of Truro, in Cornwall.*

It was settled, by a party of nine persons, to defer a certain disagreeable business as many days as they could change places at dinner each day; how long would that be?

Answered by Mr. Thomas Dodd, Mr. Lingen, and Mr. Nath. Kew. Nine hundred and ninety-three years, and 186 days. *Solution.*

The time required will be = $1 \times 2 \times 3 \times 4 \times 5 \times 6 \times 7 \times 8 \times 9 = 362880$ days; which, at 365 days to the year, come to 993ff years, H.

The following theorem will answer all questions of this kind.

Theorem. The number of permutations, or changes that can be made of any given number of things m, all different from each other, is equal to $1 \times 2 \times 3 \times 4 \times .5 \times$ &c. to m terms, L.

Iv. Question 38, *by Mr. Crabb, of fVhitlackington, in Somerset.*

An architect agreed to build an obelisk in the form of a cone, at *1d.* per cubic foot, the height was to be to the circumference of its base as 5 to 4, and if the cone were cut by a plane parallel to th« base at the height of 10 feet,

the content of the part intercepted between this plane and the vertex would be 1250 cubic feet. He moreover agreed to build a chamber in the obelisk in the form of a cube, the greatest that the cone would possibly admit of. What must be the dimensions of the cone, as also of the chamber to be formed in the same, and what will it come to at the price agreed upon?

Answered by Mr. John Newbold, Mr. Lewis Evan, Mr. Abel Ragg, Air. John Andrew, Mr. Nich, Stevens, and Mrs. Nelson. feet inch.

The circumference of the pyramid at the base.... 41 6

The whole height of the cone 51 10

The side of the room 7 11

The content in solid feet when the room is deducted, 1878-1093. The charge of the building, 5 *il.* 15s. 6d, *Solution.*

Put $a = .785398$ &c. and $5x$ and $4x$ for the altitude and circumference of the upper part whose content is 1250. Then its solidity is

——=: 1250; hence $x = 1J 750a = 8-382697$. Consequeptly the *Oil* altitude of the whole cone $= 5x + 10 = 51-913485$ feet — 51 feet 10-96182 inches, and the circumference of its base $= Ax + 8 = 41-53078$ feet $= 41$ feet 6-369156 inches: Also, by similar solids, $(5x)^3 :(3r + 10)s :: (=) 1250 : (r)3 1250 = 2375-14$ zz solidity of the whole cone.

Now, if $A = 5x + 10 = 51-913485$ the altitude of the whole cone, and z — the side of the inscribed cubical room; by similar fi cures we shall have $A ::: A - z : i z /2$: hence $z 10a = 7-921364$ feet — 7 feet 11-056368 inches — the side $1 + 6a/2$ of the room; the cube of which gives 497-05 for the vacuity.

Taking this from the whole solidity (2375-14) we obtain 1878-09 fo the solid part; which, at *7d.* a foot, produces 5 4/. 15s. Gd. 2-52g. ii.

v. Qtjestiov 39, *by Mr. Richards, of St. Thomas's, near Exon.*

The monument erected in Babylon by Queen Semiramis at her husband Ninus's tomb, is said to have been one solid block of marble in the form of a pyramid; the base was a square whose side was 20 feet and the height of the mon-

ument was 150 feet; now suppose this monument was sunk in the Euphrates, what weight would be sufficient to raise the apex of it to the surface of the water, and what weight would raise the whole of it above the water?

Answered by Mr. Newbold. Ton. cwt. qr. lb.

To raise it to the surface 939 3 2 10

To be added to raise it out 573 12 3 25

The weight in the air 1512 16 2 7

This calculus is according to Mr. Ward's tables of specific gravities, and differs considerably from those taken from the Philosophical Transactions. *Solution.*

The solidity of the pyramid will be $20'' \times TM = 20000$ feet $= 34560000$ cubic inches. Now by *JVard's* tabic of specific gravities, a cubic inch of marble weighs 1-568859 ounces avoirdupois, and an inch of salt water-594894 ounces; and their difference is-973965. Whence, the weight required to raise the point of it to the surface of the water will be-9P3965 $\times 34560000 = 33660230$-4os. = 939 ions 3cwt. 2qr. 12/6. 6-4oz.

And it is evident that the whole weight of the marble will be necessary to raise the w hole of it above the water, H.

Vi. Question 40, *by Mr. John Newbold.*

A cooper is ordered to make a tub in the form of the frustum of a cone capable of holding 19-98 ale gallons; the internal diameter of the greater end is to be 30 inches, and this is also to be the diameter of a sphere which will circumscribe the vessel. What will be the diameter of the less end and depth of the tub *Answer.*

The least diameter 18-236 inches, and depth 11-9104 inches. *Solution.*

Put $2a = 30 =$ the bottom diameter, $1x$ — the top diameter, and A — the content in ale gallons. Then, by the nature of the circle, $V(»a - xx)$ — the perpendicular depth; and, by page 159 Mensura...-78539 &c.

non, we hare $4 \times (aa + ax + xx) \times f(aa - xx) \times 3 = 282a$, where $282 =$ the inches in a gallon; or $(aa + ax + xx)$

X -/(aa — xx) — ——. Now when A = 19 98 as in the '314159 isc.
question, there is no number, taken as the value of «, will produce *io* great a content, the number 1998 being above the maximum. But to find the greatest content the case will admit of, put the fluxion of *(aa + ax +)*' X *(aa — xx)* — to nothing, and we shall have 0 — *(aa — xx)* X (« + 2a:) — *x* X *(aa + ax* + Xjt) = a3 + Bsa; — *lux* — 3a:3; or in numbers *x3* + 10a:2 — 75a: — 1125= 0; or, putting *z = ix,* z3 + 2s2 — *3z* + 9 = 0; the root 2 of this equation is = 1-9394; consequently *1x — 0z* — 19-394 = the value of the less diameter when the content is'a maximum; and then the depth /(aa —xx) is — 11-444, and the greatest content = 11-444 78i3Q&r (30 + 30 X 19-349 + 19-3492) X *tLzzl* X = 19-739 3 282 ale gallons, Ii. PRIZE QUESTION.

In gauging a spheroidical ale cask, I found the diameter of one head to measure 18-1 inches, that of the other 16, the bung diameter 20, and (he distance between the two heads 20-6 inches, also, by the cask lying a little obliquely, I observed that the liquor just rose to, or touched the upper extremities of the two heads. Having noted these dimensions, I was informed that there were in the cask a ball of iron weighing 60/6. another ball of lead weighing 90/6. and a cube of box, a foot square. Pray what quantity of liquor was in the cask?

Answered by Mr. John Newbold, *Mr.* John Edcns, *Mrs.* Anne Morgan, *Mrs.* Mary Nelson, *of Newmarket, Mr.* William Crabb, *and Mr.* R. Saudford. *inches.*

The spheroid's greatest distance from bung to head.... 12-053

The lesser distance 8-547

The content of the cask in ale gallons 20-763

The iron ball equal to cubic inches 217-048

The leaden ball 219-717

The cask's vacuity 117-814

The box emerged 1723-O0O

The sum, cubic inches, 2277-579 which are equal to ale gallons 8076 which deducted from the whole content leaves 12-687 ale gallons, the true quantify of liquor remaining in the cask.

Questions proposed in 1715 *and answered in* 1716. i. Question 41, *by Mr.* Dod.

A person who had been tippling all day, was, upon his coming home at night, questioned as to what money he had spent; in order to evade a direct answer, he made the following reply: if the square of the number of pence which he had spent were multiplied by five times their own square root, the product would be equal to the pence in 162/. What sum had he spent?

Aasucred by Mr. Richard Sandford *and* Silvia.

Tf the pence in 162/. be *b,* and the pence spent be = *a;* then this theorem solves the question; *a = $/(b--f-25) == 36* pence.

Solution.

Let *x* denote the pence spent. Then, by the question *x* X 5/ = 162 X 240 = 38880, or *a? s/x* 7776; hence, by squaring, X *x* or,r5=7776!; and consequently x=7776 = 36c/. = 3. H.

Ii. Question 42, *by Mr.* William Taylor.

A may-pole having been broken by a blast of wind, it was found that the broken part measured 63 yards, and by falling the top had made a hole or mark in the ground, at the distance of 30 yards from the foot of the pole; it is required to determine what was the height of the pole when standing upright.

Ansvsered by Mr. Jos. Peacock.

The height of the may.pole was 118 3985 yards.

Solution.

It is evident, from the question, that the part broken off (63) is the hypothenuse of a right-angled triangle, whose perpendicular is the part left standing, and base equal fo (30) the given distance which the top struck the ground from the pole; and consequently, by right-angled triangles, (63 — 302) = V3069 = 56-3985559 = the part left standing. To this adding 63 the part broken off, weobtain 118"3985559 for the whole length required, H.

Hi. Question 43, *by Mrs.* Boydell.

An aged sire, with his two daughters, came

To town, and was desir'd to tell his name.

My name, says he, 's a thousand more than yon,

And I. and if you add the other two,

The number of this present year they'll shew.

The num'ral letters of our names (well set

With the first letter of the alphabet) Make seventeen hundred, and fourteen complete.

I'll further add (to make the problem plain)

Each single name five letters doth contain.

Answered by Philo Tipperus, *and Mr.* P. Proson.

Whilst Lidia for Lydai you cunningly write,

You think you may surely ensnare us; „ *David* 100'i

But David is aged, and Lucia bright, *Lidia* 551

So 'tis easy to Philo Tipperus *Lucia* 156

The daughters who to town with David came,

Lucia was one, and Lidia's t'other's name. *P. Proson.* 1714 iv. Question 44, *by Mr.* T. Hayward.

Two men, one stronger than the other, have to remove a large stone, weighing 50olbs. with a bearing barrow, whose length is 6 feet: now the weakest cannot undertake to carry more than l0olbs. how must the stone be placed upon the barrow, so as just to allow him that weight for his share? *Answered by* Silvia.

The centre of gravity of the stone must be laid on the barrow at two feet from the strongest man.

In questions of this nature the result will be the greater strength multiplied by the shorter length, is equal to the lesser strength multiplied by the greatest length; and here the barrow's weight is not accounted for, otherwise it would require some skill in staticks to resolve it.

v. Question 45, *by Mr.* Thomas Shepheard.

Suppose a person whose height is 5 feet 7 inches, travels 10,000 miles in the arc of a great circle; how much will his head have gona farther than his feet, the circumference of the earth being 21600 miles?

Answered by Silvia.

It is evident in the case proposed, that while the feet desreibe an arch on the earth's surface equal to 10,000 miles, the head will describe a similar arch of a circle, whose radius exceeds the semi-diameter of the earth 5 teet seven inches: Therefore as the semi-diameter of the earth, is to the semi.diameter increased by 5 feet 7 inches: So is 10,000 geographical miles, to an arch exceeding 10,000 miles by 16-23 feet, according to *Van Culeri's* proportion of the diameter to the circumference, *viz.* as 1 to 3-141592C53589793.

Additional Solution.

21600

Since the earth's radius is-inches, and 5 feet 7 inches 2 X 3-14lo9 &c.' — 67 iixhes; by similar sectors, as radius: radius + 67:: 10000 ; 10000+the excess travelled by the head; or, by division, as radius : 67:: 10000: the said excess; that is, as :67:: .,,,, 10000 X 67 X 2 X 3-1459 &c. _ 6700 X 3-14159 &c. _ 100J0: 21600 urn 194-8951 inches — 16-2412 feet = the excess required, H. vi. Question 46, *by Mr.* Ed. Elphick.

Suppose a smooth inclined plane from the top of a lofty tower meets the level ground at the distance of 301 feet from the bottom of the tower, and suppose a weight of 40lbs. will sustain a weight of 56lbs. when placed upon the inclined plane: What is the height of the tower?

Anszcered by Silvia.

By a known principle in mechanics, the accelerating velocity, or weight of bodies on an inclined plane, is to their accelerating velocities or weight in their perpendicular descent, as the sine of the angle of inclination, to the radius; or as the perpendicular to the length of the plane, considered as an hypothenuse; and therefore in this the proportion of the perpendicular, and the length of the plane, being given as 40 to 56, or as 1 to 14. Let the perpendicular sought be =: x, the hypothenuse will be l"4x, and the base 301 feet — «, then l-flfte" — x-— Q-96x-— $a2$ by 47 Euclid i. and by division and evolution, x — = 310-27 feet required.

Additional Solution.

It is evident that this problem may be easily *Constructed* thus: Make a right-angled triangle whose hypothenuse and perpendicular are 56 and 40, or 7 and 5, or any two numbers proportional to these; then make another similar triangle whose base may be 301; and its perpendicular will be the height of the castle required.

And from the same principle, the *Calculation* may be given without algebra, thus: Since $f(7 - 5') = /2$ 1:= the base of the first triangle to which the other is similar, we shall have as 24: 5:: 304:-.-= — = 7-310-2687 = the castle's height, H. PRIZE QUESTION.

Two ships A and n are supposed stationary in the channel between Dover (d), and Calais (c): an observer on board the ship A, finds the Zbad r 86, and the Zcab =24: and an observer on board the ship B, finds the Zabc = 129, and the Zabd = 48. How far are the two ships distant from each other, as also from Calais and Dover, supposing an object floating on the water to be driven from Calais to Dover in 2h. 25m. 10s. 10'" 33"" 36""' by the force of the waves 45 feet distant.

To this question, besides abundance of false answers, I received ten true ones, and because I see so few amongst so many ingenious correspondents, 1 am apt to believe it was as difficult, as it was an uncommon question; for which reason I shall here give you the solution, and the algebraic method by which the same is found.

Sir *Isaac Newton,* in his *Principia,* says, Let there be a pendulum, whose length from the point of suspension, to the centre of oscillation, is the breadth of any wave; then while the pendulum makes an oscillation, the wave will pass over a distance equal to its breadth. From which, and the nature of pendulums, is raised the following theorem. Let the distance run be *a,* the length of a standard pendulum — p — 39-2 inches; the square of the vibrations in a minute f 3600, s = 45 feet or 540 inches, the breadth of the wave, and t — 2hours 25 min. &c. n 145-1696" minutes, also r 45 feet: then r *vffv* : p but /'— — to the number of vibrations it will make in a minute, and multiplied by r will be the feet the wave will move in a minute; but——,t and consequently, by reduction, *a pf rt* / — 105600 feet =: 20 miles sought, or the distance from Calais to Dover.

In this following figure c represents Calais, D Dover, A the first ship, B the second.

Then s Calais to Dover c to D 20 miles I Dover to IstshipB to A 13-5192 From *J* Dover *to* 2d ship D to B 18-1583 Calais to 1st ship c to A 22-4008 / Calais to 2d ship c to B 11-7238 V 1st ship to 2d ship A to B 13-0853 The angles Dab 86, Cab 21, Dba 48, CBA 129.

Additional Solution.

Perhaps the solution will appear a little clearer thus: *Putp* — 39-2 inches the length of the pendulum, v — 60 the number of vibrations it makes in a minute, b — 45 feet the breadth of a wave, and t — 145-1696 minutes the given time. Then, by the nature of pendulums, n *tfltb* : »Jp :: v: VV — nc number of vibrations made in a minute by the pendulum whose length is the breadth of a wave, but for every vibration the wave will pass over a distance equal to its 7 breadth b; hence the wave moves over $bv/7$ or v/ feet ia each minute, which therefore drawn into t minutes makes $iv/$— y 12 ftV-x12 = /yy'ClS X 9-8) = 7/d/3 = 145-1696 X 420 /3

— 105605-2 feet = 20 miles nearly, = the distance between Calais and Dover.

This distance being obtained, which is the side Cd of a quadrilateral Abcd, of which the angles formed by the opposite side Ab with the two diagonals Bd, Ac; as also with the other two sides Ad, Bc, being given, the figure will be *Constructed* (as in the British Oracle) thus:

At the extremities A, *b,* of any line *Ab,* make the angles 6ac, *6dt Jc, xbd* equal to the given angles, and join c, *d;* so shall *Abed* evident! ly be a quadrilateral similar to *that* formed by the two towns and two ships; and, consequently, if *dc* be produced to E, till rfE be equal to 20 the given distance between Calais and Dover, and Ec be drawn parallel to xd and meeting Ac in c, that then Cb, Cd being drawn parallel to cb, cd, and meeting xb, Ad in B and D, the points A, B will be the two ships, c Calais, and D Dover.

The *Calculation* from this construction is also evident: *viz.* assuming A6 — any number, as suppose 10, in the two triangles A6c, xbd, we have given all the angles and the side Ab, to find the other sides; and hence those sides are Ac = 17-11811 miles, be — 8-95914 miles, xd — 10-33093 miles, and bd — 13-86777 miles. Then in the triangle bed are given two sides with their included angle, to find the third side erf, which will be 15-28859 miles. Lastly, by similar triangles, as cd — 15 28859: Cd = 20 „' .ib =10:Ab = 13-03615

The latter part of the question resolved without assuming a similar figure.

Analysis. Suppose the problem solved and that Ab is the distance between the two ships as required. On Cd let a segment of a circle Dac be described to contain an angle of 62 (cad): this segment will evidently pass through the point A. Also on the the line Cd let another segment Cbd be described to contain an angle of 81 (cbd): this segment will evidently pass through the point B. Let the line Ab when produced meet the circles in P and Q, and join Cb, Cq, Dp, Dq. Then the angle Pcd is the given angle Dba — 48, and the angle Qdc is — tbe given angle Qac — 24. Hence this construction. Having described upon the line Cd the segments Dac, Cbd as in the analysis, draw Cp to make the angle Dcp =48, and Dq to make the angle Cdq — 24; join Qp meeting the circles in B and A. Then Ab is the distance required.

Calculation. In each of the triangles Cqd, Cdo, and Cpd there are given one side Cd and all the angles, to lind the other sides: *viz.* Cf, Do., Od, and oc; also op — cp— oc, Oq — Qd — on; hence in the triangle Qop, two sides and the included angle are given to find Opq — Cdb, and the angle Oqp rr Acd; then in the triangles Cda, Dbc, one side and all the-angles are given: whence Ac,

Ad, Bc, Bd, and Ac may be easily found, L. *Questions proposed in* 1716, *and answered in* 1717.

I. Question 47, *by Mr.* John Edens, *of Teneriffe, one of the Canary Islands.*

A triangular close whose sides are 20, 15, and 6 chains, is to be divided into two equal parts by a drain 3 feet wide. The drain is to be cut in such a manner as to remove the least quantity possible of the surface of the ground: how is the drain to bc cut.

Answered.

The content is easily found fo be 2 acres, 3 roods, 17 perch, and 45280 parts of a perch. The drain will cut off an isosceles triangle, whose two legs will be equal, represented by Ec, Cd. By the doctrine of fluxions, these two theorems for finding en and De will come out,

Cd = — 269-4135 yards, and 2«6 +cs—«2 — b' .....,

De —f— 51-o9457 yards.

Now 13837-97 yards the whole area — 51-59457 = 13786-37513 square yards after the drain is made.

Additional Solution.

By theorem 7 of *Simpson* on *The Maxima and Minima of Geometrical Quantities,* the required drain De will cut off an isosceles triangle Dce; and since it must cut off half the whole (or the middle being written for it in the last equation above, we hare BC /. AB — (BC — AC)2 I2ACX CB -.

From this equation it is evident that De8 is — AB. cx and hence, as in the original solution, De — V——/— = i/22 = 2-34520788 chains = 51-59457336 yards — the length of the drain, or =: its area since its breadth is one yard. (*And this is a very curious and remarkable theorem.*)

By subtracting this from the whole area, we have 13786-389 square jards for the content remaining, H. OTHERWISE.

The above solution supposes the drain to be a parallelogram, and that the middle line of it, or the line bisecting its breadth, divides the whole field into two equal parts: but, strictly and mathematical, that is not the case; for, by the question, the parts on each side of the drain

must be equal, and then the said middle line of the drain will divide the figure into unequal parts; as will thus appear.

Vol, i. D'

Let Defg represent the ditch, and Hi the middle line. Through n draw de parallel to Bc and meeting Dg, Ef in d and e: Then will be formed the two little equal isosceles triangles rfiiD, Cue, which will be both constant arid given, because the angle c and the breadth of the ditch are so; and, since the parallelograms ei, Iig are equal, as also the trapezium Af and triangle Cdg by the question, it is evident that Hi must be drawn cutting off the isosceles triangle cut = to £ the AAbc — 2 the AeiiEza given area; to do which needs no pointing out here.

The calculation from hence would bring out the lines a little different from those above, H.

The expressions in the original solution may also bc obtained as follows:

Put Ac — a, Bc — b, Ab =: c, and d — the angle Dce; then the triangle Dce being isosceles and equal to half Abc, Ac X Cb: Dc X Ce :: 12: 1, or ab : Dc2:: 2:1: hence Dc" — , and Dc = J. 7-27 2

Again, by formula 11, page 5tJ, vol. 3, of the Course,

Dk zz Dcj + Ce — 2dc X Ce X cos d n ab — ab cos d, ,. , a + b3 — c,,,, c — a' — b and ab cos d — -;hence De == «6 5 and De —fL. v ' 2 i 1 Ii. Question 48, *by Mr.* Massey.

A gentleman has his garden surrounded with walnut trees: upon gathering the fruit one season, he was informed that they had produced 2187 walnuts: upon every tree there were as many branches as there were trees in all, and upon each branch three walnuts, what was the number of trees?

Answered by Mr. Doddf *and Mr.* A, Naughley.

Let a be equal to the number of trees, then aa will be the number of all the branches; and aa X 3 2187 by the question. Therefore by division and evolution a — V(2187-r 3) = 27 the number sought.

, in. Question 49, *by Mr.* Hawney.

Find four numbers in arithmetical progression whose common difference is 4,

and their continual product 176985.
Answered by Mr. M. Moyle and Hesychia.
If the common difference be d, and the first number sought be equal to a, then $a \times (a + d) \times (a + 2d) \times (a + 3d) =$ $a^4 + 6da^3 + 11d^2V + 6d^3a = 176985$ per quest. *Now by* converging series, the value of (a) will be found — 15 just. Therefore $a + d = 19$, $a + 2d = 23$, and $a + 3d = 27$; but $15 \times 19 \times 23 \times 27 =$ 176985 as required.

Additional Solution.
Let $d = 2$, Half the common difference, and $p = 176985$. Then $x - 3d$, $x - d$, $x + d$, $x + 3d$ will denote the four numbers: the continual product of which is $x^4 - 10d^2 x^2 + 9d^4 = p$, by the question. Add $16c/4$ to both sides, and we have $x^4 - 10d^2V + 25a^4 = p + 16d$; the square roots give $x^2 - 5d^2 = \sqrt{(p + 16c/4)}$; hence $x^2 = 5d^2 + \sqrt{(p + 16d^4)}$ and $x = \sqrt{(5(P + \sqrt{(p + 16d^4)}))} = 21$. Therefore the four numbers are $x - 3d = 15$, $x - d = 19$, $x + d = 23$ and $x + 3d = 27$.

The value of a, in the original solution may also be found by the resolution of a quadratic equation. Thus, the expression $a^4 + 6da^3 + 11d^2V + 6c^3a$ being equal to $(a^2 + 3da)^2 + 'd^2 (a^2 + 3c/a)$, we shall have, putting p for the given product, $(a^2 + 3da)^2 + 2d^2 (a^2 + 3da) = p$. Hence, completing the square, &c. $a^2 + 3da (/) + c^4/4) - c^4/9$; and completing the square again, we get a $\sqrt{(HF + + P))}$ — 15j as before, L.

IV. Question 50, *by* Philomathes.
What will a weight of two pounds troy lose by being carried to the height of seven miles above the earth's surface?

Answered by Mr. Fr. Walker. Forty-seven grains. Solution.
Since the gravitation or weight of a body above the earth, is inversely as the square of its distance from the earth's centre; if the earth's radius be supposed equal to 3993 miles, we shall have 4000^2 : 3993^2 :: 2/6. : the weight at 7 miles high; hence 4000^2 : 40004 — 3993^2 :: lib. : the diminution, 7993$\times$7 Or 40009 : 7993 $\times$ 7 J : 2/6. := 006993875/6. = 36-28472 grains = the weight lost, or the decrease of gravity at that height. H.

v. Question 51, *by Mr.* Tho. Fletcher.
Find three numbers, such, that if each is subtracted from the cube of their sum, the remainder shall be a cube.

Answered by Mr, Rob. Beales, *and Mr,* Beriff.
S *SSS* and rare three numbers Which taken severally
Sfc cube of their *TMTM* lves these3 cubes,
»nd iSi whose r00ts are *it*» s§» "» w
Additional Solutions,

This problem is the nineteenth question of the fifth book of Diophantus' Arithmetic; it occupied the attention of several of the greatest mathematicians at the close of the sixteenth and the early part of the seventeenth century, some of whose solutions as well as that of Diophantus which is the basis of all the rest, we shall exhibit after remarking that the publication of Xylander's Latin translation of Diophantus in 1575, forms an æra in the history of Algebra. For we find almost every great mathematician after that time a diligent cultivator of this elegant branch of it. Vieta, for instance, resolved the problems of finding two cubes whose sum shall be equal to the difference of two given cubes, or whose difference shall be equal to the sum of the two given cubes, or whose difference shall be equal to the difference of the given cubes: it is true his solutions bring out only one answer, but it is now well understood that by means of the first a second may be obtained, and so on: it is true also that his method seemed to lie under restrictions, but these too have been done away by the foregoing observation, and it remains that every solution must begin by his method even in the improved state of the science at this day. Bachet de Mezeriac, a very learned French gentleman, published the Greek text of Diophantus with a Latin translation, and large comments in 1621, and, by the help of the algebra of Vieta with which he every where seems well acquainted, threw new light upon this difficult author, whose text had not been much illuminated by Planudes and Xylander. But the remarks which Fermat, a gentleman of Tolouse, made in the margin of his Diophantus, and which were added to the new edition which appeared in 1670, seven years after the death of Fermat; contain the largest additions which have been made to the theory of numbers in modern times, at least previous to the labours of Euler and Lagrange and the theorem of Wilson. Lord Brouuker and Dr. Wallis too, in England, distinguished themselves by solving the most difficult problems that Fermat and Frenicle were able to propose to them. Lord Brounker especially was the inventor of the method of continued fractions, and that of fending integral values of n such that $an^2 + 1$, a being a positive whole number not a square, may be a square; a theorem of great importance in this branch of mathematic science. Fermat and Wallis were the first that resalved the sum of two given cubes into two other cubes, but this problem, tho' thought a difficult one at that time, does not now seem to have required any great stretch of thought after the three problems resolved by Vieta. Descartes, a name ever memorable in the hsitory of mathematics and philosophy, was, as appears by his letters, well acquainted with the theory of rational numbers, or what Gauss calls transcendental arithmetic: but Montucla is mistaken, in saying that he did not suffer the method by which he arrived at his solutions to transpire, as there remains in the Exercitationes Mathematical of Schooten, a solution of his at full length to a problem of this kind, which was publicly proposed at Paris in 1633. It occupies the twelfth section of the fifth book of that work. Our problem too it seems was published as a challenge in 1610, at the end of Ludolph van Ceulen's or Ludolphus a Collen's book on the circle. But before we give his solution we shall set down that of Diophantus.

Diophantus, Question 19, *Book* 5.
To find three numbers such, that being severally subtracted from the cube of their sum, the remainders may be cube numbers.

For the sum of the three numbers put », and for the numbers themselves put ra9, b3, it remains that the sum of the three should be equal to «, therefore *ins — tt* divide these equals by

«, then — 1. But unity is a square. Therefore the coefficient of *n1* must be a square. And it arises from subtracting three cubes, each less than unity, from the number three. The problem is therefore reduced to this: to find three cubes each less than unity, such that their sum subtracted from the number three, may leave a remainder that is a square number. Now since each of the cubes must be less than unity, if we suppose the sum of their roots less than unity, they will each be much less than unity. Thus the square which remains will be greater than the number two. Suppose that square equal to *1*. Therefore is to be divided into three cubes, or the numerator of any fraction of equal value, with a cubic denominator.

„ 3X6' 3 X 216 3 X 54 162 sUpp0Se _j = —gr = —r-=-jr. Therefore 162 must be divided into three cubes. Now 162 is the sum of 125 a cube, and 37 the difference of the two cubes 64 and 27. But in the porisms it is shewn that the difference of every two cubes is equal to the sum of two other cubes. Let us recur to the original problem, and take each of the cubes found, and having subtracted each of them from unity, put the remainders for the numbers required and the sum will be *n*. So that the remainder after the subtraction of anyone of them will be a cube. It remains that the three together be equal to *n*. But the sum of the three is 2ra3. Therefore *n* — 2n Therefore *n* — $. Ad Positiones.

Scholium. Bachet has a long comment on this question in which he performs all the calculations that are only indicated by Diophantus, but owing to his method giving him only (g)' and (4jfS for the cubes which together are equal to 37, and his neglecting to reduce his fractions to the least common denominator, his numbers are veryhigh, when reduced by dividing their terms by 27 they are 6f'" HHii' forthe three numbers required in the question. But 37 is divisible into two cubes an infinity of ways, but perhaps not better for our present purpose than into (" J + (T The numbers required .. ,! it i GS95S 31913 j 6T229 m the question will then come out j,, and *-m*.

Bachet might have remarked that 162 is divisible not only into 125 and 37, but also into 64 a cube, and 98 the difference of the cubes 125 and 27, which would have furnished, in his own way, one other set of numbers.

We have only farther to remark, that the solutions to most problems of this kind depend upon a case being already known; and that Diophantus in fact reduces the problem to dividing 6 into three cubes, for J = £, the known case for which is 6 — 8 — 1 — 1, from which an infinity of solutions may be obtained by putting $6 = (2 —\text{fix})5 + (ac — iy + (dx — 1)3$ where $126 — 3(c + d) = 0$. If we take $c — 5$, and $d — 3$, and consequently $6 = 2, 56(c + f) — 16c$«". „. ls, „ /nX3 = 21(c+0-a/fc+d) W,U Cme Ut 5i and 6 = GO +

©' +(!)'= CS)' + (g)' + (*I*)'S -e take $c = 7, d = 5$, *b* will be equal to 3, and *x*- ± and 6 = *(t)' + ()' + (f)' = (S)' + W +* 'CiY 162 = 27-6 = (f)' + 5' + (?)«, the numbers found above.

Diophantus seems to have chosen the least square that occurred between 2 and 3. Had he taken 2£ the number instanced by Bachet, he would have had — *j* to divide into three cubes, which is just the same in effect as before, though Bachet does not seem to have perceived it. Another square — 2 subtracted from 3 leaves the remainder j-z: to be divided into three cubes, and the known case is 55=64—8—1. Again 3 — = 3— 2--= = and to divide 666 into three cubes, we have the evident case 666 =: 729 — 64 + 1. And from each of these positions for the square other sets of answers may be obtained infinite in number. It remains only to observe that the one solution to the question found out by Diophantus leads to infinite others. Thus let *a"* be a square, 6s, *c3, d3* three cubes, such that $3 — a = b3 + c3 + d3$ by putting instead of *a"*, *(a + fx)* for 6s, cs, *d3, (b + gx) (c + hx) (d + kx)* we shall have $— 2afx —fx' — 3(bg + ch + d k)x + 3(bg + chr + die) x + (g3 + h3 + ks) x3$, whence by assuming $3(tg + c'A + dk) + la — 0$, and dividing by *x'* we get *x zz f* $— 3(bg + ch + dk) g3 + h3 + P$

There is an observation of Fermat on this question of Diophantus, which very briefly indicates a solution, namely by putting *n* — 1 for the side of the square to be subtracted from the number Ji three, and 1 5, 1 + n, and —*pn* for the sidles of the three cubes; o then rejecting superfluous terms and dividing by *n* we have *n* , „„ 27p3—26 13 13-9 1 = i- & + 3 + *n P* n 5 *T-n* = T n = a-ib

In this solution n is confined to narrow limits and *p* must be taken accordingly: *n* must be greater than 1 + /2 and less than 1 + */3. n*

And when *n* is so found, (1 —-)3 is one of the three cubes, each less than unity to be subtracted from 3, and the other two are to be found by dividing the excess of $(1 + n)3$ above $p3n3$ into two cubes, after which the numbers sought in the question arc to be found by the help of these two last cubes and (1 —)3.'

It is worthy of remark that in this solution of Fermat, the assumption of *n* — 1 for the side of the square, and 1 — tj and *1* + *n* for the sides of the cubes to be subtracted from the number three, is of the same nature as Diophantus's assumption of 2 for the side of the square, *i. e.* it is justified by its success or founded upon trials or ratiocinations not expressed, it is the known case of 3 — Oj — *y3*+ *i.e.* 3 — 1 = 1+ L

We have given the solutions of Diophantus and Fermat both of them sufficiently brief, but by no means obscure or imperfect: we shall add that of Van Ceulen, remarkable for its fulness and the smallness of the numbers compared with the enormous ones of Bachet, and as Van Ceulcn's name occurs seldom but as one of those who had carried the approximation to the quadrature of the circle th« farthest, our readers nay like to see a specimen of his abilities in another kind of calculation; and Schooten's Exercitationes Mathematicas being a work of rare occurrence, we shall translate the 13th section of the 5th book, which is wholly occupied with this problem.

A translation of the 13th section of the 5th book of the Exercitationes Mathematics, of Franciscus a Schooten, 4to.

printed at Ley. den, 1657.

Question the 19lh of the 5lh book of Diophantus's Arithmetic.

To find three numbers, so that each of them being severally subtracted from the cube of their sum, the three remainders may be cubes.

Of this question the solution given by Diophantus is somewhat difficult. A different one was invented by that skilful arithmetician Ludolphus a Collen, my predecessor in the mathematical chair, in this university. This, judging it will be neither unpleasant ner out of place, I shall here briefly explain, such as I was able to gather it from his own letters, by the favour of the celebrated D. Nicolaua Huberti a Persiin, who was very intimate with him.

For the sum of the numbers sought I put $4.v$, and the cube of the sum will be $64n3$. Then by putting for the first number $56n3$, for the second $37n5$, and for the third $63n'$: there will be, each of them being subtracted from $64n3$, for the first remainder $8n3$, for the second remainder $27iN3$, and for the third remainder N Which are all cubes.

Moreover, $156n3$, the sum of $56n3$, $37n'$, and $63n'$, will bo equal to $4n$. Divide each of these equals by $4n$ and we get $39n2 — 1$.

NoWj if this number 39 were a square, the problem would be solved. But since it is not a square number, for the sides of the coefficients of the cube remainders put, $n — 1$ for the side of the first, $4 — n$ for the side of the second, and 2 for the side of the third. The cubes of which, $n'—3re + 3n—1$, $64 — 4Sn + 12wa\,i— n3$, and 8 being each severally subtracted from 64, leave the numbers $65 + 3« — n' — 3n$, $48n + n3 — 12ra2$ and 56. But since the sum of these three numbers is $121 + 45n — $ Ow: $121 --45n— 9/i$ must be a square. I put for its side $11 + n$, then $121 + 22re + n'\,z = 121 + 4on— 9ii"$, and n comes Out equal to

—.. But I supposed the side of the coefficient of the first cube remainder equal to $n — 1$, the second to $4 — n$, and the third to 2. These sides therefore are , jjj, and 2. The cubes of these are —, and 8, which subtracted from 64 leave the numbers and 56. Three numbers arc therefore found, which severally subtracted from 64 leave cubic remainders, and being added together make a square.

Hence, $4n$ being put as at first for the sum of the numbers sought, and $64n'$ for its cube, I now put for the first number 'n5, *Toss'* for the second and 563 for the third their sum $T' = 4k$. Thatis $= 1$. Whence $N = £$ and $=$ Which multiplied by jj? gives for the first number, and multiplied IT S'ves *issf* for tne second number, and lastly multiplied bjr 56, gives for the third number, and it is plain that the sum of these §-or is equal to $4n$. From the cube of which $-jlTM?$ f ii j. $4943\ 473696$ i $449000,1$ _..,.,, if you subtract 5isgs, and there will remain the

Jg, and The sides of which are £,

It is plain therefore that the numbers are rightly found.

Cujus rei soli Deo debetur gloria.

It is to be remarked, that this question is the same with the 68th of those hundred questions, which the forementioncd arithmetician Ludolphus a Collen, proposed to be solved in his Dutch work on the circle; the 69th of which is of the same kind, *vis.* to find four numbers so that if from the cube of their sum, they be severally subtracted, the remainders may be cubes.

Since the solution of this depends upon the same artifices as the foregoing. I think it sufficient to put down here only the numbers as they were found by Nicolaus Huberti.

rr,,,.1 867160 787400 13537640, $140S753S$

They are as follows: gj, -r, l257MM)l and 1257M55-t; or 13172736 11396153 9113163 4724776 fcUSliOl' 644S1301' 644SU01' 644S1S01

He found too, besides those of Ludolphus, other three numbers, lSSlT'-'SOOO 9568153000 j 8935130000 *VIZ'* 86536S34967' "86M6834967' s6fc-s6Si4967"

Who also found, to answer the question as proposed for two numbers only, the following numbers, £ and 2L, or and £2!

105045093893, 14854859747 , r &e Bwbi and ESS' and 50 of others

A solution to this question by Dr. Pell, very nearly the same as this, and in no respect better, except putting "1 11 + mn for the side of the square to which $121 + 45n — 9ks$ is to be equated, maybe found in Dr. Wallis's Algebra, Eng. ed. it. 1685, p. 219, and in Kirkby's Arithmetic (4to. 1735) page 57, prob. 86, part 6. But he, there at least, finds no other numbers than those of Van Ceulen: He has, however, a very quaint remark, if you suppose $m — 2$ or $m — 0$, one or others of the cubic remainders will come out negative. "So that you will think it was only Ludolphus's good hap to steer between those two rocks of negation, and so to light upon such a proposition, as afforded him an answer, wherein none of his numbers fall under 0. Which might giye him occasion to conclude as he did, *Constat ergo numeros rite esse inveutos. Cujus rei soli deo dcbetur gloria.*"

A little attention to Van Ceulen's Suppositions will shew that after they are made the problem is in fact solved, for if for the sum of the numbers we put a2N, and for the numbers themselves $(a6 — 63)n3$, $(a6 — C3)n'$, $(a6 — t/3)N3$ it will appear as before, that the sum of these coefficients must be a square number, *i.e.* $3«6—6s — c3 — d3 — a$. To resolve this he puts $b — n — 1$, $c — a? — n$, $d — a$, and it results that $2a6 — a3 + 1 — 3(a2 — l)n + 3(a4 — l)n$, must be a square; that this may be effected it is necessary that $2f«6 — a3 + 1$ be a square, and upon *trial* 2 the least number except one is found to succeed $2.26— 2s + 1$ being equal to 121 the square of 11. So that it was perhaps the number 4 that was the cause of Ludolphus's rejoicing. It has been found by trial that the equation $3«6— b3 — c3— d3 = Q$ may be satisfied by $a — 3$, $b — 2$, c:3, and $d — 6$, for then the expression on the left becomes $1936 = (44)9$ and from these numbers are gotten the least numbers that have yet been found to answer the original question, 1!W«7 1S954 13851

85184' 85184' 85184'

There is a synthetical answer to this question in Kersey's Algebra, vol. 2. page 111, his numbers are £ £ and =; or

1545784.1622600 j 1212416, ss37107
8966301 j 2981888. 7777016 6331625'
6331625 6331625' 1506923' 1506923
1 1506923' T 43243551'

«1s5i and *SnEi*' these are!ess than those of Bachet, even when reduced to their lowest terms by the aforesaid division by 27, and much less than than those of Nicolaus Huberti a Persiin.

Anotlier Solution.

Let x, y, and z be the numbers sought, s their sum, and a, b, c' the roots of the three cubes: Then, by the question, $s3 — x-a3$; $s3—y = b3$; $s3 — z c$ Or, $x = s3 — a3$; $y — s3 — b3$; $z — s3 —$ c3.

And by addition $s — is3 — (a3 + b3 +$ c3) (1)

Dr. Pell then shews how other answers may be derived from th« equation 4 — 121ra+ 45pra —9p by assuming lira + $qp — + 1$ or $— 2$, and is at great pains to determine between what limits q niust be taken, so as always to bring out positive answers, but his solution is much too long to be inserted here.

Different sets of answers may be obtained by assuming other square numbers, instead of 4, for the coefficients ra in the value of s. Thus if we assume $s — Qn$, $a — p — n$, $b — 9n — p$ and c 3k, we have 9 = 1432ra + 240pra — 24p'.

But here the coefficient of ra4 is not a square as in Dr. Pell's solution; therefore we must find by trial a case in which 1432k9 + 240/m—24pa shall be a square; and this evidently happens when $V-2n$; for the expression then becomes (1432 + 720 — 216)»s — 1936n = 44V. Hence 9 = 44V, Or ft = T£T; therefore $s = \%-$, _ 27 — 6' _ 19467 X 441 85184' 27'— 183 _ 13851
_ 415 85184'
-273 93 _ 18954
s — 443 — 85184'

Having obtained one solution by making /; = 3», we may find a» many other solutions as we please by assuming $p = n (3 + r)$; for then 9 = n9(44s + 96r — 24/-'), and we have only to make 44' + 9Gr — 24 r a square by assuming its roots = 44 + sr. in. Question 52, *by Mr.* Tho. Pointin.

A. malster has two cubical bins which hold together 119-998 bushels, and the side of the greater exceeds that of the less by 43 inches: What is the side of each?

Answered by Mr. Ed. Moore..

The side of the biggest cistern 62:9999314825 inches.

The side of the lesser 19 9999314825 inches.

The biggest 116-2793 bushels.

The lesser 3-7187 bushels.

Which may be found thus: Let 43 = difference of the sides, be $= d$, and the side of the greater $= a$, the side of the lesser shall be $= a — d$, and the sum of their cubes $— luaa — 3da + $ 3cPa $— d3$ = 119-9998 bush. X 2150-42, the solid inches in a Winchester bushel — 258046-099 inches, and the value of a will be found = 63 proxime; consequently a $— d—$ 20 inches. Then———
— = 116-278 bush.

2150-42 20s and giso == 3 720 bus'lels' but theirsum — 119-998 required. 1 *Additional Solution.*

This question may be otherwise more simply solved thus: Let e denote the half sum of the sides of the cubes, and $d —$ 21-f the half difference; then will the sides themselves be $z + d$ and c $— d$; and the sum of their cubes is 2:'+6rfss =119-998 X 2150-42 (the inches in a bushel), or «' + 13862 = 59 999 X 2150-42. Hence $z = 41$ nearly; and consequently the sides 63 and 2/). H.

. PRIZE QUESTION.

'"v

What were the position of the four satellites of Jupiter on October 7th, 1716, at ten in the evening, with respect to the east or west sides of the planet?

This question was answered by Mr. T. Wright, A. B. *and*

Mr. Ronkesley.

Solution.

It is evident that the difference between the geocentric place of Jupiter and the place of each of his satellites, for the given time, will give their distances from him in signs, degrees, &c. which may be turned into semi-diameters of Jupiter. To do all which is fully taught in most books of astronomical tables. These calculations made for the proposed time will give the distance in semi-diameters and tenths of Jupiter thus; *viz.* 1st satellite 08 W. the second sat. —

7-9 W. the 3d sat. = 15-0 W. and the 4th sat. = 2-2 E. Which being drawn from a scale of equal parts will appear thus

Where the configurations are adapted to the explanation given in the Nautical Almanac, H. *Questions proposed in* 1717, *and answered in* 1718.

1. Question 53, *by Mr.* Tho. Dodd.

A merchant sold sixteen diamonds at prices increasing in geometrical progression! Iie got a penny for the first, and 14348907 pence for the last. What did the sixteen diamonds come to in all, and what is the common multiplier or ratio of the progression?

Answered by Mr. J. Peirce. 15 /14348907 = 3 the ratio. Let p be $=$ first term = 1, =

Ii. Question 54, *by Mr.* Robert Boales, *of Lynn.*

Two footmen set out (to meet each other), at the same time, from the cities of London and Norwich, distant 99 miles. The footman from London goes three miles the first day, five miles the second, seven miles the third, &c.' increasing two miles each day. The footman from Norwich travels the first day a number of miles equal to one-sixth part of the number of days in which they meet, increasing each succeeding day's journey by three miles. In how many days will they meet, and how many miles will each hare travelled?

Answered by Mr. R. Hull.

Thay would meet in 6 days: The footman from Norwich travelled 48, and the Londoner 51 miles.

Solution.

Putting x for the number of days they travelled, or the number of terms in each series, of which the two common differences are 2 and 3; tbe corresponding first terms will be 3 and $ x, ... 12. (— 1) + 3 = 2a? + 1 the last terms = . ', *I* 3. $(x — 1) + x — 3x — 3$, c 2# 4-4 the sum of each pair of extremes = J

C &§X — o, r #2 4-2 T and the sum of each series, or the miles each travelled — . Then by taking the sum of these two sums, we have fars+l — 99; and hence $x — 6 = $ the number of days, and fa — 51 J

— the miles each travelled, H.

Hi. Question 55, *by* Xantippe, *of*

Ilelmsley, Yorkshire.

A legacy of 2291. 13s. 4d. is to be divided amongst three persons, M, A, N, in the following manner, namely, as often as M takes 5l. A is to take 4-fl.; and as often as A takes 4l. NL is to take 3fl. What are the respective shares?

aqd — $6V + e9 + r3\ e\sin P + r\cos p$ = —; — n, *lad* therefore $\cos p$ — , — , X $rJ(r + e2$—»s) + and the'diagonal Bd is then = $(a + i9 - 2$«$i\cos P)$. Here it may be remarked, that when the value of e is such as to 'make either?«9 or n greater than r9 + e the part under the radical becomes negative, and consequently the problem does not then admit of a solution. Therefore the limit of possibility, or the case in which the area is the greatest possible, will be when m' and w'' are each equal to r9 + e9. The values of m and n are then equal, but have a different sign, and the above expressions for cos 9 and cos p give $rm\ r\ rn$ — $r\cos 9$ = —5 or,,—jr. cos p *Ind. Geometrically.*

Suppose Abcd is the trapezium required, and p from D draw Df perpendicular to Bc and De perpendicular to Ba. Then Euclid 13, II.

BC'+CDS + 2BC CF = BD2Z=BA4 + AD4 2BA AE; B hence 2bc Cf+2ba Ae=ba2+ Ads—Bc—Cd2. Also Bc Df = twice the A Bcd, and Ba De — twice the A Bda; therefore Bc Df+ba De — twice the given area. Take He a fourth proportional to Ab, Bc and cr, and make the triangle Ekh similar to Dcf; then 2bc Cf will be — 2ba Eh, and Bc Df — Ab Ek; therefore 2ba (eh+ Ae) — 2ba. (ah) =: Ba2+ Ads—Bc2— Cd2, a given space, and Ba (ek+ Ed) — Ba Bk Zz twice the given area; . therefore Ah and Dk are given lines.

Make Hi perpendicular to Ah and = to Dk and join Id, then Khid will be a parallelogram, i a given point, and Id — Hk a given line (being a fourth proportional to Ab, Bc and Dc); hence if from the centres A and i, with distances equal to Ad and Id (or Hk), two circles be described, their intersection will determine the point D, then if Bd be drawn it will be the diagonal required.

The calculation from hence is extremely easy, for in the rightangled triangle Ahi, the side Ah is — (ba"+ad2—Bc2—Cd2)-4-2ba, the side Hi — twice the given area divided by Ba; whence Ai and the angle Hai may be found: Again in the triangle Aid, the three sides are given; whence Dai, Bab, become known, and the diagonal Bd may be found.

The construction of the problem is evidently impossible when the circles described from the centres A and i neither cut nor touch one another. But when they touch, we have the limits between which the area must be included to render the construction possible; namely, the greatest limit when they touch externally, and the least when they touch internally. In both cases the point D will be in the line Ai, and the triangle Ade similar to the triangle Cof; therefore the angle Bcd will be the supplement of Bad; consequently the trapezium will be inscribed in a circle when the area is the greatest; and will have a re-entering angle when it is the least.

Constructions and other solutions of this question may be seen in *Simpson's* Algebra and his Select Exercises. J. L.

v. Question 57, *ly Mr.* J. Symmons.

A grass-plot is to be made in the form of an ellipse, whose principal diameters are to be marked out in the following manner. The latitude of the place is 52 50' N. arifl,a pole 6 feet 8 inches long having a small ball upon the top, is to stand perpendicular to the plane of the horizon at the centre of the grass-plot; one of the semidiameters is to be the shadow of the pole at noon on the second of March, and the other scmidiameter is to be the shadow of the polo on the eleventli of June, when the sun is due west. There is then to be an elliptical step of stone five inches thick, concentrical with the grass-plot, and having the extremities of its principal axes equally-distant from the extremities of the principal axes of the grass-plot. Upon the step are to be placed four brazen lions couchant, supporting a cube, which is again to support a dodecaedron, and this again, a sphere. The contents of the cube, dodecaedron, and sphere to have the ratio of 6, 3, and 1 respectively, and to contain as many cubic inches as one third of the area of the grass-plot contains square inches. Required the sides of the cube and dodecaedron, as also the diameter of the sphere.

Answered by Ja. Peirce, Wm. Whitworth, Jos. Wilkinson, *and* Moses Bleathman.

Mar. 2. Sun's longitude 22 56' 34" X-Declin. 2 48' 28" S.

The sun's meridian altitude, 34 21' 32".

Length of the shade, 117·056 inches; which doubled, gives the the conjugate diameter of the oval 234'112 inches.

June 11. Sun's longitude 05 o 55' 41" Declination north.... 23 29 48 Sun's altitude east or west-30 1 16 Length of the shadow 1384 in.

Double is the transverse diameter 2768

The area of the oval 50916 0155

£ Taken for the 3 solid bodies 16972 0051

§ For the step 33944-0102

Transverse diam. of step 116-716

The conjugate diam. of the step 74-028

The side of the cube 21--675

Side of the dodecaedron 8-726

Diameter of the globe 14799 *Solution.*

The method of solving this question is thus:

By astronomical tables find the sun's place or longitude to the two given times; and the obliquity of the ecliptic or the greatest declination for the same: then by spherics, it will be, as radius: sine long.:: sine obliq.: sine of the present declinations. In the first case, the declin. taken from the colat. leaves the meridian altitude; and in the other, we shall have, by spherics, as s. lat.: s. obliq.:: radius: s. altitude. These altitudes being thus computed, we shall suppose to be 34 21' 32", and 30 1' 16", as in the original solution above.

Then, by plain triangles, as 1 (rad.): 80 (length of staff):: cotang. alt.: length of the shade; consequeutly 160X14622874 (cotang. 34 %l' 32") = 234-034176 inches = the conjugate diameter, and 160 X 1-7305780 (cotang.

30 1' 16") = 276-89248 — the transverse diameter: and hence the area of the green is 276-89248 X 234 034176 X-78539 &c. = 50895-58. Then of this being a number expressing the sum of the contents of the three" solids, which are in proportion to one another as 1, 3, and 6, whose sum . „ ,,,,, 508905-58 is 10; we shall have, as 10: — t I: 1696-519 — the content of the sphere y ':: 3: 5089-558 = the content of the dodecaedron r : and, by 6: 10179-116 = the content of the cube 3 mensuration %/ 10179-116 = 21-6722 = the side of the cube, / —— —-zz 87248 — the side of the dodecaedron, 7-66311890' 3 / 1696-518,. „,,,,e,,

V 4-.,,, . =: 14 /975 — the diameter of the sphere.

1 X 3-l4lo9!cc. 1

Again, for the diameters of the inner ellipse, or stone step, whose solidity is § of the area of the outer one, and the difference of its diameters = (276-89248 — 234-03418 =) 42-8583; let x — half the sum of its diameters, then the diameters will be $x \pm$ / 42 8583. x,,' 2142915 $I = J$; and their product sfi —2W1915' (per quest.) = 276 89248 X 234-03418 X f X = 8640-304; hence it = vc2142915 + 8640-304) = 95-3914, and 95-3914 ± 21-4291 = 116-8205 and 73-9623 — the diameters of the inner ellipse. H. 1 vi. Question 58, *by the Lady* Mcr. Heyshot.

A lady observes, that if the age of the younger of her two sons i« subtracted from the square of the age of the elder, the remainder will be 425: but if the age of the elder is subtracted from the square of the age of the younger the remainder will be 235. What is the age of each?

Anszsercd by Mr. Moses Bleafhman. The ages are 21 and 16 years. *Solution.* Putting x and y for the two ages, we have, per question, $x - y - 425$, and $y - x - 235$; hence $y3 - 235 + x -$ (V — 425)% or $x4 - 850s - x - -$ 180390; in which equation $x - 21$; and *tiieny*—$x2$— 425 = 16. H. PRIZE QUESTION.

There is a tctraedron standing on level ground whose content is five cubic feet; and there is also a hollow prism standing near it, capable of holding thirty-six ale gallons. The prism is open at the ends, which are equilateral triangles, and the height of the prism is equal to the side of the triangle which constitutes its end or base. Now if the hollow prism is put upon the tetraedron so as exactly to fit the end, what will be the height of the end of the prism above the base of the tetraedron? And suppose another pyramid put into the other end of the prism so as exactly to fit the same, and its height such that the vertex thereof shall just meet that of the tetraedron. What quantity of liquor will fill the space of the prism which is, left vacant?

Answered by Mr. Char. Mason. *Inches.* The side of each triangle of the tetraedron....41 "853

The perpendicular altitude 3417283136

The side and altitude ofihe prism 28-6209

Consequently the side of the base of that part 28.K909 of the tetraedron which is within the prism S

Its perpendicular altitude. 23-3683

Its content in ale-gallons 9-79793

The perpendicular altitude of the pyramid.... 5-25204

Its content in ale-gallons 220203

The content of the two pyramids 1199999

Content of the prism when placed according) 24-0000 to the import of the question in ale-gallons '

The elevation of the prism 108039 *Solution.*

Since the two ends of the prism are filled up by two pyramids whose vortexes meet within it, ihe height of the two together is just equal to the altitude of the prism; and since a pyramid is — of a prism of the same altitude and base, it is evident that f of the prism will be filled with liquor, that is, it will contain 24 gallons: which is one part of the demand. The other is to find the additional elevation of the prism, which, being evidently = the difference between the altitude of the tetraedron and of the part of it which is let into the prism, will be found thus.

By the Schol. page 403 Mensuration, 12 1/ (6 X 5 — 12 1/ (30.t/2) = 41853 inches =: the side of the whole tetraedron; 3 /l oO 6 V -j-y — 28-62092 = the side of the prism = the side of the tetraedron which is within the prism. And it is the difference of the altitudes of these two which is required, Now, from the demon stration, page 403 Mensuration, it appears that the side of a tetraedron is to its altitude, as 1 to;and since the difference between 41-85300 and 28 62092 the sides of the two tetraidrons is 13-23208, we shall have 13-23208 = 10-80394 = the additional elevation required, H. *Questions proposed in* 1718, *and answered in* 1719.

I. Question 59, *by Mr.* Doidge, *of Portsmouth.*

Required the side of a regular decagon whose area shall be 1(53 feet? *Answered by* Anna Philomathes. 5543 inches — to the polygon's side = 4-602 feet. *Solution.*

By mensuration, f *(5 + 2 or 7 6942088* drawn into the square of the side of a decagon is its area; wherefore the side will be ii. Question 60, *by Mr.* Tho. Cary, *of Lynn.*

There is a circular pond whose area is 50284 square feet, in the middle of which stood a pole 100 feet high; now the pole having been broken it was observed that the top just struck the brink of the pond, what is the height of the piece left standing?

Answered by Mr. W. Laughton.

Let r — 40-008 the radius of the pond; $k = to$ the piece broke off; and p — to standing piece. Then $h + p - a - 100$, and $hh = pp + rr$ by 47 Euclid i. Hence $hh + ihp + pp = aa$. And $hh - pp - rr$. By subtracting, $2/i/ + 2pp - aa -$ rr. „.. $aa - rr$ $aa - rr$ ThenP $= WTp$-= St = 41'9968 feet' *Additional Solutions. 1st. Algebraically.*

The square of the radius of the circle is 4 X-7b539 &c.

8800 _ = 1600-644, which put — a3; also put c = 100 the whole height of the pole, and x — the part standing. Then will c — x be the part broken off, and is the hypothenuse of a rightangled triangle whose two legs are a and x; consequently $a'' + "$

— (c — x)1 — c — lex + xs; and hence

x —— the length required.
Ind. Geometrically.
Here are given the base and the sum of the hypothenuse and perpendicular, of a right-angled triangle; to construct the same. Which will be done thus:

Making Ab the radius of the circular pond, and Bc the pole perpendicular to it; join A, c; and draw Ad making the angle Dac Z Dca; so shall Bd be the part standing, and Da or DC the part broke off.—For because of the equality of the Z's Dca, Dac, their opposite sides Da, Dc will be equal. Q. E. D. H. in. Question 61, *by Mr.* Peter Ward.

It is required to fill a magic square, consisting of 100 squares or spaces, that is, 10 in length, and as many in breadth, with numbers in such a manner that the 10 lines in length and the 10 lines in (he breadth shall each amount to 505; and also the two diagonals shall each amount to 505, and the numbers in no two squares or spaces to be alike.

Answer. There are many different zcays of answering or filing this magic square.
The following one is thus filled by Mr. J. Harris.

These numbers make 505 ten times in the lines, ten limes in the columns, and twice diagonally.

Additional Solution. A general method of Jilting Magic, Squares. By Numericus.

When an arithmetical scries of numbers are disposed in the cellsof a square, so that the sums in the horizontal, vertical, and diagonal ranks are alike, the square is called a *magic square*. It is not necessary, however, that the series should be a continued one; because it may be disjunct or broken, as 1 2 3 4 9 10 11 12.; or 2 4 6 11 13 15 20 22 24, &c.

We shall begin with squares whose roots are odd numbers; the general method of construction being more simple than in cases where the roots are even.

To make a magic square oj 25 cells with the series 1, 2, 3, §c.
Put 13 the middle number of the series in the middle cell *(Fig.* 1.); the greatest and least numbers 25 and 1 in the cells next above and below; the root 5 and its complement (21) to 26 (= 25 + 1) in the adjacent cells to the left and right; then fill one diagonal with the numbers in their natural order from 13 both ways; and let the common difference of the numbers in the other diagonal be the root 5.

(25 4-1) x 121Then each diagonal will contain =: 65 the number *Fig.* 1. required in each rank of the square.

The 3d. or middle columns, vertical and horizontal, are each 26 short of 65; but 8 + 18 (in the diagonal) — 26; consequently 8—1-f18-V-1, and 8+ 1 + 18—1 respectively make 26; hence if 8—1, 8 +1, and 18—1, 18+1 (or 7, 9, 17, 19) are in the extreme cells, those columns will each.contain 65..Now 7, 8, 9; 17, 18., 19 have the same constant difference as the numbers in that diagonal to which they are parallel. And 7, 12, 17; and 9, 14, 19 in cells parallel to the other diagonal differ by the root 5, the common difference of the numbers in that diagonal. In this manner we get the numbers for the other cells. Hence to fill a square whose root is an odd number:—Place the middle numbers and fill the diagonals as above directed; then let the other numbers in the cells parallel to the diagonals, have the same respective differences as the numbers in those diagonals. *(Fig. 2.)*

Figures 3 and 4 are magic squares whose sides are 3 and 9, constructed in this manner: *Fig.* 3. *Fig.* 4.

In these squares it is manifest that the opposite columns, equidistant from die centre, may change places, and the columns on the same side of the centre may also be changed, provided a similar variation takes place in the other half of the square.

When the root is *unevenly-even,* as 6, 10, 14, &c. Let the square be that of 6, with the series 1, 2, 3, 4, &c. to 36. » / *Arrange tlie numbers in pairs as beloa.*
1 2 3 4 5 6 7 8 9 10 11 12 13 14 15 16
17 18 36 35 34 33 32 31 30 29 28 27 26
25 24 23 22 21 20 19

Each pair being 37 or of 111 the number required in each rank of
«. (36 + i) X 18 _ the square; or = 111.

Let these pairs be regularly placed in a square *(Fig.* 5.) the greater number above the less in the alternate vertical columns. Then each verticiil column wilK belli; but the horizontal columns are alternately 102 and 120, or the defect in one column equal to the excess in the other. Now the common differences of the two middle numbers, the two next, and the two extremes in the 5th. vertical column from the left, is 9: let these change places and the vertical and horizontal ranks of the square will each be 111 *(Fig.* 6.) The diagonals, however, are 156 and 66, therefore the excess and defect are equal; and since the pairs, and also the columns may be changed at pleasure, the diagonals arc easily made equal: 20 23 thus, change *yj* for j, then let the 2d.

place of the 5th; the 3d that of the 2d; and *Fig.* 7. the 5th the place of the 3d, *(Fig.* 7). The same thing, however may be effected by shifting pairs only. In this manner a square of 10 may be constructed.

But in the case ol roots unevenly-even, an easier method seems to be that of adding a border to a square. We shall give an example of constructing a magic square of 100 cells, with borders, or *a magic square containing magic squares,* by adding three successive borders to the square of 4.

There are several methods of filling the square of 16 cells; the following, however is easily remembered:—Arrange the 16 numbers in a square thus, *(Fig.* 8*j*

One diagonal consists of the two extremes of the *Fig.* 8.

series with two other numbers equally distant from those extremes; the other of 4 numbers, two and two, which also are respectively at equal distances; consequently the diagonals are each = (16+ 1) X 2 = 34 = (16 X 8 the num 4 ber required in each rank of the square. Next, 2,

15, and 3, 14 are also equidistants, and their sum *Fig.* 9.

zz 34. The difference of the two middle perpendicular ranks is 4; and because 14 + 15 +
$t + 3 = 1 + 4 + 13 + 16 = 34$, if 15 and 2, and 14 and 3 change places, the upper

and the lower ranks, and the two middle vertical ranks, will each be 34: and when 5 and 12, and 9 and 8 are shifted in the same manner, we shall have the magic square, *(Fig. 9.)*

Now with the 16 middle numbers (or from 43 to 58) of the series 1, 2, 3, 4, &c. to 100, make the magic or central square of 16 cells (see *Fig.* 10). Then for the first border take the 10 adjacent numbers on each side of those 16 numbers, and arrange then as below: 33 34 35 36 37 38 39 40 41 42
68 67 66 65 64 63 62 61 60 59

The upper or less numbers being the complements of those below to 101 or *I* of each rank of the square of 6 when completed with the border: hence it follows, that 3 of the greater numbers and 3 of the less, which are not the complements of those 3 greater, must form a rank, and their sum be 303. Now in any arithmetical series the sum of the 3d, 5th, and 6th terms are equal to the sum of the 2d, 4th, and 8th, or the 3d, 4th, and 5th are together equal to the two first with the 9th. Adopting this latter combination, we have 68+ 67+ 60+ 35+36+37 for a rank, (because 33 + 31 +41 = 35 + 36+37). Let 68 and 67 be the corner numbers in the column (the lower for example), and put their complements in the opposite corners diagonally; also place the other numbers in the lower column, and their complements in tha opposite cells at top; and the upper and lower ranks of the border will be completed.

To fill the side columns we have 63, 62, 61, and 59, with their complements. First, 303 — (68 + 34) = 201: now 201 = 63 + 59 + 39 + 40, which are the numbers for the left column of the border; put their compclmcnts opposite in the other column, and the first border is completed.

The 2d border is constructed with the following 28 numbers, or the 14 next less than 33, and the other 14 next greater than 68.
19 20 21 22 23 24 25 26 27 28 29 30 31 32
82 81 80 79 78 77 76 75 74 73 72 71 70 69

Four of the greater numbers and 4 of the less (their sum being 404 — 4 pair) are necessary for a column of the border: now the two first terms of an arithmetical series *plus* the 7th and 8th are equal to the sum of the 3:1, 4th, 5th, and 6th, or 19 + 20+25 + 26 = 21 + 22 + 23 + 24; therefore the latter numbers with 82, 81, 76 and 75 make 404; put these numbers in the lower column of the border, and let 82 and 81 be the corner numbers, and their complements the other corner numbers diagonally; then fill the opposite cells with the complements of those below.

To fill the left hand column of this border, we have 82 + 20 — 102 which is greater than 101 by 1, therefore 3 terms of the series 27, 28, 29, 30, 31, 32 must exceed the other three by 1; now 28 + 20+31 + 1=27+30+32, Gr 28 + 27 + 32 =27+ 30+ 31 + 1; taking the first 3 will give 28, 29, 31, 74, 71, 69, with their complements, for the left, and right columns.

The remaining 36 numbers for the outward border, when arranged in pairs, will stand as below: t 2 3 4 5 6 7 8 9 10 11 12 13 14 15 16 17 18 100 99 98. 97 96 95 94 93 92 91 90 89 88 87 86 35 84 83

Here in the upper, or series of the less numbers, one of the combinations is 1 + 2+3+9+15=4+5 + 6+7+8, and therefore either five, with the complement of the other five, make 505=101X5 the number in each rank of this border.

Take 4, 5, 0, 7, 8, and 100, 9P, 98, 92, 86 for the lowest rank, and make 100 and 99 the corner numbers, then 2 and 1 will be at the oilier corners; and the other cells at top are filled with the other complements. We now have the 8 numbers 10, 11, 12, 13, 14, 10, 17, 18, with their complements, to till the two side columns. First, £05 — (100 + 2) = 403; therefore 4 of those 8 numbers together must exceed the other 4 by 1: now 12 + 13 + 14 + 16 + 1 = 10 + 11 + 17+18, (or 12+13+11+17 = 10+11 + 18+16 + 1, &c.): let 12, 13, 14, 16, and 83, 81, 90, 91, be in the left column, and their complemer'ts opposite in the right, and the square is completed; and the method is similar when the roots are odd numbers.

Hence the construction of these borders depends on the solution of this simple problem.— Having an arithmetical series, to find a proposed number of the. terms whose sum shall be equal to the sum of the like number of the other terms: or that the two sums shall have a given difference.

A singular and curious property belongs to these magic squares with borders; it is this:—The sum of the squares of the numbers in any rank of a border, is equal to the sum of the squares of the numbers in the opposite rank of that border: thus in the square *(Fig.* 10.J the sum of the squares of 100, 98, 92, 86, 4, 5, 6, 7, 8, 99 is the same as that of the numbers 2, 3, 9,. 15, 97, 96, 95, 94, 93, 1. The numbers, however, are so related, that when the differences of the least number in the lower column and the other numbers in that column are taken from the greatest number in thcupper column, the remainders are the other numbers in the upper column: in which case, when the sums arc equiil, the sums of their squares; will also be equal. See an investigation of this property in the answer to Quest. 281, No. 11, Ley bourn's Math. Repository.

Hence it appears that an arithmetical series of an even number of terms, which can be formed into a magic square, may be disposed in setts, so that their sums, and also the sums of their squares, shall respectively be equal. Thus *(Fig. 9.)* the sum of the squares of the numbers in the two upper columns, in the two lower, in the two left hand columns, in the two on the right, and also in the two diagonals, are all equal.

A. magic square whose root is any number greater than 3 may be constructed by adding a border, or borders. But there are other methods when the roots are *evenly-even,* as 4, 8, 12, 16, &c. Let it be required to make a square of 64 cells with the series 1, 2,-3, 4, &c. to 64.

Arrange the 64 numbers in 4j ranks of pairs, the pairs making alternately 66 and 64, (64 + 2, 63 + 1, 62 + 4, &c.)
A C
G H

Let the pairs on the left of Abg, and those to the right of Cdii be each —-t of the whole; then the numbers on the left of Ab, together "with those on the right of Cd are to fill one square of 16 cells; those between Ab and Cd another; the numbers on the left of Bg, and on the right of Dii, a third; and the middle numbers a 4th.

Now let the upper or less numbers be disposed in 4serics of pairs, thus 1 2 7 8 3 4 5 6 17 18 23 24 19 20 21 22 16 15 10 9 14 13 12 11 32 31 2G 25 30 29 28 27

If the vacant cells are filled with the corresponding or lower numbers 64, 63, 62, &c. and the 4 squares joined together in the or,der they stand, the square of 64 cells will be completed. *(Fig-*12. *Fig.* 12.

A corresponding number is that which, with the less number, forms it pair: thus 61 must stand above 3; 60 above 6; 64 under 2, &c.

The sum in each of the horizontal, vertical, and diagonal ,. (64+l)x32 ranks is ——— 260.
8

The sum in the bent row, or from 50 to 59, and from 31 to 22 (parallel to the diagonal is also = 260. And the sum in the next bent row, or from 9 to 5, and from 44 to 40 is also 260, &c.; and the same thing holds, taking the rows on the sides, or upwards, parallel to the diagonals. The sum of the 4 corner numbers of each of the 4 concentric squares is 130 or half a vertical rank. And the sum of every 4 contiguous numbers forming a square is also 130. Some of these properties are noticed by Dr. Franklin, (see his works, vol. 3, edit. 1806). But the Doctor's square of 64 cells is imperfect, because it fails diagonally.

In the same manner we can fill a square of 256 cells (r: 16 X 16) thus: Arrange the 256 numbers (from 1 to 256) in 4 divisions, each division containing two ranks of pairs, the pairs being alternately 258 and 256, or 256+2, 255+1, 254+4, &c. and consequently 4 of the greater pairs, together with 4 of the less, or 258x4+256x4= 2056 (J6 128) e number required in each of the hori zontal, vertical, and diagonal ranks of the square: 2 1 4 3 6 5 8 7 10 9 12 11 14 13 16 15 256 255 254 253 252 251 250 249 248 247 246 245 244 243 242 241 18 17 20 19 22 21 24 23 26 25 28 27 '30 29 32 31 S40 239 238 237 236 235 234 233 232 231 230 229 228 227 226 225 34 33 36 35 38 37 40 39 42 41 44 43 46 45 48 47 224 223 222 221 220 219 218 217 216 215 214 213 212 211 210 209 50 49 52 51 54 53 56 55 58 57 60 59 62 61 64 63 208 207 206 205 204 203 202 201 200 199 198 197 196 195 194 193 66 65 68 67 70 69 72 71 74 73 76 75 78 77 80 79 192 191 190 189 188 187 186 185 184 183 182 181 180 179 178 177 82 81 84 83 86 85 88 87 90 89 92 91 94 93 96 95 176 175 174 173 172 171 170 169 168 167 166 165 164 163 162 161 98 97 100 99 102 101 104 103 106 105 108 107 110 109 112 111 i 160 159 158 157 156 155 154 153 152 151 150 149 148 147 146 145 114 113 116 115 118 117 120 119 122121 124 123 126 125 128 127 144 143 142 141 140 139 138 137 136 135 134 133 132 131 130 129

Now with these 4 divisions make 4 magic squares of 64 cells each, exactly as the square *(Fig. 1%)* was constructed: these put together will form the magic square of 256 cells. We shall put down the process for one square with the first division, though it will appear something like a repetition:

This arrangement is similar to that for the square referred to *(Fig.* The upper or less numbers are the same as in that ex ample; therefore the four adjacent squares are copies of *Fig.* 11.

The horizontal, vertical, and diagonal ranks of the 4 squares are each 1028, or just half a rank of the great square. And if we take the numbers in any bent row of the great square parallel to the diagonals, either downwards, upwards, or sideways, their sum is 2056: thus from 247 to 200, and from 10S to 90 the sum is 2056, &c. Also the 4 confer numbers of each of the 8 concentric squares make 514 or £ of a rank: thus 46 + 131 + 82 + 255 (at the corners of the 7th square) make 514.—If the 4 outward columns all round are taken away, there will remain a magic square of 64 cells. And the sum of the numbers in every 16 contiguous cells forming a square is 2050; in other words, if a square hole be cut in a paper just the size of 16 cells, and the paper laid any where upon the square, the numbers appearing through the hole will together make 2056. Dr. Franklin's square of 256 cells answers in this respect: but here again he has failed in an essential property of a magic square; his diagonals, instead of being equal, are 1297 and 2184; this inequality seems to have been the consequence of his not having followed a regular alternation in falling the half columns .

The engrarer has made three mistakes in the Doctor's square; 181 in the comer shou'd be 185; 241 in the 7th column should be 211; and the figure 3 is wanting in the number 203 in col. 1.

Thus we have a square much more magical than the Doctor's famous square, which he sets down as ' the most magically magical of any magic square ever made by any magician."

It will not be difficult to comprehend the *rationale* of this mode of construction. The sum of each two numbers in the two squares to the left *(Vig. Vi.)* is 17, and in the other two 49, therefore the sums of their complements are respectively equal; and consequently when the latter are placed in the vacant cells, each horizontal and vertical rauk will be 17 + 497 = 514 in the two squares to the left; and 49 + 465 zr 514 in the other two (497 and 465 being the respective sums of the complemental numbers): the diagonals, however, ara 498 and 530, but 498 + 530 = 1028, therefore in joining the 4 squares *(Fig.* 13 J together, the diagonal 498 of one square, and that which is 530 of another, must make a diagonal of the square of 64 cells. And in putting together the 4 squares to form the large square, it is necessary that the sum of each 5th pair of numbers (counting from the right, or from the left, or from the top downwards) where the halves of the square join, should respectively be the same: thus 129 + 84 = 145 + 68 = 193 + 20, &c. or 52 + 157=58+151, &c. the property respecting every 16 cells evidently depends on this:

If the square be cut horizontally, or vertically, through the middle, the halves may change places, and the properties of the square will remain as before.

The construction of a common magic square of magic squares is more simple than the foregoing. Thus let the series be 1, 2, 3, 4, &c. to 64. With the 8 first numbers of the series and the 8 last, make a magic square of 16 cells *(Fig. 15.J* according to the method for *Fig. 9.* And with the eight numbers next greater than 8, and the 8 numbers next less than 57, fill another in the same manner *(Fig. 16J* rA'ne 8 numbers next greater than 16, and the 8 numbers next less than 49 are for the 3d square ; and the remaining 16 middle numbers for the 4th.

The columns and diagonals *Fig.* 15. of these 4 squares are 130 each, and consequently they may be joined together in any order so as to form a square. This is the most expeditious method of constructing magic squa-es whose roots are multiples of 4. .To make a square of this kind when the root is 9 *(Fig. 17.)* Let the series be 1, 2, 3, *4, kc.* to 81. Divide this series into 9 other series of 9 numbers each, a follow: *Fig.* 16. t 10 19 28 37 46 55 64 73 2 11 20 29 38 47 56 65 74 3 12 21 30 39 48 57 66 75

If a magic square be made *Fig. 17.* with each of these series, the ranks in the squares will respectively be 111, 114, 117, 120, 123, 126, 129, 132, 135; and a magic square constructed with these numbers would have 031±m) = 369.n 3 each rank, the same as the square *(Fig. 4.),* the 9 squares must therefore be arranged in the same order as the figures stand in *Fig.* 3, or in the squares themselves.

Four squares of 25 cells each will make the square of 10; and 4 squares of 49 cells, the square of 14, &c.

If a magic square is constructed with a geometrical progression, *the products,* instead of the sums, will be equal. /

There are other methods of constructing these squares; for (the square of 9 cells excepted) they all admit of many changes. In those squares of the most simple construction, such as *Fig.* 2, 4, and 9, we get varieties by merely transposing the columns that are equally distant from the centres of the squares. Thus in *Fig.* 2, columns 3 and 4, may take place of each other: columns 1 and 2, and 4 and 5 may be shifted to the opposite sides; or the two first, and the two last, may respectively change places and remain on the same sides of the squares, &c. In this manner any number in the square *(Fig. 9.)* may be shifted to any proposed cell in the square. And hence it is evident that the permutations which may take place, particularly in the larger squares, must be extremely numerous; but the computations for the exact number in any case are very tedious.

The earliest European authors whose works con-*Fig.* 18. tain any thing upon magic squares, are Cor. Agrippa, Stifelius, and Bachet. Afterwards came Frenicle, who wrote professedly on magic squares, and first constructed those with borders. In 1704, M. Poignard published a treatise on the subject, in which is introduced a new species of magic squares, made with progressions repeated as often as there are units in the roots. *Fig.* 18, is a square of this kind, constructed with the series 1 2 3 4 taken 4 tunes, which are *so* disposed that neither of the numbers occur twice in any rant. By substituting letters, however, it appears that the numbers for this purpose are not necessarily confined to progressions of any kind. Figures 19, 20, 21, are three squares filled with letters repeated; but the same letter is not found twice in any column or diagonal. Now it i9 evident that the letters may represent any number whatever..

Ozanam, in his Math. Recreations; and M. M. De la Hire, and Sauveur, in the Mem. of the French Acad. 1705, 1710, have als» treated the subject of magic squares at considerable length.

Among the ancients magic squares were held in great veneration, and supposed to be endowed with occult virtues; and it appears that they still are used as talismans in the East. A magic square of 16 cells stands over the door of a house in Bengal, and underneath is the following prayer or supplication in the Persian language:

O God preserve the Doctor of the Faith, surnamed Karkhy, from the calamities of this world. May he be always a favorite of heaven, whilst Moses is selected as porter to Aly.

IT. Question 62, *by Mr.* William Whitworth, *of Northampton.*

Required the.dimensions of a leaden cistern, the form a parallelopipedon, to hold just 50 bushels, the length and breadth to be in the ratio of 5 to 3, the lead half an inch thick and the least quantity possible; also, what the cistern cost at If *d.* per pound?

Answered by Anna Philomathes. Let $b — 5$, $c = 3$, and $aaa — 107520$ cubic inches in 50 bushels, also let x — length; then will — breadth, = to $7\ b\ exx\ A\ J\ it\text{-}J\ ccxxz + Ibbam + Ibcaaa \ldots c$, the depth, and —— to least superficies of tistern. „,. $Zccx'x — \ 'ibha\ x — Ibcax$ „,. „,7. lhe fluxion thereof is — $Iccx\ x — Ibba\ x\ bcxx — Zbca'x = 0$. Therefore $x\text{-}J\ M'a' + — =$ length$=78\text{-}181426\ cc\ cx\ ba3$ inches, — =: breadth $= 469088$ inches, and —— = depth $= 29\text{-}318$ inchesr

The purchase 14/. Is. *7d. Additional Solution.*

The above original solution is false as well as that given in the *Diarian Repository,* they both making the internal surface a *minimum,* which is contrary to the intention of the question; for it expressly declares "To have it that the least lead will require," and consequently the difference between the solids made up of the external and internal dimensions must be the *minimum.* Wherefore putting the C length $zz\ Bx$ 1 the external $C\ 5x + 2$ — length) internal breadth $zz\ 3x$, dimensions-?$3a; + 1 =$ breadth V.

f depth $z = y$) will be $(\_y + zz$ depth 3 And hence $Ibx'y = 107520$, and $(5x + 1). (3x + 1). + f) — J5xy$ or $xl + (Sx + 1). (y + i)\ zz$ a *minimum.* The value of *if* being exterminated out of this equation, by means of the first, and its fluxion put $= 0$, we at last obtain $15x4 + Ax' — 57344c — 14336 = 0$; in which equation the root x is $= 15\text{-}630773$. Wherefore $bx — 78\text{-}135865 =$ internal length, $3a := 46\text{-}892319\ zz$ inter v J.u A 1(47520 7168.., nal breadth, and,y —— zz r:

29338444 zz internal depth; also by adding 1 to each of the former numbers and f to the latter, we have 79-153865, 47-892319, and 29-838444 for the external length, depth, and breadth. From the continual product of these three taking 107520 the content of the inside, there remains 5594-34 for the cubic inches of lead in the cistern; and this multiplied by-409618/6. the weight of a cubic inch of lead according to *Ward*, the product is 229154/6. of lead, which at lftf. a pound, amounts to 14/. 6s. 5d. 1-24$f. H.... t" v. Question 63, *by Mr.* Lewis Evan, *from Carmarthenshire.*

Ten persons (a, B, K) purchase the hay to be produced upon a certain meadow for 40/. The first contributes a certain sum, the second 5s. more than the first, the third 5s. more than the second, and so on to the last; the form of the meadow is that of a rightangled triangle, the hypothenuse being 50, and the other two sides 30 and 40 chains. They agreed to have the meadow divided into shares, by lines perpendicular to the hypothenuse or longest sidej which should be proportional to the sums contributed. Th« share of the first to be adjacent to the less acute angle, that of the second adjacent to that of the first, &c. How must the hypothenuse be divided?
Solution.
By the nature of arithmetical progression, having given the comaion difference $5 - d$, the number of terms $10 =: n$, and the sum of the series $40 \times 20 = 800 = s$; there will be found the first term $Is - dn.hi - 1) 1600 - 450. \_. \,,, a - -i '- - - 57-k. = 11. 17s. Cd. -$ In 20 2

A's share of the money, and by the constant addition of 5s. all the rest will be found to be as in the second column of the original solution above. 1

Then, their shares of the field will be in proportion as their sums of money, and since the triangle is evidently right-angled, and its area $= 30 \times 20 - 600$ chains — 60 acres, we shall have, as 40/.: 60 acres or as 2: 3:: 2/. 17. 6rf.: 4-3125 acres = *4ac. Iro. Wpo.* rr A's share, and as *11. : 3:: 5s.: -375ac.* = lro. *lOpo.* — the common difference; which being continually added will give the several shares as in the 3d column.

Again, for the bases and perpendiculars: Since the first and last parts arc triangles similar to the whole field, and similar triangles being as the squares of their like sides, we shall have, 40 10-723 = A's base as:/4-3125:: *I* 30: 8-042 = A's perpendicular, j.,,»c 40: 14'317 = K's perpendicular and /60: 4/7'6875:: *1 v v v I* 30: 10-738 = K's base,

Then to the first and last areas add their adjacent ones, and the sums will be the next similar triangles; whose sides being calculated in the same manner, their perpendiculars will be those in the last column, and the differences of the bases will be the bases in the column next to it. H.

Vi. Question 64, *by Mr.* Rob. Beales.

A person has a legacy of 200/. left him, but which is not to be paid till the end of 9 years hence; being in want of money, he agrees to sell it for 100/. to be paid immediately: What rate per cent, per annum compound interest does the purchaser obtain for his ready money?
Answered by Anna Philomathes.
Seven pounds seven shillings and fourpence farthing per cent, per annum, compound interest.
Solution.
If *r* be put for rate of *l.* by the nature of compound interest, we shall have 100 x $(1 + r) = 200$, or $(1 + r) 4 = 2$, or $(1 + r)3 9 = 24 = 16$; and $r = 16 - 1 =$ 07368. Hence the rate per cent, is 100 X-07368 — 7-368 s *71. 7s. 4d.* 1-28. H.
PRIZE QUESTION.
Required the Sides and radii of the circumscribing circles of two regular polygons, the less of five sides and the other of seven, from the following data, *viz.* the less polygon is to the greater as 3 to 13, and the line subtending the angle formed by two adjacent sides of the pentagon is equal to the length of a pendulum which vibrates 61 times in a minute.
Ansxcered by Mr. W. Whitworth.
The lengths of pendulums are reciprocally proportionable to the squares of their vibrations.
Therefore as square $61 = 3721$: $3600 :: 30 2: 37-9252 = b$ the subtense,

whence the side a must be found by this theorem: If a quadrangle be inscribed in a circle, the rectangles of the two diagonals will be equal to both the rectangles of the opposite sides.

Now the diagonals being each equal to the subtense *b,* the theorem is era + ba = bb; ergo, a = *(bb + ±bb)* — b — 23-439062 inches, the side of the pentagon.

Then *b* being the hypothenuse of a rectangle triangle described in a circle, and *cd* part of the diameter (as far as where the perpendicular falls) the base, the perpendicular being ; we hare */(bb — — I 2 4 / = cd;* and *aa -4-cd — df* the other part of the diameter; and *cd + df* — diameter required. Also the area of the pentagon will be 945-210782. Then 3: 13:: 945-2107: 9095-91339L2 = area of heptagon, 3-633912: 1:: 4095-91 in duplicate ratio, to side of the heptagon. Then the other parts are easily found, as below.

Parts. Pentagon. Heptagon.
The area of (he 945-2107 4095-9133
Diameter of circumscribing circle.. 39-8708 76-8283
Diameter of inscribed circle 32-2611 69-1047
Circumscribing circle 125-2768 241-3637
Inscribed circle 101-3510 217-0994
Questions proposed in 1719, *and answered in* 1720.

I. Question 65, *by Mr.* Henry Walker.

There is a piece of gold in the form of a parallelopipedon, and the product of the length and depth in inches b 96; the product of the breadth arid depth is 80, and the product of the length and breadth 120; what are the dimensions themselves, and what is th« weight and value of the piece?
Answer.
The length 12, the breadth 10, and depth 8 inches, and if-10083 inch — 1 ounce, and the troy pound = 42/. *10s.* the value was 337181.19s. 9d.
Solution.
From the question it is evident that the breadth is to the length as 80 to 96, or as 5 to 6, and to the depth as 120 to 96 or as 5 to 4.

Now the product of 4 and 5 is 20,

which is similar to the product 80 in the question; and each of the proportional numbers 4, 5, 6 will be to the corresponding numbers required, as the root of 20 to the root of 80. Wherefore as $(\sqrt{20}: \sqrt{80}:: yi: \sqrt{4}::)$ f 4: 8 = the depth, 1: 2:: 5: 10 = the breadth, » t 6: 12 = the length.

Hence the content is 8 X 10 X 12 r 960 inches. And, using Ward's tables, 960 X 10-359273 ounces = 80 X 10-359273 = 828 741841b. which at 42l. 10s. per lb. amount to 35221l. 10s. 6d. 3-072q. H.

Algebraically.

Let x, y, and z represent the length, breadth, and depth of the wedge; then, by the question, $xz — 96$, $yt — 80$, and $xy — 120$. The product of these equations is $x1y1zi$ 921600, the square root of which is xyz 960. Divide this equation by each of the given ones and we have $x — 12$, $y — 10$, and $2=8$, as above, t.

Ii. Question 66, *by Mr.* W. Doidge.

In the latitude of 50 48' a beautiful rainbow was observed bearing N. E. E. What was the time of the day?

Answered by Mr. William Armstrong.

If the sun was near the equinox, which is unlimited in the question, it was 33 min. 45 seconds past 3 evening.

Solution.

In the above original solution to this question, it is justly remarked that the question is unlimited, as the declination or time of the year should have been given, and then the solution would have been very easy: For as the rainbow is formed directly opposite to the sun with regard to the observer, the bearing of the sun will be S. W. i W. so that in a spherical triangle would be given two sides (the colat. and codeclin.) and an angle (the sun's azimuth or bearing from the north) opposite to one of them (the codeclin.), to find their included angle = the measure of the time from noon required, Ii. m. Question 67, *by Mr.* W. Hawney.

How many different ways is it possible to pay oue hundred pounds with guineas and pistoles only, reckoning the guineas at 21s. 6d. and the pistoles at 17s. each.

Answered by Mrs. Hesychia.
Three; *viz.* Guineas 10, 44, 78 Pistoles 105, 62, 19.

Solution.

Put x and y for the number of guineas and pistoles respectively, then the number of sixpences in them being 43a; and 34?/, and the sixpences in 100l. = 4000, we shall have 43a; + $5ly — 4000$; 4000— 34?/ „„ $My — 1$ hence $x — — 93$ 2—— a whole number; 43, 43 a $S4y — 1$, „ iL. 170 — 5 consequently — — as also 5 times the same, *viz.* —— a 172?/ whole number: take this from the whole number —— 4?/, and » 43 2?/ 4-5 there remains the whole number —rz—: from 22 times this whole 43 number, *viz.* — 11 take the whole number ——?/, and 5 43 43 " there remains the whole number — which put — p; then y — 43p _ 110, where the least value olp is evidently 3. Substitute this , ., r,, „„ 4000—34w value of y in the value of x, and we shall have x — ———— — 180 —34p, in which the greatest value *of p* is evidently 5. So that the question admits of only three, solutions, p having only three values, *viz.* 3, 4, and 5; and by writing each of these numbers for p in the values *ofx&ndy*, we obtain x — 78, 44, and 10, and?/ =: 19, 62, and 105. H. iv. Question 68, *by Mr.* John Leddell.

There is a segment of a circle the chord of which is 60 feet, and versed sine 10 feet; what will be the versed sine of that segment of the same circle whose chord is 90 feet?

Answer.

The versed sine's length is 28-2055 feet.

I *Solution.*

The right sine being 30, and versed sine 10, by the nature of the circle, the diameter will be 10 + 30-f-10 = 100, and consequently the radius = 50. But, by right-angled triangles, the cosine of the arc whose right sine is 45, will be =. /(so9 _ 45) = 5v"(10 — 9s) = 5/19 = 21-7944947, &c. which being taken from the radius 50, there remains 28205505, &c. for the versed sine required, H. v., Question 69, *by Mr.* J. Smith.

Three persons A, E, and Y, bought a piece of land in the form of an ellipse, for 1801. The conjugate axis is 40 chains and the distance of the focus from the centre 15 chains, the abscissa of Y's part is to be 18 chains, and the rectangular ordinate of E's part 15 chains; A's share lies between those of Y and E, what is each person's share of the land, and what sum ought each to pay?

Answer.

A's part 96-65864 pounds.
E's 25-19722
It's.... 58-14413.

Solution,

By the right-angled triangles, the distance between the foens and the end of the conjugate will be Z(20S + 15s) = 25 = the semitransverse by the nature of the ellipse; then, by case 2, p. 225 Men.
„ 25 V (20s— 15s) „„ 25(4'— 3s) „„ juration, 25 v. = 25 i. = 25 —
'20 4 25 /7
———— = 8-4640543, &c. = the abscissa of E's part.

Now =-169281, and g =-36; but the tabular area for these two quotients, in the table of segments at the end of my Mensuration, are-08799586 and-25455055, whose sum taken from 78539816, there remains-44285175. Also the product of the two axes = 50 X 40 = 2000.

Then, by rule 2, p. 244 Mensuration, we shall have. 08799586 x 2000 = 175-99172 = E's part 1 25455055 X 2000 = 509-10110 = Y's part C in square chains; 44285175 X 2000 = 885 70350 = A's part) their sum being 1570-79632 = '78539816 X 2000 = the area of the 'whole ellipse.

Also, by proportion, we have as 1570-79632: 1801.
C175-99172: 20-16721. = 20l. 3s. 4d. 0-512q. = E's money, 509-10110: 58-3387 = 58 6 i 1-152 = Y's, (885-70350: 101-4941 = 101 9 10 2-336 = A's. 180 0 0 sum. So that the numbers in the original solution are false. H. iv. Question 70, *by Mr.* J. Dodd.

To find the area of a triangular piece of land there is given one of the angles 30 43 and the rectangle of the including sides 168-75 chains.

Answered by Mr. John Finch, *of Norwich.* As rad.: s. given angle:: § the rectangle given: area 4a. lr. 9p. *Solution.*

By a known rale for the area of a triangle, we have as 1:-510793 (the nat. sine of 30 43/) t: 84-375 = half the product of the including sides: 43-09817 chains = 4a. lr. 9-5707 perches. H.

Vii. Question 71, *by Mr. Alex. Naughley, of Cumberland.*

Required the dimensions of a stone trough to contain 5400 cubic Inches; and the sum of its length, breadth, and depth to be 57 inches?
Answered by Mr. Nath. Brown, Writing-master', atSleeford, in Lincolnshire.
Length 30 C 23 777
Breadth 15 C inches without-2 11-888 C within.
Depth 12 3 (9-511)
Solution. i

Put x, y, z for the length, breadth, and depth of the stone respectively: Then, by the question, $x + y + z$ 3 57, and xyz zz 5400. The question then is unlimited, there being one equation less than the number of unknown quantities. We shall therefore assume another condition, *viz.* we shall suppose the length to be double the breadth, or x zz $1y$: Then, this written for it in the two given equations, we have $3y + z = 57$, and $2\#sz =$ 5400.

Hence a — 57 — *Sy,* which written for it in the last equation,

Viii. Question 72, *by Mrs. Mary Nelson.*

A prize was divided by a captain among his crew in the following manner: the first man took 1l. and one hundredth part of the re, mainder; the second 2l. and one hundredth part of the remainder; the third 3l. and one hundredth part of the remainder; and they proceeded in this manner to the last, who took all that was left, and it was then found that the prize had by this means been equally divided amongst the crew. Now if the number of men of which the crew consisted be added to the number of pounds in each share, the square of that sum will be equal to four times the number of pounds in the chest: How many men did the crew consist of, and what was the share of each *I Answer.*

The men were 99, and had 99l. each. The whole 9801l.

Solution.

Put x for the number of pounds in the prize: Then, by the ques x gg _i_ x tion, 1 - - —— the first man's share, and conse

'100 100' .... r.,,. 99 + x 99a? — 99. quently the-sum alterwards left — x — — — H. 100 100 $99x$ — 99 — — 2 again, the second man's share will be 2 + 19701 + 99ar, and x— 19701— 9900= 9801 r: the number of gg j-$ pounds in the prize. And —j—-= 99 = each man's share.

Again, putting z = the number of men, by the question it-will be 0-+-99)2 = 4 X 9801; hence, by extracting the root, $z + 99 = 2$ X 99, and $z = 99$ = the number of men the same with the number of pounds in each man's share, H.

Ix. Question 73.

Find the least number which will divide by given divisors without leaving a remainder: and give an example by finding the least number which will divide by the nine digits without leaving a remainder?
Answered by Mr. Thomas Fletcher. Two thousand five hundred and twenty.

Mr. *Naughley* gives this canon; multiply the highest given powers together, and their products continually by every such given prime, as is no component of any of the said powers, or their product, or of any other given prime: So 9X8X7X 5 = 2520 required.
Solution.
The general rule for this kind of questions, is to begin with the greatest number and descend gradually to the least, taking the continual product of them; but omitting such of the less numbers or of their factors as are factors of any of the greater ones. So, in this example, 9 must be used as being the highest number; 8 must be used, because neither itself nor any of its factors 2, and 4, are factors of 9; 7 must be used because it is no factor either of 9 or 8; 6 must be omitted because one (3) of its factors divides 9, and the other (2) divides 8; 5 must be used as being no divisor of either 7, 8, or 9; but 4 must be omitted as being a factor of 8, 3 must be omitted as being a factor of 9, and 2 omitted as being a factor of 8. The reason of all which is extremely obvious.

Then 9x8x7X5 = 2520 = the least number required, H. x. Question 74, *by Mr. Crabb.*

The dimensions of a spheroidical cask are as follows; head diameter 31-8 inches; bung diameter 40 inches, and length 52-S inches: What is the difference between its greatest inscribed cylinder and cube in wine gallons?.
Resolved by Mr.?. Hill.
The content of the cylinder 182-2503, of the cube 84-2615; the. difference in wine gallons 97-9858.
Solution. = 19464-41 = the content of the cube. (202 + 2-26-42
The difference of these two contents is 22635-64 inches =: 97-9898 wine gallons zz the difference required, H. PRIZE QUESTION.

There is a wheel nave in the form of a frustum of a spheroid, in which it is required to mate a hole for the axletree, in the form of the frustum of a cone, capable of holding a gallon of corn; the dimensions of the hole to be as follows: the length of the hole which is also the length of the nave 18 inches, and the ratio of the diameters of its ends to be that of 13 to 16. The diameter of the nave in the middle is four times that of the greater end of the hole, and the diameter of the nave at the end is three times the diameter of the greater end of the hole. Required the solidity of the nave, also required the periphery of the two hoops, at the distance of four inches from the ends?
Answered by Mr. Whitworth.
Put b — 13, c =: 16, I — 18 the length, d — 269 the content, $g =: -78539$ &c. $a =:$ lesser base's diam. Then $b: c:: a:car$ b greater base's diam. Now the area of the greater base, lesser base, and a geometrical mean multiplied-by — d, the content, that .,, *ccaaic. aagc I .,.* is, *(aag* H — 4 —J X — = d, which reduced is $ccaa + bbaa + bcaa — 3dbb$ — gl: by this equation « = 3903886 the lesser base of the cone's frustum, and $ca — b — 4804782$ the greater base's diameter; whence the greatest thickness of the nave is 19-219128
Each end 14-414346
The solidity of the frust. the cavity

subt 4191-408136

The diameter 4 inches from'the end 17-874505

Circumference 56-154402 *Additional Solution.*

Putting 16x and 13 for the diameters of the ends of the conic frustum, and n =-785398 &c. by cor. 6, p. 156 Mensuration, we shall have the content of it = ((16 + 13)2 — 16.13) X X = 269, 269 by the question; hence x = ——-$\sqrt{Jn}$ = 3002989. Therefore 16x and 13x become 4-8047824 and 3-9038857 for the diameters of the hole.

The greater diameter drawn into 4 and 3 give 19-2191296 and 14-4143472 for the diameter at the middle and ends of the nave; and consequently, its solidity, including the hole, will be 18?£ (14-41434722+2.19-2191296s) X — = 4460-386; from which vol.. i. fi taking 269 the content of the hole, there remains 4191-386 for the quantity of the solid.

Also, by the nature of the ellipse (see the last fig.) Cb^2: Cgs:: Cd^3 — Bh^2: Cd^2 — Gi^2; and hence 2gi — _,cb'. CD^2 + CG^3. BH! $CG^2.CD^2$,, . ,,, 2 i/ 5 = 17-8745048 (cb being 9 and

Cg — 5 by the question); which multiplied by 3-14159 &c. we have 56'15441 for the circumference of the hoop. H. *Questions proposed in* 1720, *and answered in* 1721.' i. Question 75, *by Mr.* Tho. Dodd, *April* 30, 1720.

A person had 320l. due last Michaelmas, and five years from that date he will have 202l. more due; now he would be glad to know when he may equitably receive the whole 522l. allowing 5 per cent, per annum simple interest for the first sum, and rebating at the same rate for the last.

Answer. The author's solution is, the payment must be April 30, 1721. Answered by Mr. J. Jope, jun. *taken from the Introduction to the Diary for* 1722.

Put *n* for the time after Michaelmas 1719. Then 100: 5:: 320: 16, and 1: 16:: n : 16n, the interest of 320l. Then 320 + 16« — the amount of 320l. 5 — n — the time the 202l. was received before due. 1:5:: 5 — n : 25 — 5n and 125 — 5n: 100:: 202 20200 : — — = value 202l. at the day of payment.

Then by the 20200 question 16n + — — = 202, which by reduction gives *n* — 125 — 5?t 1-760076 = 1 year 277 days 10 hours. So that the day of payment should be July 4th, 1721.

Additional Solution.

The sum 320l. being due the 29th of September, and the other sum 202l. due just five years afterwards; the meaning of the question is to find such a day between these two times, as that the whole sum 522l. being then received, neither the receiver nor deliverer may suffer any loss; in which case it is evident that the interest of the 320l. for the time it is kept beyond the time when it was due, must be equal to the discount of the 202l. for the time it is received before it is due.

Hence then denoting the time for the discount by *x,* and consequently the time for the interest, or till the whole must be paid, by 5— *x;* by the rules for interest and discount, 320 X X (5—x) — 16 X (5 — x) will be the interest of 320 for the time 5 — *xy* and 202e 100+ 5x : 5x:: .202: ——— = the discount of 202 for the 20 + *x* time *x,* the rate of interest being 5 per cent. Consequently 16 X 202a =

(5 — x) ;hence x + 17x — 100, and x = 3239888.

Wherefore 5 — *x* — 1-76 years nearly — 1 year 277 days; which being added to Sept. 29, we have the 3d of July, 1721, for the day of payment, H.

Ii. Question 76, *by Mr. W.* Crabb.

If the side of the face of each of the regular solids (or platonic bodies as they are called) be 29 inches: What is the content of each in wine gallons.

Answered by Mr. Dodd.

The dodecaedron contains 809-072. the icosaedron 230-343, the hexaedron 105-58, the octaedron 49-77, and the tetraedron 12-442 wine gallons.

Solution.

By page 404, &c. of my Mensuration, it is found that the solidities ⓒf the five regular bodies, the side of each face being 1, will be thus:

Tetraedron = 0-11785113
Hexaedron = 1-00000000
Octaedron — 0-47140452
Dodecaedron = 7-66311896
Icosaedron = 2 18169499.

Then, since similar solids are as the cubes of their like sides, each of these numbers being multiplied by 24389, the cube of 29, the products will be the contents of the bodies in inches; and if these contents be divided by 231, the inches in a wine gallon, there will result the several numbers of gallons as in the original solution. H. j :..

m. Question 77, *by Mr.* W. Dcare.

In the triangular field Abc, let Bp be perpendicular to the base; then there are given the vertical angle Abc —120, the side Ab = 8 chains, the alternate segment of the base Pc = 5fJ chains: Required tho other side Bc, the remaining segment Ap and the area?

Answered by Mr. Crabb, *Mr.* Finch, *Mr.* Gurney, *Mr.* Dodd, *and Mr.* White. 24-2787 chains = 2 acres 1 rood 28 perches. *Solution.*

Put *a* = Bc = 8, *b* — Ap = 5-Jf, *s* — y'S sine of the angle Abc or 120, and *z* — Pc. Then, by right-angled triangles, Bp — »J(a3—22), and Ab zz /(&2 + a2 — z1); Ab X Bc X sine r twice the area-: Bp X Ac, that is,

Bv(3 + a' — 2s) = (b + z). JW) 5 and this, by squaring both sides, and writing the numbers instead of the letters, becomes 48 X (16745— 169z3) = (77 + 13s)2 X (64 — z3), which will be an equation of the 4th order / and by expanding it out, the root *z* may be found by converging series. But the root will be much easier found by the method of Trial and Error, from the equation as it here stands; and by this method *z* will come out 7077 or 7-A-. Hence the base Ac is 13, and the area 24-248 square chains.

Scholium. This problem is the same as to divide a given angle into two parts such, that the tangent of the one may be to the secant of the other, in a given ratio, H.

Iv. Question 78; *by Mr.* G. Hare,

In latitude 53 north, a plane declines north-west 43 15' and reclines backwards 49 20'; now suppose this plane to be carried parallel to itself along a meridian till it becomes upright; it is then required to describe a sun dial upon, it?

Answered by Mr. Hawney, *Mr.* Failes, *Mr.* White, *Mr.* Williams, *and Mr.* Finch. *Construction.* Let Elqn be the horizon and z the zenith of the place in lat. 53, P the pole, Lzn the position of the plane making the angle Ezr, = 43 15', Ezq being the prime vertical, Pzda the meridian, and Edq the equinoctial. Perpendicular to J,n draw Zb equal to 49 20' the reclination, and draw the great circle I. abn, which will be the plane of the dial, A being the new place required; also draw the great circle or meridian Cpf perpendicular to HALF.

Then Da will be equal to the" new latitude south; in which the plane will be upright, the angle Zab the co-declination, Af the distance of the substile from the meridian, re the stile's height,.al the distance of the meridian and horizon, and the angle Apf the plane' difference of longitude.

Calculation. 1. In the right-angled triangle Abz, given Zb the reclination =: 49 20', and zAzsthe declination = 43 15'. Then, As cos. Zazb = 43 15': radius:: tang, Zb = 49 20': tang, Az = 57 58'; from which taking Zd = 53, there remains Da — 4 58' the new latitude. As radius: sine Zazb:: cos. Zb: cos. Z A — 63 29', whose complement 20 31' is the new declination. As radius:sine Zb:: tang, Azb: tang, Ab S: 35 31', the complement of 54 29' the dist. of merid. and horiz.

2. In the right-angled triangle Afp, are given Ar — 94 58', and Za = (180— 63 29' =) 116 31'. Then

As radius: cos. Za:: tang, Ap: tang, Af = 78 59' the distance of the substile from the merid. As radius: sine Ap:: sinezA 5 sine Fp — 116 57',-whose supplement 63 3' is the stile's height. As radius: cos. Ap:: tang. Za: cotang. Zp = 80 9' the plane's diff. of longitude,

Now this 80 9', or plane's difference of longitude shews that the distance, on the equinoctial Hi of the hour line Pa of 12, is 80 9' from the substile Pf; and which is therefore set opposite to it in the table to the original solution. The equinoctial distances in the same column of the table belonging to the other hours, are found by the continual addition and subtraction of 15. And the several distances on the plane of the dial in the other column of the table, against the equinoctial distances are all found by this proportion, As radius: sine 63 3' the stile's height:: tang, of each equinoctial distance: tang of the corresponding distance on the plane of the dial. For if Pg be any hour circle; then in the right-angled triangle Pfg, As radius: sine Pf:: tang Z. P:tang, opposite side Fg. *Note.* In the table to the original solution, for the distance on the plane against the hour xi the author has set 84 18' instead of its supplement; or rather indeed it should be 95 46' the sup. of 84 14' as appears by calculation, H. v. Question 79, *by Mr.* John Ashton.

Upon the first of May a plane mirror being placed horizontally, at the middle of the south side of a room, it reflected the sun's rays exactly with the upper part of the east corner, just when the sun's azimuth was equal to its altitude. -Required the dimensions of the room, and the time of the day when the observation was made, the area of the end of the room being 80 square feet?

Anszoered.

This question was imperfectly proposed, no latitude being fixedto answers may vary for different places. The proposer in latitude 53 28', as also Mr. *Crabb,* Mr. *Allen,* Mr. *Finch,* Mr. *Wall,* Mrs. *Dod,* and several others, answer.

Time of the day 2b 6m altitude and azimuth 48 20', length of the opposite side of the room 7-29216 feet, height 10 97, breadth of end walls 3-245, May 1, 1719, London.

Solution.

With the above original answer, supposing the latitude to be 51 32' that of London. Then, in the annexed figure, if p be the pole, z the zenith, and 0 the sun; we have given rz = 38 28' the co-latitude, $p© = 72\ 6'$ the co-declination for May 1, old stile, or May 12, new stile, and the supplement of the angle z — the complement of zQ; to find the hour angle p.

Put *a* and *b* the sine and cosine of Pz, c — the cosine of p©, and *x* and $/(1 - xx)$ the sine and cosine of z©, or cosine and sine of the Zz.

Then, by common trigonometry, axx -f-b $/(1 - xx) - c$. Hence by completing the square and extracting the roots we obtain x = 6937742 — the cosine of 46 4' the altitude and azimuth. Also, as sine Pq: sine z:: sine z© ' sine P $(x\ \text{-j-} d) / (1 - xx)$ putting d = sine P0) — -5250344 = the sine of 31 40' which, at 15 to the hour, answers to 2'1 *6%m* afternoon.

Again, if Abcd represent the floor of the room, s the speculum in the middle of the south side Dc, and B the east corner, and Sb be drawn; then will the angle B be — 46 4' — the azimuth from the south; also the triangle formed by Sb, the height of the room, and the reflected ray, will be similar to the triangle sue, because the altitude is equal to the azimuth. Wherefore, if *s* and c denote the sine and cosine of 46 4' the azimuth, or the sines of the acute angles of the said two triangles, and s the line Sb; then will sc ba zz: sz, Cb — cz, and c: $s :: z: sz\ \text{-4-}c$ — the height of the room. Now if the area of the end Bc be 80, then *(sz -j-c)cz* = $sz2$ = 80 zz *a;* hence z $—(a-r-s)$ = 10-54, and then the breadth Bc = 7-3123, the length Dc = 15-1804, and the height = 10-94.

2sV

But if the area of the side Dc be 80; then *(sz -r c)2sz* —— *a;* hence z =r $/(ox)$ -r-s, and then the breadth — 5075, the length = 10-536, and the height = 7-5931. n.

vi. Question 80, *by* S. T.

Suppose a hollow sphere equal to the globe of the earth; and sup pose a current of water 12 yards broad, and 6 yards deep, to run at the rate of a thousand yards an hour; in what time would the cavity be filled by the current?

Answered.

In regard the diameter of the earth is variously computed, the answers to this must differ from one another: accordingly Mr *Crabb* answers 1469,982,847,541 years according to 60 miles to a degree.

Solution.

Ry the question, 6 X 12 X 1000 = 72000 cubic yards of water run in an hour, or 72000 X 24 X 36 51 = 631152000 cubic yards in a year. Now if the circumference of the earth be 21600 nautical 21600s „„., 216003X 1760,x7' m,leS thCn (3-14159 &c.)'x 6 naUtlCal m„cs' r (3-14159 &c.)X 6 cubic yards will be the content of the earth; which being divided by 631152000, the quotient is 2334289000000 for the number of years required.

So that the first figure in the original answer seems to be falsely printed 1 for 2. H.

Vii. Question 81, *by Mr.* J. Jennings.

The expence of building a house which was afterwards sold, exceeded the builder's gain by 1601. The sum of the squares of its expence and the gain amounted to 706001. Required the original cost and the gain?

Answer.
Two hundred and fifty pounds cost, and ninety pounds gain.
First Solution.

In this question, are given the difference of two numbers, and the sum of their squares, to find the numbers.

Put $d — 160$ the difference, $= 70600$ the sum of the squares, and x — the cost. Then $x — d —$ the gain, and $x1 + (x—d)3 — Itf—ldx + d = s$. Hence $x = ———$ rf8) _ 250 th cost, and $x — d z$: 90 the gain required. H.
Second Solution.

Let x represent what the house cost, and y what was gained j also let $d = 160$ and $= 70600$. Then, by the question, $x —y d$

The square of the first equation taken from the second gives $Ixy — s — $ rf. This added to the second, and the square roots taken gives
$x + y$-(25 — d).
But $x — y — d$.
Half the sum and half the difference of these equations give
$V(1s — d') + d$
$V(2«-d)-d$

Tin. Question 82, *by Mr.* William Doidge.

The slant side of a cone is 60 feet and solid content 30063 cubic feet: What is its perpendicular height?
Answer.
The perpendicular height 55-5234 feet.
Solution.
Put $a =60$ the side, 30063 the content, and $z zz$ the perpendicular height Then the radius of the base will be $/aa— zz)$, the area of the base =: $(aa — zz)$ x 3 1416, and the content =: ——-x 3"1416 zz 30063; hence $z zz$ 55'52446 zz the perpendicular required, ii.

ix. Question 83, *by Mr.* J. Plomley, *or* N. M.

Suppose two travellers set out at the same time from Bristol to go round the world; and suppose one of them to go due east at the uniform rate of 7-2miles a day; and the other to go north at the rate of 1 1-jvvy miles: how many times round the world will each have to go before they can meet again at Bristol: also required the number of days and the number of miles travelled by each?
Answer.
The first man travels 7 times round the globe, 151200 miles; the second, 11 times, or 237600 miles, and in 21535 days, or 59 years.
Solution.
It is evident that the number of times round each person travels, before they meet, will be directly as his rate of travelling. The question then only requires to be found the least two whole numbers that shall be in a given ratio; and such tvvo numbers it is clear must be the least integer terms of the said ratio. Now the given terms of the ratio are llVuV and or 7T§; and by dividing the former of these terms by 11, and the latter by 7, the quotient of each is l-jJT; therefore the least terms of the ratio are 7 and 11, and which of consequence give the number of times each travels round, H THE ritlZE QUESTION.

There is a kneading trough, the bottom of which is a rectangle; its perimeter is 11-75 feet, and area 5875 square feet: the sides, ends, and bottom have all the same breadth; and the diagonal of a section, made by a plane at right-angles to the longest edge of the bottom is equal to f of the breadth of the bottom; required the con. tent of the whole trough in wine gallons, also the content of each of the wedges made by a plane passing through the longest edge of the bottom and the opposite edge, or brim of the top?

Anszeered by Mr. J. Jope, jun.
Length at top 5"591
Breadth 2-272
Length at bottom 4-5969
Breadth, 1-2780
Depth 1-1774
Diagonal 2-1300
The whole vacuity..18563-74
Vacuity ev en with diag.12156-85
Remaining part 6406-89
Liquor, 27-735 wine gallons.
Solution.
Let Abcdehgf be the trough, its depth Di, being a perpendicular from top to the bottom. Then by comparing the words of the question with this figure, the conditions will appear to be thus: Of the rectangle Efgh the perimeter is 11-75, and the area=5-875; iiE=EK=:Jof HKthenearestdistanceof oil from Ad; and He, Ek arc also each the distance between c» and He, in consequence of which El Li will be equal to the half differenceof both the lengths and breadths at the top and bottom, and therefore the solid is a prismoid, and not the frustum of a pyramid: And it is required to find the whole content, as well as that of the wedge Adehgf. *Questions proposed in* 1721, *and answered in* 1722; i. Question 84, *by Mr.* Sam. Dicker.

In the city of Megara there were two small square temples dedicated to Bacchus and Venus, their floors were paved with stones each a foot square. The number of stones in both amounted to 2120; but each side of the floor of the temple of Venus exceeded that of the temple of Bacchus by 12 feet; what were their dimensions?
Answered by Mr. Cha. Glover.

Let a the greater side, e lesser. There's given the difference of the sides $d,$ and the sum of their squares $z;$ which by involution, subtraction, and evolution, this equation is found $a \_ j± V\&z—dd),$ s(j a _ 38j e _ 26 the solution.
Additional Solution.
Put $s =$ the half sum of the two numbers, $d — 6$ the half difference, and $s — 2120$ the sum of their squares. Then $z + d$ and $z —$ rf $—$ the two numbers; the sum of whose squares,is $2 zz + 2 dd — s.$

Hence $z — J(s — dd) — (1060—36) — 32$; and therefore 38 and 26 the two numbers, u.

Ii. Question 85, *by Mr.* Moyle.
The angle of altitude of a cloud was

observed to be 20, and that of the sun in the same direction 35; and the distance of the shadow of the cloud from the station of the obseryer measured 2304 yards; Hence the perpendicular height of the cloud above the ground is required?

Answer.
The cloud's height is 1747 yards by the prop. By some tables and rules it is 1744-8; but taking no notice of the O's alt. at the different places, 'tis 1746-3.

Solution.
Let s be the sun, c the cloud, and o the observer, all in the same vertical plane; upon the horizon Op let fall the perpendicular Cp the height of the cloud; draw sc, and produce it to cut the horizon in A the shadow of the cloud. Then Oa will be given — 2304 yards, the angle Aoc 20; and if the elevation Cap of the sun at A be supposed = the elevation Sop at o, then the angle Cap = 35, the Zoac = 145, and Zoca— 16. Hence, as s. s. 20'

Z Aco: oA:: s. / Aoc: Ac r: X Ao j and, in the triangle Apc, as 1 (rad.): s. Zcap s. 20 X s. 35 : Cp =——'0 x Ao = 1746-34 yards, or near a mile for the height of the cloud.

But as 2304 are rather above 1 minute of a degree of a great cir cle, the Zcap will be about 35 *l'* and then Cp =- 1 's. 15 1'

X Ao = 1745-17 yards the distance, a little less than before. H.

in. Question 86, *by Mr.* Jos. Dogharty.
Three ships sailed from the same place to different ports in the same parallel of latitude: the first sailed directly south 55 leagues, when she arrived at the desired port; the other two sailed upon different courses, between the south and west, till they arrived at their destined ports, which were 57 leagues asunder, and the angle included by their courses at the port sailed from was 38; required the course and distance run by each of the two latter vessels. Or in other words, given tb,e base, the perpendicular, and the vertical angle of a triangle to find the rest.' Answered by Mr. John Jope, *jun. of Loo, in Cornwall.* $x' + 1a£ + a9 + 2\&V + laVx$ = $a'\&V$-r c2 — — b'.
Where # is found = 15 103: whence the course is S. 15 21'W. and the distance = 67035 leagues. The other course is S. 53 31' W. and the distance 92-139 leagues.

The above expression is wrong printed: it should be $x4 + 2a«5 + («' + 26s)xs + lutfx$ — $as\&V$ c4 — $a b1$ — $b;$ as appears from the following solution.

Let the angle Oca (see the last figure) = 38, be denoted by P, OA 57 — a; Cp the perpendicular, =55—6, and Ap = x.

Then oc — + 2ar + a + 61) and Dc — $J(x\% + b')$.

Now the radius being supposed unity, it is well known that the rectangle of the sides oc, Ca multiplied by the sine of their included angle, gives twice (£oa X Pc —-ab) the area of the triangle Oca:

Hence + 2a + $a1$ + 6s) X $t/x'' + b$) X sin 9 — ab; or $x' + 2ax3 + (a1 + 26$-+ $tatfx + aV + b' — a'b'$-± sin'p; or $x + W + («' + 26 V + 2«6! + b = a'b siu'p$-$a'b2;$ which is Mr.JJope's expression, (r being supposed = 1).

Taking square roots we get xs $ax + b'l = ab$ cotan $t:$ therefore, completing the square, and again taking the square roots we have $x — + ab$ cotan $P — V)$ — = 13-92484. Hence, Pc: rad.::

Ap: tan Pca, therefore the angle Pca is 14 12' 27"; and, as sin Pca: Pa:,: rad. Ac = 56-735 miles: Also, as sin Aoc: Pc:: rad.: oc 5= 89-751. L. *Another Solution.*

Let c, p, A, o (see the last fig.) be the four ports; then Cp — 55 leagues, Ao = 57 leagues, and .aco =38. Now, by prop. 13, Simpson's Trigon. As 1 to cot. f Zaco:: 2aox Cp: (oc+ca)2—AO; hence oc + Ca = /(ao4 + 2ao X Cp X cot. Zaco) = V(57a + 57 X 110 X cot. 19) = 146-487 the sum of the sides. And, by prop. 14 of the same, 1: tan. Zaco:: 2ao X Cp: AO — (oc—Ca)s; and hence oc—Ca=./(Aoa— 2ao X Cp X tan. Z Aco)r: V(57a — 57 X 110 X tan. 19) = 33-016 the difference of the sides. Then, the half sum increased and diminished by the half difference, we have 89-7515 and 56-7355 for the two distances co and Ca. Again, as 146-487 (sum of sides): 33-016 (diff. of sides):: cot. 19 (j Zoca): tan. 33 12' — half the difference between the angles A and o; and from the half sum and difference those angles are found = 104 12' and 37 48' the complements of 14 12' and 52 12' the two courses required.

It is evident that this problem will be constructed, by describing on the given base Ao a segment of a circle to contain the given vertical angle; and then a line drawn parallel to the base at the distance of the perpendicular from it, will cut the circle in the vertex of a triangle, H.

Iv. Question 87, *by Mr.* T. Williams *of Middleton-Stoney.*

A person bought a quantity of land the bounds of which are to be marked out by the shadow of a tree 103 feet high, between the hours of eight and one on the 10th of march 1721: now supposing the sun should not appear on that day, how may the bounds and area be determined the latitude being 52 N.

Answered. hours 0's alt. The 10th of March. VIII 17 56' Latitude 52. IX 25 48 X 32 13 XI 36 29 XII 38 0
I 36 29

The figure will be triangular, the shadow at 8 and 1 being two of its sides, and right lines; the third (the path of the nodus or top of the tree) a curve' line, of the conic sections, about 334 feet. The content 22200 square feet — 210. 1 per. and 148 square feet. Those v/ho have taken the horizontal distances with respect to the pole, instead of the azimuths, have given false solutions.

leng. shade
318-2
212-9
163-4
13923
131-831
139-23
Feet.

As sine 17 56': log. 103:: sine 72 4': log. 318, and so for the rest. And you'll have several triangles with 2 sides and an angle between them given, to find their contents; which in one sum gives the area of the whole more exact than by taking it as one single triangle, by reason of the curve line in each of them.

Additional Solution.
The piece of land in this question is a triangle on the horizontal plane, of which two sides are the shadows of the tree at 8 and 1 o'clock, and the third side the line described by the shadow of the top of the tree between the same

two hours; and this third line will be right as well as the two former, and not a conic section, because the sun is in the equinoctial, it being the 10th of March old stile. The said third line will also be directly east-and-west, or perpendicular to the meridian or shadow of the tree at 12 o'clock.

Now, if p represent the pole, z the zenith, and © the sun at any hour: Then are given pz the co-latitude, Pq a quadrant, and Z P — the hour from 12; to find the Zpzq, the sun's azimuth or bearing at that hour. And, taking the extreme hours 8 and 1 in the question, their azimuths will come out 65 32', and 18 47'; which are the two angles A Bp, Cbp contained by the meridian shadow Bp, and the two extreme shadows Ba, Bc, the place of the tree being at B. Now the sum of these two angles is 84 19' — the Zabc, and their complements are 24 28' and 71 13' = the angles A and c. So that all the angles are then known.

Again, the meridian altitude of the sun being 38 — the complement of the latitude 52, we shall have as 1: tang. 52:: 103 feet (the height of the tree): 131-834 = Bp the length of the meridian shadow. From hence, and the given angles, Ap and PC are easily found = 289-73 and 44 837, and then the area = 22053-65 square feet — 2-0218 roods, H.

T. Question 88, *by Mr.* Chris. Harris.
A piece of land in the form of a regular heptagon was purchased for as many shilling as would surround it touching one another, the diameter of each being one inch: the number of shillings which one acre cost was equal to eleven times the number of acres inclosed: How many acres were purchased and what price per acre?
Answered by Mr. L. Evan.
If 3-633959 be the area of a heptagon, whose side is 1; then put x — the acres, 11 — shillings, the price of 1 acre. 1:Jl:: : llx — the price in shillings of all the acres bought = inches round the polygon; 6272640 inches — 1 acre.
3 633959: 1:: 6272640a;:" "" = the square of each side. o o Jo y *oy* 6272640 7 times the square root of that = 1 *lxx.* That is V = 11 6272640 1211 307359360,,,,«. , or — , or =: 121; hence 7' 3-6339 49' 3 633959' 307359360 = 439-709039', and 699006 235 = . Then 88-74999 = 88 ac. 2 ro. 39 per. — the number of acres bought. 976-24989 shill. — 481. 16s. = the price of 1 acre.
Additional Solution.
Since the price of one acre in shillings is equal to 11 times the num. ber of acres, it is plain that the price of all the acres will be 11 times the square of the number of acres; but the price of the whole is equal to the circumference in inches, therefore the circumference in inches is equal to 11 times the square of the acres.

Now if denote /he side of the heptagon in inches, a — 3-633912 the area of a heptagon whose side is 1, and b = 6272640 the inches in an acre. Then 7 will be the perimeter, and $ax2$ -4-b the acres; wherefore 7 = llaV-r $b2$; hence = *fj (ftf* -r llaa)=12377-l = the side. Then $ax2$ b zz 88:7487 the number of acres, H.

Vi. Question 89, *by* Adrastea.
Twenty four persons, consisting of captains, mates, sailors and boys, agreed to pay 21l. for a passage by sea, in the following proportions: a captain was to pay a certain sum, a mate half as much as a captain, a sailor one fourth us much as a mate, and a boy half as much as a sailor: how many of each were there, and what did each pay for his passage?
Answered.
This question is unlimited.
For zdien the number of quantities sought exceeds the number of given equations, the question is capable of innumerable anszeers. C 2 captains 41. each sr 81. *1* 2 3 4 mates 2 =8 f 1.
J 14 sailors 10s *7ƒ*24
'4 boys 5 — 1 J
Mr. *Evans* collected 10O true answers, which for brevity I omit.
Remark. In the above original answer, it is justly remarked that the data are insufficient; for, to have limited the answers, there ought to have been three more conditions; so if three of the numbers of persons had been given, the question would have been confined to one answer, and the method of solution too easy to need any pointing out here. H.
Tii. Question 90, *by Mr.* Deare.
A gentleman dying left an estate of 500001. to his two sons: the square of the pounds in the elder son's share was to be equal 50000 times the youngest son's share: What was the share of each?
Answered by Mr. Cha. Glover.
Let a eldest son's portion, e — youngest, aa — *se,* and s — a — e per quest, this equation is produced, a — *(ss* + — ±*s.* a = 30901-69943746 or 309011. 14s. « = 19098-30056251 or 190981. 6s.
Additional Solution.
In this question are to be found two numbers, of which the sum is given, and the square of the greater equal to the less multiplied by the given sum. Or, it is required-to divide a given number into two such parts, that those parts and the whole may be three numbers in geometrical progression. Or, in other words again, to divide a given number according to extreme and mean proportion; which it is well known will not admit of an answer in integer numbers.

Put s — 50000 the sum, and x the greater part. Then s — x — the less, and xx — ss — $sx;$ hence x — A s — 30901-6994375, and consequently the other part = 19098-3005625, as above determined, H.

Tin. Question 91, *by Mr.* C. Mason.
How must a horse be tethered so as to be able to graze just an acre yon. r. H ia the form of an ellipse, the ratio of the principal axes being as 7to 9?
Ansuersd by Mr. J. Andrew.
The transverse diameter 16-184053 perches — 89 01 yards.
The conjugate diameter 12-587597 perches — 69-23 yards. Distance between the focus points 55-9463; thence to the extreme parts 44505, doubled 89-01 added to the distance between the foci is the length of the tether 145 yards.

The way for the horse to graze just an elliptical acre, is thus: Set up two stakes or pins in the longest diameter of the oval, 16 yards 6 inches and a quarter from the outside. Put a string of 145 yards long round both stakes, and tie the two ends together; at which knot let the horse's mouth be fix'd: then in going about he will exactly sweep the oval, containing 4810 square yards, or one acre.

Solution.

Put $9x$ and $7x$ for the two axes in yards. Then 63a:xX-785398 *Sec.*

Tt, 4840

— 4840,the square yards in an acre. Hence $x - y = 9\text{-}890255$; consequently $9x$ and $7x$ become 89 0123 and 69-2318 for the two axes. Then 89-0123 + (89-0123" — 69-2318') = 144-96

— length of the tether, H.

The Prize Question. *The gardens of Alcinous, from the seventh book of Homer's Odysseys, translated by Mr. Pope.* Close to the gates, a spacious garden lies,
From storms defended, and inclement skies.
Four acres was th' allotted space of ground;
Fenc'd with a green inclosure all around.
Tall thriving trees confess'd the fruitful mould,
And red'ning apples ripen here to gold.
Here the blue fig with luscious juice o'erflows;
With deeper red the full pomegranate glows.
The branch here bends beneath the weighty pear
And verdant olives flourish round the year.
The balmy spirit of the western gale
Eternal, breathes on fruits untaught to fail.
Each dropping pear, a following pear supplies;
On apples, apples; figs on figs arise:
The same mild season gives the blooms to blow,
The buds to harden, and the fruits to grow.
Here order'd vine9, in equal ranks appear,
With all th' united labours of the year:
Some to unload the fertile branches run,
Some dry the black'ning clusters in the sun;
Others to tread the liquid harvest join.
The groaning presses foam with floods of wine.

Here are the Tines in early flow'r descry'd,
Here grapes discolour'd, on the sunny side,
And there in autumn's richest purple dy'd.
Beds of all various herbs, for ever green,
In beauteous order terminate the scene.
Two plenteous fountains the whole prospect crown'd,
This thro' the gardens leads its streams around,
Visits the plants, and waters all the ground;
While that in pipes, beneath the palace flows,
And thence its current to the town bestows:
To various use, their various streams they bring,
The people one, and one supplies the king.

The king's pipe delivers the water ten foot and an half (English measure) below the surface of the waterin the fountain, by an inch and three quarters bore: His brewing once a week, takes fifty hogsheads of water, (wine measure) kitchen, landry, other offices, &c. five hogsheads a-day. The people have occasion for twenty hogsheads a-day; (heir cock of two inches diameter, is below the fountain twenty-two foot. His majesty so much delights in a morning walkHo seethe waters undisturbed, that his orders are, that the cocks shall but run once every day and that in the evening; so long only, as may supply next day's consumption, and for so much in his reservoir, as supplies his brewing each week. Then if the velocity or motion of the water be equal to that of an heavy body acquired in these descents; and also, it be premised, that heavy bodies accelerate as the squares of their times, as sixteen foot the first second it falls, *kc.* How long every day ought each pipe to run, to give the king and people their due quantity?

Answer.

In answering this question in hydrostatics, the philosophy of the gravity and pressure of fluids is to be considered: That at the first moment the cock or adjutage is opened, the liquid flows out with the same velocity as a heavy body moves when fell from that height the liquor came, or the place of the reservoir. The water that enters the top, or mouth of the pipe, moves as fast as that flowing out, at what depth soever, in an equal cylinder. Whereas a heavy body moves slow at first setting out, and continually receives a new impulse of gravity, which when it has fallen the length of trie waterpipe, is equal in velocity to that column of water. Then as a body accelerates with the odd numbers 1, 3, 5, &c. the water going out as fast the first space, as a weight falls in the second; consequently must be as Gravesand, in his Mathematical Philosophy, page 188, No 378, says,

"In the time in which a body falling freely, goes through the u height of the liquid above the hole, a column oi the liquid flows u out equal in length to twice that height."

On this principle was the question composed, having Gravcsand then before me; which is plain from the question itself, the word acquired J meaning no other, than that the water moved as fast as the body, when it had fallen the height of that liquid: But the design of putting it in those words was to prevent auch who had not skill enough in philosophy, stamping a solution to it.

The king used 765 gall.n 12 hogsheads per day. The bore 175 inch squared X by 252 double height-j-29412 gives 26579 w. g.) 765 (287-9 times (the height) for the quantity. □ 60'" — 3600) 192 (-05333 inch, the space accelerated in 1 third. Then lOf feet = 126 inches —-05333 gives 48-621 thirds multiplied by 287-9 is 13994-819 thirds = 3' 53" 14'". *The answer.*

The people use 1260 gallons per day. Height dupla 528 X 4dia.sq.-294-12 = 7-18 w. g.
1260-T-7-18 = 175-49 such columns y(22-f-16) = 1-17 x 175-49 = 205-3233 = 3' 25" 32'". *The ansieer. Additional Solution.*

Put a — the altitude of the surface of the water above the delivering pipe, n the area of the orifice or pipe, and m 32J feet = 386 inches. Then proceeding as in page 4 of our new Math. Miscel. *ijlma* will be the velocity of the issuing water, upon the supposition of the question, that it is equal to that of a heavy body after falling though the space a; but if, according to Sir I. Newton and some others, the velocity be that which is acquired by falling through only §«, it will be n/ma; which is to the former as 1 to V2, and therefore the time for the one supposition may be found from that of the other, by this proportion of 1 *to* y2.

Now in the former case with the velocity t/Zma per second, we shall havenv'2wa for the quantity run out per second; and therefore *n iJlma* : o.:: 1 second: ——— — the seconds in which the ray "2m a the quantity ft will be voided.

Then, for the king, Q— 12f hogsheads = 12-f X 63 X 231 or 176715 cubic inches, n = 1-752 x-78 54, and a — 10f feet = 126 inches; with which numbers —: becomes 235565 seconds, or 3TM ny%ma 55s.

And, for the people, o. = 20 hogsheads — 291060 inches, n — 2 X-7854 = 3-1416, and a — 22 feet = 264 inches; which numbers give 205-23 seconds = 3" 25"; both nearly as in the original answer.

But if the other supposition be used, of *fma* velocity per second; then each of the above times must be multiplied by/ 2. H. *Questions proposed in* 1722, *and answered in* 1723.

I. Question 92, *by Mr.* J. Andrew.

Find the content, in ale gallons, of the greatest frustum of a cone which can be inscribed in a semi-spheroid, generated by the revolution of an ellipse whose principal axes arc 30 and 20 inches? *Answered by Mr.* C. Mason.

Let the semi-transverse 15 — h, and semi-conjugate 10 r: c, length of the frustum — a, the difference put = h — a, and the semi-head diameter — e. Then, hh : cc:: hh — aa: C = ee' Which reduced gives o= 10-606601, and e — 7-075, and 2e = less diameter — 14-15 inches; hence the content in ale gallons 8-6915.

Mr. *Ri. Tapper*, by the doctrine of fluxions, gives (his equation, i5 + %x + p:3 — fa? = -Here the flowing quantity x =-64638. Hence this general theorem,

As 1: the conjugate diameter of a spheroid::-64638: the lesser diameter of the largest conic frustum that can be inscribed. Whence

The lesser diameter 12-9277 7.. mcnes.

Height of the conic frustum 1144553

The solid content 87734 ale gallons.

But Mr. *Andrew*, the proposer, gives this general theorem, xs — 425x4 + 67500 = 3796875: and the lesser diameter = 129297, and the content — 15-4587 ale gallons.

and therefore *Additional Solution.* To find the greatest frustum Aegc of a cone that can be inscribed in a given semi-spheroid Abc, the base of the cone being the same as that of the spheroid, whether it be oblate or oblong, that is whether the revolving axe Ac be the less or the greater axe of the ellipse.

Put r — Ad the semi-revolving axe, / — Db the semi-fixed axe, and x zz Df the altitude of the frustum. Then, by the ellipse, ff : rr :: // — xx: «' = JJ X rr; hence the solidity of the frustum will be ff — xx , ff — xx 3-l416.r X (1 + 'S'-jf jj J = a maximum Or, put $j f$

«s zz jj—i tiicn xx — ff X (1 — 22), and the maximum =

V(l — 22) X (1 + z + 22); which put into fluxions and reduced, we have the equation 1 + 2 — 22 — 3za zz 0; whose root 2 is =-6464881 very exact. Hence x zz -/(I — 22) X / =-76292*ify* and the content of the greatest frustum =-762924/rr X ——X (I + 2+ 22) = l-649344/rr.

Now in the case of the oblong spheroid, f zz 15, r zz 10, x the heights-762924/ = 11-44386, and the content 1-649344/rr = 2474-016 inches = 8-773 ale gallons.

But if the spheroid were oblate, then / =: 10, r zz 15, x zz 7-62924, and the contents 3711 024 inches = 13 1597 gallons.

Corollary. From this solution it appears, that the value of *x*, or the height of the frustum, will be always the same, whatever the revolving axe Acmay be; the aid height being to the semi-fixed axe, or Df to Db, as-762924 to 1. And the content 1-649344/rr of the frustum Aegc is to the semi-spheroid Abc or 2/rr x —f M 2-474016 to 3-14159 &c. or as-787504 to 1. Also, the frustum in the oblate is to the frustum in the oblong semi-spheroid, as the longer axe to the shorter, which is the same proportions as the spheroids themselves are in by Cor. 8, page 277, of-Mensuration. 11. , 11. Question 93, *by Mr.* C. Mason.

Upon the top of a tower whose height is 253 feet, is a spire wjth a vane at the top: On the 9th of June 1721, the sun's azimuth being N.N.W. a person measured the length of the shadow of the tower and vane upon the level plane, and found it exactly equal to the height of the tower: Required *(he* height of the vane above the tower, the latitude being 54? *Answered by* Sylvia.

Jf the bearing of the shadow be N.N.W. the sun must be upon the S.S.E. point, his azimuth then being 22 30' from the south, and his declination being the 9th June 23 30'. In the latitude of 54 his . altitude is 58 *H*.

As the tangent of 45 0' 10-0000000
To the tangent of 58 2 , 10-2047732
So is the logar. 253 foot 2-4031204
Tothelogar. 403-4 2-6078937

The height of the tower and vane together, but the vane's above the tower just 152-4 foot, *Additional Solution.*

In the spherical triangle zr-0, given Pz the co-latitude = 36, P0 the codeclination — 66 30', and the angle z — the azimuth from the north — 157 3C; to find the side z© = 31 58' the co-altitude. Hence the altitude itself is 58 2' =: Zbac in the second figure, in which the shadow Ab — the tower Bd — 263: then, by plane trigonometry, as radius: tang. Zbac:: Ab: Bc the height of the tower and v ne together; from which taking away the height of the tower Bd, there remains Dc = the height of the vane as in the original solution, H.

Iji. Question 94, *by Mr.* Richard Whitehead.

There is a triangular garden, in which is inscribed a circular hedge of yew, which touches the three sides; in the south side is a door, just at the point of contact with the inscribed circle dividing the id« into two segments of 39f and 30 yards; and if a perpendicular is

drawn to this side from the opposite angle, the rectangle of the segments made thereby will be 1181-J§J£ square yards; required the other two sides of the garden, together with its area; and also the diameter of the circle?
Answered by Mr. Ri. Tapper.
Let a the greater segment taken from the perpendicular, e — lesser segment, and — their sum = 70, p their product U81$§£ yards. There comes out this equation, $a\ zz\ s + s/ss - p) = 41-6090925304966547\ 7\ e\ zzs - Vil - J$») = 28-3909074695033453 5 Y' Put x for the unknown tangent, $h\ zz$ the greater segment, $d\ zz$ the lesser, from whence this equation is brought out $x\ zz?d+ aa -,,h\ \ \ \ ee$-16-40405301497398706499445.

Hence the length of the sides are, Longest 70
Next.. 55-904530149739870499445, Shortest 46 9045 &c.
For the perpendicular's length, let g — the shortest side; then,
by Eucl. I. 47, vcss — $ee)\ zz$ 37-40536 yards.

Hence the area = 1309-1876 square yards = 1 ro. 3 per. &c. To find the angle subtended by the perpendicular, and made by the shortest side and shortest segment.

As the less segment: radius:: perpendicular: tang. 52 48'. As radius: tang, of £ last angle:: lesser segment 30-5: 15-14, half the diameter; so the diameter is 30-28.
Remark. In this solution x is put = Bh (in the figure to the following solution), $b\ zz$ Ah or Ae, and d — Gb = Ce, then Ab — $b + a$ and Bc = $d + x$: but since Ab9 — Bcs = Ad — Dc9, we have $bt - (P+ \%b - d)x$-a2— $e\%$ and therefore $x\ zz$ as m the original, L. *Additional Solutions.*
In this question wc have given, in the triangle Abc, the base Ac — 70, the rectangle of the segments of the base, made by a perpendicular, Ad X Dc 1181g J J, and the segments of the base made at the point of contact of the inscribed circle, viz. Ae = 39, and Ce = 30; to determine the triangle.
Algebraical Solution.
Put s — 35 = Ai — ic, p = 1181$g-5£

= Ad X Dc, and z = Id — half the difference between Ad and Dc. Then Ad — $s + s$, and Dc — $s - z$; hence their product M — $zz - p$, and therefore « — $i/(ss-p)$. Then Ad — Ah = s + /(w—p), and nc = Cg
— s— —p). Again, since Bh is — Bg, we shall have the difference of the sides Ab — Bc = Ah — Cg — Ae — Ec — 9; then, by a known rule, Ae — Ec: Ad — Dc:: Ac: Ab + Bc; the sum of the sides being then known, from it and their difference the sides themselves are easily found. Also Bd — (ba2— Ad2), and-BD X

Ac — the area. Lastly, the double area of the triangle being divided by its perimeter, the quotient will be the radius Fe of the inscribed circle.
Geometrical Construction,
Let i be the middle of the given base Ac, and E the point of contact with the circle. By Eucl. 11. 14, make a square equal to the givea rectangle of the segments of the base, which call s2; then take Id equal one leg of a right-angled triangle of which s is the other leg and Ai the hypothenuse; so shall Ad, Dc be the segments of the base made by the perpendicular. For, by Eucl. II. 5, Aia — Ad X nc + Id1 ss + Id2 by the construction; therefore Ai, S, and Id form a rightangled triangle by Eucl. I. 48.

Again, take Bg or Bh a fourth proportional to 2ie, Ed, and Ac; which being added to Ah Ae, and to Cg — Ce, the two sums will be the two sides Ab, Bc, of the triangle.—For, by Eucl. III. 37, Ae — Ah, Ce — Cg, and Bh = Bg; and it remains only to prove that Bg or Bh is the 4th proportional mentioned above. Now, by Simpson's Geom. Cor. 2. 9. II, as Ab — Bc: 2 Id:: Ac: Ab-fBc; but Ab — Bc (= Ah— co = Ae — Ec) = 2ie, and Ab + Bc:= (ah + Hb + Bg + Gc =:) Ac + 2bg; therefore the proportion becomes 2ie: 2id:: Ac: Ac + 2bg; hence, by division, 2ie: 2ed:: Ac: 2bg, or 2ie: Ed:: Ac: Bg. Q. E. D.

The calculation from hence is very easy and evident, n.
iv. Question 95, *bu Mr.* Alex. Naughley.
To try the skill of a gauger he is required to find the content of a tub in the form of a frustum of a cone having given the bottom diameter 32 inches, and the segments of the diagonals made by their intersection 20 and 30 inches. He however finds that he is unable to resolve the question, and therefore solicits the aid of the learned fair to help him out of his difficulty.
Answered by Mrs. Eliz. Dodd.
The greatest diameter 48. Lesser 32. Depth so inches. Content 17-764831 malt bushels.
Solution.
Abcd being the tub, we have given Dc — 32, »i = EC = 20.

Upon the middle of the base of the isosceles triangle Dec let fall the perpendicular from the angle E; and from the top of the tub let fall the perpendicular Br. Then, in the right-angled triangle Deg, Eg = /(de8 — Dgs) = (20 — lis') — 12; and in the similar triangles Deg, v. Question 96, *by Mr.* Joseph Smith.
0
There is a piece of land in the form of a triangle, the sum of the three sides is 96 chains; £ of the base or longest side is just equal to the difference of the other two; and the difference of the segments of the base made by a perpendicular from the opposite angle is 2 chains less than the shortest side. The land is to be divided amongst three men, by fences made from the angles to the centre of gravity thereof: required the lengths of the fences?
Answered.
The three sides of the triangle are 42, 34, and 20 chains. The internal fences 24-586, 18-773, and 12-238. The content 33-6 acres.

Divide each side of the triangle into two equal parts, from whence draw lines to the angles opposite; the point in which these intersect is the centre of gravity of the triangle; and where it would be, if hung up, equally poised.
Solution.
Let AC be the base or longest side of the proposed triangle ABC, and Bd the perpendicular. Put i Bc the shortest side, and y the other side Ab. Then, by the question, 2 — 2 1= Ad — DC, and the greatest side Ac (or Ad + Dc) — 3.(1/ — s), also the sum of all the three sides is $4y$ — 2s 96, or $1y$ — 3 — 48, But, by

the nature of the triangle, Ac: Ab + Bc:: Ab— Bc: Ad — Dc, or 3. $(jj — z)$

X $(= — 2) = (jf + z)$ x $(.// — z)$; hence 3. $(z — 2) = y + z$, or $Lz —y$ 6. From this equation, and the one above, viz. $ly — a — 48$, we easily find z 20, and — 34. Consequently the third side 3. $(y — z)$ is 42.,

Now the point F upon which the triangle will be in equilibrium is the centre of gravity; and lines drawn through the centre of gravity, from the angular points, bisect the opposite sides; that is, Bf produced bisects Ac in E; also the distance between the angular point and the centre of gravity is two-thirds of the whole line, that is Bf

—-jbe. But, by theor. II. book 3, Simp. Geom. it is 2be +-ac" = Ab + Bc; hence Bf (=-jbe) — f«/ — = Ti. Question 97, *by Mr.* R. Tapper.

A person observed that if twice his age in years on the 16th of January 1721, were increased by its square root, and also by 5, and the result squared and added to his age, the amount would be 2256. What was his age at that time?
Answered by Mr. C. Mason.

It is evident this question is composed from that in page 225 of Ward's Mathematician's Guide.

Suppose — to his age. *1 aa + a + 5 — 47*. Involved is $a'' + 2a3 + 12aa + 11a + 30 = 2256 =$. *b*. Then by completing the square will be produced this canon, $vw(fi + 0-25) — 6-25) — 0-5 = a$, and — = 18 years old.

Remark. The method of completing the square in the above original solution is thus. Since $a1 + 2a3 + 12a2 + 11a + 30$ is $= (aa + a + 5) + aa + a + 5 — b;$ by completing the square, we have $aa + a + 5 — + 0-25) — 0-5$; and, by completing the square again, it is $a — /(/(b + Q'\%5) — 525) — 0-5 = 6$. And then $aa — 18$. H.

Vii. Question 98, *by Mr.* T. Rasberry.

Three persons A, B, and c had the misfortune to lose considerable sums of money in the grand South Sea scheme. A lost two thousand pounds more than B, and nine thousand more than c, and the square of A's loss was equal to the sum of the squares of the losses of the other two: What sum did each lose?

Answered by Mr. Lewis Evan.
Put c, e, u — the several losses, b — 2000, and c =: 9000.
C d= b+ c f 17000 A
Then-2 e c C + Ibc — -2 15000 B C lost.
' (u — b) I 8000 c J *Additional Solution.*

The theorems, in the original solution above, for determining the values of the three quantities required, are found thus:

Denoting the two differences between the greatest and each of the other two by b and c, as above, and the least quantity itself by x; then $x + c$ — the greatest, and $x + c — b$ — the middle one: hence, by the question, $(x + c)s = x$ -f-$(x$ J-c — 6)s; from Which equation we have $x — b + /1bc$.

Then $x + c — b = c + /Zbc$, and $x+c,z:b+c + /Ibc$, which are the three quantities required, H.

The Prize Question, *by* Adrastca.

Wanting to know the depth of Eldon Hole, in the Peak in Derbyshire. I let a stone fall into it, and counted 8, vibrations of a pendulum 61 inches in length, from the instant the stone began to fall to the time the sound of its striking the bottom reached the ear: Required the depth of the pit?
Answered.

August 18, 1718, Adrastea let fall 3 several stones into Eldon Hole, which fell with little or no obstruction, and accelerated in 9, 11, and 10 seconds from their delivery to the sound's reaching the ear: Sir Isaac Newton says, heavy bodies fall 165 foot the first second, then 3, 5, 7, 9, &c. times so much in the succeeding seconds, and that sound moves 968 feet in a second. Then 10" x 10" =: 100 X 16-5, 1650 feet- by 968 = 1" 42"' for the approach'of sound. So the stone was falling but8±"; 8-25 X 8-25 — 680625 X 16-5 — 1123 feet =: 374-34 yards.

But by Dr. Halley's numbers, let $a — 16$ foot 1 inch, $h — a$ -f1142 — the time sound is in moving the distance «, t — the time, the depth; there will arise this theorem , x--$kt + ±$-$/(4M + 1) = 1265$-82 feet.

N. B. The method taught in Lexicon Technicum, and several authors, to find a depth by the falling of heavy bodies, is false. The time the sound is reaching the ear, must be deducted out of the latter part of the stone's falling. In that author's example, under the word pendulum, according to the time of the body's falling, the well is 256 feet deep; then he allows for the sound's ascending J- of 16 feet to be subtracted, makes it just 250 feet: whereas in the last second, the stone fell 112 feet, therefore-J of that (at least) must be deducted, it will be but 225 feet. *Additional Solution.*

This problem is of the nature of Sir I. Newton's 50th prob. in his Universal Arith. who has there given the true method of solution much in this manner.

Put x for the depth of the hole, $a = 16$ feet the distance fallen by a body in the first second of time, and $b — 1142$ feet — the velocity of sound per second; also t — the given time of hearing the sound, found by the experiment. Then, by the nature of falling This theorem is wrong printed in the original, and ft is put = 114? instead of a -7-1142. But, as it now stands, it agrees with the resull in prob. 50, Newton's Universal Arithmetic, and is derived immediately from the resolution of the quadratic equation + V- = t in Dr. Hutton's additional solution, by writing 2 instead of b: for then X bodies, Ja : i/x :: " : y'— — the time of the stone's falling to the bottom: and by the uniform motion of sound, $b: x :: 1$": o the time in which the sound will ascend through the space x. Then the sum of these two times will be equal to the whole time, that is, % + — Now the times in which pendulums make $b a$ an equal number of vibrations, being as the roots of the lengths, and a pendulnm 39-2 inches long vibrating 8 times in 8 seconds, we shall have-v/39-2: /6l :: 8": svni — 10" (extremely near) = t the time in which a pendulum, of 61 inches swings 8 times: then the above theorem — + /-= t becomes + V 1Sx =10.

Hence $x — 1270$-4 feet = 423 yards = the depth required, u.

Questions proposed in 1723, *and answered in* 1724. i. Question 99, *by Mr.* C. Mason.

The story of Hero and Leandcr has immortalized the names of those two lovers. Leander was a young man of Abydos, a town on the Asiatic side of the Bosphorus or Hellespont; and Hero a young damsel of Sestos, a town on the European side. Leander used to visit Hero by swimming over the straight in the night. Now supposing him to keep pace v, ith the waves, which were forty feet in breadth, how long would he be in swimming over, and what would be the breadth of the Hellespont, the angle subtended by Abydos and Sestos, at a station equally distant from both being 43, and at another station, five furlongs from the first, still equally distant from th« towns, 48?

Answered by Mr. Rich. Tapper.
As.tTtc rectangle of the radius and the sine of 2 30': the rectangle c't J&ts iines ot 24 and 21 30':: 3300 = 5 furlongs: half the breadth of the Bosphorus 11277-764613 feet. The whole breadth is 7515-1764 yards — 34 furlongs 35 yards r: 4 miles 2 furlongs 35 yards. Then (according to Sir Isaac Newton) a wave runs through its breadth, whilst a pendulum, whose length is equal to that breadth, oscillates or vibrates once. A pendulum of 40 feet in length vibrates 17-14642817 times a minute. Consequently he swam 685-85 feet per minute. From hence the time is 32' 53" 11'" 52"".

Additional Solution.
If c and D represent the two places of observation, and AB half the breadth of the Bosphorus: then we have given all the angles and the line Cd, to find Ab; viz. £c — 21 30' r: half the first observed angle, Zbda — 24 — half the latter, Zdac = (zd — Zc =) 2 30', and Cd = 5 furlongs = 3300 feet. Hence, by common trigonometry, s. Cad: s. c:: Cd: Da, and radius: s. D:: Da: Ab; hence by compounding these two proportions, &c. radius X s. Cad: ». D x s. c:: Cd: Ab, that is, radius X s. 2 30': s. 24 X s. 21 3C:: 3300 feet: half the breadth of the Bosphorus, as in the original solution.
392
Again, by the nature of pendulums, y/rzr " vo :: 1": .40 X 12 W6.
V — — 3y seconds, very nearly, = the time in 39-2 7 '"" which a pendulum of 40 feet makes one vibration, or the time in which the wave or the swimmer moves 40 feet. And, consequently, as 40 feet: 3":: the whole distance: time of swimming, H.

Ii. Question 100, *by Mr.* John Richards.
Finci the distances from Etlystone light-house to Plymouth, Start Point, and Lizard respectfully, from the following data.
f Plymouth to Lizard 60)
The distance from Lizard to Start Point 70 miles.
I Start Point to Plymouth 20)
Plymouth *)* C North
Lizard bears from Edystone rock W.S.W
Start Point 3 (E. by N.

Answered by Mr. John Topham.
This question is to be found in the Philosophical Transactions, proposed by Mr. Townlcy, with Mr. Collins's constructions to all its cases. From Edystone to Lizard 53-112 miles, to Start Point 17-134, to Plymouth 14-187.

The question being somewhat curious, I shall here give the method of solving it. Because any two of the angles answering the rumbs given in the question, exceed 180 degrees, the point where Edystone stands must fall within the triangle. Then if you suppose a circle to pass through Lizard, Edystone, and Start, and bisect the line between Lizard and Start, producing such line through the centre of that circle to the periphery, lines drawn from the point in the periphery to Lizard and Start, with the two lines from Edystone to Lizard, and from Edystone to Start will be a trapezia inscribed in a circle, which according to 22 Euclid 3, the two opposite angles taken together are equal to two right angles; consequently the angle at the periphery is 11 15', the complement to that at Edystone 168 45/ given. In like manner let a circle pass through Plymouth, Edystone, and Lizard, the angle at the periphery will be 67 30', the complement to the other rumb given, 112 so'. Again, if from the centre of the first circle you draw lines to Lizard and Start, the angle contained between them will be double to that at the circumference, by 20 prop. Euclid 3, viz. 22? 3C, and in the other circle 135. Then, s. 11 15': log. off 70 miles given:: radius: semi-diam. circle 179-4. Also s. 67 30': log. of £ 60 miles given:: radius: semi-diam. circle 32-47.

Now there is given the two semi-diameters of the circles, and the angle between them r= 116-38, to find the angle subtended by the lesser semi-diameter.

As sum sides: difference:: tang. £ opposite angles: tang, of £ the difference of the angles; which angle is 8 31'. Then radius: log. 179-3:: s. 8 31': log. of 26-52; which doubled is the distance between Edystone and Lizard 53-04 miles. For the other two, there are two sides, and an angle opposite to one of them, given, to find the other side. Hence from Edystone to Plymouth is 14333 miles, and from Edystone to Start Point 1736.'

First Additional Solution. Construction.
With the three given distances, 60, 70, and 20, make the triangle Lps, wherein P will bi; Plymouth, L the Lizard, and s the Start. Then if E be supposed to represent the Edystone, the direction Ep being north, Es being E. by N. and El being W.S.W. there will be known all the angles about the point E. Hcuce, supposing Pe produced to A, if on Ls there be described the segment of a circle Les to contain the given angle Les — 15 points or 168 45', and then there be made either the angle Sla = 9 points — Zaes, or the angle Lsa 6 points Z Ael, La or Sa cutting the circle in A; it is evident that E will be the point of intersection of Ap with the circle.

Calculation. 1. In the triangle Lps, are given all the sides, and of consequence the angle Psl. 2. In the triangle Als, are given Ls, the Zasl (by constr.) and the Za = the supplement of Z Les; to find Sa. *3*. In the triangle Psa, are given Ps, Sa, and Zs; to find Zpas — Zsle, and Zaps. 4. In the triangle Les, are given the angles and the side Ls; to find Le and Es. 5. And, lastly, in the triangle ?se, are given the angles and the side sp; to find Pe. H. *Second Additional Solution.*

Let the given sides Pl and ps be denoted by *a* and *e*; the given angles Pes and Pel by m and n; and the unknown angles Ple and pss by x and 2. Then, by trigonometry, warn: sins:: e : Pe—esinz-f-sinm; sinn: sin x:: a: PEa sin.z-j-sinn; e sin z a sin x sin 2 a sin m, ., „ therefore — = —, or— = —::and therefore sin m sm n sin x e sin n sin z + sin a; a sin m + g sin n sin z — sin x ' a sin m — e sin n'

But by Theo. xxii. p. 65, vol. 3, of the Course + Sm x J r 3 sin z — sin x tan 4(2 + x) tan 4(s — x)' . tan $(z + x)$ a sin m + e sin n,. 1 herefore — ::and therefore tan-(2 — x) a sin m — e sin n i, N a sin «i — e sin n. tan Mz — x) ——. :: X tan Uz + x). 2V J «sinm + esm« v

But the sum of the angles s and x is given, being equal to the difference between the angles Les and Lps, when the point E is within the triangle Lps, as in the present case, and equal to the difference between the sum of those angles and four right angles when it is without the triangle; therefore the difference of the angles z and x is given. Now having given the sum and difference of the angles a and x, the angles themselves are given. Hence the sides Pe, Le, and Se may be readily found, L.

Hi. Question 101, btf Mr. John Willjngham.

A person upon the top of a mountain observed the moon just rising one evening, and found her zenith distance to be 90 50': at the same time he observed a ship at sea through a tube inclined to the, TOL. I. I horizon 1 58': required the height of the mountain and the distance of the ship from its top?

Answered by Mr. Tapper.
As radius: the secant of 50':: semi-diam. earth: the semi-diam. and height of the mountain in one sum. Sem. earth: s. 88 2:: last sum: s. angle opposite 91 47'. Consequently the angle at the centre is known.

If the diameter of the earth be, as Norwood makes it, 41899310 English feet, the mountain's height will be = 2216-473 feet, the ship' distance 14-6288 miles, and from the base of the mountain on the arch of a great circle 12'726.

N. B. The proposer gives this answer, viz. The mountain's height 746 yards f, at 70 miles to a degree; the ship's distance 3 leagues 2 miles. But some others, according to the difference of miles to a degree, 881 yards and 5 leagues, &c.

Remark. The above original solution will be evident from.this figure; in which c represents the centre of the earth, Ab the hill, s the ship, and Am a " tangent to the earth directed to the rising moon. For, M being a right angle, and £_ Acm — 50', whose tangent is Ma and secant Ac, it will be as radius: sec. Z Acm: Cm:: Ca. Again, the Zsac being — 88 2', and the sides cs, Ca known; we thence find the third side As =: the distance of the ship from the top of the mountain; as also the Zsca, and consequently the arch Sb the distance of the ship from the bottom of the mountain. H.

It. Question 102, *by Mr. John Simmons.*

Wanting the dimensions of a stone, in the form of the frustum of as octagonal pyramid, which lay partly immersed in water; the greater end was just covered, but the less end only touched the water, it was known that if a line equal to the sum of the slant side and less end be divided in extreme and mean proportion, the slant side will be the greater segment of that line. The obtuse angle formed by the slant side and diameter of the circle inscribed in the less end was 100, and the solid content of the whole frustum 158821-64 cubic inches: "what are the dimensions of the frustum, and the content of the part immersed in the water?, *Answered by Mr. Tapper.* Let a =-82847, the area of an octagon whose diameter is 1, c = con 5 + x:: s s--2s fx the breadths of the two bases. And, consequently, 1 + r — the breadth of the greater base = bx. Then the area of the greatest base — $abbxx$, and the geometrical mean area $abxx$. Then, frustum dx. And by multiplication we have $adx3$ X — c zz $ of the three areas multiplied by dx the height — $mxxx$. And hence x — j (c-f-m) — 41-633534 inches. Then making the square root of the area of the lesser base — d, the greater — D, the height = H.

By *J. Painter,* 107784-57
X 1 H = 107707-75 the wet part.

Additional Solution.
The solution to this question will perhaps appear a little clearer thus.—The slant side being the greater part, and the diameter of the circle inscribed in the less end the less part of a line divided in extreme and mean proportion; the meaning of which is, that the greater part is a mean proportional between the less part and the whole, that is $xx = (x + y)$ X $y = xy + yy$, putting x = the greater part or the slant height, and y = the less or the diameter of the circle in the less end. Now from this quadratic equation is found y —

V5 —1 A/5 — 1 x — ax, putting $a J$.

Now, the slant side making an angle of 100 with the less end, or 80 with the greater, put s and c for the sine and co-sine of 80; then sx will be the altitude of the solid, and cx the half difference hence the content will be sxX— s — 158821-64 =: «, between the diameters of the two ends; and consequently y +2cr or ax + 2cx — the diameter of the circle in the greater end—bx, putting b — a + 2c.—Then, putting n for the area of the octagon, the diameter of whose inscribed circle is 1, we shall have $na'x$ and $nfi'x$ for the areas of the two ends, and $nabx$? their mean proportional, naV + $nabx$%--nbx
T
3d
from which is found x— 1/ ;;—„ Consequently all

V ns X $(au + ab + bb)$ the parts become known, and thence the content of each hoof as in the original solution, u.
v. Question 103, *by Mr. Will. Doidgc.*

In a garden is a plot of ground in the form of an ellipse, whose principal axes are 15 and 10 feet; a line cuts the transverse axis at the distance of 3-2 feet from the centre, and makes therewith an angle of 72. What are the segments of that line?

Answered by Mr. J. Painter,
The length of the greater part of the ordinate 5-18, and the lesser 4-23.
. By IVfr. *Tapper,* 5-13416 and 4 20625.
Solution.
Let Dd be the line cutting the transverse Ab in an angle of 78 degrees at the point E; draw the perpendiculars DF.

Put m semi-transverse, n — semiconjugate, a Ce, s and c = sine and cosine Z E = 72, and x De. Then Df = tx Ef cx, and Cf rz $a \pm cx$; hence, by the nature of the ellipse, «!: $n :: (m-a\pm cx)$X $(m-a+cx)$: ,,, »i4 —i $(a \pm cxY,. s x -n y. -$; this equa mm tion reduced becomes $xx \pm$ 9282248r— 21-5945; hence x — 4.206 or 5-1342 zz the two parts required. H.

Vi. Question 104, *by Mr.* Tho. Williams.

TEneas whilst contemplating with astonishment, the embellishments, of rising Carthage, observed a block of polished marble, in the form of a square pyramid, weighing 48 tons. The perpendicular height was equal to twice the diagonal of the base; what were its dimeuT rions, and how many cubic feet did it contain? *Answered.*

A cubic inch of marble weighs 1-56185 ounces avoirdupois, so the content of the pyramid is 634-5729257 solid' feet. The proportion of the side of a square to its diagonal, is as 1 to 1-4142. Multiply the solid content by 3, and divide the product by 2, gives 952-782, which multiplied by the square of 1-4142 = 1-99936, gives 1906, whose cube root is 12-319, the diagonal. Divide 952-78 by 12-31 gives 76-89, whose square root 8-768 is the side of the square sought.

Additional Solution.

The content being found as in the original solution above, put it = c, and x — the side of the square base. Then xx as *the* area of the base, xy'2 = the diagonal, and $2x2$ = the height. Hence the content $(2x3 y2)$-r-3 = c; then xzz lj $(30$-5-$22)$ the side of the base, and $(2x/2 =) / 24c$ = 2 5/ 3c = the height. H.

THE PRIZE QUESTION.

Wanting to find the height of Coventry steeple, I measured a base line, of 282-2 feet, from the bottom, along an uniform declivity, and then I could just see the top of the spire over a building; whose top was on a level with the bottom of the steeple, and distant from.it 228-75 feet. It was also found that the distance from the top of the spire to the end of the base line, and the height of the steeple, were together equal to 775-04 feet. What was the height of the steeple? *Remark.* The process for finding the equation in the above original solution, may be thus:

Put — Ac + Cd, b — Ab, d — Ad, and z Ac the height of the steeple; then i — z Cd. Draw Do, perpendicular to Ca produced in Q. Now, by right-angled triangles, Bc = /(bb + zz); (CA:CQ= V(bb +zz)Z) and, by similar triangles, Cb: Cd:: J # Ab: Questions proposed in 1724, a«J answered in 1725.

i. Question 105, *by Mr.* Williams.

The breadth of the ditch or moat of a tower is 93 feet, and if the height of the tower be multiplied by 93, and the product added to twice the length of a ladder reaching from the outside of the ditch to the top, the sum will be 14423: What is the height of the tower?

Anszeered by Mr. John Painter.

Let b — 93, c — ladder's length, a — tower's height Then is $ab + 2c$ — 14423 per question, and $aa + bb$ — cc, 47 Euc. I. There will arise this ambiguous equation $a - d \pm$ »/(dd— s) — 151-2688 the tower's height; and the ladder's length — 17757 .

Additional Solution.

The ladder being the hypothenuse of a right-angled triangle, whose base is the breadth of the moat, and perpendicular the height of the tower; if b be put = 93 the breadth of the moat, and x zz the height In rhfe solution d is put for 2i tX 14423 and. for u. Question 106, *by Mr.* John Richards.

There is a spheroidal cask, such, that whether the mean diameter of an equal cylinder be found by Oughtred's rule, or by the common method of adding ths of the bung, to-jths of the head diameter, the result will be the same. The length of the cask is 405 inches, and when full contains 98 gallons: now supposing it to want 11 inches of being full, when measured at the bung: What quantity of liquor has been drawn oflF?

Answered by Mr. John Knipe.

The bung diam. 32-1152? inches for 5 29-066? inches for The head diam. 23-3168$ ale gall. I 21103 § wine gall. 32-672 », ___ ,, 28-018 dry. 69-981 wet.

The same answered by Mr. Rich. Tapper.

Let H is the head diameter, B — bung, D the difference B — a.

By Mr. Oughtred's theorem 2bb + BH, _ tne diameter of an «s equal cylinder.

But,-7b-f-3h =: the diameter of the equal cylinder per question; by involution, transposition, and division, we have Bb — if hb = — Sj-hii, and Iib — hb — — 5? BB, Hence B = h; and H =-52b. — 73

Wherefore it will be as 53: 73:: H: B, and the contrary, universally: and the diameters 21-103 and 29-066 for wine gallons, or 23-316 and 32-115 for ale.

Let xzzditFerence of the wet and dry inches, b bung diameter. Then 2/(66 — xx) — the breadth of the surface of the liquor in the middle of the cask; and multiplying by i, the fluent will be %bx — 3 x5 x1 5x9

Q7 — zTTTf-..-pp, — 7, — &c. = the area of the middle seg36 206' 066, bib-b1 mcnt of a circle to the radius b, and the chord line's distance from the centre in the bung diameter x.

Now, to find the length of the radius, at any distance from the bung diameter.

Let a — length of the spheroid, / r: § length of the cask, h =head diameter. Then $aa: bb :: (a + /)$ X («— Q = (aa — 0: hh hence aahh — aabb — llbb; put c — bb —M, then aa —.

Let z — the distance of the circle from the bung diameter whose ra ,. w rr.i llbb,, llbb — czz llbb — czz dius is sought. Then —: bb:::7, — the c c 11 square of the radius; which raised to the power, it will give the A--h SB SSz. ccc 5c" 7cV radius _ b 2W/-gt_ i2g&7f 958M,, &c.

which raised to its several powers, and substituted in the room of b, it will give the area. The series multiplied by the fluxion of z, gives the solidity or quantity of liquor. Then find the fluent of each term, and let / z, ihe series will shew of the difference of the wet and dry parts; or, if / = the whole length, gives the difference, which added or subtracted with the contents, shews the quantity of liquor in the cask 63-5541, vacuity 32-4458 wine gallons. *Additional Solution.*

Putting b and h for the bung and head diameters; by Oughtred's ruleiy/ — the mean diameter = (by the other method mentioned in the question) o X 7 + A = "T5' rm equation is found $h - b;$ that is the bung and head diameters are exactly in proportion as 73 to 63. Now let 73; and 53 be the the two diameters; then, supposing the content 98 ale gallons, 1077-157 40 5_98, hence z_y 40. 5 x (2.73»+53' =-4399361, and consequently the two diameters 73s and 53z arc 32-11535 and 23 31662.

Then for the ullage of the cask, it may be *truly* found by the rule in Cor. 2, page 290, Mensuration. Or, to.use the approximating rule given at page 545 of the same *Xiib* = -3125155; the circular segment answering to this quotient is- 23785866; then-23785866 X J2_ = 29-68 gallons — the ullage nearly, a.

in. Question 107, *by Mr.* A. Naughley.

At an election, four candidates offered themselves, and the whole number of votes was 5219; the number for the first candidate ex.. ceeded those for the second, third, and fourth, by 22, 73, and 130 respectively: How many had each?

Answered by Sylvia.

The sum of any whole quantity and the excesses of its greatest part above each of the other, being divided by the number of parts gives the greatest, and thereby all the other parts. Hence the first had 1361, the second 1339, the third 1288, and fourth 1231 votes.

Remark. The rule mentioned in the original solution above, is thus discovered: Let the sum s be divided into *n* parts, of which the differences between the greatest and each of the rest arc a, 6, c, /, &c. Then if be the greatest, $x - a, x - b, x - c, x - /,$ &c. will be the others; and their sum $x + (x - «) + - b) + (x - c) + (x - d)$ &c. or $nx - a - b - c - d$ &c. $- s$; hence $nx - s + m$. putting *m* for the sum of the differences, and x $- \$ - - 3 n$ the greatest; which is the. rule. H.

Iv. Question 108, *by Mr.* Richard Whitehead.

There is a triangular field the two shorter sides of which are 65f and 52595 perches, and in the field is a rectangular space the longest side of which is 46§f-perches, and coincides with the third side of the field; the breadth of this space is 18 perches. Now suppose the field to be shared amongst four brothers A, B, C, D; c to have the rectangular space, B the triangular space above the. rectangle, *o* the space on the right, and A the space on the left of the rectangle: What is the quantity of land contained in each person's share?

Answered by Mr. A, Naughley.

Let $b - 65-5$ perches, $c - 52-16, d - 4698, p$ 18; *a, e,* o, u, *y,* — several segments of the lines in the triangle. Then $ee - yy - uu, aa - dd + Idy - yy = uu, cc - 2ce + ee - 00 - pp$ by 47 Euc. I. *c: e::* b*: a,* by 2 Euc. VI. and *o + y :* c*:: y : e,* by *b b Ide* 4 Euc. VI.: whence this equation $- ee - ee + .$ X 'cc c $- e$ /(ce $- pp$ f ee $- 2$ce) $= dd - 2077$-9612, which reduced and tion *x* is found $- 1$-85 nearly, and hence the other quantifies all become known, H.

v. Question 109, *by Mr.* Win. Doidge.

A father has concealed the age at which he will permit his daugh tcr to marry in the equation $a'2 - $ ciT zz 4-962ff, where *a* denotes the age. Pray ladies inform her at what age she may be a bride, the young lady andjicr lover being afraid of the time passing without their knowledge, being both unskilled in algebra?

Answered by Mr. Tapper.

Given $a - fi\ zz\ 4$-962a $= ba$ to find a. Let $x''\ zz\ a;$ then $zz\ 'aaa,$ and $'\ zz\ aa,$ also $x - xX\ zz\ bxc,$ which when coa. tracted is $x - x - bxe,$ and by transposition and division $x'' - bx - 1.$ Here *x* will be found $== 1$-7425615449 +, and $x'' - a - 27$-9981125 $= 27$ years, 364 days, 13 hours and *i fere,* or 28 years *proxime.*

vi. Question 110, *by Mr.* George Brown.

A ship at sea having been long tossed by a tempest, at length the storm abated, and, to the great joy of the crew, the sun made his appearance on the 10th of May, when his altitude was observed to be 39 7'; and in an hour and fifty minutes afterwards, the ship lying in the same place, his altitude was found to be 55 57'. Required the latitude of the ship, and the times at which the altitudes were taken?

Answered by Mr. Nat. Browne.

The latitude 46 33', the hours 8" 24m and 10h 15TM.

Solution.

Here are given two observed altitudes of the sun (supposed to be freed from the errors of refraction), with the (supposed) true interval of time between the observations, as also the declination of the sun'; to find the latitude and true times of observation. It is admitted that the watch or timc-keeper may be too fast or two slow, but yet however it is supposed to go true for the interval of time between the observations. The declination for the supposed middle true time between the times of observation, may be used for the common declination at both times, unless the interval of time be great; but if this be thought not sufficiently accurate, let the declination be taken for the two supposed true times themselves, and used in the calculation.

Construction.

On a proper plane, as a primitive, describe the triangle op©, making 0 P, Op equal to the co-declinations for the two times, and the angle at p equal to the given interval of time; then will P be the pole, and ©, o the places of the sun at the first and second observations. Again, about the poles O, o describe two circles at the distance of the two observed co-altitudes and intersecting in z the zenith of the place. Then a great circle described through P, z will be the meridian, the arc Pz — the co-latitude, and the angles Zp©, zro the measures of the times required.

Calculation.

Drawing the great circles, zo, z ©. In the triangle Op© are given the two sides Op, Q P equal the two co-declinations, and the included Z.opq — the interval of time; to find o© and tiie Zo©p. Then in the triangle oz ©, are known the three sides; to find the Zo0z; which taken from the Zo0p, there remains the /z0p. Lastly, in the triangle z©p, are known the two sides z0, ©p, and included Zz0p; to find the side rz the latitude, and the Zzp© the time for the first observation from noon; from which taking the given difference or©, there remains the time of the second observation from noon. H.

The Prize Question, *hi)* Adrastea

Two military roads, called by the Romans Watling-Street, and the Fosse, intersected each other at a place formerly named Benones, now called High-Cross. Dove-Bridge or Tripontium, bears nearly south-cast by south, from High-Cross, and distant from it 8A miles; at Dove-Bridge the angle subtended by High-Cross, and another place upon the Fosse, called liathorpe, is a right angle. BrinklowHill is another place upon the Fosse, between High-Cross and Eathorpe, and distant from the latter place 8 J miles; and at Brink low-Hill the line to Dove-Bridge is perpendicular to the Fosse. The above data are sufficient for determining the distances of Brink lowHill and High-Cross, and of Eathorpe and Dove-Bridge. At a place called Newbold, the angle subtended by High-Cross and Dove. Bridge was 88 15'; and the angle subtended by Dove-Bridge and Eathorpe 149 45'. Required the distance of Newbold from each of the places, High-Cross, Brinklow-hill, Eathorpe, and DovaBridge?

Answered.

In the first part of the question there is given in a right-angled triangle Abc, the ca-; thetus Ab, and the alternate segment of the j hypothenuse Cd, (made by a perpendicular; Bd, let fall from the right angle); to find the other segment Da. Put c — Ab, b — Cd, and there will arise this theorem,, a = $\sqrt{cc + \pm bb}$) — b — 4-81903, and by 47 Euc. I. the base — 11-0836, the perpendicular Db G'55; which completes the triangle.

Then from E where Newbold stands, there is given the angle Aeb 88 15'; Bec 149 45'; and Cea 122. To find the dis tances Ea, Eb, Ec, and Ed. And here we must note, as in the answer to question 100, that as any two of the angles given, together exceed 180 degrees, the point w here New hold stands will fall within the triangle Abc.

Now if you suppose a circle to pass through c Eathorpe, E Newl)old, and B Tripontium, and bisect the line Cb, producing that bisection through the centre of the circle, it will cut the periphery in a point from whence lines drawn to B and c, w ill complete a trapezia inscribed in a circle; which by 2? Euc. III. has the two opposite angles taken to gether equal to two right angles: hence the angle at the periphery will be 30 15'. In like manner proceed with the 3 points Aeb, and the ang!e at the periphery will be 91 45'.

Then if from the centre of the first circle you draw lines to B and c, the angle contained between them will, by 20 Euc. III. be double to that at the circumference, *viz.* 60 30', and in the other circle it will be 183 30'.

But it will be needless to explain the matter.any farther, having already, in the last year's diary, given as clear a demonstration as could be, without a large scheme that would admit of all those lines and circles requisite thereto; what remains being purely trigonometrical, from whence I have deduced this following answer.

Mr. Rich. Tapper *answers in (lie manner following.*

Let a r: the distance of Tripontium and Eathorpe; c — the distance of Tripontium and High-Croas — 2605 poles; n — the distance of Brinklow from Eathorpe = 2862 poles; then a — $/((cc?in+ n4)"$ — nn) — 3549-9109 poles; which call d. Let s = sine of 30 15'; m its cosine, or sine of 149 45'; z — the sine of 88 15', x its cosine, 1 — radius.

Imagine the line which joins Newbold and Tripontium to be extended through the Fosse, and a perpendicular let fall from Eathorpe upon it; also a perpendicular from High-Cross upon the said line. Then $d:s::a: at-d$ — the sine of the angle made by the lines which join Tripontium and Newbold, and Tripontium and Eathorpe, 1: d :: as -j-d: as — the length of the first perpendicular, 1: d: i m: ma — the distance from Newbold to the place where the said perpendicular cuts the extended line; and $/(dd—aass — ma)$ — the distance of Newbold from Tripontium, by 47 Euc. I. Now $l/(dd—aass)$,,. .as _,, $/(dd—aass)$

—1; — the cosine of -r. Then, z : c:: ; $d d 1 d : — i/(dd— aass)$ — the distance from Newbold to High-Cross; 1: os cos —:: c: — the distance from Tripontium to the place where the perpendicular from High-Cross would cut the line between Newbold and Tripontium, and 1: c:: $)£SitL$ $ssaa$). $c(dd-ssaa)$ — the perp. also $z:-dd$ — $ssaa$) :: $x:$ -$n/(dd$ — $ssaa$) = the distance of the perpendicular from Newbold. Hence this equation, xc sea j __ — x / $(dd — ssaa)$ — ma + —, which reduced gives this cx d — — theorem a = -jy-=2612-7383poles.

Additional Solution.

In the first place we have given, in a right-angled triangle, one leg Ab, and the alternate segment Cd of the hypothenuse made by the perpendicular Bd; and the triangle will be constructed as question 28, page 24. Again, the point E, where three lines Ae, Be, Ce make given angles with each other, will be determined as in question 100, j;age 127. H..

Questions proposed in 1725, *and answered in* 1726.

I. Question 111, *by Mr.* Rich. Whitehead.

Suppose D, c and G to be the respective positions of a house, a tre« and a boat on the borders of a lake, the distances of which from one another are to be determined. For this purpose the following lines were measured, *viz.*

Bb zr 117, the prolongation of a line joining D and c

Ba — 474 a perpendicular drawn to Dc, meeting Cg produced in A

Ag — 579 the prolongation of Cg

Cf = 674-J the prolongation of a line drawn from D to a.

Fe zz 507 a perpendicular let fall from F on Dc produced

Ce — 259 the distance of the perpendicular from c.

Hence it is required to find Dc, Dg, and Gc?

Anszccred by Mr. C. Mason. 1 2 3 4 5 6 7 8 9 10 11 12 13

Which equation reduced, and the sums collected, &c. gives a zz 1078-0833: Then a—/is the distance between the house and boat Dg = 4037499, and Dc the distance between the house and tree r= 692-2499, and Gc between the boat and tree = 386. Q. E. I.

N. B. *The Idler G is omitted at the boat in the prcccdiiigjiurc. Additional Solution.* The final equation will be simpler by substituting x for the unknown.

perpendicular Gc, the known quantities being as in the original solution j for then, by similar triangles, $fg\ g — x:g::f$ = Df, , "cd and $c — x : c:: d: = Ac$; $c — x$ bence, by right-angled triangles and subtraction,

$\sqrt{\text{te-o-»}}=/G£W\text{-»}$.

And here if Ce or h be supposed equal to Bd or b, as those distances are arbitrary, and might as well be measured equal as unequal, then .... i *cedd* o *ffss* the final equation will become barely — c9 — —g in which a; is easily found, H.

Ii. Question 112, *by Mr.* Tho. Dodd.

From what height above the surface of the earth must a heavy body fall, that the time of its descent may be equal to the time of ascent of sound to the same height, the velocity of which is known to be uniform and 1142 feet per second.

Answered by Mr. Sam. Rouse.

Sound moves 1142 feet per second: heavy bodies fall 16 feet in the fir«t second, according to Dr. Hallcy. Then put $a — 16$-jL, $b — l''y\ x —$ height, $d —$ the time sound flics 16-jfeet; $a: x :: bboc\ lb :—$ = square of the time of the descent of the body. Ajid $dx\ a: ve :: /: —$ =; the time sound moved to the height x. Conse $dv{,}xbb$, $bbx\ ddxx\ bba$ niiently — = /— whence — -, v x —,, — $J\ a\ a\ a\ aa\ dd$ 81088-085 feet = 27029-36 yards — 15 miles, 2 furlongs, 34 perches 7 feet.

Additional Solution. The solution will be a little clearer thus: Putting $a — 16$-jsj, $c = 1142$, and«'= the height. Then ya: *tfx :: '':* = time of falling x feet; and c: $x::$ 1":-= time of sound's passing ., ,, ,, $xx\ x\ cc$ 1142s over x feet; therefore — = and $x — =$-r—— = 81088 cc $a\ a$ 16-jij feet. ir. m. Question 113, *by Mr.* Tho. Grant.

A father at his death left an estate of 50001. per annum to his three daughters to be shared in the proportion of their several ages: now the square of each age added to the product of the other two, will make the three sums 1000, 980, and 920; required their age and fortunes?

Answered by Mr. John Turner.

C aa 4-i

Let then *ttaymn + n) zz* c, or aa —— , $mm + n\ uaUin + m) — d$, or $aa — mi$ - m

Whence — — —— and — _ " —— .

$1 + nni\ mm + n\ mi + m\ mm$ -f n or $bmm + bit\ zz\ c + enm$ and $dmm + dn — enn + cm$. _,.., bmm — c.....

From the first of these equations n — — —, winch bein?

$cm — b'$ B substituted in the second gives ,, $dbmm — dr.\ /bmm—c$ V' dmm 4-7— — c I —)-f $cm.\ cm — 0\ cm — 0$ J

And, by reduction, $(hb — cd)m + (bd + cc)$«!-4ta! + $(bb\ \text{-}dc)m + (c' — db)$-0, or in numbers, and dividing by 400, 246w' + 4701»»3— osoow' + 4754m + 101 r: 0; whence $m — \text{-}9683$, $n — \text{-W}$—— — 833, and the values of c, $e\ cm — b$ and u are found the same as above nearly.

This problem is the same (except the numbers) as one proposed to Dr. Wallis, in the year 1062, by Colonel Titus, to whom it had been originally proposed by Dr. John Pell, the famous algebraist of that time. Dr. Wallis inserted a solution of it in his Algebra, but it is exceedingly tedious and laborious, and leads to an equation of the 12th power; it reduces, however, by division, to one of the 8th power.

Mr. Baron Maseres has inserted it in a volume of Tracts on the resolution of algebraic equations published in 1800, and has set forth every step of the solution in the fullest and clearest manner possible. Mr. Maseres has also inserted another solution by Mr. Frend, which is much simpler than Dr. Wallis's and produces only a biquadratic equation. It is similar to one given by Ronayne, in his Algebra, and is founded on the same principle as that which we have given above. There is likewise a very ingenious solution of Col. Titus's problem, by Mr. Ivory, in the 3d vol. of the first series of the Mathematical Repository, which also leads to an equation of the fourth power, but the coefficients are smaller, and the equation easier to resolve than Mr. Frend's, but it is only adapted to Col. Titus's numbers. This problem is also resolved by Kirkby in his Arithmetic. i.

iv. Question 114, *by Mr.* Christ. Mason. What would a body equal to ten pounds troy at the earth's surface, weigh, if carried to the surface of each of the planets?

Answered by Mr. Rich. Whitehead.

Suppose the sun's parallax 10 seconds, and the magnitude of the earth according to Norwood's observations; then let $a —$ the distance of the earth from the sun, $p —$ the periodical revolution of the earth, $s —$ the periodical revolution of one of % satellites. To oV find its distance from % say $p : s2:: as: =$ the cube of the dis ' PP tance sought.

And as the squares of these periods recip. so are the centrip. forces towards their respective central bodies.

Then for the weight of bodies on their surfaces, if the distances are equal, the weights will be as the quantity of matter the bodies contain. If the quantities of matter are equal, the weights will be reciprocally as the squares of the distances: *Ergo,* If neither are equal, the weight will be in a compound ratio. For, as the distance between the sun and the earth, and the quantity of matter in the earth, is to ten pounds, so is the distance of Jupiter, and quantity of matter, to the weight ten pounds would weigh on his surface; and so for the rest. Hence ten pounds of our troy weight will weigh on the surface of the sun 244 pounds, on Jupiter 20, on Saturn 1275, on the empire of the bedlamites, *viz.* the moon 345.

Mr. Alexander Naughley's *answer.*

On the surface of the sun 240, % 19 9, rj 6, J) 5-15, § 215, 9 2-08, Tj 17.

Mr. *Tho. Dod* computes them from © % hi

Mr. Whiston's numbers-245 19-6 13-0 3'2

And Dr. Cheyne's theory 79-3 64 4-2 5 *Additional Solution.*

The proportions of the force of gravity at the surfaces of the planets, or the proportions of the weights of an equal quantity of matter at each, are now stated thus:

Sun Moon Mercury Venus Earth Mars Jupiter Saturn

These being severally multiplied by 10, we have 250 3$ '8 10 3$ 20 13J for the weights required, H. v. Question 115, *by Mr.* Bernard Annely.

On the 1st of June, 1724, at 55 minutes past seven in. the evening, it then wanting 7-f minutes of sun-set, a person observed the sun in a direct line with the top of a lofty building, 97 feet high, which stood upon the same level with himself: What was the distance of the building?

Answered by Mr. John Turner.
The time was 7 55', and © setting in that latitude was 811 2m 30". The longitude TJ 21 5C 17". Declination 23 13' 53". Ascensional difference 30 37' 30". To find the latitude, having the declination and ascensional difference, tan. declination 23 13': radius:: s. ascensional difference 30 37': tan. lai. 49 52' 53". Then there are given two sides and an angle included, to find the third side-the cosine of the sun's altitude 57' 52". Then s. © altitude: height of the object:: cosine of sun's altitude: length of the shadow 5762'4 feet = 1920 yards.

Additional Solution.
The time 8 2fra of sun-set is found by adding 7§m the half quarter to 7h 55m the time when the sun is directly behind the top of the edifice; at which time let o denote the sun's place, and © the point of sun-set; also let z be the zenith, and P the pole; and let the great circles be drawn as in the figure.

Then will Zpo be the hour angle of 7h 55'" and Z.P0 the hour angle of 8'1 2'" Pq or Po the given co-declination, rz the co-latitude, zo the co-altitude at the time of observation, and zQ the co-altitude at the time of setting, which will be a quadrant, it being the distance between the zenith and horizon.

Wherefore, in the triangle Zp© are given z©, Pq, and the Zzp©; to find Zp the co-latitude. Then in the triangle Zpo, will be given Zp, Po, and their included Z Zpo; to find zo the co-altitude at the time of observation. And, lastly, the distance will be equal to the length of the shadow, which is the base of a right-angled plane triangle whose perpendicular is the height of the building, and the angle at the base the sun's altitude; whence appears the reason of the last stating in the original solution; H.

Vi. Question 116, *by Mr.* John Simmons.

There is a piece of land in the form of a rectangle, the sum of whose perimeter and diagonal is just half a mile: and it was remarked by a surveyor who had measured it, that if a right line equal length = V(a-w) = =4/(l-(-iY)==v/'i So that the breadth, length, and diagonal, are to each other as / —-5 and 1; and therefore are in continual proportion.

Now the sum of this diagonal with twice the length and breadth is $A/5 + /(2 — 2)$; and then, by proportion, as this sum is to half a mile (the sum given in the question), so is each of the above proportional quantities to the breadth, length, and diagonal of the figure required. Wherefore half a mile or 880 yards drawn

V5— 1 75 — 1 2 *v* 2 into each of the fractions —-, —..

V5+/(2V5 — 2) /5+ (25-2) and yf5 _ — »)' produce the required breadth, length, and diagonal, H. THE PRIZE QUESTION.

When the Romans under Marcellus besieged Syracuse we are told that Archimedes contributed greatly to the defence of the place by the invention of curious and, powerful warlike engines. Let us suppose that one of them, for throwing large stones, was placed upon the city wall, to annoy the nearest point of the Roman camp, and that the distance of the camp from the ditch' at this place was 260 yards; also that at a corner of the wall, distant from the engine 400 yards, Archimedes stood viewing the point assailed, and found the distance across the ditch in the direction of that point to be 200 yards. What distance would he have stood from the point assailed?

Ansisered by Mr. Sam. Marriot.
In this right-angled triangle wherein a line is drawn parallel to the base, there is given the base = 400; that segment of the hypo-*p*,-, thenuse next the base 200 — *c*; and the alter--"I nate segment of the cathetus 260 *d.* To find the cathetus, &c.

$d + a: b:: d: -\!-\!-y$,
Here a will be found 141-7005; $a + b$ = 401-7005 the distance of the camp of Marcellus from Syracuse.

The solution of this question may more fully be seen in Ward's Introduction, p. 334.

Questions proposed in 1726, *and answered in* 1727.

I. Question 117, *by Mr.* Richard Whitehead.

A company of mathematicians, after emptying an elegant glass punch bowl, found themselves quite at leisure to contemplate its figure, &c. The inside had the form of an hyperbolic conoid, the transverse diameter of the generating hyperbola being 6-93 inches, and the conjugate 5-29 inches; the form of the outside of the bowl was that of a cone generated by the revolution of the asymptote of the hyperbola, and the length of the outside was 8££inches; also the depth of the bowl was 5-98 inches. Required the internal diameter at the brim, weight of the bowl, and what liquor it contained when full?

Answered by Mr. Christ. Mason. -Ac?'
$bb — 26a + aa$

Which equation reduced, &c. gives *a* — 2-93, from which all the other dimensions may be easily found. Then *per Archim. de Conoid if Spheriod, Def.* 3, the truncated cone *Adenbta* will be r a cylinder generated by the parallelogram *cteg.* Ergo, from the frustum AdeBA, take that cylinder, the remainder will be =: the solidity of the hyper, bolic conoid *atba;* to which cylinder add the frmtum *dzed,* the 111. Question 119, *by Mr.* John Turner.

In surveying an elliptical inclosure, three lines of 200, 31362, and 870-62 feet, were measured from one of the foci to the curve; the first and second made an angle of 25 with each other, and the second and third an angle of 65. Required the area; also the length of a ditch, which cuts the transverse axis 200 feet from the centre, the lesser segment of the ditch being the least line that can possibly be drawn from the point of intersection to the curve?

Answered by Mr. W. Gill.
Dr. Keil, in his Astro. Loct. gives a method of determining an ellipse from 3 lines given in length and position, cutting each other in the focus.

The transverse diameter 1000 feet, conjugate 600, the content of the field 10 a. 3r. 10 perches, the angle of inclination of the transTerse 64 21'. From the doctrine of fluxions, if the lesser segment be supposed to be the hypothenuse of a right-angled triangle, also a minimum, and a perpendicular let fall upon the transverse diameter, the base of the said triangle will be a fourth proportional to the transverse, the latus rectum, and the distance of the perpendicular from the centra of the ellipsis, that is 1000: 360:: 200 + x: x — 112-5. Hence the lesser part of the ditch =: 259-8, greater =: 330-66, and the whole length 590-46.

Additional Solution. that if c be the
It is demonstrated, by the writers on conies centre and F the focus of an ellipse, and in the transverse axe Ba produced there be taken Cd a third proportional to Cp and Ca, and from any point G in the curve Ge be drawn parallel to. Ed and meeting De perpendicular to it in E, and Fg be drawn; then Fg will always be to Ge, in the constant ratio of Cf to Ca.—Wherefore, if G, H, I be the three given points, or ends of the given lines Fg, Fii, Fij drawn from the focus F; and there be drawn Hg, Ih, and produced to K and L So that Hk be to Gk as Fh to Fg, and Il to Hl as Fi to Fh; and then if Ki be drawn, and perpendicular to it In, Hm, Ge, Fd; and lastly Fd be divided in A in the given ratio of Fg to Ge; then A will be the end of the transverse, and the whole of the ellipse is thence determined.——For, Eh being to Kg as Fh to Fg by the construction, and Kh to Kg as Mh to Eg by similar triangles, therefore Fh will be to Fg as Mh to Eg, or Fh to Hm as Fg to Ge; and in the same manner Fi: In:: Fii: Hm; wherefore in general Fi: in:: Fh: Hm:: Fg: Ge:: (by the above cited property) Cf: Ca; whence the centre c and the whole ellipse becomes known.

Again, for the shortest line Op that can be drawn from the given point o in the axe to the curve; since it must evidently be perpendicular to the curve pr to the tangent in the point p, it may be determined from that consideration alone and the property of the curve, independent of fluxions j and from thence will easily arise the property of it mentioned in the original solution, and as is actually determined at *prop.* 10; *lib.* 5, *Apol. Con.* viz. Ab: latus rect.:: Cq: Oq; hence the point Q is found, and of consequence Oq; and then Or as in question 103, page 132. H.

IV. Question 120, *by Mr.* John Simmons.

A gentleman wants to have an elliptical cistern in his garden to hold 60 hogsheads, wine measure, the dimensions to be determined by the shade of *a. jet d'eau* on the 6th of June, 1726, which throws the water 10 feet perpendicularly above the level of the brim of the cistern. The semi-con jugate diameter to be the shade of the *jet d'eau* at noon, and at 5 minutes past two, the extremity of the shade to extend 10 inches beyond the point where the shade cuts the brim of the cistern. Required the transverse diameter, and the quantity of sheet lead, 4-15ths of an inch thick, necessary to line the same?

Let $ea - b$ — 52-4, $dc\ zz\ c$ = 67-989 $de - d$ — 64 53 and $et\ zz\ a$, Qttccre $a?\ dd + 2d« + aa: cc :: da\ ccdd\ dd + Ida + ati$ Reduced, $bbaa + Ibbda - ccdazzbbdd$. In numbers produces a — 36-86. Then 1: 7854.": T x cc: 21640-4668 inches = the area, by which divide the given content, gives the depth 40-35 inches. Add twice the thickness of the lead to each diameter, aHd once to the depth: from which elliptical cylinder subtract the given content, gives the inches of lead 11614, which according to Ward's specific gravity of lead, is equal to 76116 ounces avoirdupois zz 2 ton, 2 hund. 1 quar. 25lb. weight.

Remark. The spherical calculations, in the original solution above, will be evident by applying the given declination, latitude, and hour to the spheric triangle in page 119; for if Zp represent the co-latitude, p© the co-declination, and their included angle p the hour from noon, all which are given; then zQ will be the coaltitude, and the Zz the azimuth, both which are hence easily found.

Again, for the ellipse, instead of the *jet d'eau* suppose a pole of 10 feet high erected in the centre d of the ellipse; then will the shadow of it at noon be the semi-conjugate axe dc, and 10 inches less than the shadow of it when the azimuth is equal to the Z_udc will be the semi-diameter $db - da$. Which are easily determined as in the original solution.

Every thing else in the original solution is very well determined except the transverse axe, which may be better found thus, by the common property of the ellipse, as $i/dc1$ — ac!): $de :: dc : dt$ the semi-transverse. H.

V. Question 121, *by Mr.* Tho. Grant.
Not far from the city of Cairo, in Egypt, is a small round temple, whose outside is curiously ornamented with hieroglyphical figures, and encompassed by a spiral tube, sloping from the bottom to the top, in an angle of 61 5'. The circumference of the temple is 1007 yards, and it is known that a perfectly smooth heavy ball would descend through the tube in 8 seconds. Required its height? *Answered by Mr.* Whitehead.
The proposer has either unlimited or unhinged the question, by giving the circumference of the tower incoherent with the time; either alone would have limited it.

According to Gallila;us, and experiments made by several ingerilous artists of late, as 1: 16-Jj:: 8" X 8"=64: 1029J = the space a body will describe a perpendicular descent in 8" of time. Then,

As-the sine of given angle Acb Zz 61 5'
Is to the side.. Ab = 1029-$
So is the radius
To the hypothenuse Ac = 1175-81

Then let fall the perpendicular *an,* and while a body accllerates the space Ab, another will describe the space An, along the inclined plane Ac, as has been demonstrated by the illustrious Sir Isaac Newton.
Ab
Having found the segment ha — — — 901, &c.

Say, as radius: $xa\ zz$ 901, the length of the tube:: s. of the given angle $xab\ zz$ 61 b': $b\ zz$ 788-72 feet, the height required.

Mr. Grant's *solution to the* 12 W *question, taken from the Diary for* 1759, *and icho thinks Mr.* Whitehead's *solution zcas not right.*

As 1: 193: 61:: 12352 inches = the perpendicular descent of the body by gravity in 8" of time: Then as the radius: sine of 61 5':: 12352: 10812 inches = the space described in 8" by a body descending along a plane that makes an angle of 61 5' with the horizon, which would be the tube's length were *it* a right line, but being a spiral to the temple which the question supposes a cylinder whose periphery is 100-7 yards; it is evident, that as the ball descends, it will also, by the tube's curvature, be carried in the said periphery, therefore it will be acted on by a *vis centralis,* in a direction parallel to the horizon, which will not forward the ball's descent, but will constantly diminish it, and consequently the velocity that would arise therefrom, which will occasion the ratio of the spaces described by the ball descending in the tube, to the times of their description to be always variable. Wherefore, I compare in a ratio, as the semi-ordinates of a conic parabola to their respective abscissas, whence the following analysis: where x zz tube's length the ball runs in 8".

Radius: cos 61 b' :: x: -483537a: zz to an arch described in 8", in the periphery, which squared, divided by the diameter, gives 0002026167xz zz the space in 8", agitate4 only by the central force; which multiply by $x1$, and make it the abscissa of a parabola convex to its axis, x its ordinate, and the parameter will come out — 4935427 inches = «, the parabolic curve, by compounding the motions along the ordinate and abscissa, will be = 10812 inches = the space in 8", by a body descending along the inclined plane. Then, by the doctrine of fluxions, x zz 6175 inches zz 514TV feet the tube's length, and radius: s. 61 b' :: 6175: 5105 inches s= 450 feet, the temple's height.
Remark. After all Mr. Grant's labour and time spent in the solution of this question, Mr. Whitehead's solution is right. For the side of the tube, by impelling the ball in the horizontal direction, does not alter its perpendicular velocity or descent; and therefore "the spiral may be considered as a straight inclined plane in the solution, H. vi. Question 122, *by Mr.* Sam. Marriot.

A person was possessed of a rectangular close, the fences of which had been destroyed, and the only mark left was an oak tree in the east corner; he however recollected the following particulars of the dimensions. It had once been resolved to divide the close into two by a hedge diagonally, and he recollected that a segment of the diagonal intercepted by a perpendicular from one of the corners was 16 chains, and the same perpendicular produced 2 chains, met the other side of the close. Now the owner has bequeathed it to four grand children, whose shares are to be bounded by the diagonal and perpendicular produced. What are the several shares?
Answered by Mr. Sam. Rouse. Draw Da. Then Adab = A Fab by Eucl. I. 37,..
Adac r:
A FBC.
Put Ac = $b - 2$, Cf = a, Cd — 16 — _pf d, Cb —-e.
Total 16 0 0
This question is in page 367 Hill's Arithmetic.
THE PRIZE QUESTION.
A person travelling towards York, discovered, by means of a telescope, the top of the tower of St. Peter's Cathedral, when just in the horizon; and upon approaching 20 miles nearer, he found the top of the tower elevated one degree. What is its height, that of tho observer's eye being 5 feet 6 inches?

Then find the angle *tee,* and line *te;* the angles *tec,* and *etc;* subtract the angle *etc* from 90, it leaves the angle *eta.* Again, to the angle *tec* add /.cca, which sura subtract from 360, leaves the angle *tea.* Then the angles *tea* and *ate* subtracted from 180, As sine *tae: te* :: sine *tea* 260 feet, the height sought; which is something more than the real height of the tower of York Cathedral.
Questions proposed in 1727, *and answered in* 1728.
I. Question 123, *by Mr.* Richard Whitehead.

A surveyor put the following question to an impertinent fellow who had interrupted him when busy. Suppose four towns B, C, D, and L, the distance from L to each of the other towns being as follows: Bl — 12848, Cl = 11440, and Bl = 7744 yards; the Zb = 65 10/-96766, Zc = 77 C-07237, Zd — 37" 49'. Required th distances Bc, Bd and DC?
Additional Solution.
Describe the triangle *jicd* similar to the proposed one, or whose angles shall be equal to the given ones: then, by prob. 31, Simpson's Geometry, determine the point / such that the three lines B/, *cl, d/*may be in proportion to each other as the three given distances Bl, ex, Dl: upon *ul* take Bl — the given distance of B from t; and draw Ld, Lc parallel to *Id, Ic;* and join D, c: so shall B, Cs J, L be the four points required.

Which is too evident to need a formal demonstration, u.
Another Additional Solution.
In the triangle Bcd there are given all the angles and the length of the lines Bl, Dl, and Cl drawn from the angles to a point within the figure to construct the triangle. Suppose it done. Draw Be, Le to make the triangle Ble similar to the triangle Bcd, namely, the angle Lbe = Dec, the angle Ble — Bdc, and the angle Bel = Bcd, and join Ec; then Bd: Bc:: Bl: Be, and because the angle Lbe — Dbc, the triangles Bld, Bec are similar (Euc. VI. 6); therefore Bd: Bc:: Dl: Ec, or Bl: Be:: Dl: Ec: whence we have this construction.

On the given line Bl describe a. triangle Lbe, similar to the required one, and take Ec a fourth proportional to Bl, Be, and Ld; then with the distances Ec, Lc and centres E, L describe two arcs to intersect in c. Make the angle Bed =r Bec, and take Ld of the given length; join Bc, Bd, and Cd, and the triangle will be constructed.

For the lines Bl, Cl, and Dl are evidently of the given lengths: and since the angle Bld _. Bec and Bl: Be:: Dl: Ec, or Bl: Dl:: Be: Ec, the triangles Bld and Bec are similar; therefore the angle Dcl = Cbe, and adding the common angle Cbl, the angla Dbc =: Lbe. Also Bd: Bl:: Bc: Be, or Bd: Bc:: Bl: Be, and consequently the triangle Bdc is similar to Ble.

The calculation is extremely easy, for in the triangle Ble we have the side Bl and all the angles to find Be and Le; then in the triangle Lce all the sides arc known to find the angle Cel, and then the whole angle Bec becomes known, and we have two sides and the included angle to find Bc. Now all the angles of the triangle Bc» being known, the sides Cd and Bd are easily found. J. L.

Ii. Question 124, *by* Philosophicus.

Suppose a point to more upon the spherical surface of the earth from a place in latitude 48, with the following compound motion, viz. along a meridian with the uniform velocity of 14 miles per hour, whilst at the same time the meridian revolves about its axis with the uniform angular velocity of *15* per hour. Required the latitude and difference of longitude of another point in the curve so described, that the intercepted part may be of a given length; suppose 4503 miles?

the difference of latitude, and the latitude, arrived in will be 46 5 north.

This may likewise be solved trigonometrically, and has some affinity to current sailing, the motion of the earth representing the current's motion, the point being carried by the compound motion from p to s: but each point of the parallel of 48 does not run through 1039 miles per hour, and the line Ps will indeed be a spiral line upon the globe.

Mr. *Geo. Broun* has well answered and demonstrated this question, and found the latitude to be 46 16': but the operation and scheme my room will not admit.

The original solution to this question is not right, because the motion in the parallel is made constantly equal to that at the equator; whereas the intent of the question seems to be, to find the spiral de. scribed on the globe by a point, which is urged with a given constant velocity in the direction of the meridian, and a given constant angular velocity around the pole in the direction perpendicular to the meridian; the rates being 14 miles on the meridian to the 24th part of the parallel of latitude.—Or it may be conceived by supposing a point to move along the brass meridian of a globe at the rate of 14 miles while the globe turns round 15 degrees, the motion answering to an hour; lor then the parts of the globe passing directly under the point, will trace out the spiral.

Wherefore, if x be put for the cosine of the variable latitude, and consequently $\sqrt{(1-xx)}$ its sine to the radius 1; also $a := 11$ mjlrt, VOL. I. L *Additional Solution.* and b — 1-15th part of the equator: since bx — the motion per hour x in the parallel of latitude, and $-\dot{j}jz$ r the fluxion of the arch

©f the meridian or abscissa of the spiral, wc shall hare as $a : bx ::$

——: *ff.* — the fluxion of the parallel or ordinate

$\sqrt{(1-xx)}$ $a/(1-xx)$ of the spiral; then the sum of the squares of these fluxions of the ordinate and abscissa will be equal to the square of the fluxion of „... ../ $aa + bbxx$ the curve of the spiral, or fluxion of the spiral $z - x f U\_L / 1-4-QXX$ or $= y$ — by putting q for —. Now, by Cor. 2, p.

Mensuration, it will be found that this expression is the fluxion of an $/aa$ 4-bb elliptic arc whose semi-axes are 1 and W———.

y aa the circle whose radius is 1 be circumscribed by the ellipse whose transverse semi-axe Ac is — and Bd be the degrees or arc of the latitude, and Edf be drawn parallel to Ac;

then Cf will be $x,$ and the arc Ae Z the above fluent, or length of the spiral from the pole: Also Ee will be the length of the spiral between any iwo latitudes Bd, *ml.* So that if Bd be the given latitude of 48, and De be drawn parallel to Ac; then take Ee — 4503 miles the proposed length of the spiral, and draw *ed* parallel to Ed; so shall Bd be the latitude required, H.

m. Question 125, *by Mr.* John Turner.

Suppose three lofty poles standing perpendicular to the horizon, at points denoted by A, L, C; the height of the pole at«A being 32 feet, that at 1 96, and that at c 53 feet, and the distance of A and L 200 feet. Now suppose that upon a certain day the shadow of the top of the pole at A passed through the points c and L; and the shadow of the top of the pole at L passed through A and c; and the shadow of the top of the pole at c passed through A. Upon what day, and in what northern latitude might this happen?

Answered by Mr. Brown.

There is a demonstration of this in Sir Isaac Newton's Universal Arithmetic, too large to insert, by which I make the latitude 81 30', and sun's declination 70 22'.

Mr. *Mason,* Mr. *Whitehead,* and some others say this question is unlimited, or at least admits of more true answers than one; but having received none but the above, I shall not here give my judgment till further trial be made at a more leisure time, except Mr. *Bent's* latitude 80 45', declination 19 27'.

Remark. This question has evidently been made from prob. 55. Sir Isaac Newton's Arithmetic, where a full solution may be seen. H. iv. Question 126, *by Mr.* Tho. Dodd.

It is required to dispose the under written 16 numbers into the form of a magic square, so that the sum of each horizontal, vertical, and diagonal row may amount 74. 'The numbers to be disposed in the square are 8, 9, 10, 11, 14, 15, 16, 17, 20, 21, 22, 23, 26, 27, 28, 29. *Answered.*

Mr. *Elias Colbourn* says, if the numbers as given be placed in four rows, you need only let the diagonals stand, and cross places with the other numbers as in these squares: *Aspatia* says, the method of filling all sorts of magical squares with the magic cubes, may be seen at large in the memoirs of the Royal Academy of Sciences for 1710, page 124, by Mons. Saurier, in his Construction Generate des Quarres Magiques.

See also question 61, *page* 73. v. Question 127, *by Mr.* Tho. Williams.

Our modern nat'ralists dispute— Whence came

The water that destroy'd the earth's first frame?

Some bring it from the moon; and some have thought

That from above, the firmament, 'twas brought:

Others—that 'twas created for that end,

Or from a deep abyss did then ascend.

The last the sacred writ doth intimate,

As Woodward has explain'd it to's of late:

The which abyss (with Hal ley) he wou'd have

Concentric with the earth, an orb concave.
If so—an alternative change suppose;
Let air subside, whilst water earth o'erflows;
And while the earth's a sea, let air in place
Of water fill up the orbicular space.
For present use (with Burnet) we'll agree,
That the antidiluvian earth might be
Of mathematical rotundity;
And that th' abyss did hold this weight in air,
Which we'll admit no heavy'er there than here.
From hence, fair ladies, these two things unfold:
Hqw deep the flood; how much th' abyss might hold?
1000000000000000 tons avoird.
Ansizered, by Mr. Whitehead.

According to Mr. Boyle, the weight of water is to that of air as 1000 to 1. Mr. Ward makes a cubic inch of water to weigh 578697 ounces avoirdupois. Mr. Norwood makes a degree of the great circle — 69 miles; hence the diameter of the earth is — 504606222 inches fere. And thence 35840000000000000000 ounces of air will fill the abyss; and thence 3584019 ounces of water will fill the same. Then as 578697 ounces: 1 inch:: 35840, &c. ounces: 61932237423038308475765 = number of inches in the abyss, which added to those which are in the earth, the sum will be equal to the solid inches in the sphere of the flooded earth: from the diameter of which take that of the earth, and divide the remainder by 2, the quotient is 77397-7752 inches = 6449-8146 feet = 2149-9382 yards. ± 1 mile 389 yards,

This answer agrees pretty near with the proposer of the question. There were many others who solved it: but in answers to questions of this nature, there will be some considerable difference, by reason the' proportions are taken from authors which do not exactly agree; as (1) In the proportion of air to water, (2) In the weight of water, (3) The geometrical miles in a degree, (4) in the diameter to the circumference.

VI. Question 128, *by Mr.* Christ, Mason, Given the quantities of matter in the earth and moon, together with the distance of their centres, to determine their common centre of gravity. *Answered by Mr.* T. Williams.

The common centre of gravity of the earth and moon goes through the magnis orbis so, that the areas described by the radii to the sun are proportional to the times; the accelerating gravities are as the quantities of matter in those bodies; the mass of the earth is given equal to 39008956283823202513476 cubic feet; the diameter of the *J*) to the diameter of the 0, as her apparent semi-diameter to her horizontal parallax. Hence her magnitude801682492916446916225 feet: The attractive force will be the same in respect to their distance from the common centre of gravity, as in respect of the whole distance between them.

Let s denote the sun, Mc the magnis orbis describ'd by the common centre of gravity of the earth T, and the moon L, c the J in octant, her mean distance 60f semi-diameters = 1309095 060 feet — Tl. Now as the D and 0 tend to c as to one another, Ct: Cl:: mass in L: mass in T.

Therefore Ct = 26361759 feet = 4083 miles, and Cl = 1282733200 feet = 242752 miles.

Mr. *Mason,* the proposer, answers thus: *d* — mean diameter — 268923 miles, 9 — the quantity of matter in the earth, and In *J, a* distance of the common centre from the sun; *q* : 1:: mass 0 *d* : mass *i,qa — d — a* per statics, and50 *+ a — d;* hence *a ——* = 5899-34 miles.

Mr. *Turner,* has curiously explain'd this, and says the author ought to have told whether in 5 or £, &c. but that nothing certain can be laid down, since we cannot truly determine the distance and magnitude of the sun; and that regard should be had to their densities, and specific gravities, &c.

Additional Solution.

If *-e* be the quantity of matter in the earth, and *m* that in the moon, or any other two bodies, and *d* their distance asunder. Then, per statics, as e + *m* : *d*

V *m 1 . —2 —* the distance of the earth :: K "J *y* from the common f *e: —*
; = the distance of the moon V *e + in J* centre of gravity, H. ii. Question 129, *bjj Mr.* Sam. Rouse.

A golden candlestick is suspended by a chain from the roof of a Jofty building; If put in motion it would make 1000 vibrations in an hour: it is also known that the distance from the roof to the candlestick, is a mean proportional between the height of the roof, and the height of the candlestick above the floor. What is the height of the building on the inside?

Ansicered by Mr. Da. Nairne.

The pendulum vibrates 1000 per hour =r 16$ per minute, and one of 39-2 inches vibrates 60 per minute; also they being in a duplicate ratio of their vibrations, therefore the length of the candlestick will be found 508 inches; and the candlestick above the floor 314. Hence the whole height *zz* 822 inches = 68-5 feet.

Additional Solution.

As 1000': 3600 or as 102: 36":: 39-2: 39-2 X 3-6 = 503 inches the length of the cord or line. Again, if *x* the whole height, and *a —* 508 — the greater part.

Then *x :a :: a: « — a:* hence *xx — ax — aa,* and — 2

X *a* = 821-96 inches = 68J feet nearly, H..

I

THE PRIZE QUESTION.

In a beautiful garden is a circular grass plot whose radius is 50 feet; from the centre two rectilinear walks branch ofi, forming an angle of 55; their lengths are 108 and 80 feet respectively. It is required to find a point in the circumference, to which lines being drawn from the extremities of the walks, they shall form equal angles with the tangent at the point of concourse.

aa — cc put *dd,* and transposing *rrx — —yy — — -jt* Proceeding finds *x* = 45-8068 = As.

Then the angle *sAtn* may be found; and two sides and a contained angle given in each to find *sin —* 7032, and *cm —* 39-63 feet ths answer. /. T. *Additional Solution.*

This question may be otherwise solved thus:

Putting *a — Ab, b — Ac,* and *r — Am,*

as above; and also s and a — sine and cos. ∠ Bac, a and $//(1-x)$ — sine and cos. ∠baw, and. t and $-2s) = z$ sine and cos. ∠caot, to the radius 1.

Another Additional Solution.
Iu this question it is required to find a point m in the circumference of a circle, given in magnitude and position, so that the two lines drawn from it to the given points B and c may make equal angles with a tangent to the circle at m. Now let A be the centre of the circle, and draw Ba, Ca in which let the points E and D be so taken that the rectangles Bae, Cad may be each equal to the square of the radius Aot; and join Em, Dot and Ed, and draw *mil* parallel to Bc meeting Ca in s and Ed in H. Then because Ba: Aw :: *Am* : Ae, and Ca: *Am* :: *Ant* : Ad, the triangle Aotb is similar to Aeot, and the triangle Awe to Adot, therefore the angle Aotb — Aeot and the angle Aotc — Adot: but by hypothesis the angle Aotb — Aotc, therefore the angle Aeot — Adot. And since the rectangle Bae — Cad, the points E, D, B, C are in a circle, therefore the angle Aed Acb — *Ann,* and consequently the angle Deot Aeot — Aed — Adot — Afot Dotf; therefore the triangles Hote and Hdot are similar, ai)d He:Hot:: *urn*: Iid, which is the property of the equilateral hyperbola whose diameter is De: Hence if an equilateral hyperbola be described to the diameter De and whose ordinates are parallel to Bc it will cut the circle in the point m required, and likewise in another point which will also answer the question. And moreover if the opposite hyperbola be described it will also intersect the circle in two other points, either of which will answer; so that there are four points, in the circumference of the given circle, to which lines may be drawn from the given points so as to make equal angles witii the circle at the point of concourse.

When the given points are equally distant from the centre of the circle the hyperbolas degenerate into two right lines, the one passing through the points E, D and the other through the centre perpendicular to ED.

It may be remarked that this question is the same as the famous problem of Alhazen relating to the reflection of light; namely, to find the ray which, issuing from a given point, shall be reflected by a a spherical surface to the eye in any given position. Which problem has, at different times, engaged the attention of some of the most eminent mathematicians of the 16th and 17th centuries, as Slusius, Huyghens, Barrow, L'Hospital, R. Simson, Robins, &c. Their solutions are all effected by means of the hyperbola, and the greater part of them are not essentially different in principle from the solution which we have just given.

There is also a neat analytical solution by Mr. Wales in the Philosophical Transactions for 1781, where the angles Baot, $c.m$ are calculated by means of the trigonometrical tables and the method of trial and error. Indeed those angles may be very readily found by this method, from Dr. Hutton's solution above; for we have only to divide the given angle Bac into two parts U(bam) and v(cAm) so that a sinu b sin u ....,.

—, which may be easily done from the $r-a\ co\&v\ r-b\ cos\ u$ tables, by a few trials. And in general this way of resolving questions of this kind is much better than by reducing the result to a final equation, L. *Questions proposed in* 1728, *and answered in* 1729.

i. Question 130, *by Mr.* Rich. Whitehead.

Three persons owned a field, which they had used so Jong *ip* common, as to have quite forgotten the bounds of their respective shares; at length, after much searching, an old plan of the field was found; but it was so much obliterated, that only the following particulars could be collected therefrom towards determining the three shares. The form M as a trapezium Adkc, the side Ad *6'4* chains, Ae — 14 chains, Fx — 101 chains. The three shares were triangular, formed by two right lines drawn from A and c to a. point B in De; ∠-Abc was 78; the ratio of B.c to Ba as 3 to 4; and the ratio of Ed to Be as 3 to *1.* Required the sides of the triangles?

Here being given of the trapezium the three sides Ad, Ac, and Ce, the angle Abc formed in the other side, the ratio (;» to *ri)* of its legs Ab, Bc, and the ratio (*p* to *q*) of the segments Bd, Be o£the other side; from which the figure will be constructed thus: *Construction.* On the given base Ac (by Prob. 3 of Simpson's Algebra) constitute a triangle Abc whose sides shall be in the given ratio of m to w, and whose vertical angle shall bc equal to the given one. Then with the centres A and c, and radii equal to the other two given sides of the trapezium, describe two circles. Produce Cb, and make *as q: p:: Cb: Bf* and also:: Ce: Fd; which apply to the circumference of the circle whose centre is A. Draw Db, and continue it to meet the circumference of c in E; and Adec is the trapezium required.

Demonstration. The triangles Bce, Bfd are similar by Eucl. VI. 7, and therefore Be: Bd:: Bc: Bf:: q :p by the construction; and the rest is also evident from the construction. *Calculation.* As $m+n$: $m-n$ :: cotang. i ∠ Abc: tang. dif. of the angles Bac, Bca at the base; which added to and taken from half their sum, we obtain those angles themselves; and consequently the triangle Abc becomes all known, which is one part of the field. Then in the trapezium Badf, are known all the sides and the ∠abf; to find the diagonal Bb; for Ad is given, and Ab and the ∠b have been Cb: Bf — — X Cb found; then by the construction $q:p::$ 'L /ce: Df =-X CE 9

To determine Bd, draw Af; then in the triangle Abf,_ given two sides Ab, Bf, and their included ∠, to find the third side Af and the ∠ Afb. Then in the triangle Abf, are given all the sides, to find the /afd; and the sum or difference of Afb and Afd will be the ∠dfb. Wherefore in the triangle Dfb, are known two sides Df, Fb, and their included angle, and consequently the whole triangle; which k the 2d portion. Lastly, as *m: n:: Db* : Be; hence the 3d portion eBE is known, H.

Ii. Question 131, *by Mr.* Tho. Dodd.

Suppose that in two geometrical series continued *ad infinitum,* the sum of all the terms of the first is to the sum of all the terms of second as 4 to 9; also, that the first two terms of the *first* series are 40 and 35, and that the second term of the *second* series is 46$, Required the first term and ratio of the *second* series? *Ansicered by Mr.* Tho. Grant,

The sum of the first geometrical progression, continued *ad infinitum,* is 320 (the first term being 40 and the second 35). Then by the question, as 4: 9:: 320: 720 = the sum of the decreasing geometrical progression, whose second term is 4Gg, and last term = 0.

Let x — the first term of the same; then, per Euclid, 5, 12, it will be as x: 46-J-?:: 720: 720 — x. This, turned into an equation, gives $720x - xx = 33500$; whence $x - 50$. and the common ratio as 6 to 5, or as 1 to f.

in. Question 131, *by Mr.* John Hartley. Amongst the other ornaments of the famous temple of Solomon was the curious Molten Sea, which stood upon twelve brazen oxen: 'its form was cylindrical, and it contained 2000 baths; the outer circumference of the cylinder was 30 cubits, and its internal depth 5 cubits, and the thickness of the metal was a hand breadth or palm. Now, supposing the Jewish cubit 21-888 inches, and the palm 3-648 inches; what was the measure of one bath in wine gallons? AnJ, supposing the Molten Sea made of copper, what would be its weight; and what weight would press upon the oxen, when the cylinder was full of water? *Answered by Mr.* Turner.

If a line of 30 cubits, or 656-64 inches, would surround the Molten Sea on the outside; then the outside diameter was but 209 015 inches.

Twice the thickness of the copper or 2 *f* hand br. sub J 7'296

Remains the inside diameter 201-719

The depth 109-44 inches, area of the base 34311-982

The whole solid content from outside... 3755103-31 cubic inches.

Add the copper's bottom 125170-11

The sum is 3880273-42

Content of the inside 3497523-126

Difference... 382750-294

Equal to the cubic inches of copper. Divide the last sum but one by 2000, the number of baths it contained, gives the quotient 1748'76 cubic inches, the content of one bath as 7 'gallons wine measure; the whole contained 1514008 gal-

lons wine measure, or 60 tuns 20 gallons. Then according to Mr. Ward,

A cubic inch of JgKJ!— f water 56 tuns 8 hund. 12 pounds

Hence the weight of- copper 55 12 40 13 n the oxen 112 0 52 13 *Answered by Mr.* John Clark.

f cubit is 21-888 inches By Harris's Lexicon, a-? palm 3-648 (bath 1747-700 ishei.ee the quantity of 2000 baths 3495400 water in the sea 3497504 difference 2104, which is but T£ of art inch in (he depth, or little more than one bath.

T. c. st. lb. dw. gr.

Then by Mr. Boyle's (of water is 57 0 5 11 205 8 proportion the wt. t sides of the copper... 37 2 7 4 59 19 and the bottom in proportion to the sides.... 18 1 0 1 173 9 The whole weight in avoirdupois 112 4 5 4 146 6 iv. Question 132, *by Mr.*Tho. Williams.

Supposing that Xcm is the sector of a conic parabola, of which x is the focus, and c the principal vertex: there are given xc — 26 poles, and the area of the sector 676 square poles. Required the length and position of Xm?j *Anszeered by Mr.* W. Milward.

Let fall the ordinate Mp, which call a, and put cxz=6rz26 poles. As 46: a :: a: £T*tw*, . 2cp x Pm,,

— Cp per conies. — — the area *40 r* 3 ,.,, 2«aa *aaa* ot the semi-parabola Cpm ———-or —-; r 126 *6b Abb* — *aa* ,. *-2C cx* — Cp — rx — —, and Px X 4mp *4b* — the area of the triangle Pxm.

The A Pxm + area of the semi-parabola =; the area of the sector,. *aaa, 4bba* — *aua*

Ti*z.*-r-r + — — *bb* per question. *ob 8b aaa* + 1266*a* — 24666; here *a* is = 42-55 poles. Hence Mx =r 43-445. *Additional Solution.* Putting 6 — cx, and *x* = the ordinate Pm; then, by the nature of the parabola, Cp = *;*and, by prob. 7, page 321, Mensuration, (cx + £cp) X pm = the area = *b'* by the question; that is, v. Question 133, *by* Texcuvw Ti-aXaci.

Find such a right-angled triangle that if double the *ale area*, be severally subtracted from each of its sides, the three remainders shall be rational squares. *Anszeered by Mr.* Geo. Brown.

Let a — side of the triangle; then — the double area. And *Qua* suppose a— — 3 which will admit of many answers, for vi. Question 134, *by Mr.* Tho. Grant.

Required the greatest space or area which can be included by four right lines, whose lengths are 20, 16, 12, and 10?

therefore De =

Retaining the same substitutions as in the first of those solutions, we have *ad* sin *p--be* sin a *e...* .(1). *ad* cos *p* — 6c cos 8 = *r*.... (2).
-*i be* cos 8

Taking fluxions, we get from the first equation-5— — — s J & i e *ad* cos 9

Tii. Question 135, *by Mr.* John Turner.

There is a very lofty mountain whose height is such, that when cubed and multiplied into three times the square root of the length of a tangent from its vertex to the earth's surface, the product will be 1005-9309 miles. What is the mountain's height, the semi-diameter of the earth being 3963 miles? *Answered by Mr.* John Bulman. Let x — Ba — the mountain's height.

Then $x + 3963$ — Ac. *See Fig. to Quest. 10U*

Hence $xx + 7926 + 15705369 =$ Ac'. *page* 130.

Or $xx + 7926 =$ Am.

Consequently t/ *(Six'* + 642006x13) = 1005-9309.

Then if the latter part of the equation at the last step be involved to the fourth power, and the radical sign taken away from the first part, the equation will be clear of surds, and may be found = 3 miles, the mountain's height required. *The same answered by Mr.* R. Fearnside. Pat a = AB, b — Cb = 3963, e = Am, c = 1005-9309. Theft TOL, I. M *Questions proposed in* 1729, *and answered in* 1730.

i. Question 136, *by Mr.* John Bulman. The distance from London to York is 150 miles, and Stilton divides the distance in extreme and mean proportion, the greater part being the distance from Stilton to York: Now suppose two messengers, dispatched at the same time from London, to travel uniformly to

Stilton and York, how must their rates of travelling be adjusted so as to arrive, at those two places at the same time *1* Answered by Mr. Rob. Fearnside.

The distance between York and London given 150 miles; from London to Stilton will be easily found 572940 miles; and Stilton to York 92-7051. Put y the space passed over by the courier bound to Stilton, in any moment of time; and x — the space passed over by him bound for York in the same moment of time. Then, per question, $xx - 2xy + yy - xy$, in fluxions $2\#i - 3xy - 9tfx + lyy = 0$. Reduced to an analogy, $y:x$ (the fluxion of any flowing quantity being taken for its velocity):: $2r - 3y : 3x - ky$. That is, as 128-1242 to 335-4161.

Additional Solution.
The meaning of this question is, To divide 150 miles into two parts in extreme and mean proportion j and to find the ratio of the equable velocities, by which the less part and the whole length may be passed over in the same time.

Put x — the less part, and $a = 150$ the whole. Then $a - x$ — the greater part; and, by the question, $x: a - x :: a - x : a$; hence $ax - «2 - lax + x2$, $nn\&x \times a$ — the less part.
$f 5 - 1$' Therefore $a - x - ' \times a =$ the greater part. Hence
The two parts of any quantity which is divided into extreme and mean proportion, are in the ratio of — y-to ——, or of 3— to — 1, or of 1 to $I?-? + 2$, or of V'5-to 1.
3 i/5

And the less part to the whole, as to 1; which is the ratio of their velocities or rates of travelling required, H. II. Question 137, *by Mr.* John Simmons.

Suppose the side or edge of each of the five regular solids to be 30 inches, what will be the content of each in wine gallons; also what will be the content of each of their respective inscribed and circumscribing spheres?
Remark. In the *Scholia* at page 403, &c. of my Mensuration, the true values of the content of each regular solid, with that of the radius of the inscribed and of the circumscribed sphere, are expressed in terms of the linear edge or side;

whence the numbers, as above,, may be easily found, n. in. Question 138, *by Mr.* Tlio. Grant.
A vessel under sail goes 25 Grecian feet in seconds, and in the ame time it was observed that a ball fell from the mast head upon th deck. What was the space through which the ball fell?
Answered.
The ball descending with a compound force, that is, an horizontal force by the motion of the ship, and by the force of gravity; the spaces described by such motions are analogous to the abscissas and their respective senii-oidinates, in the conic parabola, and the motion will be in the curve of the same.

Then there is gi en the abscissa — x — 434'25 inches — the space described in three halt seconds by the force of gravity only; and its emi-ordinate —yz-zlb Grecian leet =302-1 indies English. Whenca by fluxions 5«! 3y4 $3i/ v'' +$-f $+$--3 — —3 + ";&c. = 567-42 inch, or 47-285 feet, the space the ball descended.
Additional Solution.
The 25 Grecian feet are = 25 X 1-007 or 25-175 English feet = the horizontal motion, or the ordinate of the parabola, which call $1y$; and as l3: (f)8, or as 4: 9:: 16 feet: 36TV feet = the perpendicular descent, or the abscissa of the parabola, which call x. Then, by Cor. 1, page 310, of my Mensuration, the true length of the curve will be $/(x + y1) + X$ hyp. log. of $x + (x2+ il - 45-9578$ feet — the length of the line described by the ball. H. sum of these two angles, we have 118 41' =r the Zadis; and this taken from 180, there remains 61 19' for the Zadc. Then, as s. Zbda: s. Zbad:: Ab: Bd — 12-967; the f ds of which is Dc — 8-645. Hence ad X Dc X S. Zadc — 41-648 chains = 4-164S acres for the other part Acd. And, lastly, as s. Zcad: s. Zd:: Cd: Ca = 10-0135.
Construction.
Having drawn the given side Ab, and the lines An, Ac making the given angles Bad, Dac; in Ba produced take Ag to Ab in the given ratio of Cd to Db, that is, of 2 to 3; draw Ec parallel to Ad; lastly draw Cb, and it is done.

For, by sim. A s, Ab: Ae:: Bd : DC. H.

T. Question 140, *by Mr.* John Lowe.
Suppose there be a pyramid erected upon a triangular base, whose longest side is eighty-eight inches, and the angle, opposite to the longest side is eighty-five degrees and one minute, and the rectangle of the other two sides added to their sum is four thousand one hundred and three inches; and the pyramid's greatest angle of altitude, is in proportion to its least, as seven is to six: What is the difference, in ale gallons, betwixt the greatest cylinder and sphere that may be inscribed in the said pyramid?
Ansuered by Mr. Lowe, *the proposer.*
Put $Ab = b$, the sine of the angle $Acd = s$, its cosine — c, 4103 p, $Ac - a$, and $Bc - e$; the radius — 1. As 1: a :: s: $sa - Ad$; and 1: a :: c: $A E ca - Cd$: but $ae + a + e - p$; hence e —
»—a , $p - a v - a - ca1 - ca$
—-7—and—$cn = bd = $—: $a+ V a + 1$
$a+ 1$ oil. . $p - oca - jca$
Put $1 + c = x$, then — Bd. $a+1$
Hence $ca4+ 2aca' - 2pca'+ xxaa - Zpxa+pp A$.
"'$aa + la + 1 + ssaa = bb$. Which equation reduced gives $a = 75$; and thence e 53.
$1 + m n + n m + mn n + n$
or $b(n + ri) = rf(1 + m)$
and $c(rc' + w) = + $»$m$).
From the first of these equations $m - H$ —, which substituted for in in the second equation gives $c(ra4-n) = (bn+ bn - d) (— — J$.
And by reduction $bn' + db+lb2) + (b - db - dc)n - (T+2M+cd)« + d2 = 0$, or in numbers and dividing by 400, $n4 + 4$»' — $4na - 1ln + 4=0$.
From whence n is found = 1-6369136; then »» = — $d - 1$-1581999; $a = /$—$r - =3$-0441718; $e = $»»$a = 3$-5257595; 1 + » and $y - na - 4$-983462. i

Tii. Question 142, *by Mr.* John Ingleborough.
The great tun at Heidelberg, an author says, held as much wine in its entrails as the Colossus of Rhodes held water between its thighs. It is 31 feet long and 21 high.

Now supposing the tun to be of the same shape with Parson's cask, mentioned last year, so far as may agree with the dimensions above; how many gallons of wine would it contain? Secondly, supposing Parsou's cask of stout to equiponderate with the Heidelberg tun of wine, suspending from a balance 60 feet long; what would the difference of the brachia of the balance be? And thirdly, supposing it were required that each vessel should evacuate itself exactly in two hours by a hole in the lowest place; what must the diameter of each bore be, that so the vessels may hang in equilibrio all the time the liquor is running out, not admitting the weight of the Tessels to interfere or make any variation?

Answered by Mr. Rich. Lovatt.

The length 372 inches = d, bung diameter = 252 = b. If the eask be the same shape as Parson's, the head is the latus rectum; then $i/(dd-bb):b::b:$ 111-334 = the head per conies: finding an infinite number of ordinates betwixt head and bung, will constitute the solidity = 59780-4 wine gallons, and a mean of all those ordinates will give an equal cylinder = 217-3072 inches. A gallon of wine weighs 8-29645 pounds avoirdupois. Then 8-296 X 59780-4 =: 495965 1593604, avoird. the whole weight. A gallon of stout-weigh 10-25 pounds avoird. X 5760 = 59040, the weight of the liquor in Parson's cask. Then as the sum of the weights is to the difference,fso is the length of the balance to the difference of brachia = 47-2348 feet. From Parsons's cask the liquor flows 128-8 inches, equal bung diameter, in 34-218 thirds of the time. Heidelberg cask flows 252 inches in 47-863 thirds. Then put d — 432000, the thirds in 2 hours, n — 34-218, a — the drain of the bore in Parsons's cask.

And then = 5760: hence a — 1-127 inch. And by the 35!J-05«' same way the bore is found 2-78119 inches in Heidelberg cask. Mr. *Tho. Grant* makes the bores 3 387 and 1-3518 inches.

Remark. The dimensions of the apertures, as determined in the solution to this question, may perhaps be pretty near the truth: but as for the mathematical certainty, there does not seem to be a possibility of it in the case, n. THE PRIZE QUESTION.

A courier at Montpellier receives orders to proceed with all possible expedition to Turin: Now Montpellier is situated 40 miles directly west of the Rhone, and Turin is 150 miles east of that river, whose course is directly south. The shortest distance between the two cities is 200 miles, but this is not the most expeditious route: for on the western side of the river the courier can travel at the rate of three miles an hour; but on the other side, on account of the difficulty of the roads he can only travel at the rate of two miles an hour. It is required to determine to what point of the river the courier must direct his course, so as to perform the journey in the least time possible?

Answered by Mr. John Fearnside.

Put AB — c, Cd c= d, nc — b, and Ce

Euc. I. Ae = $/(cc + xx)$; and De = $/(dd + bb — \%bx + xx)$. Then, by the question, 2:1:: $/(dd+bb—2bx-xx)$,$dd + bb — 25x + xx$, : y':-, and 3: 1:: $»/(cc + Xx)$: $/———$. Therefore fluxions, and reduced, x = 18-5723, Ce = 43-8776, AE = 44-1015, and De zz 156-286; and the time in going the whole journey 92h 50TM 30".

Remark. This problem may be seen applied to various and very curious purposes in *Hayes's* Fluxions, H. *Questions proposed in* 1730, *and answered in* 1731. V. Question 143, *by Mr.* Tho. Battersbye.

There is a right-lined triangle, in which a circle is inscribed; and in the corners of the triangle are placed three little circles, so drawn as to touch the adjacent sides of the triangle, and the greater circle, whose diameters are 484, 441, and 400. It is required to find the sides of the triangle, and the diameter of the greater circle?

Answered by Mr. Rich. Lovet. $(aa—dd)$ x $(«a — hk)$

But $aa + nn$: 1:: $aa — nn$: z s. Z Egd: and, by $aa + nn$ 7 that curious theorem 31, in Spherical Triangles explained by Ozanam, vol. II. p. 142, which holds good in all triangles, we have $a'cm — aack — aamp + pk.,$ „$f aa — nn3$ TT 5 — 4—:1:: *Adh:* I ——;Hence $a — c2aann + n aa + nn)$ $a'cm — Aa'dh — aack — aamp — 8aanndh — An'dh —$ hp. Put $b — ck + mp + Simdh,$ and $I — cm — Adh;$. $b / (Andh — kp, bb$ Then $aa= V j- + j = 661 =$ nr..

And the lines are 2««« = 1322, Ib = 2407-85, Eq — 2188-48, m = 2304-72.'

Additional Solution.

Instead of supposing the figure a triangle, we may, without increasing the difficulty, suppose it to have any number of sides whatever. The problem thus generalized may be expressed thus.

A figure of any number of sides being such as to admit of having a circle inscribed in it: let there be given the radii of circles inscribed in each of its corners, so as to touch the adjacent sides of the figure and the inscribed circle: it is thence required to determine the sides of the figure and the radius of the inscribed circle?

Suppose perpendiculars to be drawn from the centre of the inscribed circle to all the sides of the figure; these will be radii of that circle, and the angle contained by every two adjoining perpendiculars will be the supplement of the opposite angle of the figure.

Let the fourths of these supplements be denoted by the letters a, *of-,* a", a.''', &c. the tangents of these angles by $t, t', t'', t''',$ &c.

Let the radii of the circles inscribed in the corners of the figure be $r, r', r'', r''',$ &c.

And let x be the radius of the circle which touches them all artd also the sides of the figure.

Then, by a little consideration, it will readily appear that rad: tans«:: x: r; hence wc have the following series of equations; $xt — r$ $xt'1 — iJ$ $xt''' — r'' r$ W
&c

the number of which is equal to the number of sides of the figure. Moreover, because

« 4. *of* + a'' 4. 4-&c. = a right angle, if B be put for the sum of the products of the tangents $t, t', t'', if'',$ &c. taken two by two, (that is, let B=$tt'+tt''+$&c.$+?t''$ + &c.), n for the sum of their products taken four by four; F for the sum of their products taken six by six, &c. then, by a theorem in the arithmetic of sines which is demonstrated in the solution to question 388. (Also in the Mathematical Repository, quest. 273, vol. 3.).

$1 - n + D - F + \&c. = 0$ (2).

By taking the products of the equations (1) two by two, four by four, &c. we get $xW - A/qy)$, $xt't'' - s/rJr'')$ &c. $xtt''-V(rM)$, $xt't''' - VXrV'')$ &c
&c. &c.
$xH't''i'''$-rrVV" &c.
&c.

Let b be now put for the sum of the square roots of the products of the known quantities r, rJ, r", &c. taken two by two (that is let $b - rrl) 4-V(rr'') +$ &c. $4-Vir'') + Sec.$) also let d be put for the sum of the square roots of the products taken four by four, and / for the sum of the square roots of their products taken six by six, &c. then it is manifest that $xB - bX'd - dX'f = f$
&c.

Let the values of B, D, F, &c. deduced from these be now substituted in equation (2) and there will result ,. &c. $= 0, xxx'$

An equation involving only one unknown quantity x, which is therefore determined.

The remaining unknown quantities t, t', t'', &c. may now be found from the series of equations (1); accordingly we get

The angles of the figure and the radius of its inscribed circle being known, the manner of determining its sides is sufficiently obvious. In the diary question, the number of sides being three, D F, &c. also d,f, &c. are each $=0$; therefore $1 --- = 0$, or, since $6 - (rrl) + V(jt'') + A/(rV')$, $x = (rrl) + V(r»J/) + vWh$
$r rl r''$
as' $v xl x$

If the number of sides be four, or six, then F, / &c. are each = ©, and x is to be determined from the quadratic equation
$b d$
$1 h-r = 0. w.$

X K ii. Question 144, *by Mr.* Will. Massey.

A labourer was hired for a year upon the following conditions, *viz,* for every day he worked he was to receive seven shillings, but for every day he absented himself or was idle, he was to forfeit three shillings: Now at the expiration of the time it was found that he had nothing to receive, his forfeitures being exactly equal to his earnings; how many days had he worked and how many days had he been idle?

Answered by Mr. Geo. Auderson.

Let $b - 365 =$: the number of days in a year, $a -$ the number of days wrought; then $b - a$ the number of days played; therefore $7a - 3b - 3a$ per question. Whence a will be found:$= 109\text{-}5$ days wrought; and $255\text{-}5 =$: the days played.

Additional Solution.

A,10(=7+3):365:: f 7:-7 X 365 = 255-5, v' 3:-3 X 365 = 109-5. H.

in. Question 145, *by Mr.* Rob. Fearnside.

Two ships A and n, lying west and'east of each other, are bound to a port D which could not be seen from their stations: The ship A takes her course between east and north leagues and then dis. covers the port D, directly to the north of herself and the place where she left B: The ship B proceeded directly east 12-8 leagues, and then despairing to find the port D lay to. The ship A continued her first course till she came within 5 leagues of D, when the two ships and the port were in the same right line. The angle formed at o N. B. The above method will find x to any degree of accuracy by only assuming n nearly to x, and even without that if the logarithm of a and n be made to a sufficient number of places.

Remark. Though the above be a very complete and masterly solntion, the method of trial-and-error would sooner approximate t« the value of the root. H.

v. Question 147, *by Mr.* Tho. Williams. On the 9th of June 1731, there will happen a small eclipse of the moon. The centres of the moon and shadow at the beginning, and the centres of the moon and shadow at the middle of the eclipse, form a right-angled triangle, the sum of whose base and perpendicular will be 83 minutes, and the sum of the base and hypothenuse = 116 minutes; and the diameter will exceed the perpendicular by 4 minutes. Required the diameter of the earth's shadow and the diameter of the moon, and what part of the moon will be covered at the middle of the eclipse?

: *Ansxacred by Mr.* W. Grimmet.

Let $a - Ac$ the base, $b - Ac + An$ the sum of the base and perpendicular, $c - Ac + Bc$ the sum of the base and hypothenuse: Then $b - azz$ the perpendicular; and, per 47 Eucl. I. $/(2aa - 1ba + bb) = Cb$ the hypothenuse. Therefore $laa - 'Zba + bb) 4-t - c$: which equation solved, a will be found $- 54\text{-}4985$ the base, and perpendicular $- 285015$, to which add 4 gives the moon's diameter =: 325015; and if from the hypothenuse $- 61\text{-}5015$, be subtracted the moon's semi-diameter, it leaves cn $- 45\text{-}2508$ --semidiameter of the earth's shadow; also from the hypothenuse subtract the base, remains the opaque part of moon $= 7\text{-}0028 = 2$ digits 35' 7".

First Additional Solution.

This question is the same as, *In a right-angled triangle, having given the tzco sums of the base and hypothenuse, and base and perpendicular; to determine the triangle.* Of which this is the *Construction.*

The difference between the two given suny will evidently be equal to the difference between the hypothenuse and the perpendicular: Take Ea equal to this difference, and Eac $-$ a mean proportional between 2ea and the greater of the above two sums; and Ac will be the base of the triangle. Then the hypothenuse and perpendicular are easily found by subtraction.

,-*Demonstration.*

Since $Ce = (ca + Ae) = Ca + 2ca \times Ae + ae8$, by Eucl. II. 4,

And $Ae - Cb - Ba$ by the construction,

Also $Ae'' - Cbs - 2cb \times Ba + BA$ by Eucl. II. 7,

We have $Cej = Ca'' + 2ca \times Cb - 2ca \times Ab + cb - 2cb \times Ba + ba$;

Again $Cb5 - Ca2 + Ba'$ by Eucl. I. 47,

Therefore $Ce = 2cb2' + 2cb \times Ca - 2cb \times Ba - 2ca \times AB = (cb + Ca) \times (2cb - 2ba)$ (by Eucl. II. 1.) $= (cb + Ca) \times 2ae$ Q.E.D. V,. *Second Additional Solution.*

Take na $-$ the sum of the base and perpendicular, and Bd $-$ that of the base and hypothenusc; draw Gc to make the angle Gcb Z: half a right angle, and produce it to meet a perpendicular, drawn to Bd at D, in F: join Fb, and apply Gezod; draw Bc parallel to ou meeting Gc in c, and demit the perpendicular Ca; then Acb is the triangle required.

For if Ce be drawn parallel to Ad, then by reason of the parallels, and because Gh — Cd by construction, Be is = Ce = Ad; therefore Bc + Ba = Bd the given sum. Also because Agc is half a right angle Ag is = Ac; therefore Ba-JAC is ma the other given sum. L.

Ti. Question 148, *by Mr.* Tho. Sparrow.

To determine a point in the line joining the centres of the earth and moon, where a heavy body would be kept in *equilibrio* by their attraction.

Answered by Mr. John Fearnside.

Two bodies gravitating towards each other, the distances of fh» common centre of attraction, are directly as the quantities of matter in the bodies: Whence the quantity of matter in the earth being, according to Sir Isaac Newton, to that of the moon, as 39-778 to 1 And the mean distance of the earth and moon — 1271018757 English feet, the distance required from the earth 215882 miles, and from the moon 59018 miles.

Additional Solution.

The above answer to this question is wrong. For, the gravitation towards any body being as its quantity of matter directly and square of its distance inversely; if e to m denote the proportion of the quantity of matter in the earth to that in the moon, d the distance of their centres, and x and 2 the respective distances from their centres, of a body placed between them; then the gravitation towards the earth will be as , and towards the moon as-j: that the body be at rest between them then, or gravitate equally towards them, c tn we must make — — —, and hence $/e : »Jm :: x$:s: that is, $x z'$ the distances from them must be as the roots of the masses, which in the present case are nearly as 6 to 1.

TOL. I. M

Vii. Question 149, *by Mr.* Rich. Lovatt.

On the 3d of June 1730, the sun's altitude was 33 at the time the hour angle was equal to the co-latitude of the place: what was the time of the day?

Answered by Copt. Wm. Scarth.
The latitude 26 33' N. the hour 4h 13n 48".

Additional Solution.

Here are given z ☉ the co-altitude — 57 (see the spherical triangle on page 119) p☉ the co-declination = 66 31', and Zp — the angle p. Put a — s. altitude = cos. zQ, d — s. declination = cos. 0, c — its cos. — s. p0, and s =; cos. pz or Zp

Then, per spherics — K = z:
$r c«/(l — z)$

Hence $ccz' — cczz + ddzz — ladz —$
— aay the root of which equation will answer the question, H. vm. Question 150, *by Mr.* John. Turner.

There is a meadow in the form of a parabola, the abscissa of which is equal to 40 chains, and the greatest ordinate (that which bounds the meadow) is 72 chains, from whence the latus rectum will foe found 324 chains. It is required to inscribe such a parallelogram in this parabola, as that its area may be greater than the area of anyother parallelogram that can possibly be inscribed in the said parabola, and to give the analytical investigation of the same?

This in fluxions, 2 toj $zz\ 0, dd\ zz\ 3xx$, Hence = d = 20-7846, and— = 1108-512, &c. square chains = 110 acres 3 roods 16 perches.

Additional Solution.

If to the point b there be drawn a tangent meeting the abscissa and ordinate, produced in r and Q: Then, in all curves that are concave towards their axes, it is 09 r: Sd, and therefore De = Ep by similar'triangles; but, by the nature of the parabola, Ae is — ep; therefore Ae = £ed or = ad; and consequently the height of the parallelogram Ed zz f Ad. Also, since the ordinates of a parabola are as the square roots of their abscissas, and the abscissas being as 3 to 1, therefore the ordinates are as *3* to 1.

So that Ad: Ae:: 3:1,
and Bd: £e:: /3 : 1. H.
ix. Question 151, *by Mr.* Chr. Mason.

Required the ages of two persons from the following equations $aaae + aaeee\ zz\ 3800000000 = b,\ eeea + eeaaa — 4067442500 = c$; where a represents the age of the older and e that of the younger?

. C a — 85-379 7.,. *Answer.* J $g \_ 7g.$
sgg j the.rages. *Additional Solutions.* 1.
Of the two given equations Jjy + J, the latter being multiplied by a, and the former taken from the product, there .,,,,, a ± V(a' +4ac— 4b) remains $e\ a — ea — ca — b$: hence $e\ zz$ ———3: this being substituted in one of the original equations, there will result an equation with only one letter in it, and which from it may be found, u. *1.* Take two near values of a and e, as 85 and 80, and call the differences x and s; then $a\ zz\ 85 + x$, and $e = 80 — z$: substitute these in the two original equations, neglecting all the terms which rise to above two dimensions, and there will result two quadratic equations, from which x and z may be found, u. THE PRIZE QUESTION.
At the time of the last eclipse of the moon, when lunar affairs were of course the subject of general conversation, the following question was proposed. Suppose that A, B, and c make a stock of 22650 hundred weight, and it sold at the moon for 23361931. 9s. 7£d. being sold at a hundred times more per ton than it cost; and suppose the price of A's stock in pounds to be the square root of the stock of B; and the stock of A and B, the square root of the stock of c. Quere each man's stock and gain, and the weight of the goods at the moon; and because if the same goods, at the same price, had been sold at the globe of Jupiter, the amount had been 91089241.? Quere weight at his body also?

Answered.

This question may admit of some differences in the answer as the proportions vary in authors. I shall therefore first give you the proposer Mr. *Tho. Pointin's* answer.

The distance of the earth and ☉ 80015040 miles.

From the centre of 0 to (— 236350
From centre ☉ to *d* surface — 80251390

The weight of a body at the☉ and as 1 to "516; the force of the 0 at d-516 — 000284; =-515716 X 22650= 11680-96 the weight at the (; by which the prime cost is 21. per hundred: for-515716 X 100 X 22650= 1168096-74) 2336193-48 (2. Let, 2a=A's cash, *4aa* = B's, and

16a1 + 8a3 + *aa* — c's stock. Therefore 16a" + 8a3 + *bua* + *a* — sum. A — 6 price 12 lib. B 150, c 2250, and total stock. = 22650. The total gain 2290893, of which A's gain = 606-8592 lib. B's = 14564-6208, c's = 2275722: the weight at the earth and Jupiter as 1 to 2-0108. So the weight will be 4554462 = 2033 ton, 4 cwt. 941b. Mr. *Grimmef,* Mr. *Sideboltom,* Mr. *Bullman,* Mr. *Fearnside,* Mr. *Pilgrim,* and some others, make the weight at the moon 567 tons, at Jupiter 2210 tons. Mr. *Richards,* Mr. *Fairchild,* Mr. *Hale,* Mr. *Lowe,* Mr. *Mason,* Mr. *Grant,* and some others, 386 ton at , and 15071 at Jupiter: several of whom have wrought this question very curiously, and in an algebraic method, but my room will not permit inserting them.

Questions proposed in 1731, *and answered in* 1732. i. Question 152, *by Mr.* Tho. Williams.

A ball projected at the elevation of 31 above the horizon, from the top of a lofty tower, in 9-J seconds fell 2000 feet from the base. Query, the tower's height?

Answered by Mr. Rob. Fearnside.

In the same time the ball describes Be, another body let fall from E would fall the space Ef, and consequently in 9" 10"' time, when the ball is at H, a heavy body will describe Ch — 1351-4 feet. Then as cosine 31: Bd = 2000 feet:: sine 31: Cd 1201-7 feet; consequently the tower's height — Ck — Cd — 149-72 feet

± AM. The same answered by Mr. Wm. Grimmctt.

Let Ba represent the pillar, Ah the distance the ball falls from the base of pillar equal to 2000 feet. Let Ch be perpendicular to Ah; BC the line in which the projectile is directed, in which it would move equal spaces in equal times, were it not deflected downwards by the force of gravity. 'Tis known all projectiles will (rejecting the resistance of the medium) describe parabolas: therefore Bc is the tangent of that parabola, Bd is parallel to Ah the horizon: draw Mh parallel and equal to Bc: consequently Mh is an ordinate to the diameter Bm. Then in the right-angled triangle Bdc there is sufficient given to find the sides. And since the velocities of all projectiles in the several points of the curve, are as the lengths of the tangents to the parabola in those points, intercepted between any two diameters; therefore Bc — 233333 divided by 9£ (= number of seconds the ball was in motion) gives 25454 the velocity in a second; and the square of the Telocity divided by 16T feet, the space a body describes in a second by gravity, gives the parameter to the diameter Ba. That is (per conies) the rectangle under the intercepted part of tlie diameter taken from its origin B towards A, and the parameter, is the square of its correspondent semi-ordinate: whence the parameter is = 4028-43; and the square of Mh divided by the parameter, gives Bm — 13515, But Bm Am Ba = 1495 the height of the tower.

n. Question 153, *by Mr.* Geo. Auderson. Mr. Euclid Speidell, in his Geometrical Extractions, p. 59, says, if upon c, one end of the base Ca, of the triangle Abc, you raise a perpendicular Cd, equal to the perpendicular Bp, let fall from B to Ca, and join Da; that the right line Ce bisecting the angle Acd, being produced, shall cut Da in such a point *v* through which, if the right line Gh be drawn parallel to the base Ca, the part Gh intercepted between the two sides Bc and Ba, shall be the side of the square made in the aforesaid triangle. Quere, the geometrical demon-. stration? *Answered.*

Produce Ug to L, and draw Fm and Gk parallel to Fb.

Per. step 7. (8) Dc: Dl:: Ca: Ch.
But per fig. (9) Dc: »l:: Ca: Lf.
U(10) Ca:gh:: Ca: If.
Therefore Oh — Lf =: Gk. Q. E. Z.,v
Answered by Mr. Will. Grimmett.

The geometrical demonstration of this problem may be easily seen from the proposer's own scheme, without any previous construction, (viz). Since there cannot be but one square inscribed in tbat position, and that Lc is equal to Lf each subtending an angle of 45 (per prob.); therefore if we prove that Lf is Gh universally, it is demonstrated; for Lc is equal to Gh (which is supposed to be a side of a square.) *Demonstration.* From 37 Euc. 1, the triangles Dcb and Dab are equal; and if an infinite number of right lines as Lh be drawn parallel to the common base Db, the parts of those lines which are intercepted by the respective sides of the triangles, will also be equal, that is Lg — Fh J which is Cavalerius's method of proving the triangles to be equal (which is the method of indivisibles;) therefore if to both be added or subtracted (as the case requires) Gf, Lf Gh. Q. E. D. *Additional Demonstration.*

This construction may be otherwise demonstrated thus: As Dc or Bp: Ca;: Df: Fa (EucL VI. 3.):: Dl: Lc or *ex,* (Eucl. VI. 2), but Bf: Ca:: Bn or Dl: Gh;.. Gk — Gh.

Why the proposer of the question calls *Speidell* by the name of *Euclid,* I know not. His name was *John,* as appears by the book, which was published in the year 1617. H.

in. Question 154, *by Mr.* John Turner.

Let a stone be whirl'd round in a sling, whose length is equal to 33 inches, performing each revolution in the time of two thirds of one second. Required the ratio of the centrifugal force to the weight of the stone? That is, the ratio of the tension of the string whirled round in this manner, to the tension arising from the force of the same weight hanging freely, and without motion?

Answered by the Proposer.

As 113: 355:: 66: 207-35 inches, (he arch described in f of 1"; and 207-35 squared and divided by 66, the double length of the sling, is — 651-03 the centrifugal force. But the descent of a heavy body in-J of *I"* is =86-208 inches: whence the centrifugal force is to the force of gravity as 651-4 to 85-7 or as 7-6 to 1.

The same answered by Mr. John Ommanney.

The stone, if let fall out of the sling when at rest, by the force of gravity would descend 85j inches; which call *b.* Now let F be the force of the stone or tension of the string when at rest; and E that when in motion. The lengths gone over are always propor.

%*b* tional to the force impressed. Therefore r: E:: *b:—* the space descended through with the force E in the same time. Let *c* — the circumference of the sling = 207-344, and *d* — diameter = 66; then, *cc* E6 by Sir Isaac Newton, — — —. Whence F: E:: *db* : cc. That *J 'd* F is as 5659-5 to 42991-9, or as 1 to 7-596. Q. E. I. iv. Question 155, *by Mr.* John Turner,

Suppose the earth's radius — 6982000 yards, and that there is a mountain upon its superficies of such an height, and that a clock when on the earth's surface, shall point out equal time; but when carried to the top of the mountain, shall be so retarded as to err 2 minutes every day. 'Tis required to give that mountain's elevation?

Answered.
The number of oscillations in each place being equal, will be as the time in one place to the time in the other, viz. as 1440 to 1442. Let *n* — earth's radius, and *a* — radius and the height of the mount tain together; the force of gravity being inversely as the square of 1442a the distance from the centre, we shall have 1442«s: 1440a, and

''1440 — 6991698 — *a;* from which subtracting the radius of the earth 6982000, remains the mountain's height = 9698 yards 5 miles 18 yards.

Answered by Mr. Geo, Auderson,
The length of the pendulum vibrating seconds on the mountain's top will be — 39-09 inches; therefore by Huygen's proportions the space descended in a second of time on the top of the mountain will be 192 9009 inches; and the space descended in a vibration of the clock is 193-4437 inches: And the gravity being defined by the space passed over in a second of time. From corol. 2, prop. 5? theor. 5, Principia Philosophise; put r = earth's radius, a; — mountain's height.

r' + 2ir + : r:: 193-44: 192-9. And therefore *x* =-0014059/-= 353375-7768 inches, or 9815-99 yards, or 5-5773 miles.
Additional Solution.
Universally, the lengths of pendulums being directly as the force of gravity drawn into the squares of the times of vibration, and the pendulum being of the same length in both cases, we shall

have *ft1* — Fts, putting/and *t* for the force of gravity and time of vibration at the earth's surface, and F and T for the same at the top of the hill. But the force of gravity is inversely as the square of the distance from the earth's centre: that is *f* is as-v, and F as;———., putting r for *J* r' *(r+x)" r* the earth's radius, and *x* for the height of the hill; then the above *t' T t .* T equation becomes— or-=. Again, the time *r (/ + x) / 7 + x '* of a vibration being inversely as the number of vibrations in a given iSme, and the number of vibrations being as 1440 to 1438; the same equation will become — —————-. Hence a: 1440r 1438 X (r + *x*) 2r r
—*rrr.* = ;= 9710-7 yards — the height of the mountain required *Corollary.*

Hence it appears in general, that if / be the time lost in the time *t*; then 24 hours — /: *I* :: r: *x*; or, because 24 hours — / is nearly — 24 hours, it will be nearly as 24 hours: /:: *r* : *x*; that is, the whole time is to the time lost, as the radius pf the earth to the height of the hill. u. v. Question 156, *by Mr.* William Grimmett.

Required the greatest parallelogram that can be inscribed in an ellipsis, whose transverse is 10, and conjugate 8. And supposing the ellipsis to revolve upon its transverse axis, required also the greatest cylinder that can be inscribed in the spheroid that is generated by the revolving ellipsis; and to shew the analytical investigation of the same?
Answered by Mr. John Turner.
Let Sd = *t* = 5; Be — *c* == 4; *si* = *a; vt* — *I* + *a;* and *At zz t — a.* Then we hare *yy.* Ergo jf _ *y -M lecrx* Which substituted in the former, we have *decx — ccxx decx — Iccxx* be found = 7-071, and *my* — 5-6568: and the area of the greatest parallelogram = 39-999999. Q. E. I. *Additional Solution.*

In the solution of question 74, at page 96, it is proved that Ce cAv'i-j *(see fig-t that solution)* and Ef Cd *A/* Ce being half the height, and Ef half the diameter of the cylinder, whea Ca is the semi-transverse, and Cd the semi-conjugate axe.

Again, supposing Ce and Ef to be the

halves of the length and breadth of the greatest inscribed parallelogram, by page 201 Simpson's Geom. 2d edit, Ce is — fcT, and Ef =: £ Ck; but, by the nature of the ellipse, Ce is: Ca:: Ca: Ct or 2ce; hence Ce — Ca V *h* And in like manner Ef *Z:* Cd y.
Corollary.
Hence, if *t* and c denote the whole transverse and conjugate axes. Then — length of the greatest rectangle, *c/* — breadth of the same,
ct — area of the same.
And — length of the greatest cylinder, cy'-j — diameter of it,
2c4 *fn*
—— — content of it, putting *n —* "78539, See. v.
3y 3
vi. Question 157, *by Mr.* Christ. Hale.

On the evening of the 9th of May, 1730, a person viewing the heavens, in latitude 29 22' N. observed a star whose altitude was equal to the hour-angle from noon, and also equal to the azimuth. Query, the name of the star?
Answered by Mr. Geo. Auderson.
In contemplating on the solution of the 159th question, I hit upon the following lemma, which I find to be so useful in solving astronomical questions of that kind, that I believe there can no such question be proposed, but it will be found an useful instrument in solving it.

In the spherical triangle let p be the north pole, z the zenith, 0 the place of the sun: and '1 =.radius, a — tangent of zp, is — cosine of Zp, Put *d* — right sine 0 P,. 1 *e* — cosine of © p, y *g* —' cosine of ©z, = cosine of © Pz Lemma; (» + *dax*) Xf = f. *Corollary.*

In question 157 there is given the latitude of the place, and the altitude equal to the hour from noon and to the azimuth, to find the latitude of the star (or declination with respect to the sun); therefore in the room of *g* in the lemma put —*xx) (*— sine of the hour) and there will be had (e + *dax*) x s = »/(1 —*xx),* from the equality of the hour and altitude. And now to answer the other parts of the question, because the azimuth is equal to the hour, therefore the same *x* still represents the cosine of the angle © Zp, and the theorem must be so transposed that ☉ Zp may be the angle contained: wherefore since Zp is one of the containing sides of the angle ☉ Zp, as well as of the angle ☉pz, therefore a and s may still retain their former office, but for d must be wrote $/(1 - gg)$, and 1or e put g, and for g write e, and for e put x, and then the lemma will stand thus, $(x + ax/(1 - gg)) \times s - e$. But because $-gg) x$, the theorem will be $sx + saxx\ e$; therefore from the two equations $(e + ax »/(1 - ec)) \times s - «/(1 - xx)$ and $x + saxx - e$, exterminate e you will have this equation $ssa"xu\ 4-4s'a7x" +84ax$ f l2,a + lw c + i2,v c TfXc ' j OS" fit J 4V f,

Which in $1 - aa$ "'" $1 - aa$
— versed sine Zzqp, and — =: cosine Zz☉p. Hence $1 - aa$
— $nlM - = 1 - aa - aV$. Reduced we have a =:-7493411 $1 - aa$ — sine of 48 33" = to the altitude and latitude of Perseus's right side.

Additional Solution.
In this question is given zp, the Z.Z — Zp = comp. ☉z or 0p, the triangle being isosceles. Then supposing a perpendicular demitted from ☉ upon and bisecting Zp, and thereby dividing ☉zp into two equal right-angled triangles; put-a — the tangent of the base of each or half pz the given colatitude, and x — sine of the hypothenuse ☉p or ☉z =: cos. Zp or z; then, by right-angled triangles, (radius =) $1:x :: - (=$ tang. Zp or z): $V(l-x3)\ x-a$; hence $a4-as-oV$, and #=: $4/fa/(£a +1)-a)$ = the cosine of the declination, H. vn. Question 158, *by Mr.* John Fearnside.

There is a garden of a triangular form, the three sides are ornamented with the statues of Bacchus, Apollo, and Hermes; there are also straight walks between each of the statues; the walk from Bacchus to Hermes is 216-4074 feet, that from Apollo to Bacchus 192-1 306 feet, and the walk from Apollo to Hermes is 209-694 feet. The length of that side of the garden in which the statue of Hermes is placed is 363 feet, and one of the angles adjacent to this side is 55. Required the two unknown sides of the garden, one of the walks being perpendicular to one of them?
— m. Which reduced gives $x - 233$-1047 i.

Therefore Df — 412-5, Cf = 427-4, and the area 1 ac. 1 r. 20 p.

This question being unlimited, as not determined on which wall Bacchus or Apollo stands, will admit of another answer.

Remark. In this question it is required, about a given triangle to circumscribe another triangle such, that one of its angles, and one of tha sides about that angle, shall be each of a given magnitude; and tiie side opposite to the given angle perpendicular to a side of the given inscribed triangle.

And hence if upon the given line Bii be described the segment of a circle capable of containing the given angle n, the problem is reduced to this: To apply a line Cd of a given length between the circumference of that circle and the line Cf given in position, and so as to pass through the given point H. H. *Solution of the problem indicated in the preceding remark.*

Suppose the thing done. Let o be the centre of the circle; join no, draw the radius Op parallel to Hd, and Pe perpendicular to no. The chord Hb is twice the cosine of the angle Poe, to the radius Op, and Oe is the cosine of the same angle, therefore Oe — m. Take 01 the given line Cd, then i will be a given point and Ei — ca. Through o drawn Not. parallel to Cf. Draw Mun and Il perpendicular to Hi, the former meeting cr, Nl in M and N, the latter meeting Nl in L; and produce Pe to meet Nl in K.

Because of the similar triangles Hcm, Pok, and the parallel lines Il, Ek, Un, we have
Iim: Hc or 2ie:: Kp: Po or OH,
2ie: 2lk:: Oh: On;
therefore Em: 2lk:: Kp: On:
Hence 2lk × Kp = Hm × On.

Now from the disposition of the lines, it is manifest that Iim and. On are both given in magnitude; and the point L and the line Ol given by position, this last making with Pk a given angle; therefore the point p is evidently in a given hyperbola of which Ol and Li are the asymptotes. And this curve being described, the point or points in which it cuts the circle will determine the point p, and consequently the position of Cd which is parallel to op.

The composition is easily deduced from the analysis, and for the sake of brevity is omitted, w.

vm. Question 159, *by Mr.* John Fearnside.
What time of the day is the hottest at York on the 8th of June, supposing it to be as the sine of the sun's altitude, and the time of his continuance above the horizon?
Answered by Mr. Auderson.
Given the latitude, the sun's declination, and the sun's heat, as the sine of his altitude and continuance above the horizon (viz. as their product) for so I take it, and was so informed by E. Stone, who proposed the same question in his preface to de l'Hospital's fluxions.

Lemma $(e + dax) \times s$ — sine sun's altitude, as in question 157. But $+ xs + j5\#s + i7 +$ &c. is the arch belonging to x, and $b - x" - xs - -x$ &c. (putting b = J of the circumference) is the complement of it, and therefore the hour from noon: Put r =: the time (viz. the length of the arch of the equinoctial) passed over from sun-rising to noon: Now it is manifest the aforesaid phenomenon will not happen before the sun's arrival at the meridian, therefore $r + b - x - xs - x5 - xl -$ &c.
is the sun's continuance above the horizon, and this multiplied bjr $se + sdax$ the sine of the altitude, and thrown into fluxions and reduced gives $Zsdax + isex + \%sdaxs + pex + fasdax +-fasex6 + fc\ sdax7$ &c. — $sdar + sdab - se - m$. And therefore x: Ise X lsdaf· Ada (tsdaf
The proposer's answer.
Let m as the rectangle of the sine com. lat. and co-declinatlon, p — sun's alt. at 6, n — the length of the semi-diurnal arch, and z the length of the arch from noon. The cosine of the hour angle $zz\ s\ z"$ from noon is $=1 - - + - - -$ &c and, putting m + $p=a$, the sine of the sun's altitude will be $- a - + - -,$ &c.
2 24 720
Which multiplied by $n + z$, and thrown into fluxions, &c. gives $3m.\ mn, 5m\ .\,,\ \_,\ mnz + -z -a - -z +$ &c. Reversed z will be =-50614 2 o 24 (the

radius being 1) consequently the hour is 1h 56' afternoon. '*Additional Solution.*

Put s and c = the sine and cosine of Pz, d and e =: sine and cosine of P0, m — the semi-diurnal arc, x — the hour arc or Zp y — its sine, and z — sine of the altitude or cosine of z Q. /0-2)"

Wherefore-=St-£%BL + dsj, + ,,f =0, or ce — dsmy — dsxy + di —?/) = 0, and hence = Ce !g +/'ɪZjfl.

Now this equation may be resolved after several different maimers. One method is to substitute in it the value of x in terms of y in an infinite series, and this will be like the two original solutions: Or a finite approximate value of x in terms of y may be substituted for it, and then the resulting equation will be finite: Or some method may be used for approximating to the values of x and y immediately from Ihe equation as it stands above, which will be easiest and soonest done; and the best method for that purpose seems to be this; by a few trials find y — 5 nearly, which substituted in the above form, a near value of x will be found; from a table of sines, to this value of ar take the correspondent value of y, which written in the above form again, there will be had a nearer value of x; and so on as far as necessary, H. *See also question* 241.

ix. Question 160, *by Mr.* Christ. Mason. A surveyor wants to determine the distances from a certain station to two objects, 40 chains asunder, and the angle which they subtend 30: accordingly he measures 23 chains directly south of the station, and then finds the objects exactly west, and in the same right line. What are the distances from the said station.
Answered by the author Mr. Mason.
Let Ad = b = 40, Bc = c zz 23, d — s. Zabd = 30, a =z Dc —?

Per 47 E. 1, $S(b + Iba + aa + cc)$ zz Ab; for which substitute y : then
V: 1:: c:-= s. Z Bac: and d: b :: c be .
_ ,,, bbcc -:-r — Db: per 47 h. 1, — — cc if dy v ddyy — aa i. c. bbcc — ceddyy — ddyyaa: for yy put its value..Then a' + Zba' + bbaa — Ibca — ——r-c'

— bbcc: which reduced gives a— 183, Ab =62-672, Db=29'392. Answered by Mr. John Bulman.

On the given segment Ad == 40 chains (per 33 Eucl. 3.) describe a segment of a circle which shall contain the given angle Abd — 30. And from F the centre thereof let fall the perpendicular Fp upon Ad; make Ph = 23, and draw Eb parallel to Ad meeting the circle in B; and let fall the perpendicular Bc. Then the lines Fb, Fd, Fa will all be equal as being radius's of the same circle.

The angle Afd is double the angle Abd (per 20 E. 2); therefore the triangle Afd is equilateral, and consequently equiangular, each side being 40 chains, and each angle 60. Then Fds — Pds — Fp4 (per 47 E. 1); whence Fp — 34-641, and Fp — Bc =: Fr =: 11-641. Again, FBa — Frs == Rb2; whence Rb 38-2686, and Rb— Pd =dc
— 18-2686 — the distance of the nearest mark from the end of the first line: Hence Bd may csaily be found = 29-3628 chains, and Ba = 62-6438. Q. E. 1. x. Question 161) *by Mr.* Tho. Pointon.

In th' Atlantic ocean an island is found,
Neither oblong nor square, but perfectly round;
In the centre of which a tower's erected,
From whence, with much ease, their foes are detected:
For if Neptune but smile, and the sky be serene,
Four leagues from the shore is the horizon seen;
We being at anchor, o'er the top o'th' mast
From the top o'th' tower a line being past.
Did bound the utmost stretch of sight at last.
From thence we set sail, and I'll tell you in short,
The distance + we ran, to arrive at our port:
And also our course J as corrected at noon,
Perform'd with great care by the height of the sun:
Which, to my surprize, neither higher nor lower,
Was cut in two halves by the fore-mentioned tower.
The height of our mast from the water's here shown,
And whatever else is most fit to be known §;
Note, 69 *miles to a degree, three of which are a league.* T *Our distance of a degree.* t *Our course N. by E.* 2 45' *E. or 4from N. to E.* Tlie *height of the mast from the water 4b feet, Lat.* 64» 20' *N. of tht temer* 63 5&. *Tht ship's distance from the shore is* 1-363244 *leagues.* VOL. I. O
Which being supposed, what I want to be found,
Is the tower's just height, and land's compass round.
Besides, when you're got in this fig'ring strain,
Let's know the square miles the whole doth contain.
Answered by the Author.

The longitude is 20' 23" X'' 14""; from which, and two latitudes, is found the tower's distance 26' 12". The arch of distance between the ship and horizon is 7' 5" 16"' 48"" +.26' 12" = 33" 17" 16"' 48"". By which 326-15204 yards is the tower's height, and 566202 leagues the island's compass; also the area 21932553 square miles.

It is not easy to say what the proposer's real meaning is in this question, but we have printed it, and the solution, exactly as thay stand in the original, L.

Xi. Question 162, *by Mr.* C. Mason.
It is required to find two such numbers, viz. A and B, that the sum of the aliquot parts in A may be equal to f of D, and the sum of the aliquot parts in B equal to of A. *Answered by the proposer Mr.* Mason.
A = 404: B — 465.
Mr. Robert Fearnside's answer.

Let 1y — sum of the aliquot parts in A; and 3s sum of the aliquot parts in B: Then $3y$ will be — second number B; and 4s= A. Now 1+ 2 + 4+ 2+ 2a — 1y; and 1 + 3+ = 3s = $2y$ — 7. Consequently the first number A will be found to be 20, and B — 33.

For 1 + 2 + 4 + 5 + 10 is =-j-b; and 1 + 3 + 11 is = a. *Mr. Grimmett's answer.*

It is supposed that of A is an integer, because the sum of the aliquot parts of B is — to it; and likewise £ of B is an integer for the same reason; therefore the number A must be a multiple of 4; and the number B a multiple of 3. Make therefore A — $4a$; its aliquot parts are $2a, o, 4, 2, 1$ the sum of which is $3a+7$. Put also BrrSej the sum of the aliquot parts of which is $e + 4$; and per question $3a + 7 = 2e (= \$B)$; also $e + 4 = 3a (= a)$. Whence a is found — 5, and e zz 11. Consequently $4a = 20$ zz the number A j and Se s= 33 zz B. $x + 3xxz+ 3xzz+z'$ $101'730562'$ c = 67-820375; the value of the estate 169-550937; the annuity or income = 22-577929.

Additional Solution.

In this question for determining the three quantities, x, y, s, there are given the two equations $x + y = $ t, and $y +- xt$ o

And the third equation is to be made out from these following conditions, *vis.* that /xz is the present value of a yearly rent which is expressed by $1/yz$, to continue for 7 years, but the first payment not to become due till the end of the 8th year; the interest of money being reckoned at 6 per cent.

» 'Sz

From the two first equations we easily find x zz , and y — —; consequently the yearly rent becomes --y aI,d the present value 3s 3 of it *if*——or s /-. But by any calculated table of reversions at 5 a. 6 per cent, it appears that the present worth of one pound due 8 years hence is-6214, the present value due 9 years hence-5919, the same for 10 years-5584, for 11 years-5268, for 12 years-4970, for 13 years 4688, and for 14 years-4423; the sum of these is 3-7128 which is the present value of 1 for those 7 years, and consequently

"5-7126 V-r-=the present value of v —annuity for the same time, *Questions proposed in* 1732, *and answered in* 1733.

i. Question 163, *by Mr.* Sam. Ashby.

There is a park in the form of a right-angled triangle, having a round walk touching the sides: there are also four straight paths terminating in the round walk, forming therein a trapezium Abcd J the side Ab = 152-99 chains, Bc = 191-11, Cd = 93-03, and Da — 41-56: Also the area of the park — 55296 square chains. It is required to determine the lengths of the three sides.

Answered by Mr. W. Grimmett, Draw the diagonals Bd and Ca; and from the centre of the in. 167-65 = Be; and then Bd will + *ddcs* + *bbcs* + *ccdb* be found = 189-81.

Again, from the circle and its inscribed triangle Bad, in which the perpendicular Ah is let fall, it will be as Ah: Da:: Ba: the diameter of the circle zz 191-6832; and consequently Mo the radius is 95-8416.

Put b — area of the triangle Pnr; n zz Mo; x = Rn. Then 2d. *Geometrically.*

In this question it is required to inscribe a quadrilateral whose sides are given in a circle, which may be done as follows: Suppose Abcd to be the quadrilateral required; join Ac, Bd and draw Df parallel to Ac, meeting Bc produced in F; then because the angles Abe, Dce are equal; and also those at E, the triangles Abe, Dce are similar; therefore Ab: Dc:: Be: Ce (by the parallels):: Bd: Df; therefore Bd has to Df a given ratio. Again, because the angle Bcf is — Dab, and the angle Cdf — Acd — Abd, the triangles Abd, Dcf are similar, and therefore Ab: Ad:: Dc: Cf: Wherefore Cf is a given line, and consequently Bf is a given line; and since Bd has to Df a given ratio, the locus of D is a given circle (Apoll. Loci Plani ii. 2.), and Cd being also a given line, we have this construction.

On Bc produced take Cf a fourth proportional to Ab, Ad and Dc, and describe the circle which is the locus of D, so that any two lines being inflected to it from B and F they may have the given ratio of Ab to Dc; then from the centre c, with the distance Cd, describe an arc to intersect the other circle in n, lastly from the centres D and B, with distances equal to the given sides Da, Ba, describe arcs to intersect in A; join Da, Ba, and the quadrilateral will be constructed, j. t.

Ii. Question 164, *by Mr.* John Turner.

Two men, A and B, buy a piece of ground in an unknown northern latitude: but it was observed that on a certain day in the year, also unknown, the sun's altitude upon the south part of the meridian, at the said place, was 42 30'; and upon the north part of the meridian,

his altitude above the horizon was 4 30': The limits of the ground were to be marked out by the shadow of the vertex of a tree 20 yards high, on that same day when the altitude of the sun on each part of the meadow was observed as above-mentioned. It is required hence to find the latitude of the place, and the sun's declination; and also the share of the ground belonging to each man» A being to have for his part the greatest triangle that can be cut out of the said conic section described by the shadow_of the tree's top, and B to have the remainder.

Answered by Mr. Rob. Fearnside.

It is obvious that the declination of the sun is equal to half the sun of the meridian altitudes, which consequently is 23 30'; and the latitude 71. property of the ellipsis, (as per Ward's Introduct. p. 448.) therefore $ttmm + Ztmmx + Imrnxx$ — $ttnn$ — $itnnx$ — $nnxx$ — $ttmm$ — $Ztmmx + mmxx$—$ttss+ltssx$—$ssxx$; by reduction and transposition, $ssxx$— $nnxx$ $+ 4invilx$ — $Itnnx$ — $2wx = ttnn$ —$ttss$.

Now the tree being supposed to be placed in H, it is evident, as the sun does not set, that its summit will describe the ellipsis Agfdbda; therefore, by plain trigonometry, Ah will be found = 21-826, and Bh = 254-121; and (finding the altitude of the sun when due cast or west) au — 43, and consequently Fc the semiconjugate diameter 79-5.

Then put Ab = 2a, Fc = b, Ce = x, and De zzy. Thdh, per conies, aa— xx: yy :: $aa : bb$: therefore $y = . — (aa— xx)$. Now $(a + x) \times -i/(aa — xx)$ — the area of the triangle Dad, must be a maximum; a which put into fluxions and ordered, x will be $= a$, and the area of the greatest triangle will be — 7124-37 — 2 a. 3 r. 32 p. = A's share.

and 27335-88 = 4 0 29 = B's share.

Mr. *Grimmelt* having discovered a new property of the ellipsis, after a solution to this question, concludes with this other following method:

Supposing a circle inscribed in the ellipsis, then it will be as the radius of the inscribed circle, is to the perpendicular height of the equilateral triangle inscribed therein; so is the semi-transverse of the ellipsis, to the perpendicular of the greatest triangle inscribed in the ellipsis = 206-9652.

The answer will be 14277-7 = 2 a. 3r. 32 p. = A's share.

20251-5 = 4 0 29 = B's share. *Remark.* Having found the declination and latitude as in the first solution above, viz. by taking half the sum of the greatest and least altitudes for the declination, and then by taking the complement of the difference between this declination and the greatest altitude for the latitude of the place, which are general rules; next compute the altitude when due east or west, and then say as radius: the height of the tree:: the cotangent of each of these three altitudes: each of the three lines Ha, Hb, Iig. All the rest of the first solution above is

Tery clear.

The truth of Mr. Grimmett's theorem above may appear thus: From Mr. Fearnside's solution we find that the altitude of the greatest triangle is 3-4fhs of the transverse axe; and by geometry we know that the altitude of an equilateral triangle is also 3-4ths of the diameter of its circumscribed circle; wherefore as the diameter of any circle is to the altitude of its inscribed equilateral triangle, so is the transverse axe of an ellipse to the altitude of its greatest inscribed triangle. We may hence remark also that the equilateral is the greatest triangle that can be inscribed in a circle. H.

nr. Question 165, *by Mr. Tho. Grant.*

There is a cask in the form of the frustum of a spheroid; the length is 45 inches; the bung diameter is 36 inches; greater head diameter 32, and less head diameter 27 inches. Required a general theorem expressing the content of the cask; and find what part of the length lies on each side of the bung diameter.

Answered, by Mr. R, Lovatt.

Put $ss - nn - - b$, and $4mnit - linn - Zttss - c$, and $ttnn - ttss\ zz\ d$; then $- bxx + cx = d$; and, extracting the root, $x - - 4$-10 inches; then $2 = 8$-20 inches = the part wanting Dc: from whence we find irr the distance from the greatest bulk of the cask to the lesser head to be $- 266$ inches, and en to the greater head 18-4 inches. And the content is 143-9 ale gallons.

Mr. *Grimmett,* after two different solutions to this question, delivers this theorem:

Theorem. The square root of each difference between the square of half the bung diameter and the square of half the diameter of each head,,put into one sum: It will be as the sum is to either of those roots, so is the length of the cask to the distance of the respective head from the bung.

Remark. By the nature of the ellipse, /(I!If2—cb9) *VOTM*—Fe8):: en: Hf; and, by composition, &c. (hn—Cbj) (un-Fej) : Cf:: J (H£» Fe2) Hf ' wnich therefore both becomeknown; and this is Mr. Grimmett's theorem, mentioned above. Again, by the nature of the ellipse, *(un — Cbs): Ch::Un:* Ha the semi-transverse: which being thus found, the contents of the two parts Bnrg, Neor, of the cask being computed separately by the common rules, their sum will be the whole content Or indeed their contents are easily computed without the transverse axe by rule 1, page 278, of my Mensuration.

N. B. The two expressions marked in Mr. Lovatt's solution are wrong printed; but they are here given as they stand in the original, as it is not easy to distinguish what are the true expressions meant, H.

Iv. Question 166, *by Mr.* Christ. Mason.

Required a theorem or formula expressing all perfect numbers; and give an example in finding all such numbers from l to 10000000.

Answered by Mr. Grimmett.

If from unity be taken how many numbers soever in double proportion continually, until the whole added together be a prime number; and if this whole be multiplied by the last term of the series which constitutes the prime, the product will be a perfect number. 36 Euclid 9.

From such a series it may be observed, that any term made less by unity, will be s= the sum of all the preceding terms. Put therelore $a - 2$; and $x -$ its variable exponent (for in the first operalion it wijl represent 1, in the next 2, and then 3, &c, till it be raised to a""1 and. being lessened by unity may be a prime number. Thus 6 -num.

.a J 5 I J — abounding,

«f 6 1 #8128 perf. num.

„&c. / V &c.

Whence the perfect numbers are 6, 28, 496, and 8128, all the perfect numbers required per question.

Mr. C. Mason, the proposer, gives this rule: $(1 + 12) \times 2 = 6$; $(1 + 2 + 4) \times 4 = 28$; $(1 + 2 + 4 + 8) X8 = 120$, &c. *Mr.* Sam. Ashby *answers thus:*

The canon. If from any power of 2 be subtracted unity, and that remainder be a prime number, multiply it by half the said power, and that product will be a perfect number.

Mr. Robert Fearnside's *ansxoer.*

Let ynx be the number sought; its aliquot parts will be $1 + y + y'+y3$, &c. till the exponent becomes n; and $x+yx +yx+yx$, &c till the number of terms be likewise n; then, from the nature of a perfect number, $1+iy+3/!i+y+$ &c. $+x +yx+yv+yx+$ &c. $= ynx$;

I I y $y\%$ y"i and consequently $x -- -$: Now, that may b« a whole number, it is requisite that $yn - 1 - y -$ &c. be I, which only happens when y is $- 2$; whence the canon required becomes 2TMa?. If $n - 1$, x will be $=: 1 + 2$, and the first perfect number $= 6$. If $n - 2$, x will he zz $1 + 2+4$, and the second perfect number will be $- 28$. If $n - 4$, the third perfect number f= 496. If $n - 6$, the fourth perfect number is 812S. Which are all the perfect numbers from unity to ten millions.

Woolfius, in his Elem. Math, supposes n to be successively the numbers 1, 2, 3, 4, 5, &c. which will not hold when n is supposed =; the odd numbers 3, 5, 7, 9, &c. and Mr. *Cunn's* rule for finding a perfect number will npt find all the above numbers: See p. 12 of his Decimals. *Additional Solution.*

By *Eucl.* IX. $36,:? + 2 + 2! + 2' + 2 +$ &c. to 2B: X 2s is a perfect number when the sum of the series is a prime number; but the sum of the geometrical series is $2B+1 - 1$, therefore $(2B+1 -1) \times ''$ is a perfect number when $2n''''1 - 1$ is a prime number. Taking $n - 0$; then $2n+1 - 1$ is $= 1$ a prime, and $1 \times 2 = 1 \times 1 = 1$ the first perfect number: If $n - 1$; then $2n+1 - 1 = 3$ a prime, and 3 × 2' = 6 the next perfect number: If $n = 2$; then — 1 = 7 a prime, and 7 × 2 zz, 28 the 3d perfect number: If $n\ zz\ 3$; then $2'''1 - 1 = 15$ which is net a prime, and therefore 15 × 2' = 120 is not a perfect number: In like manner it will appear that no other greater odd number can be put for n so as to make the expression $(2\ 1— 1) × 2n$ a perfect number; n must therefore be always an even number for finding the other perfect numbers; but it cannot be any even number, as some have falsely asserted. Dr. Harris says that there are only ten perfect numbers between 1 and 1,000,000,000,000.

This rule of Euclid's only demonstrates that a number found by it will be a perfect number; but neither it nor any other that I know of, shews that there may not be other perfect numbers besides those found by this rule. H. v.

Question 167, *by Mr.* Turner.

Let there be a triangle whose three sides are given, viz. 415, 353, and 488: And upon the three angular points, as centres, let there he described three circles whose radii are 130, 80, and 70: Let a fourth circle be drawn, which shall touch these three circles. It is required to find its diameter?

Answered by Mr. Turner, *the proposer. Mr.* Rich. Lovatt's *answer to the same.*

„ ,. 488s — 130 — 70, 130 — 70 Put b -;a s —: n 488 × 2' 4S8 353' — (80 — 70) 80 — 70 Dpe.

—: m =:p z:;and a — Cf. 353 × 2' 353 '*1 2*'

Then, per axiom 4, ft — *adzz.pv.;* and $n — am$ — *Uif:* and Cf will be the diameter of a circle, whose periphery will pass through *met*; and (20Eucl. 3.) the angle at the centre, v, is double to the angle, F, at the periphery; also (5 Eucl. 1.) the angle $ipm — vmp$. Put $ft = s$. */Lvmp* — 33 34'; k — s. *£mvp* = 112 56'; then $h: -:: k: = mp$. And by that noble theorem which I mentioned 2 2A *1 1* in the Diary of 1731, quest. 143, we have this analogy: $(b — ad)\ A\ b — ad — n + am\ ak — i + ad--n — am\ (n-am): + Jj × + —:: 1 :pp;$ and/jp × $(b — ad)$ x $(it — am)\ 6 — ad — n +$ am «fc — & + $ad + « — «ot\ ak — 2 + 2/t × 2\ 1th$' In numbers, 1682«a + 9071« = 9473-58 + 1023-9, and a =

V63140-3—27 = 224-273; hence 224-273— 70 = 154273 = cr, which doubled is the diameter 308-56 of the circle required.

Remark. This is one of the problems of Apollonius on Tangencies, and is constructed by his restorers Vieta, and our countryman the Rev. Mr. John Lawson, who has lately published an English restoration of this piece of Apollonius's works, where it appears that the problem hath several cases, according as the fourth circle is to touch the other three, either all internally or all externally, or else some internally and the rest externally.

This problem has also been attended to by several other respectable persons, it being constructed by Sir Isaac Newton, in lemma 16, lib. 1. of the Principiaj and his Universal Arith. prob. 47; by the Marquis de l'Hospital in his Sectiones Conique, lib. 10, ex. 4, cor. 1; and by Mr. Tho. Simpson, at the end of his Geometry.

Concerning this problem I shall also insert the following extract from the Histoire des Mathematiques, par M. Montucla, tom. i. p. 263.

Vieta, in a dispute which he had-with Adrianus Romanus, proposed to him this question. The solution which Romanus gave to it, though obvious, was very indifferent, viz. by determining the centre of the circle sought in the point of intersection of two hyperbolas; for as the problem is a plane one, it may be solved by plane geometry; by this Vieta solved it, and very elegantly: his solution is the same as that given in Newton's Universal Arithmetic. Another solution may also be seen in the 1st book of the Principia (this question being there necessary for some determinations in Physical Astronomy), wherein Newton, by a remarkable dexterity, reduces the two solid loci of Romanus to the intersection of two right lines.—Moreover, Descartes attempted to solve this problem by the help of the Algebraical Analysis, but without success; for of the two solutions which he derived from thence, he himself acknowledges (see Lett. tom. iii. let. 80, 81.) that one furnished him with so complicated an expression, that he would not undertake to construct it in a month; whilst the other, though somewhat less complicated, was not so very simple, as to encourage him to set about a construction of it. Lastly, the

Princess Elizabeth of Bohemia, who, it is well known, honoured Descartes with her correspondence, deigned to communicate a solution to this Philosopher; but as it is deduced from the algebraical calculus, it labours under the same incoveniencies as that of Descartes, u.

vi. Question 168, *by Mr.* Chr. Mason.

Three persons, A, B, c, each staked a guinea to play for at dice, the game to be 15; when growing tired they agreed to part the money according to the chance which each had of winning at the time: now A had got 10, B 8, and c 5; what part of the money ought each to have.

Answered by Mr. Rob. Feamside.

Let A, B, c, represent the three players; A wants 5 of being up, B 7, and c 10. Now it is plain the game will be ended in 20 throws at most; then A + B + c must be raised to the 20th power; and as the players here are supposed equal, the co-efficients of every term where the 5th power of A and upwards, including the 20th, is found, are to be added together, as also the co-efficients where the 7th power of B and upwards is found, and the co-efficients of the 10th power of c and upwards are to be added also together; these three totals will be in proportion to one another as the respective shares they are to have of the guineas.,

l. s. d.

He who got 10 must have 2 3 10 + He who got 8 must have 0 16 1 + He who got 5 must have 0 3 0 +

Mr. *John Ommanney* numbers are the same.

Remark. The method of solving questions of this kind, may be seen at page 43 or 192, of De Moivre, or in some other books on Chances, u.

The Prize Question, *by Mr.* Rob. Fearnside.

To determine the longest cylindrical pole, 1 foot diameter, that can be put up a chimney, whose width at the mantle tree is 4 feet, and height of the mantle tree from the floor 8 feet. It is also required to determine the greatest conical pole that can be put up the said chimney, the slant side of the cone being to the diameter of its base as 4 to 1?

Anmered.

Let Fi represent the floor, and Adem the chimney; then put

$C = d$, $Ed - b$, $Di =: c$; $Lb - x$. Now, ... dd Ml AA. per similar triangles, $x: d:: d: = $ Au; and $d : -:: 6: - =$ Ad. After the same $x \times d$ manner of reasoning we shall find Ac $= 272$ fluxions, &c. the following equation will come out, viz. $x1\ 4\ x + = c - i$ brought into numbers and reduced, gives $x - 4488$ inches, and Gc $- 16848$ inches $- 14$ feet 0 inches, 48, the length of the conical pole required.

Remark. It is true the process above will bring out the longest pole which can be put quite into or up the chimney, but some of the expressions used in it are very improper: thus the expression for cat in the former case, and Cg in the latter, is not a maximum, but a minimum; for it has no maximum but infinity; and the thing to be found, though it be the longest pole that can be put quite up the chimney, is the minimum of Ch or Cg, that is the shortest pole which can rest with one end on Fi, the other on AT, and its side touch one point E: for it is evident that whatever way this line be moved from this narrowest or shortest position, its side will fall below the point E, and so it may be put up the chimney; but a longer cannot be put into the said shortest position, and therefore not up the chimney.

The former1 part of the process, for determining the length of the cylinder, when considered of no thickness, may be brought out by a simple cubic equation thus:

Put Ad $- z$; also De $=: 6$, and Di $=: c$, as above. Then Ai:= $c + z$ and $z : b :: c + z: S\ 6\ zz$ If; hence $-t(bb+zz)\ z\ z - Af$, which must be a minimum. This put into fluxions, &c. we get $z' - 62t0;$ hence $z\ zzl/Vczz$ Ad. And therefore the length of the rod or line Af in this case is-+ 99)» where $q\ r: 5 / C$ Questions proposed in 1733, *and anszcered in* 1734.

'i. Question 169, *by Mr.* Will. Grimmett,

In a certain dictionary, under the word *Conoid,* it is said the solidity of an hyperbolic conoid is to its circumscribing cylinder as 3 to 10; and in ah appendix of fluxions the same is also asserted; which is certainly false. Be pleased therefore to investigate the expression that does expound their ratio; and when you are in this VOL. i. p way of thinking, suppose the generating hyperbola to become the plane of a west declining dial, in the latitude of 50 north, and the focus to be the centre of the same, in which, if you erect a wire perpendicular to the plane, the sun on its first shining on the plane, the 12th of May, will cast the shadow of the wire, so erected, exactly on the hour line of 8. Quere, the declination of the plane?

Answered.

Let the abscissa of the hyperbola be x, the ordinate $- y$, the parameter $= b$, and the transverse $- a;$ then the nature of the curve will be expressed by $yy = bx + -;$ then by the doctrine of fluxions $Sff\ \_l.\ Pxrv$ eXpres8 the solidity of a conoid whose $4r\ 6ru$ altitude is $- x$, and the radius of its base $= y$: And the solidity of i ii $pbxx\ pbxxx$ „ its circumscribing cylinder will be expressed by $+ j$ gm: t-onf sequently their ratio will He expressed by $fa + x\ to\ 3a + 3x$, which is agreeable to that deduced from the method of indivisibles.

If we consider such a one whose altitude is equal to the transverse axis of the generating hyperbola; the ratio will be expounded by that of 5 to 12.

When the sun is in the plane of any dial, the shadow of the style, and that of a wire erected perpendicular to the plane in the centre of that dial, will be coincident.

Demonstration. Let Abcd represent the plane of a dial coincident with the plane of the paper; then the point E will be the perpendicular wire, Ef the hour line of 12, Eh the style, Eg the substyle; ss a parallel the sun describes, which will here become an ellipsis. Now the sun in some point of the orbit will be in the plane of the dial, suppose at s or s; then its plane by the line drawn from the sun through the centre of the dial will give the shadow of the style on the plane, as Sp or Sp; for a line drawn from the sun through any other point of the style more remote from the plane will not fall on the plane. Again the shadow of a wire erected perpendicular on a plane, when the sun is in that plane will be coincident with a line drawn from the sun through the intersection of the wire with that plane (which is here said to be the centre of that dial) consequently when the sun is in the plane, the shadow of a style (however inclined) and the shadow of the wire erected perpendicular in the centre will be coincident, *Q. E. D.* Therefore from the latitude of 50 N. the declination on the 12th of May and hour of 8, the azimuth will be found 99 48' from the north, which is the declination of the plane from the point.

4

Ii. Question 170, *by Mr.* Sam. Ashby.

If upon each leg Ab and Bc, including the right angle, be drawn a square Bd and Be; and the lines nc and EAj which cut the said legs at F and G. I say, Bf and Bg are equal, and are each a mean proportional between the segments Af and Cg; that is, as Af: Fb:: Fb: Cg, &c. Quere, the demonstration geometrically?

Answered by Mr. Rob. Fearnside.

It is plain, by similar triangles, that Cb + Ab: Ab:: Bc: Fb. Again Cb + Ab: Bc:: Ab: Cb. Pcrmutando Cb + Ab:: Bc: Gb. Ergo Fb — GB.

For the other part of the demonstration; by similar triangles Ab (z= Ad): Af:: Bc: Bf; and Ab: Bg:: Bc (:= Ce): Cg. Therefore, *exequo* Af: Bg:: Bf: cc. *Q. E. D. A Grubean Lady's answer to the same.*

The triangles Ape and Abg, being similar, it is Ap: Pe:: Ab: Bg, (by Euclid 4. VI.); that is Ab + Bc:Bc:: Ab:Bg, because all the sides of a square are equal. In like manner the triangles Cqd and Cbf, being similar, it is Qc: Cb:: Dq: Fb; *t. e.* Ab + Bc: Bc:: Ab: Fb. Therefore Fb is — Bg. Again, the triangles Daf and Fbc, and the triangles Abg and Ecg are similar; therefore (da or) Ab: Bc:: Af: Fb; and Ab: Bc (=: Ce):: Bg: Gc.

Whence Af: TB:: Bg (or Bf): Gc (by Euc 11. V.) *Q. E. D.* in. Question 171, *by Mr.* Geo. Brown.

Three ships departed from a certain port in latitude 51 N. The first sailed S. E. 33-8, the second S.S.E. 49, and the third S.S.W. 355 leagues, then each vessel changed her course, and after sailing an equal distance they all met again. Required the second course and distance of each of the ships, with the latitude of the place arrived at. Required also the course and distance from the port first cailed from?

Answered by Mr. J. Turner.

This is altogether solved by trigonometry For, first, in the triangles Bas, Cas, there is given two sides and a contained angle, to find Bs, and the Zbsa, and cs and the Z Csa; add these two angles together, and then you have in the Absc two sides and a contained angle, to find Bc: Now in the A B«c, the angle at *n* is double the Zbsc, and being isosceles, it is easy to find B« — era — Sn — 19-44 leagues, each ship's 2d distance run, from B, S, c, to meet atra. Again, in the Aabc, find the Zs Abc and Acb, to which add the Zs Cb?i, Bcra, we find that the 2d course of the first ship steered

S.S. W. from B to *n* is E. by N. 5 26' easterly, 2nd ship S.E. c to *n* is W.S.W. 1 37 westerly, 3rd ship S.S.E, s to *n* is N.W. 3 12 northerly.

Lastly, in the A BAra, there is given Ba, Bn, and the angle contained; to find Ara — 314 leagues, the distance from the port A to where they all meet: And by the Zbak found, the course from A to *n* is S. by E. 34' southerly. The difference of latitude of the ships when at «, 30'7 leagues.

iv; Question 172, *by Mr.* Chr. Hale.

Let the rectangle of two right lines be 2332800 square inches; then the length of a third right line, which together with the other two shall include the greatest area possible, will be equal to the height of All Saints Steeple, Derby: Required the steeple's height?

Answered.

I have received a great many answers to this question, but they generally agree that it is unlimited, or else they do not rightly understand the proposer's meaning; but if that product be broke into two equal lines, making the legs of a right-angled triangle, the hypothenuse will be 180 feet. I shall here give you the proposer's own solution.

Put dd = 2332800, and a ss Ac. $a : d + d :: d — d : 0st$

In fluxions, $Sddaa — 4a'a = 0$: Reduced gives « = 2160 inches. The exact height of All Saints tower 60 yards.

Additional Solution.

Since the product of any two sides of a triangle drawn into the sine of their included angle produces double the area; therefore when the product of the sides is given, the area will be as the sine of the angle; but the right angle has the greatest sine, therefore the triangle is right-angled when a maximum. And then into whatever two parts the given product is broken, the area will be still the same; but then the hypothenuse will vary, and is shortest when the triangle is isosceles, in which case it is jfc *Jl* $2332800 — 2160$ inches =: 60 yards, H.

v. Question 173, *by Mr.* John Turner.

Two ships sail from a certain port to two other ports in the same latitude, *viz.* 35 34' N. The first ship sails between the south and east, and the other between the south and west, the ratio of the distances run are as 12 to 5, and the angle formed by the two courses 112 29'; the departure of the ship which went to the westward is 2297 miles. Required the latitude of the port sailed from and the course and distance run by each ship?

Though this question may be solved by a simple quadratic equation, yet I always prefer conciseness iii mathematics, and send you the geometric construction, and trigonometric calculation, which are vastly easier than the algebraic operation.

Construction. Assume any two lines as As, At, in the ratio of 12 to 5, and let them contain the given angle *sAt,* produce the line:: indefinitely, and let fall Av perpendicular to *st,* and at the distance of 230 draw a parallel to Av, as Vp, and from where it cuts At produced as at D, draw Dc parallel to *ts,* and where it meets As produced will form the triangle required. *Solution. As, At,* being assume;! any numbers.in the ratio of 12 to 5, and the angle contained given: Find *st,* and thence *vt* and *Va.* And then it will be as'si: Da:: Cd: Ca, from whence all the rest are easily known. *Miles.*

The course of one ship isS. 71 38' westerly, dist. run 8437 the otherS. 40 52 easterly, 351-5

Latitude of the port sailed from 40 north. Difference of latitude 266 miles.

vi. Question 174, *by Mr.* Richard Lovatt.

Having given the lengths of three right lines, 3000, 2000, and i 500, to find the length of a fourth right line, which together with the three former shall include the greatest possible area.' *Solution.*

The original solution given in the Diary being erroneous, as well as another afterwards substituted in its stead, it will be proper to give one that is correct, or rather instead of the original problem, let it be E/i required *to inclose the greatest possible space by any proposed number of straight lines all H which except one arc given in magnitude. Q Ji*

Let Adbc be the maximum figure, of which the sides Ad, Db, Bc, are given in magnitude and let Ac be the side to be determined. From the ends of Ac draw lines to B, any angle of the figure; then as the triangle ABC may vary without changing the magnitude of the remainder of the figure, *viz.* by the part Bda revolving on B as a centre, while the lines Ba, Bc retain the same magnitude, it is evident that the figure can only be a maximum when the triangle is a maximum, which will be the case when Cba is a right angle. Hence it follows that when the figure is a maximum lines drawn from A and c to each of its angles *must contain* right angles, therefore whatever be the number of ks sides *it Kill always*

The Prize Question, *by Mr.* Fearnside.

There is a meadow in the form of a right-angled triangle, the base is 95-23 chains, but the other two sides being overflowed with water cannot be measured, however it was observed that a ditch which ended at the acute angle at the base, and crossed the meadow, made

with the hypothenuse an angle of 15; there is also a tree growing exactly in the middle of that part of the perpendicular intercepted between the ditch and the right angle, and it is known that a right line from the tree to the acute angle at the base divides that angle into two equal parts. Required the other leg or perpendicular of the triangle?
Anszcered.
Given Bc = 95-23 chains —*b,* sine abdss 15 = s, ∠ Abe = Ebc, and De = Ec. Put x = s. ∠ Ebc; then.
/(1 — xx):b :: x : Ce = ;hence $Y(1 - xx)$ £bx
——— = Dc. Then, per Euc. 47. I. Bd = b √(1 — xx) j.,. Again the cosine of double the
∠ Ebc = sine of the ∠ A will be found to be = bs 1— %3? 3« + 1 t. Then by 3d prop. 6 Euclid, Bc:Ba:: Ec: Ae; which analytically expressed, and the equation ordered becomes 48 — 3sV — ss—0. Reduced, the sine of the ∠ Ebc will be found to be that of 34 27' 47", and Ca = 247-13; consequently the area of the meadow will be = 1176-709 acres.

Questions proposed in 1734, *and answered in* 1735. r. Question 175, *by Mr.* Rob. Fearnside. A lady of wit, youth, and beauty beside,
Remote from all cares, but of being a bride,
Surpriz'd her fond lover one morning in May,
And dispatch'd him for parson and licence away.
But how great her confusion, when Strephon brought news
That the parson a licence to grant did refuse!
Her age, which the lady nor lover cou'd tell,
Was the cause that this fatal disaster befel.
Therefore, ladies, their humble request is, you'll show
The way how to do't from the data below.
And this by a general method explain,
So that lovers may never be non-plus'd again.
Cycle of ☉ 18, golden number 8, Roman indiction 10, that year the lady was bom. *Answered by Mr.* Richard Dunthorne.

The solution to this question is in Keil's Astronomy, lect. 29, p. 379 and 380, by finding three numbers 285a;, 420y, and 532s; so that the first divided by 28 leaves the cycle of the sun a remainder, the second by 19 leaves the golden number, the third by 15 leaves the indiction. Then if the sum of these numbers be divided by 7980, the remainder will be the year of the Julian period required. Or,
The cycle 0 18 mult, by 4845 = 87210 J The sum
Goldennumb. 8 4200 = 33600 I J
Indiction 10 6916 = 69160 3
Which divided by 7980, there remains 6430, the Julian period; from which subtract 4713, the Julian period at our Saviour's birth, remains 1717, the year required in answer to the question.
Answered by Mr. John Ommanney.
Dr. Keil in his Astron. Lectures, p. 380, says, if 4845 be multiplied by the cycle of the sun, and 4200 by the golden number, and 6916 by the Roman indiction, and the sum of their products divided by 7980, the remainder (neglecting the quotient) will be the year of the Julian period; from which subtract 4713, there will remain the year of the christian sera. And in thin question/ the answer 1717, as above.
Additional Solution.
The solar cycle is a period of 28 years, the lunar of 19, and the indiction a period of 15. The year before the christian aera was the 9th of the solar cycle, the 1st of the lunar, and the 3d of the indiction cycle. Wherefore 9, 1, and 3 being severally added to any year x of Christ, and the sums divided respectively by 28, 19, and 15, the remainders will shew the several years of the cycles for that year. But, in the present case proposed, the remainders are 18, 8, and 10; $x+9$ — 18 $x+l$—8-$X+3$ —10 t..
hence then —, ———, and — must be in 28' 19' 15 tegers; or———, ?and —— integers. Put the first of C g these equal to the integer m that is — $m;$ then x — 28jw + 9 a value of x answering the first condition. Write this in the 2d, 28m + 9 — 7 28m + 2, 9m + 2 then — or — = m fg— = an Integcr; 9m + 2 18m + 4 m—4 therefore —— or — — — m — an integer; tfi — 4 therefore ——— — n an integer; hence m — 9n + 4; which substituted in the value of.r, we have x — X (19re + 4) + 9 532ra+ 121 a value of x answering the two first conditions. This value of 532« + 121 — 7 x being written in the 3d original integer, we have — 532n + 114 Qr, „, 7n + 9... 7»i+9 or — = 35m + 7 + —— — = an integer; hence 15 15 15 14n + 18„ n — 3.. ... n — 3 — n + 1 -r— — an integer; therefore 15 ' 15 — ' 15 = p an integer; consequently n— 15p + 3; this written in the last value of x, it becomes x — 532 X (15p + 3) + 121 = 7980p + 1717 a general expression for the year answering all the three conditions, in which p may be either nothing or any whole number. In the present case it is evident that the value $o(p$ must be nothing, and then$x$ = 1717, the year of the lady's birth.
It is evident that such a combination cannot happen again till the year 9697 = 7980 + 1717, when the value of p is 1; and that the successive years of its happening are found by the continual addition of 7980. H.

H., Question 176, *by Mr.* John Gundy.
Whilst I was surveying for his Grace the Duke of Bucclcugh, it was my chance to meet with a piece of land in the form of a rectangle, or long square; and the proportions were such, that if it had been two perches broader, and three longer, it would hare been sixty-four perches larger than before. But, on the contrary, if it had been three perches broader, and two longer, it would then be sixty-eight perches larger than it was by my survey. Quere, what was tie area of the said piece of land?
Answered by Eumencs Pamphilus.
Let x — length, z = breadth. Then per quest. xs + 3z + 1x + 6 = xz + 6 4, and xz + 1z + 3x + 6 = xz 4-68. Their difference is x — z = 4, hence x — 4 = s; which being substituted for r, there comes out, by the 1st equation, xx + if — 6 = xx — 4x + 64, or bx = 70. Hence x = TM = 14 perches the length, and X = x — 4 ss 10 perches the breadth, also xz = 140 perches, or 3 roods 20 perches the

content.

Mr. *Turner's* answer is in substance the same.

in. Question 177, *by Mr.* John Turner. Required the greatest cylinder that can be inscribed in a frustum of a cone whose dimensions are as follows: the diameter of the greater end 44 Inches, that of the less end 20, and the length 30 inches. Also suppose the frustum to be cut by a plane, parallel to the axis, through the extremity of the less end. What is the content of each of the parts so formed?

Ansicered by the Proposer.
In order to find the height of the whole cone *m*. Put *sm* s *x*, the solidity of the cylinder = *bbxx — Ibbpx + bbpp*,. ",. *i — X dx;* in fluxions, *PP* it is *Sdbbxxx — Adbbpxi + dbbppi —* 0. Divide all by *dbbx,* and *3xx — 4px + pp* = 0; Ergo *x = p* = 18-3333 inches, the cylinder's height; and the diameter of its base 29-3333. Again, from *kg —* 12, and *Tg —* 32, being given, *gv — ge* is found r (y'W x 32) 19-6 inches, and *ve —* 39-2: the area of the segment *Aev* (by page 404 of "Ward, or much easier by a table of segments) is found to be 335-88 square inches. Which multiplied by ura — 18-333, gives the solidity of the pyramid Ase»A — 6157-8 cubic inches.

Now the base of the pyramid coeBC is an hyperbola, whose area is thus found: *ng* = 10 is the hyperbola's conjugate semi-diameter — *b, ve —* 39-2 — *g* its bounding ordinate, eg — 30 the abscissa, Cq the transverse semi-diameter — 25, *Qg — p —* 55, Ap — *d* = 44. The *fl* _1_ *IT* hyperbolic logarithm of or 4-16 is 1-4255142 — s. I say the *pg tiiT)bbs* area of the hyperbola is — *i— —* 721-62 square inches, which is a contraction of Dr. Wallis's quadrature of the hyperbola, p. 328, of his Algebra. This multiplied by *ng,* the perpendicular altitude of the pyramid, or 3-333, gives 2405-40 its solidity. Subtract this pyramid creisc from the pyramid ABetiA, the remainder is the content of the ungula or cuneus ArecA — 3752-4 cubic inches, which was required. And lastly, if you subtract this from the content of the conic frustum Acdp, which is easily found — 25258-4(5, the remainder is the solidity of the other part or ungula *pevce —* 21506-06 inches.

Answered by Mr. Geo. Brown.
Who projects the scheme, and all its parts exactly the same as above,"and carries the process through the whole, from whence I shall only collect such parts as are essential to the answer. The area of the segment *Aev* = 335-915 square inches, The solidity of the inclined pyr. *ABg*= 615S-45 cubic inches,

The area of the hyperbola = 721-45,
Solidity of the inclined pyramid *cng* — 240495,
Which taken from *Acg,*
Leaves the solidify of the hoof Ac»e = 3753-49 = 2-1721 feet.
Which taken from the given frustum of the cone 14-6171,
Leaves the content of the part PDcrep = 12-445.
The height of the greatest cylinder *wn* = 18-333
And its base's diameter 29-333 r Ill-cl" s iv. Question 178, *by Mr.* Chr. Mason.

What is the solid content of a piece of timber bounded by four equal planes, each of which is an isosceles triangle, the longest side 5 and the shortest 3 feet *I Answered by* Juvenis Malhcmaticus.

This body seems to agree with Euclid's definition of a pyramid Per 47 Euc. I. cc — *bb —* £(4cc— *bb)* = to the perpendicular of one of the isosceles triangles; and if the body be conceived to be divided into two equal parts by a triangular plane, two sides of which are the perpendiculars above, and the 3d = *b* = 3. Then by the 14th prop, of Keil's Plain Trigonometry, *(4cc— bb)* : %/(4cc—*bb)* + *b* :: /(4cc — *bb) — b:* the difference of the segments of the base. The rectangle of the means divided by the first extreme = /(4cc — *bb) — bb* -r-%i/(4cc— *bb)* = the difference of the segments. Hence then %/(4cc—*bb)* —-*bb* /(4cc — *bb) —* the greater segment, and *bb* -J-/(4cc—*bb)* — the less segment; also *lib — b4* (4cc — *bb)* = the square of the perpendicular height of / 4cc — *bb* this triangle. But *b y —* = area of one of the isosceles triangles or base of the solid body. Wherefore /(bb — *Trj tCC DO I / 4cc — bb*

X by -= 6-791536716428 cubic feet, the solid content required.
The same answered by Mr. Ed. Golding. *A general Rule to find the Solidity.* From the square of one of the legs, abate the square of half the base; and multiply the square root of the remainder by the square of the base: The last product divide by 6, and the quotient shall be the content of the proposed solid. *For the perpendicular Height.* The square of the side or leg 5 = 25; subtract twice the square of half the base 1'5 — 45; there remains 20-51 whose.square root 4-5277 is the perpendicular height. *For the Solidity.* Multiply the square of the base 3=9, by the perpendicular 4-5777, and the product 40-7493 is the solidity of the circumscribing prism. As 6: 1:: 40-7493: 6-79155 the solid feet in the alabrum, by which name I call this solid till a fitter name be imposed. And to prove it but J of the prism. Suppose the first figure, being a square prism, be 3 feet square at the ends, and 6 feet high, the content will be 54. Cut off from the prism (I.) the two prismatic wedges *a* and *b;* which both together contain 9 upon 3 — 27 feet; leaving the wedge c, which suppose to be the second figure; from it cut off the two pyramids e and *f,* which both together contain 9 upon 2 — 18. Leaving the alabrum only behind: The two wedges 27, and two pyramids — 18, make 45, which taken from 54, remains the alabrum 9 *i of* the prism. Q. E. D. *The same answered by Mr.* J. Bulman.

From the square of the given side of the isosceles triangle — 25j subtract the square of half the given base 2-25, the remainder 22-75 is the square of the perpendicular to the triangle: from which subtract again the square of half the base, the square root of the remainder 4-527692 =: the length of the circumscribing square prism: whose solidity is 40-749228 feet, £ of which is 6-791538 feet, the solidity of the body required.

This solid may easily be cut from a prism having square bases. Or if a piece of stiff paper or pasteboard be cut according to the following figure, and folded in the lines *ab, be,* and *ca,* so as *cf* and *ce* coincide or make but one line, and *g* touches the joined points *e* and /, it will perfectly represent the body proposed in the question.

v. Question 179, *by Mr.* J. Bulman.

At a certain place in northern latitude, the sun was observed to rise exactly at 3" 58TM and at 6 o'clock his altitude was taken the same morning, and found to be 15 deg. 20 min. his declination being then north. Required the latitude of the place where, and day of the year when, those observations were made?

$V(1-ss) ''/(ss-aa)' '8/(ss-aa)$

Reduced, it is $s - aass + aa - ss + ff - 0$: hence $s - .835728$ *ad* — the sine lat. = 56 41' 32". And the decimation = 18 26' 45", answering to May 2, or Aug. 4.

Additional Solution. liet *x* and *y* — sine and cosine of the latitude, *v* and 2 — sine and cosine of the declination, *s* — sine of the altitude at 6; and *a* — sine of the ascensional difference. Then per spherics rad.: :::-: a, and rad.:*v* :: S *t if »* .-. *vx — azy* and r.r — *s*, and.. *azy s* or *zy — s a*.

Therefore by addition and subtraction *zy + vx* the cosine of the difference of the latitude and declination, and *zy — vx* the cosine of the sum of the latitude and declination are known, and consequently the sum and difference of the latitude and declination are known. Half the sum is the latitude and half the difference is the declination. *i»*

vi. Question 180, *by Mr.* John Gundy.

A gentleman, who was a great lover of the mathematics, had a large estate, which lay in four several entire manors, of which he had drawn four several maps. Now he, by his often looking over the contents of these maps, found the quantities of acres belonging to each of these, would make four numbers in continued proportion; whereof the sum of the two middlemost numbers is 1152, and that of the two extremes 1728. He lying on his death-bed, called his four sons to him, saying, My dear children, my glass being almost run, and the estate I have to leave amongst you was for the most part gained by my own industry, and so entirely at my own disposal, I shall leave it amongst you with this proviso, that he that answers the abovesaid question first, shall have the largest manor for his share; and so the rest of you the others, according to your birthright. It is demanded the quantity of acres that each manor does Contain.?

Jtnsrsered by Mr. Bcachatn.

This question is composed out of Sir Isaac Newton's Arith. or Ronayne's Algebra. The first share is 1536, the second 768, the third 384, and the fourth 102 acres.

First Solution.

Let *v, x, y,* and denote the numbers sought, and put *a — 1728* and *b — 1152*. Then by the question, *v + z = a, x + y = b,* and by the nature of continued proportion *v : x:: x:y,* or *vy — xx* and *x: y :: y: z,* or *xz — zz.*

Batz — a—v and 3/ *— b — x;* therefore *v(b—x) — xx* and *x(a — v) — (b — x).*

xx (ix (I)

Therefore *v —*, *v —*: 6 — x x' and therefore »3 — *ax(b — x) — (i — x) b*

Reduced xs — *bx zz — r——*.

3o + *a*

Hence $x = \pm /= 576(1 \pm 4)-768$ or 384. And the four shares are 1536, 768, 384, and 192 acres, i.

Second Solution.

Let the numbers sought be denoted by *x, rx,* r'ar, and *r'x,* which numbers are evidently in continued proportion, and put *a — 1728* and *p =: 1152*: then by the question *x (1 + r3) = a* and *x(r + rs) r = b.* Multiply the second equation by *r* and subtract the product from the first, and there results x(r2—1) — *br—a;* but from the second equation x = ———„, therefore by substitution fr2 — 1) — 1 *r + r' r + r v J br — a,* or £ (r — 1) i *br — a:* whence ir' — (a + *b)rz=. — b,* j»nd by completing the square, &c.

The. Prize Question, *by Mr.* Mason.

A gentleman wants a garden of ten acres, of an oblong form, to embellish the front of his house. In the middle there is to be an elliptical fountain, 3 feet deep and 20 rods in area: the principal axes of the ellipse to have the same proportion as the length and breadth of the garden, and the transverse axis to be parallel to the longest side. The garden is also to be surrounded on three sides by a canal, the breadtli and depth of which are to have the ratio of 7 to 1; the earth from the canal together with that from the fountain, to be spread over the garden and to raise it a foot. The nearest distance from the edge of the fountain to the edge of the canal to be 238 feet. Required the dimensions of (he garden, fountain, and canal?

Questions proposed in 1735, *and answered in* 1736. 1. Question 181, *by Mr.* John Turner.

In the triangle Abc there is given the side Ab = 65 feet, and the side Bc = 74; and in this triangle there is an equilateral triangle inscribed as Swh, whose side Sh is parallel to the base Ac: And lastly, in the equilateral triangle there is a circle inscribed, whose area is known to be:r 3079 square feet. It is required to find the side of the equilateral, and the base of the external triangle?

Ii. Question 182, *by Mr.* Chr. Mason.

A surveyor measured a field in the form of a trapezium, the longest side was 25 chains. The two angles subtended by the given side at the extremities of the opposite side were 118 and 108; and the perpendiculars from the said angles to the given side were 9 and 7 chains respectively. Required the three unknown sides of the trapezium?

Answered by the Proposer Mr. Mason.

The obtuse angles given arc *adb* — 108 and *aob* — 118; the perpendiculars *pd* 9 chains, and *eo* 7 chains; and the base *ab* — 25 chains. Required *bd, do,* and *oa;* the other three sides of the trapezium? Which will be found trigonometrically, viz. *ad* — 16-61; *db* =. 14-23; *bo* = 17-71; *ao*= 11-15; *do* = 5-76.

Additional Solution.

In this question are concerned two triangles *aob, adb,* on the same given base, and whose perpendiculars and vertical angles are also given; to find their sides and the distance of their vertexes.

Construction. On the given base describe two segments of circlet capable of containing the given vertical angles; then at distances equal to the two perpendiculars draw two parallels to the base, and they will cut the respective circles in the required vertexes *o* and *d* of the two triangles. As is too evident to need a demonstration. *Calculation.* Let c be the centre of the circle passing through one of the vertexes; and Cab perpendicular and Ob parallel to *ab*, and the other lines as per figure. Then Ac6 = 62 = the supplement of the given Z. *aob*, and Aco is — the difference of the Zs *(pab, oba)* at the base. But s. Zac6:: cos. Zac6:: *sb(ab)* : Ac; hence Cb cr Ac + oe; then (since *sb* and Cb are the sines of the Zs Aciand *cob* to the same radius *cb* or co) *b:* Cb:: s. Zac6: s. Zcob r: the complement of the difference of the Z s *oab, oba,* at the base. Hence their sum and difference being known, the angles themselves Then, by the question, *aeu* — *b;* « + w = c; and *au* — *ee*: by the become known; and thence the sides *ao, bo.* In like manner are found the sides arf, *bd.* And thence *od.* H.

Hi. Question 183, *by Mr.* Tho. Fearn.

A General disposing his army into a square battle, finds he has 284 soldiers over-and-above; but increasing each side with one man, he wanted 25 to fill up the square. Quere, the number of soldiers?

Answered by Russellus.

Put *a* =: side of the first square; the overplus (284); and c z: 25 the number wanting to fill up the second square. Then *aa + b — an + la + 1 — c* the number of soldiers per question .". *b —* %a + 1 — c; *b + c —* 1 = 20; and — 1 — *a —* 154; *aa--b —* 24000 — the number of soldiers.

The answer by *Eumenes Pamphilus,* being nearly the same as the above, is omitted.

iv. Question 184, *by* Eumenes Pamphilus.

There are three numbers in continued proportion; the product of the three multiplied into one another is 512, and the sum of the extremes 34. Three-fourths of the greater extreme being called years, and the other fourth weeks, will exactly shew my age; the mean, the month, and the less extreme, the day of the month I was born: Whence you are desired to shew the year, month, and day on which I was brought to light? Sep. 27, 1733.

Answered by Mr. Ed. Golding.

The three numbers in continual proportion are 2, 8, 32; for 2 X 8 X 32 = 512, and 2 + 32 = 34; which exactly agrees with the proposal: three-fourths of the greater extreme is 24 for years; and one-fourth is 8 weeks; so he was 24 years 8 weeks old; and he was born August 2, 1709.

The same answered by Mr. John Turner. first *au* — (in the 3d step) — *ee;* hence *ece — b;* and *e —jb* — 8 the mean. And from hence *u* is found — 32, and *a =z 1;* so he was 24 years and 8 weeks old.

Mr. *Mason's* answer is omitted, being nearly the same as Mr. *Turner's.* v. Question 185, *by Mr.* Rob. Fearnside.

To determine the greatest area included by the curve of a parabola, whose equation is *ax1 — J/* and a rectangular double ordinate, the length of the curve being 100 feet?

Answered by Mr. Fearnside *the Proposer.*

Putting the equation *axi — ys* of the curve into fluxions, we haTe *laxx-3yy;* hence *i — L -& V-.* Then the fluxion of the *2,ux* 2 a area = *yxh* whose fluent-V—is the area a maxi 2 a 5 *a* mum. Again, the fluxion of the curve */(x + y5)* will become *y* X whose correct fluent j + -1 X £is = 50 r: c. Then the value of either a or *y* being found from this equation, and written for it in the above area or maximum, the maximum will then contain only one of the letters *a* or *y,* and whose fluxion being made equal to 0, that letter will be determined, and thence all the rest.

vi. Question 186, *by Mr.* Ed. Hauxley.

The use of a meridian line in astronomy, geography, dialling, &C is very great, and on its exactness all depends: whence infinite pains have been taken by divers astronomers to have it to the last precision. M. Cassini has distinguished himself by "a meridian line drawn on a copper-plate on the pavement of the church of St. Petronia, at Bologna in Italy, the largest and most accurate in the world. In the arched roof of the church, at a great height above the pavement, is a little hole, through which the sun's image when in the meridian, falling upon the line marks his progress all the year. When finished, Mr. Cassini, in a public writing, informed the mathematicians of Europe of a new oracle of Apollo, or the sun, established in a tem pic-, which might be consulted-with entire confidence as to all difficulties in astronomy.

Bologna, by some tables, lies in the latitude of 44 8' north; and Dr. Burnet, late bishop of Salisbury, in his letters many years ago, has given us an account of this meridian line, from whencs the height of the hole in a perpendicular above the pavement, and the length of that copper meridian from that perpendicular, under the said hole, to its utmost extent,-where the sun's image marks the tropic of Capricorn, in one sum makes 285 feet 10 inches. From hence the height of the hole, or nodus above the floor, and the length of the meridian line, and the distances of the tropics from the equinoxes may be severally known,-and are here required?

Answered by Mr. E. Golding.

There is given Ab + Bc =. 285 feet 10 inches; required Ab, Bc, Be, and Bd. I here use 23 307 for the greatest declination: then 90 — 44 8' 45 52" the elevation of the equinoctial; and the tropics and equinoctial will have the same angles in respect to each,/ other. Of all which Bd, Be, Bc are tan-*g B _D 12* gents to the radius Ab. Produce the line Cb till Bd = Ba; then, per question, *cd* = 285 feet 10 inches = 3430 inches. Then the angle *dAB* = angle *d* = 45, and (cab =) 68 31' + 45 = 113 31' = *cAd.*

As s. *cAd : cd::* s. *d* : Ca — 264924 inches.

Rad.: Ac:: s. Cab: Cb = 2453-95 = 204 feet 5 inch. 95 par.

Rad.: Ac:: s. Acb: Ab = 976 05 = 81 feet 4 inch. 05 par.

And proceeding in the same manner we shall find

Inches Feet Inch. Parts.
»d = 380-7423 = 31 8 7423 sB & De 588-8556 = 49 0 8556 T Vf Eb 1484-3521 = 123 8 3521

The sum = Bc = 2453-95 = 204 5 95
To which add Ab = 976-05 = 81 4 05
Total 3430-Be 285 10 0 *N. B.* No notice is taken of the distance pf Bologna's longitude in time from the 0's entering the first scruple of the equa-

tor or tropics, nor of the ☉'s refraction, in the answer to this question, as being too curious.

Additional Solution.

The above calculation of this question is hot very accurate with regard to the angles; however any one may easily make it as accurate as he pleases by the same method, or rather by this following.

In the above figure, we have given all the angles formed at the point A, and the sum of the legs Ab, Bc; to find the rest. For A represents the hole, Bc the meridian, Ab the perpendicular on it, Ae a ray from the sun in the equinoctial, and Ad, Ac rays from him when in the two tropics: therefore the Z Bae = the lat.=44 8'; to and from which adding and subtracting the declination (23 = Z Eac = Zead, the sum (67 37') will be the Zbac, and the difference (20 390 the Zbad.

But, by plain trigonometry, 1 (rad.): t (tang. Zbac):: Ab: Bc i 1: Ab, then, by composition, &c. 1 + t : Ab + Bc:: l (tang. Zbae: Be, Which being known, then J.: Ab:: J

£ tang. Zbad: Bd. H.

The Prize Question, *communicated by Mr. Samuel Ashby, in a Letter to* Tho. Grubbian.

If in any plain triangle, as Abc, you draw lines from each angle through any point E (o) within the triangle, till they cut the opposite sides, as Ca, Ab, and Bc. The rectangles of the alternate segments at those sides will be equal.

viz. Aj x cs x Bc=4c x Ob x *ax,*

The demonstration of this curious proposition is required?

Answered by Mr. C. Mason.

Per 31 Eucl. I. draw lines parallel to the given sides through o the given point, as *dg, eh, fi.* Then, per 2 Eucl. VI. will be the following proportions, *viz.* do: og:: Ab: bc; and io: of :: Ac; Cb; also eo: oh:: Ba : ac; from which will proceed the following compound proportions, *viz.* do X io X Eo: og X *of* X oh :: Ab X Ac x Bs: ic X t'B X ac; and, per 4 Eucl. VI. *ho : eo :: to:de*; and *og: od :: of: de; eo* X to *do* X *of* ,.,

§ —Ao— = —oTM—— which, reduced, gives Jo X *fo* X *ho* = eo x *io* X *go*; permt.

alteina. & comp. ergo Ac X Ba X *bc* =

Cb X *ac* X *bx*. Q. E. D. a.

Mr. J. Turner's answer is omitted, as being nearly the same.

The letter o is omitted at the point of intersection.

Questions proposed in 1736, *and anszsercd in* 1737.

1. Question 187, *by Mr.* Tho. Simpson.

 By reading your di'ry a croud of strange notions
Crept into my head, of your rules, laws, and motions;
Your extravagant fancies my senses confound;
Can the unwieldy-earth at the sun caper round?
But you say, she's an atom, each star a huge sun,
And attendant worlds with their moons round 'em run.
Such a tott'ring strange whirligig you've set's upon,
We wonder ere now we're not shak'd off and gone:
If what eyes ne'er saw you so soon can disclose,
Then pray solve this question; The earth, we'll suppose,
Round her axis in thirty-eight minutes to roll;
Shou'd we, who're degrees thirty-eight from the pole,
Be hurl'd thro' the air; where should we descend?
How long wou'd it be ere our circuit did end?
How far from the centre in six hours time
Wou'd they be, who live in the midst o'th' hot clime?
 Kind artist, be pleas'd these things to let's know?
We'd rather believe you, than e'er find them so.
The equator. N. B. We suppose the earth sole actor, and to continue inviolate, and that we shall acquire the same velocity as the place of our residence. 52 deg. lat.

Answered by Mr. J. Turner.

The circumference of the earth being 25080 miles, at the equator, if it revokes round its axis in 38 minutes, each point of tho equator will go through 11 miles each second, with this velocity the body is projected from P. Let Sp =: 1: then the velocity of a body moving in a circle vq, at the distance of one semi-diameter from the.earth's centre, is such, as would make it go 4-92 miles each second uniformly; and according to Mr. Abr. de Moivre, in Philos. Transact. Abridged, p. 5. vol. 4.

Putting a — 11, Q — 4-92; Rr —2w: Rr:: Sp:Pf. *i. e.* 72-6: 121:: 1: 1-666, and the point F will be the other focus; and because Fc — ps — 1, therefore Cp-666 the transverse axis of the section, which is an hyperbola. (jo.: Rr:: 2sp: Lr; that is, 242: 121:: 2: 10; hence the latus-rectum of the hyperbola is 10 semi-diameters of the earth.

Again, each point in the parallel of 52 degrees goes through 6'773 miles each second, put this — R; 2«q — Rr: Rr:: Sp: *vj;* that is, 2-53: 45-87:: 1: 18-13, and the point / will be the other focus: and because *fc* — Ps — 1, therefore Cp — 19-13, the transverse axis of the section, which in this case is an ellipsis, and Qq,: Rr:: 2sp: *lr* — 3-791 its latus rectum.

Merones says that the body in 6 hours will be 8 of the earth's diameters from the centre. Mr. Lowe says the equator will go 10-9 miles, the parallel of 52, 6-7; and in 6 hours the moving body would be 1486709 miles from the earth's centre. Mr. Abr. Lord 246321, Mr. Geo. Brown 204660, and Mr, Hauxlcy 400589 miles. I have not the ingenious author's olution by me, to the intricate and difficult question, so shall say no more of it till I can procure it,

Additional Solution,

The above computations of Mr. Turner's are rightly made as far as they are carried, but he has left some part of the question undetermined, which we shall here supply.

The body projected from the latitude of 52 will describe an ellipse whose focus is the centre of the earlh, its transverse axem 19-13 (semi-diameters of the earth), and its parameter 3-791, as determined above. So that the ellipse, no where touching the earth but in the place from whence the body is projected, the body will revolve about the earth without falling upon it again, or touching it except in the place from whence it was projected, supposing the earth's revolution to cease at the instant when the body is projected; buj, if the revolution be contiuncd, the body will touch some other part of the same parallel of latitude, or will return to the vertex of its orbit again wen some other point of the said parallel passes under it in revolv-»jng; and which point will be thus found: Putting $s - 16\text{TV}$ ee p=o'77,3Xo28Q feet velocity in the vertex, and/ =si':z:3992 X 5280, feet; then the periodic time, or time of one revolution, is known to be 3141.6 X —. — 132277 seconds; this being divided by *(lfs — vv)i* 38' or) 2280'', the quotient 58 shews the number of compleat revolutions the earth makes in the same time, and the remainder 37 shews what part of another revolution is made; wherefore as 2280: 37:: 360: 53 50' — the difference of longitude required from the point of projection.

Again, with regard to the body projected from the equator, the path will be anhyperbola whose focus is also the earth's centre, its 2 transverse axe —, and latus-rectum 10, as determined above; and consequently its conjugate axe = $2/j$. Then to find at what distance from the focus it will be in 6 hours — 21600 seconds: Since the body describes equal areas in equal times, and the rate of description being 3999 — ygj square semi-diameters of the earth per second, therefore —-7—— will be the area described in 6 hours, or the area included by the curve, and the focal distances from the vertex and the other end of the curve, viz. the space Spt, and in which ps r 1.

Now if the ordinate Tv be drawn, and Pv be put zz x, the trans $2. / b$ verse Pc - *t,* the conjugate 2 A/ ——— c, and the area Pts — 21600 X 11, $C/(tx + xx)$ ——— — A; am sy = x— 1, Tv = v and the *oc* ——— 1 c / *(fx -sex) fi,* Stv ——— x;consequently the hyperbolic seg *jnent* will be expressed by A + X — ——-But by

Jtule IV. p. 376 Mensuration, the area of the same segment is ex ,. 21 *tf(tx +* 4xx) + *4i/tx* 4c.r *x,* pressed by 1)— X-j—; these two expressions l?eing made equal to each other, and reduced, we have 168 X $X/(tx + \text{f } xx) + 32$ $Xtx = 1$ A + $(x — 1) X 7 o /(x + xx);$ pr, by restoring the values of t and c, it will be 168 $x/(lZx + 2ixx) + 32x\%v = 30a/5 + (—$ 1) X 75(2 + 3xx); and the root x is easily found 3 083 3 rv. Then St Z=. V(ty + vs) = ccx- — + (— 1) J = 4x + 1 = 13 semi-diameters — 53227 miles, the distance required, H.

Ii. Question 188, *by* Eumcnes Pamphilus.

Find the third side of a triangular field, whose area is 138 acres, and tw o of its sides 296 and 201 poles?

Ansicered by the Proposer.

Let x — the side sought, then.will x + 250 half the sum of the sides; each side being subtracted from it, and the three remainders multiplied into it, will give the square of the content, and will produce 16154xx — — 132250000 rz 487526400 poles; which, reduced, gives x 400 poles, the side required.

Mr. Turner's solution is omitted, as being on the same principles.

Additional Solution.

Let the two given sides be a, *b,* and the given area A. Then 2A-j-*ab* — the sine of the included angle, whose cosine call c; then, by trigonometry /(aa + bb— 2abc) or /(aa+ bb—Z/(aubb—4as) s *zz* the side required, H. in. Question 189, *by Mr.* Rob. Beighton.

Solomon, we are assured in Holy Writ, was a man of the most extensive judgment, and the wisest of all mankind in his days. How great a philosopher he was, may be gathered from his writings; and amongst them are some indications that he was acquainted with the circulation of the blood, (not rightly described to us before Dr. Harvey wrote of it in 1628) the composition and frame of the human bodies, as well as others. His skill in architecture is sufficiently evident from the account we have of his building that most magnificent, beautiful, and perfect pile, the temple, and its furniture: but I cannot learn from the Divine writings, or from Josephus's fabulous history, how persons can form an idea in what orders, and in what manner exactly the workmanship was performed, as to give us exact draughts and models thereof: whether of the Corinthian or Ionic orders, with their members and mouldings, such, as we have had transmitted down to us from the Greeks and Romans, and copy at this day. Solomon, no doubt, would have rejoiced to have added to him one blessing which we have enjoyed, the acquaintl ance of (the glory of the age) Sir Isaac Newton, who, we may say, has exceeded all men since Solomon's time. It may, perhaps, be thought a presumption too nice and curious, to examine any of Solomon's great works mathematically: but as nothing is intended, nor can be said to lessen his wisdom or stupendous work, I shall only suppose a question was taken from that description the inspired writer has given us of his Molten Sea, 1 Kings vii. 23. 'And he made a 'Molten Sea ten cubits wide from brim to brim, round in compass, *e* and five cubits high, and a line of thirty cubits did compass it about. ' It is evident it could not be a circle; for then the line that compassed it must have been more than 30 cubits, viz. 31-4159265359. Therefore we may suppose it to be elliptical, (or that the workmen were not very curious in their measures, or not skilled in geometry) and the transverse diameter ten cubits, and its periphery thirty. What then would be the least triangle that could circumscribe, the same? and how analytically to investigate the solution?

jV, *B.* A cubit is equal to 21-888 inches. *Answered bi/ Mr.* Turner.

Let Bo — 10 cubits — *b; x* — the conjugate axis *Da;* the periphery — 30 cubits — *d;* therefore a quadrant Bgd — 7-5.

The gentlemen of the Weekly Oracle have given us a theorem, by which nearly to find the periphery of an ellipsis, viz. To twice the square root of the sum of the squares of the two principal diameters, add one-third of the conjugate diameter, and it will give the circumference within less than one-hundredth part of the whole. Hence 2y'(i6+.rr) + % $x = d;$ the *rootx*= 9-056 cubits = 198-22 inches.

But by fluxions, put Bc = a=:5; *Dc* — c; *b* — 7'5; *x* — *Gn* = Fc: Then, by the property of the ellipsis, Fg *y*—-/(aa— xx),

Jlength of the arch Gd; and supposing x to flow till it becomes $x — a$, Additional Solution.

Put $a — 10$ — transverse, z — conjugate, and $c = 30 = $ cir $+$
4
cumference. Then, by Rule VI. p. 233 Mensuration, $" + x p$

Ob ' *an;* consequently Ha X flK — - dc X Ob X — 118-05 the least triangle Hex required.

The proposer also solved this question, but the solution is omitted as it was so very falsely printed, H.

IV. Question 190, *by Mr.* John Bulman.

There is a cask, supposed the frustum of a parabolic conoid, or a cask of the 2d variety. The bung diameter is 38-4 inches; the head diameters are unequal, the greater 33-5, the lesser 28-8; the length of the cask 54-27. Required the content of the cask in ale gallons, the distance of each head diameter from the bung; it being supposed that there had been a decay in the cask, and cut off, and a new and larger head put in at one end; and to let us know the diameter, length, and content of the greatest cylinder (hat can be inscribed therein, the circumference of each base touching that of the cask around?

The content of j NEOR - *I* ale gallons, or *i* NBCit 5 69-3193 i &' 5137-483?.,.
I 84-623 £ w'neSalIons
The whole content 181-9384 ale gallons, or 222-106 wine gallons. The diameter of the greatest cylinder inscribed Bg — 33-5, length 38-33, and its content 119 8304 ale gallons, or 146-2842 wine gallons.

V. (jtuestion 191, *by Mr.* J. Turner.

There is a stone in the form of a parallelopipedon, whose depth, breadth, and length are in arithmetical progression: the solid content is 5184 feet, and the common difference of the dimensions is l-48th part of the product of the length and depth. Required the dimensions of the stone?

Anszsered by Mr. Duuthome.

Put $x, y,$ and $s = $ the depth, breadth, and length of the stone, $b — 5184$, and $c = 48$: then $— =: xz,$ and $— = — = $ the com y *CU c* mon difference per question.

Whence $y — — — x;$ and$;/ + — cy cy — z;$ consequently $y" = b;$ reduced y— by $— —$. Solved, $cctj cc y = 18;$ whence $x — 12,$ and $z — 24.$

vr. Question 192, *by Mr.* C. Mason.
Find three such cube numbers, whose sum may be both a square and cube number; and if that sum be squared, to be a cube; also if cubed, shall be a square?

AnsKerjd by Mr. J. Hill. *xe 8x6* 125a?6
The three numbers are —, ——, and-; x being any number at pleasure. Hence if $x — 216,$ we haye three whole numbers for the answer. / *Solution.*

Let $a', 6",$ and $c',$ be any three cubes whose sum is a rational cube; that is, let $a' + b' + c' = 3,$ then will $as', bs',$ and $cs3$ be the roots of three cubes whose sum is a 12th power, for $oV + dV$-f $eV = s9 (a3 + b3 + c3) = s9$ X $s3 = su;$ and therefore $asjfl, bs'x\%$ csV will obviously be the roots of three cubes whose sum is a sixth power.

Now $33 + 43 + 5s — 63,$ therefore we may take $a — 3, 6 = 4, c — 5,$ and $s — 6,$ and hence the preceding expressions for the roots of the three cubes will become 3 X 6V, 4 X 6V, and 5 X 6V, in which x may be expounded by any rational number whatever.

Take $x — $ -J, and then we shall have 18, 24, and 30 for the roots of the three cubes.

Again, $13 + 6" + 8s = 93,$ therefore we may take a 1, $b = 6, c — 8,$ and $s = 9;$ and hence 1 x 9V, 6 X 9V, and 8 X 9V will be the roots of the three cubes in which x may be expounded by any rational number.

Take $x — $ and the three roots will be 9, 54, and 72.

It will be perceived that the question admits of an infinite number f answers, but those brought out above are perhaps the lowest, L.

The Prize Question, *by Mr.* Tho. Simpson.

Young Strephon, long bless'd with his charming fair,
In happy consort liv'd devoid of care;
Till cruel fate call'd the fair nymph away
From his kind arms, to cross the raging sea;
Where horrid tempests, in thick darkness, roar,
And toss'd his dearest to an unknown shore.
He mourns, is restless, wanders day and night,
In ev'ry clime to find his dear delight.
Her lovely aspect his wing'd soul inspires;
He longs, sighs, wishes, melts in soft desires.
Propitious Venus pities his sad moan,
Glides shining down from her etherial throne,
And smiling says, (in a majestic tone)
'Thrice ten degrees north of th'equator lies
'This place, from which, as Sol due east doth rise,
Set out; and keep him always in your face;
'Move not too fast, but such an equal pace,
'To be eight miles more south at four hours end,
1 And you'll arrive to th' arms of your dear friend.'
Thus said, she vanish'd from his wond'ring sight:
But still the swain is in a mournful plight,
Unless, fair nymphs, you'll vouchsafe to explain,
And shew the place, that must the fair regain.
i. e. the distance required to move in an hour.

A/iswered by Mr. Tho. Simpson, *the Proposer.*

Let the radius be $= 1;$ then the sine of the latitude $— i$ for the versed sine of the hour from 6 put $x;$ then the $1 — x$ sine of the sun's azimuth will be —— —, 5—:-,,—rj n 4/(1 — $p + Ixx$) «: x now whilst x flows x the arch of time flows $— 5$ $jtf(tx—xx)$ which (because the man's motion is equal) must be in a constant ratio to the lineola $(rv) — $ the distance 0
moved by the man in the same time: therefore by putting Yd) for the said ratio, we have (rv) $—;$;5 and be
B ' 'K' V(x $—xx$ cause the angle (mrv) is the complement of the sun's

azimuth, it is as radius: sine of *(jnrv)*:: *(vr)*: (ms) — — *zrs* » the

I. Question 193, *by Mr. Merones.*

Ye bright sons of art, that a rule did impart In the Diary 1735, to obtain
The solid content of a conic segment,
Cut off by a vertical plane. +
Since ye're so expert, proceed in like sort,
x To compute us the surface convex
Of a segment the lesser, and all such to measure
A general theorem annex.

Answered by the Proposer.
Through the axis Bra, and any two points infinitely near each other as r, *s*, draw two planes Bra, *Bsn,* cutting the base in the lines ra, wt, and the plane of the hyperbola in the lines *ot, qi,* parallel to the axis B«.

The ratio of the As *nti, Boq,* to each other, is compounded of the ratios of A *nti* to A *nrs,* and A *nrs* to A Br, and of the A Br to ABog, that is, of the ratio of nt'' to wr% and of nr to Br, and of (Bra to Bos, or of J wr4 to *nts.* Whence A *nti*: A Bog:: *nr* : Br. And since A *nrs*: A Br:: *nr* : Br. Therefore the A *nrs* — A *nti*: A Br — A Bog:: *nr* : Br. That is, area *trsi*: area orsg:: nr: Br. And since Questoin 177, proposed in the Diary 1734, and answered in 1735. t Perpendicular to the base. TOE. I. R this always holds for any small correspondent parts of the circle and the conic surface it follows that the wholes are in the same ratio. Hence this theorem,

As the radius of the base: side of the cone:: segment of the base: surface of the segment of the cone. And the area of the segment ewee will be found to be 904-38 square inches. The answer.

Mr. Ri. Dunthornc's answer to the same.
The curve surfaces of cones may be considered as made up of an infinite number of infinitely narrow annuli, whose radii are in arithmetic progression, and the cosines of their segments equal.

Let r — radius, d — 3-14159 &c. and b — the cosine of any indefinite segment, then by (he arithmetic of infinites, dr—26— b' 3bs bb1 35b „, 1 — j —
—— j — &c. = the arch of that segment.
3rr 56V" 576V &
Put it — *An,* B — cm, A — *p,* c Ac; and let *c*-the infinitely small breadth of one aimulus. Then will *dre* — 2ne — 3-t—
; — —*r-r* — Tr-» — &c. = superficies of any lnden *3rr* 20r4 56/ 576r8 1 nite annular segment, constituting the curve surface of such conic segment.

Therefore such curve surface will be composed of an infinite number of such series, having B constant, and r increasing in arithmetic progression, from B to its greatest K, and—— the number of terms. Con .„ (zr'c /bc B3c B'c Bjc B5c sequently — — 2bc - 1-——: =
H '2a 2a 3ra 3ba 20r'a 20b 3a
B7c B7c 5bc 5b"c 4-TS-J V« ' + 7. — ; + &c. = the curve surface 56r A 56b A 576r A 576b A of such conic segment, which from the numbers in question 177, gives 905 square inches, the answer nearly the same as the proposer's above.

If we suppose *r* radius, and *a* — versed sine of any indefinite segment of a circle; we shall, by the arithmetic of infinites, have
„T, 4ba2c, 7ac 7lArc. 319a2c 5419a2c 2-1 + — + — -+ + &c.
840bt 10080b 354816b the curve superficies of such conic segment, in numbers above.

Ii. Question 194, *by Mr.* J. Turner.

An elliptical field, whose principal axes are 40 and 60 chains, is, by a father's will, to be divided between his two sons in the following manner. A semi-ordiuatc is to be drawn at right angles to the transverse axis at the distance of 15 chains from one end thereof, and the parting fence to be the shortest line possible bisecting the semi-ordinate. Required the shares and the length of the parting fence?
38 p. The greater Cmindc = 159 2 1, the shares; and the whole 188 1 39. in.
Question 195, *by Mr.* Rich. Lycctt.

There is an oak tree (the frustum of a cone) whose length is ten yards, the diameter at the top one foot, at the bottom three feet; and an ivy twisteth round it in the manner of a spiral screw, so that each twist is ten inches distant; three-sevenths of the ivy is eat into the tree; the diameter of the ivy is at the bottom one foot, at the top three inches. Quere the length of the ivy, and the content of both?

Answered bjj the Proposer.
The centre of the ivy will be found to lie without the periphery of the oak at the bottom-055, and at top-015 parts of a foot; which doubled and added to the diameters, at the bottom 3-11, and at top 103. Then the frustum's length on the outside is 3091, and the angle with the base is 88 0' 52". The circumference at bottom 9-77, and at top 3235 feet. Then a line being drawn through,the extremity of the top diameter and parallel to the central line is a mean arith. proportional; which multiplied by the number of twists 36-02 gives 234-0, which let be one leg of a triangle, 30-01 the other, with the angle between them 88 07 52". The other side will be found 235-3 feet the length of the ivy: Hence the content of the ivy is 80-87 feet, three-sevenths of which is 34-6: the content of the tree with the ivy growing into it is = 102 1; consequently 102-1 — 34-6 = 67-5 feet, the real content of the tree.

Merones's *Answer to the same.*

In the cone compleated, let s = the length of the side, c the circumference at the base, d — the distance of the spiral threads, z — the spiral line, and x — the distance from the vertex to the top of the first helix or turn.

Then d : c:: ai *C,* and *s:* % :: x : =z a small space the *d7 d ds* ivy moves round. And let the hypothenuse line the ivy move round in be =: z: then x — *A/(x' -* I —— 4/ (*rxx*). v d s J u s" cc

And, finding the fluent, z = 237-746 the length of the spiral ivy.

Hence the content of the oak = 102-102; of the ivy = 81-6925 feet.

Remark. The fluent of 1/ (+ *xx*) is — to — + X /+ *xx*), by Emerson's 13th form, where *t* is =2-30258 x / log. i+U (— + *xx),* the fluent of - by the 9th form. L.

It. Question 196, % Mr. Robert Heath.

Three ships, A, B, and c, sailed from a certain port in north latitude, un.til they armed at three different ports, all lying under the equinoctial j A sailed on a direct course, between the south and the west 175-62 leagues j c sailed 133 leagues between the south and east; B sailed a course between A and c 102 leagues, making the angle or rhumb with A, equal the angle that c made with the equinoctial. Hence it is required to find the port sailed from, each ship's course, and distance from each other, and their respective ports? and to solve it by an equation not higher than a quadratic?

Answered by the Proposer.
As 102: 175-62:: 133: 22899 leagues: The port sailed from is in 5 5' north latitude.

Additional Solution.
The reason of the proportion, in the above original solution, for finding the distance (228-99) between the extreme ports, will clearly appear from the annexed figure, in which p represents the port sailed from, and A, B, c the ports arrived at by the respective ships. For, since the Zc=Z APBby the question, and the Z A common to the two A S Apb, Apc, therefore the third angles are equal, and those triangles equiangular. Hence then Pb (102): Pa (17562):: rc (133): Ac = 22899. And in like manner as AC: Ap:: Ap: Ab. Hence the perpendicular and the angles are easily found.

Hence also the problem will be easily constructed. For it is only taking AC a fourth proportional to the three given lines, H,

T. Question 197, *by Mr.* Ant. Thackcr.

Let Ab = 1000, Bc — 2000, Cd — 3000, De = 4000, and Ae

Whence by reduction and the converging series a is found = 6646 316, &c.

But the diameter Ae or radius Aq, may be more expeditiously found by a table of natural sines (which is an invention of my own) by finding out four chords, in the proportion of the chords given Ab, Bc, Cd, De. By a few trials, I find the angle Aqjb under half the chord — 8 39' the next less to a minute; and 8 40' the next greater. The operation is thus: vi. Question 198, *by Mr.* Christ. Mason.

There is a high cliff from the top of which a heavy body is suffered to fall, the time of descent is 11 times as much as the ascent of sound from the bottom to the top. What is the height of the cliff?

Answered by Mr. Mason,
Let « be the time a heavy body requires in falling from the top of the cliff; then $a - 11 -$ the time that sound requires to move that space; $b - 16$ feet; c 968 feet.

Then $baa - ca$ 11 per quest, and $ll-baa - ca$, which divide by a, and it is $lha - c$; therefore $a - c - b - 5$-5 seconds, the time sought. Then 5-5 X 55 X $b - 484$ feet, the height sought, But if $b = 16$-jjj the answer is 481-417.

The Prize Question, *by Mr.* Turner.
In the triangle Bad, Bd 55, Da — 53, and Ba rz 40 feet; about A as a centre a circle is described with a radius of 15 feet; it is required to determine a point F, in the periphery of this circle to which if right lines Bf and Df are drawn the angle Bfd may be the greatest possible?

Answered by Mr. Rob. Heath.
In the triangle Abd, there is given Ab 40 5, AD — 53 =: c, Bd = 55 = 2rf, Ps = 30 = 2/.

Make rs parallel to Bd; draw mc perpendicular. On the centre c describe a circle, to touch the given one at F, through the points B, D; the point of contact p, from which lines must be drawn to B and D to constitute the greatest angle, which is a maximum. Draw Ca, Cd, and p the perpendicular of the triangle. In order to investigate the centre c, and the lines Bf and Df, find the perpendicular $Ap - 86$-4342 — $mq - h$; qp as $Km = 10$-991 = g; and let $qc = a$.

Then per 47 Eucl. I. $/(aa + dd) - Cd - Cf$; $/(aa + dd) + f = $ AC; and $(gg + hh + 2As + aa) - $ Ac = $J(aa + dd) + /.$ Whence $gg + hh + dd - ff + 2ha - 2/ /(aa \pm dd)$ by involution and transposition, or $k + 2$fia $2 = 2/ /(aa + dd)$ by substitution, will do. When the angle is to be a maximum or a minimum, the circle Bfd must touch the given circle Pfs respectively below or above the vertex A; which is very "well done in the 12th prob. of Lawson's Apollonius on Tangcncies. H. *Anszceered by Mr.* 3. May, *jun. of Amsterdam.*

The ship will arrive at the north pole, and the leagues run, will be the length of the loxodromic beginning at the latitude of 51 north, and ending at the pole, after having performed infinite revolutions about the said pole; the length of the said loxodromic will be 1278-56 leagues, supposing the earth to be a true spherical figure; and the circumference according to Norwood's observations, likewise the ship infinite small.

The same anszeered by Mr. Walter Trott, *per Corollary to Prob.* XIIi Stone' *Appendix.*

Suppose a line drawn infinitely near to Tb; then may the triangle made thereby be looked on as rectilinear; and making nm radius, mr will be the secant of the course, and a Pa Pb; $Am - y$; and $mn - i -$ fluxion of the diff. latitude; then per plain trigonometry, K: sec. course:: £ : y. Hence, taking the fluents, $y -$ secant of the course multiplied by divided by the radius. The ship's distance sailed is 103-08 leagues, and then coincides with the pole.

Mr. Tho. Bird answers thus:
The small decrements of the spiral, or the distance the ship runs while it passes through small, but equal angles of longitude (as at every 0-01 deg.) are a series of geometrical proportionals continued decreasing and ending inO, in the pole: whose ratio (1-0001745) together with the first or greatest term (0-57736) and last or least (0) being known; the sum of all the series or length of the spiral is easily found zz 3309 minutes of a degree, or 1103 leagues; which may more easily be done by fluxions. However it may be solved to a geometrical exactness by this easy and known analogy.

As the cosine of the course co. ar. 0. 150515
To dift. lat. 780 leagues 2-192095
So radius 10-000000
To dist. run 1103 leagues 3-042610

After the ship has passed through all the degrees of longitude, and is arrived to the same meridian itself, it will be but 4632 minutes from the pole, according to artificial tangents (for Wright's meridional parts being made from false secants, are not to be trusted) alter which it Will be no deviation from mathematical exactness to suppose the remainder to the pole a plane, in which case the proportion of the velocity of the ship's approach towards the pole, is nearly as 10000000 to 18151, she in the next round will be but 0-00841 min. from the pole, and the next revolution falls into the pole itself, contrary to what the ingenious Oughtred supposed in his Cir. Prop. of Nav. p. 37.

Mr. Chr. Mason, *the Proposer, answers in this manner.*

Let P denote the north pole, A the place whence the ship set sail, Amp its course, Ap the meridian, and Bp, Cp two other meridians infinitely near. ir a parallel of latitude. Let Ap = co. lat. — b; r = rad. c cosine of the course, $urn - a$; $Amp - x -$ dist. run.

Then by plain trigonometry, $a : TM :: b : = = x = 1277$-$73$ leagues.

The same answered by Mr. R. Dunthornc.

Since parts of rhumbs are every where to (heir corresponding parts of the meridians, as radius to the cosine of the course, it will be S. 45: rad.:: 9O025 leagues (the dist. of 51 from tiie pole): 127314 leagues the answer.

Additional Solution, taken from the Third Volume of the Course.

Problem. *Suppose a ship to sail from the Orkney Islands, in. latitude* 59 3' *north, on a N.N.E. course, at the rate of* 10 *miles an hour; it is required to determine how long it will be before she arrives at the pole, the distance she will have sailed, and the difference of longitude she will have made when she arrives thefc?*

Let Abc represent part of the equator; P the pole; $xmrv$ a loxodromic or rhumb line, or the path of the ship continued to the equator; Pb, Pc, any two meridians indefinitely near each other; nr, or mt the part of a parallel of latitude intercepted between them.

Put c for the cosine, and t for the tangent of the course, or angle nmr to the radius r; Am any yariable part of the rhumb from the equator, zz v; the latitude $nmzzw$; its sine x, and cosine y; and Ab, the difference of longitude from A, $= z$. Then since the elementary triangle mnr may be considered as a right-angled plane triangle, it is, as rad. r: $c -$ sin. /.mm :: $i - mr$:w $- mn$:: v rw sw : rs; therefore $cv - rw$, or $ti = ---$, by putting s for the secant of the Ln-mr the ship's course. In like manner, if w be any other latitude, and v its corresponding length of the rhumb; then v 'rw w $-$ to rd
---; and hence v—$v - r$ X———,
or n ———, by putting

D = v $- v$ the distance, and d w $-$ to the difference of latitude; which is the common rule.

The same is evident without fluxions: for since the Z.mrn is the same in whatever point of the path $xmrv$ the point m is taken, each indefinitely small particle of Amrp, must be to the corresponding indefinitely small part Bot, in the constant ratio of radius to the cosine of the course; and therefore tlie whole lines, or any corresponding parts of them, must be in the same ratio also, as above determined. In the same manner it is proved that radius: sine of the course:: distance: the departure.

Again, as radius r: $t -$ tang, nmr :: to mn : nr or tnt, and as r :y:: Pb: Pot:: z — Bc: mt; hence, as the extremes of these proportions are the same, the rectangles of the means must be equal, viz. tVX 'Tx $y'z - tto$ because to ——— by the property of the circle; y y trx trx therefore z ———5 the general fluents of these are $z - yy$ $r - x b r + x t$ x hyp. log. + c; which corrected by supposing $z - 0$ when $x -$ «, are $2 - t$ X (hyp. log. — hyp. log. y'———J; but r X (hyp. log. y'-- —— hyp. log. y-J is the meridional parts of the difference of the latitudes whose sines are x and a, which call b; then is: =, the same as it is by Mercator's sailing.

Further, putting $m - 2$-71828 the number whose hyp. log. is 1, 2s . $r + x$ and $n -$ then, when z begins at A, m'', and there t $r - x$ m $- 1 2r$.
fore $x - r$ X zz $r - ———$-; hence it appears that as $m + 1 m + 1 m$, or rather n or z increases (since m is constant), that x approxi mates to an equality with r, because $-$ decreases or converges tn + 1 to 0, which is its limit; consequently r is the limit or ultimate value of x: but when $x - r$, the ship will be at the pole; therefore the pole must bc the limit, or evanescent state of the rhumb or course: so that the ship may be said to arrive at the pole after making an infinite number of revolutions round it; for the above expression —— vanishes when n, and consequently is infinite, in whichquently the height of the lowest mountain = 16468 yards; that of the highest = 283-68 yards. $m'' + 1$
case a; is zz r.
Tit £t
Now, from the equation D =—=:—, it is found, that, when d zz 30 57' the complement of the given latitude 59 3', and c zz sinn of 67 30/ the complement of the course, D will be 2010 geograyphical miles, the required ultimate distance, which at the rate of 10 miles an hour, will be passed over in 201 hours or 8$ days. The difference of longitude is shewn above to be infinite. When the ship has made one revolution, she will be but about a yard from the pole, considering her as a point.

When the ship has arrived infinitely near the pole, she will go round in the manner of a top, with an infinite velocity; which at once accounts for this paradox, viz. that though she make an infinite number of revolutions round the pole, yet her distance run will have an ultimate and definite value, as above determined: for it is evident that however great the number of revolutions of a top may be, Hue space passed over by its pivot or bottom point, while it continues on or nearly on the same point, must be infinitely small, or less than a. certain assignable quantity.

iv. Question 202, *by Mr.* Tho. Cooper.
There are two mountains, the higher situated in Iat. 65, and the other in lat. 64 307; the difference of their heights is 119 yards;, a straight line joining their summits is a tangent to the earth's surface and 63 miles in length. Required the time the sun first begins to illuminate the top of each mountain on the shortest day, reckoning that the earth's radius is 6980000 yards.

The time when the sun first begins to shine on the highest mountain (m) is when he cuts the tangent to the earth's surface (sm) below the horizon (iimh) in the angle Hms (found by trig.) r: 31TM also he first begins to shine on the top of the lowest mountain (m) when he cuts the tang, (mot) below the horizon (iimh) in the Z Moth — 23m. Now if the sun's refraction be allowed for near the horizon — 33', the angle Hms will be 1 4'; and angle Hotm — 56m, which the sun is below the horizon of each mountain when he first shines on their tops.

The hour or times will be found by spheric trigonometry; thus, at 10" 8ni 38s on the highest mountain, at 10" 2m 4" on the lowest.

N. B. Sun rises in lat. 65, at 10" 35m 16", in 64 3(/, at 10" 22» 56s. This shews how much those are mistaken, who suppose the sun would first shine on them, nearly at his rising. *Additional Solutions.*

In this problem we have given the base Mot, the perpendicular eg and the difference of the sides Cm — cm, to construct the triangle which is reducible to one of the simpler cases of *Tangencies,* viz. to describe a circle through two given points to touch a circle given in magnitude and posi. tion. See Art. 4, Vol. I. of the Mathematical Repository.

It may also be constructed as follows: Bisect the given base at E, and take M» — the given difference of the sides; then Mc + Cot — 2mc — *un,* and (2mc — *un) un —* Mot. 2e7, Theor. 35, Cor. Vol. I. Course, or 2m c. *yin Mm* . 2EJ + Mn. Make *vim* . 2ef = Mm!; then Mc. *Mn — Mm* . Fjr, or Mc: *vq* :: Mot: *Mn,* a given ratio. Draw F» perpendicular and Gc parallel to *Mm,* and draw Mh parallel to Mg meeting Mc produced (if needful) in H: then Gc is — *vq,* and by similar triangles Mc: Gc z: *rq;*:: Mh: *Mn;* therefore Mh = Mot. Whence this construction; having bisected the base Mot in E, take Ef a third proportional to twice Mot, and *Mn* the' difference of the sides; draw Fg perpendicular to *Mm* and of a length rz to the given perpendicular; draw Gc parallel to Mm and Mh to Mg; from M as a centre, with a radius equal to Mot, describe an arc to cut *nn* in H; draw Mh cutting Gc in c; then join mc and the triangle is constructed, the demonstration is obvious from the analysis.

The problem may also be resolved in the following manner.

If we conceive the triangle to be circumscribed by a circle, and a diameter drawn through the middle of the base, and a line through the vertex parallel to the base to intersect the diameter; then if *v* be put for the segment of the diameter above that line, and s for the

Vol. i. s segment below the base; *p* for the perpendicular, *d* for half the difference of the sides, and 6 for half the base; we have, by well known theorems, $vz — fl"2$ and $z(p + v) — 6a$; whence $v :p + v :: dl: 62$ or $v: p:: d\%: b —$ if, a giren ratio; therefore v is given, consequently 2 is also given, and the method of construction is obvious. _ *The same Analytically.*

Put $a —$ the perpendicular, $b —$ the base, $d —$ the difference of the sides, 9 — the angle at the vertex made by the greater side and the perpendicular, 8 the angle made by the less side and the perpendicular; then the sides will be denoted by a sec. 9 and a sec. , and the segments of the base by a tan. 9 and a tau. ; and we have a tan. $9 + a$ tan. $9=6$, a sec. $9 — a$ sec. $9 = d$ Whence a' tan.$2,, = b$ —lab tan. $8 + a2$ tan.'fl *di* sec"? $= d + lad$ sec. $9 + «2$ sec.2 8; subtracting the first equation from the second, and remarking that sec — tan.8 rad.2, we have $a = d2 — i2 + 2a\&$ tan. 9 f lad sec. $8 + a$ or 2od sec. $8 — b — d2 — lab$ tan. 8; and squaring $4o'd2$ sec.2fl $= (62 — d')1 — 4ab(b — ds)$ tan. $8 + 4a'b$ tan'9; or putting for sec.2 8 its equal tan.2 9+1 and dividing by $4a5(6J—tT)$, tan. 9 tan. $9 — — a$ $bl— d$ $4a3'$ therefore by completing the square, &c.

tan. $9 = — \pm — 1/ 3. 2a — la$ y $b — d'$ Whence the greater segment of the base $= +-4/ 4a -t, 2 2 K » — d ..... b d/4a+b — d'$ and the lesser segment $=-.— -W$.
J. t

T. QUE3TI0N 203, 6y J. B. S.

A ball of lead hanging from the top of a hall by a string, drawn over a pulley, which is 20 feet long between the centre of the ball and pulley, is set a swinging: The moment it begins to swing, a person, holding the other end of the string, begins to pull it, and draws tip the ball, and continues so to do, at an uniform ratio of 5 feet in a minute, until he has pulled the ball quite up to the pulley. Quere, how many oscillations will the ball make before it reach the top?
Answered by Mr. Ri. Dunthome.

Let $a —$ 20 feet, £ = 4 minutes, c = number of vibrations which the pendulum whose length is a makes in the time b, and $e —$ a $C6$ small particle of time. Then $b: c:: e : —$ ss number of vibrations b ae which the pendulum a makes in the time $e;$ and $b: a :: «: — =$ portion of the string drawn up in the time $e;$ then will $a — — =$ length of the pendulum after the first time $e;$ $a — — =$ that after the second time e, &c. And $-,—,-r——: —$ tne square of the $o(o — e)$ number of vibrations in the second time e. Consequently its squard root — number of vibrations in the second time e. In like manner $ce —r,—--r$ number of vibrations in the third time e. i/b $y(6 — 2e) C$

$——r$, s-t = number in the fourth, &c. Whence it is manifest tliat the number of vibrations in the several times e, as above, are a series of fractions, whose numerators are equal, and their denominators arc square roots, whose sides are single powers, decreasing ia arithmetical progression from b, and b e the number of terms. So that by the arithmetic of infinites, 2c will be the sura of all the terms in the series. But c — 97, whence 2c = 194, the number of vibrations required.

See also Question 681.

Ti. Question 204, *by Mr.* Mason.

Soon after a hard gale of wind, some persons strolling along shore, upon the look-out, found a large cask just driving ashore, which proved a piece of old Jamaica rum:. They soon boarded it, and racked olf forty-one gallons, and filled up the cask again with water, and acquainted some more 9f their party with their success, who went and racked off the same quantity of the mixture, and filled it up again with water: In like manner it was served so twice more; and at last, by the proof, there was found 25-JA gallons of rum remaining, the rest water. How much did the whole piece contain, and how many gallons of

rum was drawn out at each evacuation? *Answered by Mr. Rob. Heath.*
Let $b = 25\text{fi-}\S = 25\text{-}2935528$ gallons of rum left in the cask. $5 = 41$ gallons, the liquor drawn off each time. n — the number of times of drawing. And $x =$ the quantity of neat liquor the cask held. *fx Qy*
Say x: $x - q :: x - q : v - =$ rum left at 2d drawing. x : (f H. :: $x - \ll$: ($x =$ rum left at 3d drawing.
$XXXx : --- :: x - a : --- =$ rum left at 4th drawing. $xx\ xxx$
Whence it is evident, that the quantity of neat liquor, left at any ($x -$ oV number of times draw ingi off, will be universally ———; conse ($x\ pY\ 2$. £ quently — =6. Reduced $x - a - bx$. In numbers $xxx\ x - 41 = 2\text{-}1426\text{-e'}5$; solved, according to a new method of managing exponentials $Jx - 124671$, &c.
Now, if each quantity left in the cask, at any time of drawing off, be subtracted from the quantity left the time preceding, the neat rum at each time drawn off will be found; and is as follows:
Rum drawn off I. 41-000) 2. 27-516f 3. 18-467 gallons 4. 12-394 i Total 124-67. add gallons left.... 25-293J

The Peize Question, *by Mr. Ri. Dunthorne.*
Let Afk be the conchoid of Nicomedes, which is continually approaching nearer to the line Bc, yet if continued *ad infinitum* could never meet; which at first setting out to generate the line Afk, the distance Ba is 16 inches; and the distance Bp is 24 inches from the pole P to the asymptote Bc. It is required to find the distance of F, the point of inflection of the curve, from the line Bc?
Answered by Mr. Hen. Travis. Let Pb and Ab be called b and c, the abcissa and ordinate x and *Questions proposed in* 1739, *and answered in* 1740. 1. auESTioN 205, *by Mr. John Turner.*
There is a piece of ground in the form of a triangle, as Acb, side Ac = 14, and side Bc Zz 22 chains; and a circular drain Ce, centre A, radius Ac, cuts the side Ab in E so that 2 Ab — 5ce. Required Ab?
Answered by the proposer, Mr. J. Turner.

Let Ab — x, Ac — 14 = 6, Cb — 22 = c, $cc - bb - 288 = m$. Then the cosine of the angle Bac — $(xx - m)$ -7-lx: but the arch Ce —-$4x - nx$; and the radius — b; consequently the cosine of the said arch — b — comes out 28 9443: And the angle Bac — 47 degrees 17 min.
Merones *answers this question thus:*
Let the radius Ac = r, Cb — s; take an arch p, as near Ce as possible, let a its sine, $b =$ its cosine to the radius r; and let $p + z -$ Ce: and per quest. -$\$p +$ fs zz. Ab J also the cosine Ap — + + &c. And Ba — Ap-p + fa — 26 + r *Irr* or 52 4— 2 — — &c. different segments of the base. But by $r\ rr\ 3r\ Ax$. 4th of plain trigonometry, f/ + f s: s + r:: s — r: different segments. Whence we have 5ap 5bp '$f\ zrr$ Sap +
— 56 + —
» 4 180t?
Now assume $p = 11$: and then-3. 141592 = tnG degrees of the arch p; from whence is had $a = 10\text{-}249675$; $b = 9\text{-}536464$; all which substituted in the foregoing series, and putting A, B, c, &c, for the known co-efficients, and reversing the series, we shall have z-2. + 2bca?R', &c. = 0-704043, an he arch Ce = 11-5704043; and Ab = 28-92601J.
Mr. Robert Heath
Says, by a table of natural sines and a few trials, I find the angle Cab — 47 21'; whence the required side Ab — 28925, &c. The method of solving this by infinite series, which converges so slow, renders it more tedious than useful.
Answered by Mr. Hen. Travis. Let Cb = 6, ci = o, Ap y; and as in Simpson's Flux. p. 121, we have the arch $c = y +$ L-+ + c and ?a x $iX6$ — the side je = 21-991 = j; from which take «c, ii. Question 206, *by* Merones.
If a cannon ball be projected upwards in 'a direction perpendicular to the horizon, half a mile high, and in the latitude of 53 degrees; where will it fall?
Answered by Merones.
Let the ball be projected from A, the time of its flight will be 25f seconds, in which time the point A will be carried to B, through a space Ab, of 23666 feet, by the earth's rotation. Now the ball (carried by a compound motion of its pro-

jection and the earth's rotation) will describe an ellipsis whose focus is in the centre of the earth; in which the elliptic area *Arte* — the circular sector Abc: Or the area *Artx* = area Bc; but by reason of the small ratio of rs -to Ac the portion *Art* may be taken for a parabola. Let Ac = b — 21000000 feet, AB = d — 23666 feet, $rs = h - 2640$, $a - Bt$; then will $ba = A\ (d-a)$; and 35a + 4ha = 4hd, whence $a = +4h\ W$ nearly = 3'967 feet. Near 4 feet to the west.
31r. Hen. Travis's *answer.*
The time of the ball's ascending is equal to the time of its descending, according to the writers on projectiles; which time call (x) and the number of feet a heavy body will fall or descend freely, by the force of its own gravity, in one second of time r: n. Then will 2640 2640 $nxx -$ 2640 = the feet in half a mile: $xs = -$ —rj-, = 163-98 nearly, V $x - 12'\ 48"$ = the time the ball is ascending or descending; and consequently the ball will fall near 4 feet from the place it was projected.
m. Question 207, *by Mr.* John May, *jun.*
Ther# came three Dutchmen of my acquaintance to see me, being lately married; they brought their wives with them. The men's names were Hendrick, Claas, and Cornelius; the women's, Geertruii, Catriin, and Anna: but I forgot the name of each man's wife. They told rae they had been at market to buy hogs; each person bought as many hogs as they gave shillings for each hog: Hendrick bought 23 hogs more than Catriin, and Claas bought 11 more than Geertruii; likewise, each man laid out 3 guineas more than his wife. I desire to know the name of each man's wife?
Answered by Mr. J. Hill.
Call the number of hogs any woman bought x; the number her husband bought $x + n$; money laid out by the woman is xx shillings; money laid out by the husbaud is $xx + Inx + vn$ shillings. Equation $xx + 2/\text{i.r} + nn - xx + 63$. $x - n$. If n r: 1, then $x - 31$, and x - f-«=32: hence some woman bought 31 hogs, and her husband 32: If $n = 3$, then $x = 9$, and $x + n = 12$; therefore some other woman bought 9, and her husband 12: If $n - 7$, then $n + x - 8$; some

woman bought 1, and her husband 8. Consequently

Henthick bought 32, and his wife Anna 31

Claas 12, Catriin 9

Cornelius 8, Geertruii 1 *Answered by* Merones.

Men. Women. For the persons put A, n, c, p, Q, R,

Hogs $a, e, y, e — c, a — b, u$, Money $aa, ee, yy, (e — c)\%, (a — 6)', uu$. Let $h = 23, c\ 11$. Compare B with Q, then per question $ee — (a — i) = 63$ shillings; that is, putting $e — a + z;\ 2«s + zz + 46a = 592$; therefore $a — — 1 —$; now it is evident the last term cannot be a whole number; therefore 2 in the first term must be an even number: so the last term—must be $2j$-+ 4B 03 63 the half of' a whole number: let $— o$. Whence $z — 2+23\ v\ 23$; hence v must be either 1, 3, 7, 9, 21, or 63; from each of ....,., J a 54, 32, 14, 22, 24 t .,.-.... which is had 32' » J2 g' g£. And again comparing c with p, then yy-$ee + 22e = 184$; and we find 1 J» 32.

Whence e must be the same in both suppositions; therefore it is 12, If the question be possible in whole numbers. But since the other two persons A, R, must be compared, therefore $aa — uu = z\ 63$: From hence $a — 32, u =: 31, e — 12$, and,?/ =: 8; but comparing the men and women in any other manner, it will appear there is no other answer in whole numbers. Therefore ilendrick and Anna, Claas and Catriin, and Cornelius aud Geertruii, are man and wife.

The same answered by Mr. Rob. Heath. Let $x —$ the hogs bought by either Hendrick, Claas, or Cornelius; then xx will be the shillings they cost, and $xx — 63$ the shillings their wives hogs cost, which (as whole hogs) must always be a square number; because the square root of the shillings laid out for each parcel is equal to the number of hogs, $hetx$—y — the side of that square, then $xx — 63$ $xx — Ixy + yy$. Consequently, by reduction,

'63 + 30.-.

cr ": whence we find y may be iy' 3 Hogs.

X / Consc f 32 bought by thef *311 3 -j*l*2-raen,* coupled 9 bought by their wives.

7 3 X I 8)with (I) Whence are joined Hendrick and Anna, Claas and Catriin, Cornelius and Geertruii. *Mr.* N. Farrer Observes, that the number of hogs the three men and their respective wives bought will be expressed by three pair of numbers, the difference of whose squares must be 63. Now all the whole numbers whose squares will produce this difference are 1 and 8, 9 and 12, 31 and 32; there 8, 12, 32, the men bought; 1, 9, 31 the women.

iv. Question 208, *by Mr.* Hen. Travis. Given this equation, viz. $xy + Bm + Z — c\ 0$; expressing the relation of the sides of a trapezium inscribed in a circle whose diameter is known to be 75 feet (or d). Required the sides separately, and area, by a general method that will resolve all such problems?

N. B. A $=z$ 100; B = 5; c = 432246. From the first, second, and third steps, by common algebra we get $x — 12, y = 6$, and $u = 3$; and by the very same method of reasoning,-the sides of the trapezium are found to be $— 60, y — 72, u — 45$, and z—1 and the area = 2106 square feet. This trapezium may be placed 4 or 5 different ways in a circle, which I hava proved by a large geometrical projection, and every way justly contain the remaining chords of the circle, and measured, amount to each the same area 2106 square feet. (1) In the first fig. the several lines are obvious; and the diagonal Bd =75, multiplied by the half of the two perpendiculars (ce =: 1965, Af — 3652) will give the area as above. (2) In the second fig. Bc =: y 72, Bd z = 21, Da = x — 60, and Ac = u — 45. And the diagonal Bc (=7496) multiplied by half the perpendiculars (af — 3575, and Be — 202) gives nearly the same area. (3) In the third fig. y is the line Cb, X is Ab, Z is Ad, and u is The diagonal Bd = 7001, the perpendicular At — 16'6j ce 431 nearly; and (4) in the same fig. s is represented by Bo, u by Oa, and x by Ac; the diagonal oc is nearly 7495, which by the perpendiculars gives the area as before.

Mr. Paul Sharp has found the sides 72, 60, 45, and 21, in answer.

Mr. Tho. Robinson gives the sides 72, 2, 59, 9, 45, 1, 20, 7, nearly true. In this question it does seem to appear, that the number of quantities sought exceed the number of given equations, and fas my ingenious correspondents have observed) is unlimited. But I presume since the numbers given in the question, viz. A = 100, B zzb and err 432216; and the four numbers sought are together obliged to extend the chords of 360 degrees, and the diameter of the circle is given; it may be said to be limited; but I shall rather leave it to the speculation of those ingenious persons who are pleased to appear in the emendata next year.

v. Question 209, *by Mr.* Robert Heath. (v

I ind ar2, when I xJ is a minimum. i-$ddiinxx$—$2dnjx$—jJ—$ddmmddmmxx$-$lldmm\ i/\ i$-$xx)$—$udmjy/$ (I $-xx$)' which when all the terms affected with —xx) arc brought to one side of the equation, and involved, will produce an equation, of the 8th power; in which x -87719. Consequently the Zdac — 28 42'; Bac = 44 18'; side Dc = 29 19'; and Bc = 53 59'.

Viii. Question 212, *by Mr.* Chr. Mason.

There is a triangular piece of ground, whose centre of gravity measures from each angle 12, 16, and 20 chains: It is required to find the periphery of the greatest inscribed ellipsis; and also the content of each angular piece without the ellipsis *I Ansitered.*

There is no solution printed to this question this year; but in the Emendations in the next yea/ the Diary Author says, the printer omitted it for want of room, and that of several who answered it, Mr. Hill's numbers for the sides of the triangle are 34-151, 28521, and 19-549.

Again in the Emendations in the year 1744 he mentions it, saying that Mr. Heath had fully answered it at first; and that Mr. James Tercy now puts the side sought — from one angle to the inter, section = d, another = c, the 3d = b then $x — (2dd + 2cc$ —$hb)$: Whence he gives tiie sides 34-176, 28 844, and 20; the area = 288. Then 1:-6046:: area of the equilateral A: area inscr. circle. Hence area of inscr. ellipsis = 174-124, and each angular piece = 37-95; diam. inscr. circle 10-88 = conjugate of the ellipse; longest 50-36.

Solution.

The method of finding the sides of the triangle may be thus: Put , y, and z for the three sides, and a, b, c, (= 12, 16, and 20) for the distances between the angular points and the centre of gravity; then because the lines a, b, c, if produced would bisect the opposite sides, and are each § of the whole bisecting line, by a known theorem in geometry, we have $f + r\text{-}K = K + z!\text{-}W = W$, $y + $'— K = «s; the sum of these beijig taken, and cleared of fractions, we have $xx\text{--}yy + zz - 3aa + 3bb + 3cc$ which is a very curious theorem; from this last each of the three former equations being subtracted, &c; we have $x - J(1bb + 2cc - aa) = 4\ 73 = 34\text{-}176$, $y = V(2ao + 2cc - 66) - 4\ Jb1 = 28\text{-}8444$, $s = (2aa + 266 - cc) = 4f1\$ - 20$. *Otherwise.* Or the triangle might be easily constructed. For, since the three lines drawn to the centre of gravity divide the whole triangle into three equal parts or triangles, and each triangle being equal to half the sine of its angle at the centre of gravity drawn int» the product of the two sides or lines about it, therefore the sines of the three angles formed by those three given lines are reciprocally as the products of each two about them; but those sides being 12, 16 and 20, are as 3, 4, and 5; therefore the sines of the angles are as

——, —i—, and,-.; or as 5, 4, and 3; and so univer3X4' 3X5' 4X5' ''' sally the sines of the three angles are always as the three given lines.

But the three angles about one point are equal to four right angles, or 360; whence the problem is to divide 360, or a circle into three such parts, that their sines shall obtain the given ratio. In the present case the ratios 5, 4, and 3 form a right-angled triangle; let it be Abc; then the supplements of the Zs A, B, and c, of this triangle are the angles required to be formed by the given lines at the centre of gravity. For, with the centre A *J)* and radius Ac describe the circle; then it is evident that Cb is the sine of the arc Dc or

ZoAc,;that ABor Ce is the sine of CFor Zcaf,

and that Ac is the sine of the remaining quadrant Fd or Z Fad; and these are respectively the supplements of the three angles of the triangle Abc.

The other parts of this question will be done as quest. 430, proposed in the year 1757, where the subject is resumed, and to which therefore we refer, H.

The Prize Question, *by Mr.* R. Heath.

Given the latitude of three places, Moscow 55 307, Vienna 48 12', Gibraltar 35 30', all lying directly in the same arc of a great circle: The difference of longitude between Vienna (situated in the middle) and Moscow, easterly, is equal to that between Vienna and Gibraltar, westerly: It is required to find the true bearing and distance of each place from the other, and the difference of longitude, according to the convexity of the globe?

Questions proposed in 1740, *and answered in* 1741. i. Question 213, *by Mr.* Rob. Heath.

What sum of money x, will double itself in x years at x per cent.-per annum, compound interest *I Answered by Mr.* J. Turner.

Let x — principal, rate, and time; as 100: x :: 1:-Ola:. And putting $b = $"01; what Ward in his Comp. Interest calls H, will be $= 1 + 6$; consequently by his 1st prop, and per quest, $x\ (1 + bx) = 2a$?; or $1 + bxf = 2$. Hence x x log. $(1 + bx)$ — log. 2, = 6V b'x' 693147 (or c). But the log. of $(1 + bx)$ is $= bx - + -$

—— $+ -$, &c. which multiplied by x is $= c$. Reverted, it gives x z= 84983 the time and rate, with which any sum will gain the principal.

Answered by Mr. Peter Kay. x

Let a; be the number sought; therefore $(1 + "iqq) = 2$ Per TOLi I. T quest, this in log. gives x X + «, &c. $z:$ 1 8 100 20000 3000000' 693147, whence $x - 8\text{-}4983$, &c.

Ii. Question 214, *by Mr.* Nich. Farrer.

Sometime in the spring quarter, in 1739, in the forenoon, an obserVation being made of the sun, his altitude was found 33 41' 40"; and azimuth from the north 102 40' 52"; and sometime after, on the same forenoon, his altitude was found 48 46' 53", and azimuth 134 39' 56". Froni whence the latitude of the place of observation, month, day, and hours of observation may be found and are here required? With a general theorem for all questions of this nature.

Answered by Mr. Ant. Thacker. *Construction.* With radius =: sine of 90 describe the primitive circle on the plane of the meridian Hzhn; draw Hh through the centre for the horizon, and Zn the east azimuth at right angles thereto; with the versed sines of 102 40' 52" and 134 39' 56", set off *nt* and Ht: And with the sines of 33 41' 40" and 4846' 53" lay down *ck*and Ck; then diiaw *kq* and Kq parallel to Hh: make Nm and Ne = *kq* and Kq; join Tn and *tx*; and draw w» and *he* parallel to Hh; then make *k* 0 and K0=fflM and *he*; through QQ draw *oQQmngf* and draw the equator *mem* parallel thereto; and *enp* the elevation of the pole at right angles to it. From whence *cn* will be the sine of the sun's declination, and *vb* the sine of the latitude, &c. 1. From which projection, the investigation of a general theorem will easily arise. For per similar triangles, say as Nc (radius 1): *ct* (z):: *mi (q)* : *qz — uzs — kQ*. And Nc (1): Ct *(m)* :: Nc *(s): ms — he — K0*; v *ms — qz — 0*«. Also as 0a $((-p)$: Qa (ms— qz):: *cz* (1): Az — *(ms —qz) -7-(s —p)* — the tang, of the required latitude. 2. *For the Sun's Declination.* As *vb* (x): cb (y) :: 0 *k (qz) z km* rs *qzy — x*; and as *mc (p — qzy* -r*-x): cn (d)* :: CP (1): *vb* (x) j therefore *px— qyz = d*, the sun's declination. 3. *Lastly, for the hour of the day.* Put c = cosine of sun's declination; and *s* and *e* for the sine and cosine of the hour from noon; then will *px — qyz — d; and dx + eye — p* ; and by substitution *xxp — xqzy + eye — p;* but $1 - yy - $ xx; ce *zz py + xqz*; and as *s: q :: n* (sineof 0 azimuth):*c*;: *qn-r-s —* c; which substituted for c, gives *qne* -r *s — py + xqz*; therefore *e* -r-*s (py + xqz)-r-qn—* cotangent of the hour from noon, at the first observation. *N. B.* If the sun's azimuth is less than 90 (from the north) then *tc* must be taken on the contrary side of c, and therefore negative with respect to what it is (in this quest.)

Hence — TM?; px + qyz — d; and -= are general expressions for the quest, as above. Only whenever any angle or side exceeds 90, its cosine must be expressed by a negative sine.

This theorem +,qyz — d, will be found to answer all the ends proposed by that of Mr. Auderson, in the Diary, 1732. And is indeed more simple, and is better adapted to the uses than his; though I freely own, that the above method of deriving it was first hinted to me some years ago by my ingenious friend Mr. T. Simpson.

This theorem, viz. -= — X is found to be more useful than 's qn the other, e. g. In the solution of the prize question, 1739, solved by it, comes out st — 26c =: x; where the sine s Gp + Mp — sine 89; and t — tangent Pv; and all the others as by Mr. Turner, Diary, 1740. Also quest. 211 may readily be answered by this theorem, and will come out xx + 2px n.

These theorems above being brought out in numbers, by help of the artificial and natural sines, to facilitate the labour; gave, 1. The latitude = 54 51'. 2. The sun's declination = 20 24' answering to the 10th day of May. And 3d, the hour 60 rr 4h or 8 in the morning, and 30 = 2h or 10 o'clock, agreeing precisely with that of the ingenious proposer's true answer.

in. Question 215, by Mr. J. May.

Going to pass a leisure hour at billiards, I wondered to find the table an irregular hexagon, when seeing the balls fly very strangely in striking the several gins, made me think, If two balls A and B, lay on the said table, and the ball A was struck against the gin Rs, from thence reversing to St, from thence to Tv, then to vw, then to wx, thence to Xr, thence reversed, and struck the ball B; to find geometrically the points in the several gins, where the ball A will strike; and that by a general construction for all polygons, supposing the balls to be geometrical points?

iv. Question 216, by Mr. Henry Travis.

At Matlock, near the Peak in Derbyshire, where there are many surprising curiosities in nature, is a rock by the side of the river Dcrwent, rising perpendicularly to a wonderful height; which being inaccessible, I endeavoured to measure in a mathematical method. From a station at some distance, (nearly level with the bottom Of the rock) I took an angle of altitude to its top 47 3(/; and having designed a second station, I took an horizontal angle 87 5', between the foot of the rock and that station; the measured distance between the stations was 4 chains and 29 links, (per Gunter) or 283 274 feet At that place I had an angle of altitude 40 12', but forgot from hence to take an angle between my first station and the foot of the rock; yet am in hopes some curious artist will, from this data, determine the perpendicular height of this stupendous rock?

Answered by Mr. N. Farrer.

In the annexed figure, if Bt, Bt, represent the height of the rock perpendicular to the horizontal plane Abc; the points T and T (on the turning up the two triangles to which and the plane they are perpendicular) are supposed coincident; A and c the two stations, and Bac the horizontal angle given: by letting fall a perp. Cd by plain trigonom. I find Cd = m, and Ad = p. Then put 9= sine Zbat, (the angle at the first observation) and s = its cosine; h = sine Zbct (Z altit. at the second observation) and d — its cosine. Let x — Db, then (per 47 Eucl. I.) /(xx +mm) Cb and x+p — Ab; then n» cosine L Bat; its sine:: Ab: St cos. Bct: its sine:: Bc: Bt;

T. ftUESTiON 217, by Mr. Ant. Thacker.

Given the equation of the exponential curve Mdseb, together with the axis Ab = 6 = 1000; to find the greatest ordinate (sr) and inscribed parallelogram Deqp, and to give the analytical investigation of the same?

Pba' =.PDri; i.e. (b — xf

Answered by Mr. Rob. Heath.

When an ordinate (or any quantity) is a maximum, the logarithm of it, or any power of it is a maximum; consequently the log. of Rsrs Zz log. of Rbar zz x X log. of b — x is a maximum.

In fluxions —-+ X log. (6 — x) zz 0; where is easily determined 836-0532 &c. by a new method of solving exponential equations; v (163-9468)863'052 = y, *undy* = 657-1442 &c. very true to a decimal, the length of the greatest ordinate Rs required, By drawing the true figure, or trying the increase of the parallelogram, it appears that Ap is greater than 400, when the C=jq,edp — Dp X Pojs a maximum; and by the table of logarithms, it also appears that Dp — Eq is greater than 420, and Aq less than 987. This must be observed in order to have the following logarithmetic series converge Put 400 + x — Ap, 420 + y — Dp Zz Eq, and 987 —z zz Aq.; to find Dp and Pq. By the equation of the curve, PBAP = Pdpd = $wFzz$, or (600-)400+x = (4$0+y)i20+y zz (13 + zf7 % or m-xf -(p + y)P + » = (?+)r— by substitution; in logar.

m f lmm f 3 m

Now the value of any two ingle quantities may be found in terms of the other. The above in numbers *(g)* 21-8648 + (a) 5-730263 v vr. Question 218, *by Mr. Rich. Gibbons.*

I will undertake,-with 12 fair dice, to throw 42 once in 15 times; and between 37 and 47, at every throw. Quere, whether I shall be a g:;iner or loser by these chances, and the exact odds?

Anszeered by Mr. Peter Kay.

It is found from theorem 2, page 53, of Simpson's Laws of Chance, that the odds between 37 and 47 coming up at any assigned throw, with 12 dice, is as 1162 &c. to 1, or as 7 to 6 very nearly; which is an answer to one part of the question. And by theorem 1 in the same page, the probability of throwing just 42 comes out = 7Tq &c.

Therefore (1 — - &c.)15 =-3604 is the probability of losing in the other part of the question; and consequently the required odds for winning as 6396 to 3601, or as 16 to 9 nearly.

which is about 71199 to 128801. tluced from the above series, and chances to win, against 776299422 included; but if excluded, then 982355142 to lose.

The second query is easily dethe proposer has 1400482914 to lose*; i. e.* if 37 and 47 are 1194427194 to win, against *Mr. Rob. Heath answers this Quesiion.*

Thenumber of chances for 42 happening in one throw with 12 dice (by his theorem) will be 144840476; which taken from all the chances on all the dice, leaves 2031941860 chances for failing in one throw. The advantage in wagering to throw 42, once in 15 times with 12 fair dice, will be 6440045 to 3569955; or nearly as 9 to 5. To find the number of throws to make an equal wager; make ——— — i, which comes to x n; log-2 when $(a + bf$ l.o+b— 1.6 reduced; and solved x 100666 throws by common logarithms:

Mr. De Moivre says X '7 shews the trials requisite to that effect, when b is pretty large in respect of a; but in this case it shews it to happen in 982 throws; very near the truth: but his Table of Limits at p. 42 Doct. Chances, 2d edit, is not very exact, as being not deduced from exponential equations truly solved.

The sum of the chances for each party, N. in one throw (by the series) are found = 1194307074; which taken from all the chances on all the dice, leaves 982475262 chances for missing; therefore the odds are nearly 6 to 5. Q. E. F.

The Prize Question, *by Mr.* Rob. Heath.

It is proposed to enclose a park, the greatest possible, in the following manner: The straight bank of a river, having two trees growing at its extremities, at the distance of three furlongs, is to form one part of the boundary, and the other part is to be a mile in length. Two equal circular coverts or shades are to be made so as to touch the boundary of the park, and the longest right line that can be drawn from each of the trees to the opposite side of the park. Required the form and area of the park, and also the area of each of the coverts?
Answered by Mr. H. Travis.

Put 1 = radius of the circle; Tmait the park; q — 1570796 *The same anszcered by Mr.* Heath, *the Proposer.*

Since the river Tt (part of the boundary) is given straight, therefore the nearest the park can approach the form of a circle, is the segment Tmait the true form; which comprehends for its area a maximum. Put b = 320 poles = Tmait; d — 60 poles Tlt; p =: 6-28318 &c. x = arch Jot; then $(b+\%x)\, p$ — rad. = ©t. And, by a series for finding the sine from the radius, and arch given, d — *Questions proposed in* 1741, *and answered in* 1742.

i. Question 219, *by Mr.* J. May, *of Amsterdam.*

Here, in Holland, the land lying so very low, they are obliged to raise banks or dikes to keep the sea from overflowing it; yet some time ago a great storm, with a high tide, broke through one of. the banks, and laid the country for some miles under water. Going with some friends to the place where this inundation happened, and walk, ing upon one of these narrow banks, we saw at a distance three trees (a, B, c) standing in the water, which we were told stood at an equal distance from each other, at the corners of a triangular field; and a pole equidistant from each tree, that formerly was used as a mark'to shoot at with bows and arrows. Now one of our party proposed to find the content of the inundated field by the help of a staff, or measuring rod only, which we had with us. As we walked along this bank in a straight line (dp) at D we came in a straight line with the trees c and A; thence measuring 304 feet, at E we came in a right line with the trees c and B; thence continuing straight 1216 feet, at it we made a right line with the pole in the middle of the field, and the tree at the farther corner B; lastly, from R measuring right forward 1596 feet, at p we came in the line of Ba. From this, which was all we were then capable of doing, is required the content of the field Abc *l* (peb = 73 10'); the half sum (60) —" less difference is the lesser angle (epb = 46 50'.)

Then say, as sine Zb (60): Pe (281-2):: s. p (46 50'): Be (236 9). Again, s. Zecd (60): Ed (304):: s. Zn (13-10): Ec (79-959); v Be — Ec — 156-94 — Bc the side of the triangle required. Which squared and multiplied by V' give 10664-857 square feet, the area of the triangle Abc required.

There is a great many wfiys this problem may be solved, which I I shall reserve for another place, where the solutions to the questions in the Diaries shall be further discussed and illustrated. Only here observe, that by 3 Eucl. 6, the line Blr bisecting the Zb, cuts the opposite side into two segments PR and RE, in proportion to the other two sides (bp and Pe*)*, and consequently the sines of the angles they subtend in like ratio.
Construction. Upon Pe describe the segment of a circle capable of containing an Zof 60; and having completed the circle, from p, the middle ol the lower segment, through R draw a line to cut the circumference in B; join the points P, B, and E, B, and J_ Fb draw Dl, cutting Eb and Fb in c and A, and Abc will be the triangle whose area is required. For the Z Abc being, by construction = 60, the Z Fbe

—the half of it or 30, and the Zdlb aright one, the Zbcl will also be = 60, and of course the A Abc equilateral, H. *N. B.* The letter L is wanting in the figure at the intersection of the lines Ac, Br. *Answered by Mr.* R. Fall, *of Dunbar.*

As PR + Re (281-2) is to PR — RE (38), so is the tang, of half the sum of the (opposite) angles P and E; to tangent of half their difference (13 10'); and half the sum more the difference is equal to the greater angle *Additional Solution.* ii. Question 220, *by* Merones.

Being at sea on the first of May, and a clear forenoon, I made two observations of the sun, and found the difference of altitudes 16 30', the difference of azimuths 34 dcg. and the difference, of the times 2h 15m. Required the latitude of the place and hours of the day? *Ansvsered by Mr.* Ant. Thacker.

As sine 90: cosine sun's declin. (71 47'):: s. diff. of time (211 15'): 32 a fourth number = ©o the distance in the parallel of declin. Then tothenat. cos. of the diff. of azimuths (34—S29037) add radius, the sum is 1-829037,-which multiplied by the nat. cos. 16 31'=-958819) the difference of altitudes gives 1-753717282920, which made less by twice the cosine (32=2x-848048)=l-696096, leaves-057621082920; which divided by the versed sine of the difference of azimuths (34 =-170963) quotes-337453; which answers to the nat. sine of 70 18'; one half of which 35 9' made less by half the given difference of altit. (8 15') leaves 26 54' the altititude of the sun at the first observation, and more by 8 15' is = 43 24' the altit. at the second observation. Whence there is now sufficient given to find, by the common canons in trigonometry, the latitude = 57 5', and that the time of the first observation was at 7 26', and the second at 9h 41'.

The analytical Investigation of the abovesaid Theorem.
Given ⊙p = 71 47' comp. declination, the Z 0po = *33* 45' diff. time, whence ⊙o is found = 32, whose cosine call tn, put 2 cosine Qzo the diff. azim. *a* and *b* for sine and cosine of diff. alt. then will *bb — aa* or 1 — *laa*, or *Ibb* — 1 (= *n*) be the cosine of the diff. of the altitudes. Also let *x* and *y* express the sine and cosine of half the sum of the altitudes: then *yy — xx (— v)* will stand for the sum, *xb + ya* and *yb — ax* the sine and cosine of the greater altitude, *xb— ya* and *yb + ax* the sine and cosine of the lesser. Then by a theorem in page 176 of Simpson's fluxions, *xxbb — aayy+yyb-bz — aaxxz* 1—*xx* for*yyf* and reducing the equation we hare *xx —* in. Question 221, *by Mr.* Peter Kay.

One with six dice undertakes to bring up four faces of a sort at a throw; that is, either four aces, four duces, &c. in seven trials? What is the odds against him?
Answered by Mr. Farrer.
First (per p. 7 Simpson's Laws of Chance) 6!x!xf X X 6 — *a* = the probability that one face of a sort comes 3125 up at one throw with 6 dice. Then-" is the probability of four faces of a sort coming up at the first throw with six dice; and that 777fi4 _ 31254 of the contrary, and the odds 7776 — 31254 to 3125, or as a to A. Ihen by page 13, X-X —1 (a + B)b *71* — 2

X ———, &c. to *p*, factors: here *n* — 7, and *p — ;* which substi *t* ,.,.,,.
.. (31254X7776'—3125)6 tute in the above theorem, and it becomes = i 7776'

X 7 == the required probability = '8134, and that on the contrary 1866, and the odds 8134 to 1866, or as 4067 to 933, I. e. 2-1954 to 1.
Answered by Mr. Rob. Heath.
Raise the binomial *a* (1) + *b* (5) to the 6th power, the three first terms of which (a6 + *6a5b* + 15a46s) will be the chances for 6, 5, and 4 aces to come up, which (in this case) being multiplied by C,— 2436 chances for 6, 5, and 4 aces, duces, trays, &c. to come up 442207 at one throw; wherefore r———a are the chances for failing to throw 46656 3 6, 5, and 4 like faces in 7 trials; whence the wager's disadvantage is 687033 to 312967, or 11 to 5 nearly, viz. 2-197 to 1.

The same ansicered by Mcroncs.
The number of combinations of 4 aces out of 6 is 15; and in anyone case of these 15, any two left out are capable of 25 variation where no ace is found; therefore 375 gives all the cases where only 4 aces can be cast. But since 5 or 6 aces must be cast, the number of chances for these, which is 31, must be added; therefore all the cases wherein 4 aces can be cast with 6 dice, is 406. Now since there is the same variety for duces, trays, &c. therefore 2436 is the whole number of cases wherein 4 points of any one sort can be cast: Let the whole number of chances 46656 = *s*; 46656— 2436 *q — q;* the odds against the thrower for 7 casts will be as to 1 — , or as 2-1954 to 1.

It. Question 222, *by Mr.* Daniel Boote.

Some time in the spring quarter 1740, an observation was made of the sun, at 24 minutes past eight o'clock in the morning, and his altitude found 39 *7'.* Also at 15 minutes past ten o'clock (on the same forenoon) the altitude was 55 57'. From whence the latitude of the place of observation, month, and day may be found; and are required, with a general theorem for all questions of this nature.
Answered by Mr. J. May.
Let *a* be = sine of sun's alt. at the first observation; *b —* that of the second; c sine of the hour angle from 6 o'clock at the first observation; *d —* that at the second; and let r= radius; *b — a p; d — c — q; r — c — h;* and *r + d — k;* then the sine of the sun's *hp* southern altitude will be *a+* the degrees of which put = *in:* Likewise the sine of the sun's depression under the horizon in the north will be — whose degrees let be *zz n*; then the sun's declina*m — n* tion will be ——— — 20 25' N. answering to the 11th day of May; and the latitude is 90 — *m — n* — 46 58' north.

This question was answered by Mr. *Boote,* the proposer, and several others. But that we might shew what may be expected from the intended treatise of the Diary questions, &c. where this and other questions will be solved by simple equations, which have their origin *Answered by the Proposer Mr.* P. Kay, *and by* Merones.

Since the Telocity with which the ball is projected is sufficient to carry it over a space of 6 miles per second; and the velocity of the place of projection through the earth's rotation round its axis is 0-1802 miles per second; the absolute velocity compounded of these two will be 61115 miles per second; and the angle which the true direction of the ball makes with the horizon 29 24', and the azimuth or bearing from the south 46 22'. Let Pqko represent the earth, R. the place of projection, Achb the required trajectory, Aoh its transverse axis, Cb is conjugate, and ns a tangent to it at the point R. Putting Or = *d;* 6"1115z:»; nat. sine of Ors (119 24') — s; radius = 1; and the distance descended in one second, in parts of a mile, = r. Then by p. 23, of Mr. Simple son's Mathematical Essays, the transverse Ah will be = d-h (1 *vs f* AH — 17165 miles, the conjugate Cb ———— — 12633 miles; and *yr* the time of one entire revolution — 4h 27"" 13s from whence the time that the ball is in motion will be found 4h 6' 24s and the arch Rpq described, in the plane of a great circle round the centre of the earth, in that time will be 209 14'; but the angle, which that circle makes with the meridian, is found above to be 46 22'; from which angle, and the two given sides including it, the third side of the triangle, or the latitude of the place where the ball descends, may be found, and comes out 28 16' south: Also the angle at the pole, from the solution of the same spherical triangle, will be 156 30', which being added to 61 42' the arch described by the earth about its axis during the time the ball is in motion, gives 218 13' westerly, for the difference of longitude required.

Merones's *Answer.*

To answer every part of this problem at large, would require too much room: I shall therefore ouly explain the method of calculation: 1. Compounding the earth's motion, with the projectile's motion, I find its true velocity to be 6'11228, at an angle of elevation (above the horizon supposed at rest) 29 23', making an angle w ith the meridian 46 22'.

2. By propositions 15 and 17 Princip. I. the latus of the orbit is — 0301-53; the transverse axis of the ellipsis — 17252-42; and the periodic time — 4h 29B. 3. By measuring the area of the ellipsis, and part cut off by the earth's radius; the time of the flight above the earth will be found 4'' *Sm* 32-4 in which time it comprehends an arch of the earth (between its rising and falling) = 208 37'.
4. Therefore, by spherical trigonometry, the body falls in south latitude 28 48'; and the difference of longitude east is 226 29', from the point of projection supposed at rest. 5. But since the earth's motion in the time of the flight, transfers the place of projection 62 23' eastwards; therefore the place the body falls in will be in 164 6' east longitude from the place of projection. *ft.* Question 224, *by Mr.* Nich. Farrer.

Two ports bear north and south of each other, and distant 50 leagues: A ship sails from the south port to gain the other, and after running a certain distance upon the larboard tack, alters her course, and reaches the north port. On comparing the distances run, it was found that the distance upon the first course exceeded that upon the other by 10 leagues; and the space included by the distance of the ports and the distances run was 796 square leagues. Required the two courses, with the distance run upon each?

Now let us, suppose the ship to hare sailed uniformly at the rate of 4 miles an hour, and at the same time that she sailed from the south port, another ship sails from the north port, directly south, at the rate of 5--miles an hour, till she arrives at a port under the same meridian with the former ports, and is then known to be at the nearest distance from the first ship that she could possibly have been during the whole passage, if she had continued her course to the south port. Required the bearing and distance of the middlemost port from the first ship when she brought her starboard tacks on board?

Anszcered by Mr. V. Daniel.

From an analytical process (which shall be published elsewhere) is deduced this theorem. The sq. _ 796 root of — -p + 25s; that is, 4/(1681-026, = 41 nearly, made more by (5) half the compared distances, makes 46 leagues, the distance between the south and middle port; and less by (5) half the compared distance — 36, between the middle and north port: therefore 82 leagues is the distance run. The area 796 by 25 gives 31-84= Pe the perpendicular. Which squared and taken from the square of Se, *Additional Solution. Construction.* Since the perpendicular of the A Nes is given, being a 3d proportional to ns and the side of the square expressing the given area, the triangle itself may be constructed by prob. 76 of Simpson's Algebra, 2d edit. Or, perhaps, more elegantly thus: At N-L to Ns erect No = the given perpendicular, and continue it to H so that Gh — Ng; with centre s and radius Sk = Se —Ne describe a circle; then by prob. 12 of Mr. Lawson's Tangencies, find the the centre of a circle which shall touch that already described, and likewise pass through the points N and H, and that centre will be the vertex of the triangle. By cither of these methods the A being described; on Es, produced and parallel to Ns, take sc and ci proportional *to* the uniform velocities with which the ships move from s and N; then on an indefinite line drawn through the points I, s, let fall the J_ Nf, and complete the parallelogram Nfba, So will Ba be the minimum sought.—For constituting any other parallelogram *xfba*; then since, by sim. As, *sb: bf* or (Euc. I. 34.) No:: sc: ci, and likewise Sb: Bf — Na:: sc: ci, the points 6 and o, B and A will be contemporaneous positions of the two ships; and by Euc. I. 18, *nf* or *ba* is greater that Nf or Ba.

Had Ba been required of a given length, Nf need only have been taken equal to that length, and, it is manifest, the remainder of th« construction would have been performed as above, H.

Vii. Question 225, *by Mr. 3.* Corbctt.

In order to survey and divide the triangular field Abc, I bid my men measure the three sides round, whilst I took the angles. The owner would have it in three equal parts nearly divided, but as there was no water but one spring near the middle, in order to have the three fences run straight from it to the three corners, I took the angles there, as well as those at the spring to each corner, as in the scheme are set down; for he would have the content of each part separate. Having thus much, as angles, sides, &c. I thought surely I might from hencefind the lines to the corners (and areas) as well as Mr. Beighton, in his survey of Warwickshire, could find the situation of Newbold, and distance to High Cross, Tripontium, Eathorpe, &c. as he sets forth in the compartment of bis map j for that besides angles I should have three sides measured, whereas he had but one and a piece. As soon as we had done, night approaching, I repaired home: where I found they, blundering, had taken the three lines all in one sum just 100 chains. And I, being ambitious to match this mapmaker, have been puzzling to find a theorem less complex than his; $V(kVy + r) + -r$-is » minimum; the fluxion of this made $=z$ 0, 1 Vs

And the content of the whole field Abc 47 0 2046 *Mr.* John Jackson's *ansrcer.*

Calling Ac (a); Ab (6); Bc (c). And finding the sides as above. Putting *m zz* s. A () c — Cba, and *d* — cosine; *n* — s. Zc(t)b; and » = s. A©b. Thenj/zzs. Zboazz Ca0; —*if)* zzz — /1 — *vl* cosine; and tang. $= y$ ——7—— $1 = $ s. Cb 0 zz Ac ©. Then *n: c:: x*: _—c 0; and m: a:: «: — — c 0: consequently *n n n ay any., any* — :. *x* — —, and *mz* — *ay* — —: transposed, *mz* — *m cm cm any any* + *cmdy any* + *demy z an* + *dem cm cm'* — Cot" 'y cm2 — /*Xiy;* consequently $q = -f''' = 1-999 = 63\ 25'$, B0A — 26 35'. Whence the lines and areas as above.

Additional Solution.

The A Abc itself may be determined by the construction given to prob. 44, in the *Mathematician,* or by first describing a triangle similar to it; after which, if on Ab and Ac two segments of circles capable of containing Zs zz to 130 and 120 be described, their point of intersection will, it is plain, give the place of the spring, H.

The Prize Question, *by Mr.* J. Turner.

Dvf and Cvf are two different Apollonian P-. parabolas; v the vertex, and Vb the trans, Jj'S verse diameter of both; «b and As, ordinates /& "V" rightly applied: There is given the area Bfv r"-*jL* equal to 1473 poles, and Vf Zz Fb; F being the focus of the parabola Dvb.

Again, Vac is the other Apollonian parabola, whose arch Av, is to the arch Dv, as 1 to 2. And the ordinate As (rightly applied) being let fall on the common axis Vb, makes the area Asv a maximum. Required its parameter, and the area of the wood in statute measure by a simple equation?

Answered by Mr. Ant. Thacker.

Putting $x - rv$ the focal distance, and proceeding with the nature of the parabola, we get $1 =: 25\ z\ Fv$, Tb $Z= 50$, and Bb = 70-71.

there comes out $5 = -V(1 + \_\ )$; or $-/n + 4x4) = h$. L $3yy\ yyJ\ 3\ Ixx + (1 + 4x)$; whence by reversion of series, $x =z$ -986408; $g - 1$-01378; the curve = 1-4787; and in the parabola Av, where the curve is 44-9459; we shall have vs — 29-9823; Sa = 30-8142; and the area Vas = 615-921.

This question has exercised the faculties of a great number of persons versed in the most abstruse and higher parts of the mathematics, has occasioned a good deal of speculation and controversy; and the best of artists have been doubtful whether it is possible to be solved by any scientific method; nor can I apprehend I have received any such solutions, unless these two above.

The latter, by Merones, a person so profound in these sciences, that he is equal to the most arduous task; by his difference between the *absciss* and *ordinate* seems to be right, yet do not readily enough comprehend his process: And as I have long wished I could discover who he is, or how to direct to him; I would now heartily beg that favour, that he would please a little further to exemplify how the expression above, $Jyy + -$) + put into fluxions $yy / 4$ makes z (1 + 4a:4).

Remark. The Diary Author having, as above expressed, a desire of having some parts of the solution by Merones (Mr. Emerson) explained to him, and it no where appearing, that I know of, that he received any farther account of it; I think it my *duty,* as an Editor, to supply a particular explanation of the said solution, npthwithstanding the Editor of the Repository has thought fit to pass thia question by in silence; though his declared intention at the beginning was to ' supply defects by rendering the questions perfectly clear, and their subsequent answers as easy to be understood as the nature of the subject will admit.' The first principle of the solution is to find the curve a minimum under a given area, instead of the area a maximum and the curve given, as in the question, which is the same thing. Mr. Emerson assumes another curve similar to the curve required, whose area is-J, or xy — 1; and if a = the parameter, then $ax\ y\%$; from

X' these two equations we have = — , and $a\ rr\ rr$-$= y'$; also $- y\ x\ J\ a\ v\ 1$ — =: — — xx. Nbw the general expression for the length of the $y\ y$ writing y' for a in this expression, it becomes + —J + 2 4 X h. I.-s + —j) — a minimum; the fluxion of which be $y\ y\ J$ ing found in the common way, and made = 0, the equation gives:or h.l. $4 + + A$) = — V'O +-r) 5 that is (putting in$y\ y\ J\ yy\ y\ f$ stead of-) + 4) = 1-2x5 + /(+ 44), which y « thrown into a series, and reverted, # is found; thence y, and the curve. Then, by sim. figures, he proportions thus, as the length of the curve thus found is to the length given in the question, so is x and y here found, to the abscissa and ordinate required, H. *Questions proposed in* 1742, *and answered in* 1743.

i. Question 226, *by Mr.* Tho. Ramsey.

There is a triangular field, near to two trees, an oak and a pine. One of the fences of the field, if produced 18 chains, would touch the oak; and another, if produced 12 chains, would touch the pine. The trees are 40 chains asunder, and a right line joining them is parallel to the third side of the field. Required the area when a maximum *I Answered by* Hurlothrumbo.

Let Ac. be parallel to Cp; or =: $a - 40$; Oa zz $6 - 18$; AQ = pc =: c =: 12, and Oq = x. Then the area of the A Aoq is. /26V + 26 V + 2cV — b' — c4 — $x\ y$ — ";therefore, as xx (oq): (a — $\$y$ (ac5):: the said area: the area of the A Abc, which, by the question, is a maximum; v *(XT.* x: 26V + 26V + x 3eV — 64 — c4 x' is also a maximum: Whence a (fib — ccf — (66 + cc) a2 — (66 + cc) xi + weight 27 pounds; to find at what part of the rod of that pendulum, a weight of one pound must be fixed, so as to have the greatest effect in accelerating the pendulum; or, so that the time of the vibration may be the shortest possible? The rod itself being supposed void of gravity.

Anszcered by Mr. Kay.

Pnt a — the length of the pendulum — 29'2 inches; *to* — weight of the bob *17* pounds; o = the weight to be fixed to the rod — 1 pound; and x — the required distance thereof from the point of suspension*;* then the distance of the centre of oscillation from that .,,, aazc + xxv ,.,,, point will be -aw xv which by the question ought to be a mi nimnm; and therefore lixv X (arc-f-xv) — vx (aaza + xxv) = 0, whence xis — *a (klc* 'r"L—— 14.4(386 inches.

V The same anszcered by Mr. J. Watts.

The momenta of all moving bodies are as a rectangle of their celerity and mass, and the celerity of a pendulum as its length, &c. Then the centre of oscillation of any compound pendulum (by Colin Mac Laurin's Fluxions, lib. 2, p. 453) is equal to the squares of the distances multiplied into their respective weights, and their aggregate divided by the sum of the momenta; therefore (the answer as above.)

Hi. Question 228, *by Mr.* J. May.

The great inundations we have had here lately in Holland, has laid above six hundred thousand acres of land under water; and hath ruined and washed away the boundaries, that it is almost impossible again to determine each man's possessions; but to help a fricud, and prevent disputes, your assistance is desired.

He had a piece of land, Afpvd, which was divided into two equal parts by the right line Vf; of which the part Advf was a geometrical square; and the other part Vpf an apollonian parabola, v the vertex, and F its focus: but all was defaced except the side Ad; which we with some difficulty measured fifty-two chains. So that to fix the boundaries again there is required the lengths of the sides vp and Fp: It is also expected that the points v, r, r, &c. be determined by a geometrical construction.

Answered by Hurlothrumbo.

Upon the given line Ad describe the square Advf, and from the focus F, and vertex v, the parabola Vp; bisect Fv with the perpendicular Hg, and take Iig — f Ad, and from the centre G with the radiu9 Gv describe the circle Vpf, and from the point p, where it cuts the parabola, draw Fp, then will Advpfa (by book 1, prop. 30, Newton's Princip.) be the figure required.

In this Jig. a line drawn from F to p is omitted, which the reader may supply; the letter v *is also wanting. Answered by Mr. Farrer.*

Let w =: Vf = 52 chains, $x - Vb$; then $m - x$ = Bf, and per conies, Pb= %fmx, and the area of Vpf $- mx\ 4{-}m\ {-}x$) t/mx $-$ mm; this equation reduced is $x'' + 6mx + Qrn'x - 9tn - 0$; hence x = 34-77163, Bp =85-044, Fp = 86-77157, and the arch Vp = 93-7442 chains. And the points v, p, and F, will be determined by the following construction.

Let Hg — of Vf bisect at right a»gles the side of the square, and on the centre G, with Gf describe the circle, which will cut the carve in p.

Mr. J. May, the Proposer,
After an analytic answer, gives this geometrical construction: Having $xx = Aay$ from the property of the parabola, and $yx - 6aa$ — Sax then $yxx - 4ayy$, and $yxx - 6aax - Saxx$, whence $4ayy - 6aax - 3axx$, divided by 4a is yy — far — £xx, for xx put it value Say, we haveyy — %ax — Say, to which add $xx - 4ay$, is yy-xx — %ax+ ay an equation to a circle, an&$y - a\pm /(aa$ + fa$x$); put the surd zz 0, then is $y - a$; bisect Fv in H, and draw Hgi perpendicular to Vf, in which the centre of the circle will be; then $m - a$ + vCrJaa); make Hg — fa; draw Vg, this is V(ilaa) and the centre is G; put$x$ = 0, then = ay+0, and$y$ = $a + a$, or $y - 0$, or $- a$, then v, F are two points in the periphery. On the centre G with Gv draw the circle which cuts the given parabola in the required points.

iv. Question 229, *by* Hurlothrumbo.

Supposing an homogenous fluid, equal in density and magnitude to the earth, to revolve uniformly about an axis; so that the greatest diameter thereof may be just double the axis from pole to pole; to find the time of one entire revolution; with a general theorem for the solution of other questions of this nature? or that of $(266 + a)' (aa - (b + xf) = 0$; we get $1ax - 26'\ 2\ 2'$ *Answered by the Proposer.*

Let r be the time wherein a body would describe a circle about the earth, just above the surface, by means of its own gravity = lh 24m 45"? and let a be the arch of a circle whose radius is 1, and secant n, supposing the given ratio of the equatorial diameter to the axis be as n to 1. Theii by Simpson's Mathematical Disserta tions, we shall have r X W—, n. „ „,, —7-. for the 7 V (nn + 2) 3a — 9 /(nn — 1) exact time of one entire revolution; which therefore, when $n - 2$, or the equatorial diameter is just double the axis, will be 2h 31"1 20".

Meroncs's *Answer.*
Let r = earth's radius, / = 16 feet. That the equinoctial diameter may double the polar one, the centrifugal force must take away half the gravity; to do which any point in the equinoctial must in X''' describe the arch whose versed sine is f; or which is the same thing, the arch itself will be /rf; and the periodic time 3-1416 Jv/(4r-;-/) = 7147" = 2" fere; and therefore the body will revolve 12 times as fast as our earth. But to give an accurate solution to this problem, the decrease of gravity arising from the earth's figure, ought to be taken into consideration; but this would render the calculus very intricate, and too long for this place.

v. Question 230, *by Mr. J. Turner.*
Suppose the bung diameter of a spheroidal cask were 40 inches, and its diagonal 48 inches; it is required to find the head diameter of the least spheroidal cask possible, having the abovesaid dimensions; and its content in ale gallons?

Answered by Hurlothrumbo. — 48 — a, half the bung d half the head diameter = x; then the content will be
— 46a — 5bxl — 3'=0; that is, in numbers — 16000+ 3008a; — 100xJ — Sz5 = 6; whence x — 7-85, or x — 12-63, ori =-53'8, but none of these roots is the required value of x.

For. let Bdfh be a curve, whose abscissa Ac is, and ordinate (26" + xy (aa — (b + xf), and it is evident _ that when,the ordinate of this curve is a minimum, the cask will be so too; but it appears from what has been found above, that the ordinate Cd grows less and less, till x or Ac becomes 7-85 (because till then its iiuxion, or
— 16000 — 3008 — 100x2 _ 3X35 is a nega-A. C C tive quantity) after which it increases till x becomes 1263 (the fluxion being affirmative) and then decreases again continually, till x arrives at 20, its greatest value; in which circumstance it will be less than in any former position, as will easily appear upon trial; therefore the head diameter is equal to the bung diameter indefinitely near, and the required content 236-468 ale gallons.

Mr. N. Farrer's Answer.
If $m - 40$, $n - 48$, y = head diameter; then m -is the base ,. „. i i i „ , . , x w / Ann-mm—lmy-yy f the right-angled triangle, and (per 47 hue. 1.)/ — semilength. Let Ann— mm — d; then its length is $(d - lmy - yy)$, and its solidity = $(1mm + yy) /(d - lmy - yy)$ X 2618; whose fluxion lyy $(d - lmy - yy) (1mm$ -f $yy)$ $my - W$—. — 0. Reduced, 3«' + 5my-+ Immy — Idu /(d— my—yy) J J J + 1ms — 0. Hence y — 15-701465 — head diameter, 78-

187894 = length; 250-174 ale gall, the content. And farther observes, 1. The cask will be greatest when it becomes a spheroid, (whose length is then 87-266 inches, and content 259-28 a. g.) and least when a cylinder (length 53-066, content 236-46 a. g.); therefore the question, properly speaking, does not admit of either maximum or minimum, for the least spheroidal cask will be infinitely near the cylinder, greatest near the spheroid. 2. If the length be 76, the content is 252' 18 a. g. If 84 inches long, the content is 252-85, between these two the least is that found above. 3. Between this least and the cylinder, there is another, whose capacity is a maximum.

Mr. Hemingway,

After his answer, remarks, That when any expression is put into

fluxions, the roots of the equation determine so many limits of increase and decrease of the (lowinn quantity; whence if there's but one root which answers the conditions ot the problem, wc obtain a maximum or minimum; but if there be more than one, the limits those roots exhibit may not determine cither. In the present cafe, if the semidiff. of diam. — x increases gradually from its first value 73749, till it arrives at its second value 12-149, the cask continually decreases from 250-87 to 250-174; but x still increasing, the cask will increase again till it becomes a whole spheroid, whose content is 259259 a. g. Again, let x gradually decrease from its first value, and the cask will decrease likew ise, till it becomes a cjlindcr, w hose length is 53-066 inches, and content, 236-47, which is the minimum, and may be considered as the middle frustum of a spheroid of an infinite length.

Til. Question 232, *by Mr.* Ant. Thacker.

If $a;' + y' - 945yx - 0$, express the nature of the curve Am, and 150400 be the area of the space Amp; it is required to find the area of the greatest parallelogram that can be inscribed in the said figure AMP?

Answered by Hurlothrumbo.

Put $a = 945$, $b - 150400$, Pm = y, Ap = $-vy$, then, by writing vy instead of x in the equation of the av curve, &c. we shall have $y - \underline{\quad} x$ zz $2aVp -$ whose fluent

$\underline{\quad}$, &c. = 0: that is, $- 407728$ 4 200 80000 24000000' '' 6578-982 + 5-29832 —-0058333s —-0000125s4 = 0; or 6578-98 + 5-2983s8 —-005833s5 —-0000125s4 = 407728; which divided by the coefficient of s, (per Simpson's Flux. p. 101.) gives $z + 00080543'$ — 0000008s3 — 000000001s4 = 619742, compared with the series, in the same page, we have $b - -0008054$, $c = 0000008$, $d = 000000001$, &c. and $s = 61-9742$ which call y, then will $z = y - by' + (266 - c) x y'\&c. = 59-37973$, which added to 800, gives = 859-37973.

IX. Question 234.

A father at his death bequeathed to his daughters these portions, *viz.*

To the eldest he gave 2- of 1000 pounds.

To the second -3-' of 1000 pounds.

To the youngest 4-4 of 1000 pounds.

How much was each daughter's portion?

Answered by Mr. J. Watts.

Subtract the log. of 2= 0-3010300 from the log. of 10 = 1-0000000, the remainder is-69897000, which multiplied by 2 is-1397940 = the log. of-2-2, which subtract from unity, and the difference is-8602060, which sought in the logarithm tables, gives the absolute number answering-72478. And proceeding in like manner with-3' and-4-4, we shall have the eldest daughter's portion 724-78 = 7241. 16s. 4d. the second zz 696-84 = 6961. 16s. lid. and the youngest = 693-14 = 6931. 2s. 8d.

The Prize Question, *by Mr.* Heath.

Admiral Vernon sailing on a south course, from Jamaica to Carthagena, sees Don Blass right 'before him, steering due west, along the shore. He now continually bears directly upon him, in a right line; when coming up with him, it appears that the Don had sailed 8 leagues during the chace, and that the said admiral was 7 leagues distant from him when the chace began: Now, supposing each ship' motion to be uniform during the whole chace, to find from thence the distance sailed by Admiral Vernon?j *Questions proposed in* 1743, *and answered in* 1744.

1. Question 235, *by Mr.* Thomas Cowper. On the longest day, the distance from the branch of a tree to the

Then by trigonometry, as s. efd: Ed:: s. Zedf: Ef, i. e. x: d :: y: c; therefore $y\&S$ r» cx zz. dfi and $x y d$ —-c — tangent of /P

42 23' 51" the angle Ekd, or half the sum of the angles Bad and Baf = half the sum of the two altitudes of the sun. Again, sine

Edf: Ef:: rad.: Df, i. e.:C:: 1: e Uj y and as Ad: radius:: fd: sine of half $A £ C$ $r.$ c the angle Daf, viz. 6:1:: —: —-; or as 26: c:: i:-4-, viz. 26: c:: secant 42 23' 51": sine $5 y lby$ 31' 39" equal to half the angle Daf, which is half the difference of the required altitudes; whence the altitude Caf = 47 55' 30", and Cad = 36 52' 12", and the times of the day 8h and 9'1 16m, the latitude 52 197 37", the answer required.

Additional Solution.

Make Db = the given diff. of the shadow Fig. 1., and perpendicular thereto De = the given diff. of the heights of the boughs; then from E and B as centres, with the same given distance from each bough as a radius, describe two circular arcs, and having drawn Ea, and Ba to the point of intersection, A, draw DC j and Ea, and Ac drawn to meet Db, produced, in G, will determine Cg and AG for the two required heights of the boughs. Dc being, by construction, — Ea — Ba, AC (by Euc. I. 34.) =: and De and consequently the angle at G == the angle at D a right one. H.

H. Question 236, *by* Hurlothrumbo.

If two bodies, L and T, whose masses are respectively equal to those of the moon and earth, were projected at the same time, and in the same plane, from two places, A and B, at the distance of » hundred thousand miles from each other; the former, L, with a velocity of 5 miles per second, making an angle with Ab of 100 degrees, and the latter with a velocity of 2 miles per second, an angle (on the same side Ab) of 60 degrees; it is required to find the distance 'and position of the two bodies with respect to each other, also with respect to the points A and B, after they have been 48 hours in motion; supposing them, when in motion, to be only acted upon by each other, N *Answered.*

After the two bodies have been 48 hour in motion, t is distant from the point of projection (b) 393270 miles, and makes an angle with it of 59 55'. Also L makes with A an angle of 98 2S7, and is distant from it 861570 miles. Through the industrious labours of some of our correspondents we have got an answer to this abstruse and curious philosophical problem; but as it is doubted whether some errors are not in it, and believing no one so equal to the task as the author, whose knowledge and penetrability in such difficult and uncommon problems, is scarce to be rivalled in an age; we have given only the numbers above (besides the scheme and answer we have inserted in our first vol. of Diary Questions, p. 193,) till such time as the proposer favours us with his. *Solution taken from the Mathematician.* Let L and T represent the bodies as projected, whose masses are respectively equal to those of the moon and earth, or in the ratio of unity to 39-778; and let At and Bv, the absolute directions of the two bodies meet each other in v: then, in the triangle Abv are given all the angles and the side Ab (— 10000 miles) whence Av will be found equal to 253208 8163, and Bv = 287938-4609 miles respectively.

Now as 5 miles, the absolute space described by the body L in one second, is to 2 miles, the space described by the body T in the same time, so is the measure of Av, in miles, to 101283-5265, the measure of the space in miles, which T would uniformly describe in the time that L uniformly describes the space A v.

Let this space be denoted by Bt7, then it is manifest, when the body L, by an uniform motion hath described the space Av, and is arrived at v, the body T will have described the space Bt' in the same time, and arrived at T'; therefore if T'y Bv — Bt' =: 287938-4609

— 101283-5265:= 186654-9344) be divided at c' in the given ratio of their masses inversely, or cV be taken to T'v in the ratio of unity to 1 + 39-778, then r? will be the common centre of gravity (of the two bodies) in this position, and the distance cV will be found — 4577-344; 'which added to Bt/ gives Bc' = 105860-8705, whence vc' = 18077-5904.

Moreover, let Bc be taken to Ba, in the ratio of unity to 1 + 39-778, and then c will be the point of cquilibrio, or centre of gravity of the two bodies L and T, at the instant'of projection, and consequently the space Cb will be found = 2452-3027 and Ac = 97547-6973. Now, if the right line cc' be drawn, it is plain that in the time the bodies L and T would respectively describe the space The first vol. of questions here referred to, is *Thaekrft* Mtscel.-wheie ths calculation of this question is given, a.

Av and Bt', their common centre of gravity will describe the space cc'; therefore in the triangle Bcc', there being given the two sides Bc, Bc', and the included angle Cbc' = 60, the angle Bcc', shewing the direction of the path of the centre of gravity, will be found = 118 52', as also the space cc'(104656-2697 miles) described by the same centre in the time that L uniformly describes the space Av. Hence, it will be as Av: cc':: 5 miles the space described by L in one second, to 2-0666 miles the space described by the centre ot gravity in the same time.

Furthermore, draw Bf equal and parallel to cc/ and let the pa. rallelogram be completed, and join v, F' and r, F'; then in the triangle Fvv are given the two sides cV (ac), c'v and the include angle F'c'v *(60)* whence the angle cVv the relative direction of L with regard to the common centre of gravity, will be found 86 44' 50" and the side F'v = 157938 2168 miles the relative distances; hence it will be Av: Vf':: 5 miles the absolute velocity of the body L in one second: 3-118735 miles, the relative velocity in the same time.

Moreover, since the triangles Vc'f', and Fc't' have one angle c' common, and the sides about that angle proportional, those triangles are similar, therefore the bodies L and T will describe similar figure (which in this case are hyperbolas) about their common centre of gravity; and the space C'f being to cV as 1:39-778; the relative velocity of T will be that of L in the same ratio.

Let now F'lu represent the trajectory, or conic section described by the body t, to which F'v will be a tangent at the point F/; and let F'c'l be the area described about c' the focus, or centre of force, in 48 hours the proposed time, and let cc' (Af/ = Bf) be the distance which the common centre of gravity, or the plane where the motions are performed, is carried uniformly in that time; also let «Tbe the vertex of the trajectory and draw C'q. to which draw F'i and Ln perpendicular, putting the sine of 86 44' 50", the angle cVv (to the radius 1) (=-9983897 — s; 3982 the number of miles in the earth's radius $=yb$; 0003046, the parts of a mile which a heavy body will descend in a second of time at the earth's surface — r; yV = 0-0051913; 97547-6973 (cV) the distance of the point of projection from the centre of force $=di$ 3-118735, the relative velocity of L in a second, = v; the trans-' ——, from whence y will be fouud = 4996512 and consequently the distance (lc') of the body L from c' the centre of force = 502296: but Lc': Tv:: 39-778: 1, therefore rV = ——g = 12627, and consequently Tv + Lc7 the absolute distance of the bodies L from each-other = 514923.

Since in the two right-angled triangles C'ln, C'y'y there are given two sides in each of them, the angles I.c'n and Ncv will be found 84 7' and 3 40'respectively; the sum of both wl.icli is 87 56' the true anomaly of each body, or the angle described about the centre c'in the given time; but the distance c'c uniformly described by the centre of gravity of the two bodies in that time is 2-06G6 X 48 X 60 X 60 = 35710-848 miles; therefore if Ac' and Bt7 be drawn, in the triangle Acv will be given the two sides *Ay' (— cc'),* Fvand the angle Afv (= 180 — 118 52') 61 8'; whence Ac = 103020, the angle C'af7 — 56 2', and consequently the angle Acv = 62" 50'; therefore in the triangle Ac'l are giv n ihe two sides Ac', C'l and the included angle Ac'l — 150 46', whence the distance of the body *i.* from the place of projection A will be found

— 594320 and the angle C/al = 24 23' and consequently the angle Bai,, or the position of the bod) T. = 87 13': Lastly, in the triangle Acv are given the two sides Ac', cV and the included angle Ac/t/, whence At' = 97489 and the angle T'ac' — 6 C/; therefore in the triangle Abt are given the two sides Ab, At' and the contained angle Bat', whence Bt' the distance of the body T/ from the place of projection B will be found = 93785 and angle of position Abt' — 60 17'.

in. Question 237, *by Mr.* Ivich. Oats.

A fleet of ships, at Portsmouth, is bound with military stores, &c. for our brave admiral in the West Indies; and being informed, by experienced navigators, that a ship, in sailing upon a wind, having her larboard tacks on board, which makes her way good six miles an hour, will, when got into a trade wind (which blows in the latitude of thirty) make her way nine miles an hQur; now admit the fleet can sail at the rate above, I demand the course and distance, before and after their arrival in the trade wind, to be performed in the shortest time possible, from the Lizard to Jamaica, and the minimum, according to Wright's projection. Lizard in lat. 49 56', long. 5 14' west, Jamaica 18 and 76?

Answered by Bironnos. Let Lm represent the enlarged diflf. lat. between the Lizard and

Let =: 3-14159; a — length of the pendulum; c =-= the versed sine ol the arch described in the descend; then the time of descent, or i half the time of vibration, will be — x: 1 + V 2.2.2a c«

&c. and the time along the chord by 2/2«; (as demon.

2.2.4.4.4a v p. 140, 141, of Simpson's Flux.) which two expressions must by f X the question be equal to each other; divide both by ,,and put $e \times S\ 4\ x$ — — and the equation will become 1 + h —' &c. = —. 2a 1 2.3 2.2.4.4 / + r — l and rn —, consequently «is found = and $r\ zz$ jj therefore a — / zz 15, e = ma = 18, u = na = 21, and $y\ zz\ ra\ zz$ 25. i» *The solution of this question, as given by Mr. Ash, is omitted, at being so very erroneous.* vi. Question 240, *by* F. R. S.

Let there be the frustum of a cone, whose less diameter is 20 inches, its greater 40, and length 90; which being cut by a plane diagonally through the contrary extremities of its two diameters, will divide it into two parts (called hoofs) a greater and a less. There is required a scientific theorem for finding the solid content of each part; there being none yet given by any author (except perhaps those got from a tedious series) which will give the contents precisely true, when at the same time we have found by an analytical method, the true solidity of each. All which may be made fully appear, and shall be demonstrated in the next year's Diary.

vii. Question 241, *by Mr.* Will. Daniel.

It is universally agreed, that the heat at any moment of time, on any day, is proportionable to the rectangle made of the sine of the sun's altitude, and the arc of time expressing his continuance above the horizon: which being allowed, it is required to find what time of the day will be the hottest at Coventry, (lat. 52 30') on August 14, 1743.

N. B. This is one of the two problems which Mr. Stone (in his translation of L'Hospital's Fluxions) challenges the mathematicians of Europe to answer.

Tol. 1. T

—: which series reverted will give the value of t — tangent 14 28'.' *ca* vm.

Question 242, *by Mr.* J. May, *jun.*

Last spring, 1742, being at sea in north latitude, we had great storms for several days together, succeeded with cloudy weather, which hindered our making observations; at last when it cleared, up, with Mr. Hadley's octant, upon deck, I endeavoured to take the sun's meridian altitude, but unfortunately thick clouds prevented it. Now being at a great loss to know where we were, we endeavoured to contrive some other way; and accordingly waiting a few minutes, it cleared up again, and we took the sun's altitude (after allowance for refraction and dip of horizon, &c.) 57 24'52"; tarrying 26 *The same answered by* F. R. S.

Let the quantities be represented as above; also let r and s — sine and coiine of the latitude; and a and c the sine and cosine of the sun's distance from the pole. Then in the three triangles by the spheric theorem, we have *()* $er + asy = c$, (2) er -f wpy — $ashx = t$, (3) er -f-$asny$ — $asmx =$; d.

In the (1) er — c — asy, which substituted in the other two, make (4) c— asy + Ry — as Ax = t, (5) c — ay + $asny$ — $asmx$ — d; per (4) — asy + $aspy$ — $ashx = t$— c = g,.. as =—— g — T,—'—; r: ca" 1 — P = o = versed sine 6 30', then rr will as = _; by the (5) — $asii$ + asnu — $asmx$ — d — c

— yv — hx — k, as — 1 — —;and if 1 —

—y ny —mx —y ('—n) — mx k n — w = vers, sine 12 45', then will as — :conse

— yw — mx qilently —r-r=, or *f-r*— —.which J —yv—hx —yw — mx yv + hx yw+mx out of fractions *gyta + gmx* — kyv + kpx ——— £f? — y gm — kli tangent of the Znpl = 12 *10'-36"* = time 49m22s. Whence the answer will come out as above.

I cannot but be persuaded that this curious problem will point out a way to be very useful in navigation for determining the longitudes as well as latitudes: for, supposing at sea we know neither, or had not the time of the day, but were furnished with a quadrant to take altitudes of the sun, and could find the difference in time between each observation, which a common pocket watch with a minute hand would give us very well, or with a second hand better. For though that watch or a clock was incapable of keeping true time at sea, yet it might very well measure a few minutes between one observation and another, in which space the error must be very inconsiderable. Now when this was done, by solving this problem, we get the latitude and the true times of the day, and then it would be no very difficult task to rectify the longitude pretty near. In order to this we shall deduce a theorem in words, by which any one that is but skilled in the common cases in trigonometry may put it in practice.

A Theorem for the Hour of the Day.

1. The difference between the first and second altitude, drawn into (t. *e.* multiplied by) the versed sine of the arch of time between the first and second obser-

vation; made less by the difference between the first and second altitude, multiplied into the versed sine of the arch of time between the first and third observations. 2. The difference between the first and second altitude, drawn into the right sine of the arch of time, between the first and third observations; minus the difference between the first and third altitude, i drawn into the right sine of the arch of time between the first and second observations.

Lastly, Divide the former difference by the latter, and the quotient will be the tangent of the arch of the time from noon.

The same anszcered by Mr. J. May, the Proposer.

Put a = sine 57 24' 52", b = that of 55" 35' 19", c = that of 53 15' 16", the sine of 26m or 6 30' = m, cos. = n, f — sine 12 42' (= 51"') the time between the first and last observ. its cos.

— g, radius zz 1. Then put $a - b - h$, $a - c - i$, $r - n s$, $r - g - t$; then the tangent of the hour angle from noon when the *Jit jg j* greatest altitude was taken will be — — r - -2190328 = 12'

D $mi - hj$ 21' 16", which in time is 49m 25', or after 12 o'clock; the second lh 15m25s; and the last at 1h 40" 25", according to the altitude's decrease.

Now put the cosine of 12 21' 16" = d; of 25 6' 16" (the arc of 1h 40TM 25s time of the last observation) — e; put likewise $d - e - q$, $r - e I$, and $r + d - p$.

Then the sine of the sun's southern altitude will be — $b + R$ -f (see his answer to quest. 222, Diary 1742) the degrees of which put — w. Likewise the sine of the sun's depression in the north will be pi-r-q — a; the degrees of it put = u; then the sun's declination will be $(w + u)$ — 20 47' nearly; and the cosine of the latitude i(jo —M)-38 4' 45", and 51 55' 15" the latitude required.

ix. Question 243, *by Mr* John Powle.

Let there be three spherical and perfectly elastic bodies, A, B, c: the weight of A — 3 pounds, and of c = 27. Now it is required to find the weight, of the intermediate body B, so that A striking B at rest, and B, with the motion acquired by the stroke, striking c at rest, the motion produced in c, shall be a maximum?

Answered by Mr. J. Landen.

Theirbweighr 3,' x, 27. Thcn accordinS- to Mr-Neil's Introduct, *la*

Fhys. we have——-= the celerity wherewith the body B will approach c, and, —,— = the velocity of c after the im pulse; the fluxion of which being made — 0, and reduced, we har« $x = 9$, a mean proportional between A and c.

Mr. Tho. Cowper's *answer.'*

The bodies and weights denoted as above, and putting 1 to express the velocity of A: from Dr. Keil's demonstration about the motions of elastic bodies is deduced this analogy: As the sum of the bodies: twice the weight of the moving or striking body:: the velocity of the striking body before percussion: the velocity of the quiescent body after it. That is, $x + a$: 2a:: 1: 2a

———1 = velocity of B after the stroke. Again, $x + c$: 2x:: 2a $4ax$ —:— :;; — the celerity of c after the stroke; $x + a\ xx + cx + ax + at$ which, per question, is a maximum, and the fluxion thereof $4ax,x + Aaexx + 4aaxx — 8axx — Aacxx — 4aax = 0$. Reduced, gives $x — A/uc$ pounds.

The Prize Question, *by the late illustrious Sir* I. Newton.

Three staves being erected, or set up on end, in some certain place of the earth, perpendicular to the plane of the horizon, ia the points A, n, and c; whereof that which is at A, is 6 feet long; that in B, 18; that in c, 8; the line Ab being 33 feet long: It hap. pens on a certain day in the year, that the end of the shadow of the staff A passes through the points B and c: and of the staff B, through A and c; and of the staff c, through the point A.

To find the sun's declination, and the elevation of the pole or day, and tho place where this shall happen. *Note*, this is the 42d problem in Sir Isaac Newton's Universal Arithmetic; and it may seem a piece of vanity in attempting to give a solution after the greatest of men; but having in the winter 1740, taken a great deal of pains to bring out a solution, and never being able to get his numbers for the declination and latitude precisely the same, I was fond to think his were exdet, and wrought it over and over again; at first it came out an adfected equation, then a quadratic, and at last happily by a simple equation; and having taking the pains to prove all the numbers (not depending on the logarithms) fifund them agree in every particular, and by construction to form a true conic section. We therefore humbly presume, that in a calculus so prolix and difficult (in Sir Isaac's method) there might happen a small error, or at least some press fault of the editions, or in the translation; which we hope to make more fully appear in the next year's Diary.

,,,,, — = 1-948315, the versed sine of an are $1 + hh + kk — Ihkv — vv$ which is double the latitude 161 30/; whose half is = 80 45', the true latitude required.

Now calling the sine of the latitude p, then will $P0\ Pa\ \_\ s + m$ 33309 =: the sine of 19 27', the sun's declination north.

Sir I. Newton, the author of this problem finds the lat. 80 20", and declination 19 27' 20", as may be seen in the 42d prob. of his Universal Arithmetic, in the English edit. 1720, p. 151, where the translator Mr. Raphson, Mr. Cunn, or the printer, committed a blunder, making the line Ab = 30, instead of 33. By reason of which disappointment, the solution is here shortrr than was designed; but the investigation of the theorem above wc have pr.nted in the first vo. lume of Diary Questions Thacker's Miscel. If the line Ab was 30, then *Ilerg follows the Solution from* Thacker's *Miscellany alluded to above.*

Call height of the staff in the point A, (a); that in B, (b); that in c, (c); the line Ab (d); the distance betwixt the top of the staff in A, and the bottom of thfe staff in B, (e); the distance betwixt the top of the staff in B, and the bottom of the staff in A, (/); and let Ac — x, Cb 2; then /($xx + ad$) s, and /($xx + $ cc) — tn, the distances betwixt the top of the staff in A and bottom of the staff in c, and top of the staff in c and bottom of the staff in A, respectively. And suppose us the meridian line, radius n 1; then will $a\ e$ and d -7-e be the sine and cosine of the sun's altitude when he makes the shade Ab by the staff A; for the cosine of the angle Abn (or Ban) — cosine of the un's azimuth from the north at that time, put q= v. Again, b -r/ and d--f express the sine and cosine of the sun's altitude when he makes the shade Ba by the staff B; the cosine of Ban (or Abn) = cosine of the sun's azimuth from the north at that time + v. Also a -f- and x -f- will be the sine and cosine of the sun's altitude when he makes the shade Ac by the staff A; and let + y be put to denote the cosine of the angle Acn (or Can r:) the sun's aziniuth from the north at that time; again, c-r-m and x -f-m will express the sine and cosine of the sun's altitude when he makes the shade Ca by the staff c; and + y the cosine of the angle Can (or Acn) =: the cosine of the sun's azimuth at that time from the north. Lastly, let p and q be put to express the sine and cosine of (he required latitude; and g, the sine of the sun's declination. Then (1) — +:

— g. Whence, by equation (1), we have ± qdv — ge—pa; m and by equation (2) pb — gf — + qdv; consequently ge — pa — pb —gf; and$g$ = pb pa; again, by equation (3), we get + qxy — gs — /«, and by equation (4), pc — gm — + qxy: consequently gs — pa — pc — gm, .. g — therefore pc + pa pb + pa c + ab + a _ (c + «) (e + /) + m e+f 5 s + m e + f b + a (c 4-a) (e + f) zz s + m: .;—r — — m — s. which squared is b + a , „, 2Mrp.,, hV kp squared, &c. makes — + v 1 — — —, or, by writing 1-p' for ?,-+ = 1

And by reduction 2ps =-+ y +.r_2Mg _ p» the versed sine of an-arc, which is double the required latitude. And the sine of the sun's declination is known to be g — we Pa _ + m Another Solution, by Mr. Skene, taken jrom Davis's Mathemdtical Companion for 1805,

Among a variety of problems, which, were proposed, about the time of Des Cartes, as instances of the excellence of the modern analysis, and its superiority to the ancient, the following appears to be the most abs'ruse, as well as the most curious and remarkable. Des Cartes speaks of it in his Epistles as a problem of the greatest difficulty, and eminently fitted ad notandam industriam bene disscrendi equationes. From Francis a Schooten we learn that it was first published in the year 1640, in a very ingenious book, entitled Den Onwissen Wis-konstenaerl. I. Stampioenius.+ The solution there exhibited, is revised, corrected, and improved in Schooten's Additamentum to his Commentary on Des Cartes's Geometry. J The Additamentum, indeed, is principally occupied with this problem, which is placed at the end of the Commentary as a proof, as he himself expresses it, non facile problema aliquod datum iri, quod hanc geometriam atfugiat, aut ejusdam methodo solvi'non possit. Sir Isaac Newton has likewise given a solution to this problem in his Arithmetica Universalis, published by Whiston 1707. It may be justly concluded, that it would be in vain to seek for a more elegant solution of a problem which has passed through the hands of such eminent men. Newton's, in particular, is one of the finest specimens of algebraic analysis in the whole circle of the mathematical sciences. But as the question has been supposed to be beyond the reach of the ancient geometry, I shall make no apology for giving the following solution, which is etfected without the assistance of algebra.—1—The problem is thus enunciated by Des Cartes.

"Tres baculi erecti sunt ad perpendiculum in horizontal piano, ex punctis A, B, c; et baculus A est 6 pedum, B 18 pedum, c 8 pedum, et linea Ab est 33 pedum; et una atque eadem die extremitas umbra? Solaris, quam facit baculus A, transit per puncta B & c, extremitas umbrae baculi B per A & c, et ex consequent! etiam baculi c per A & B. Quaeritur in quaenam poli altitudine, & qua die anni it Ren Pes Cartes, Epist. Part II. Epist. Lxxi. page 257, Francf. Ed. f Edited by Jacob a Waessenaer. L.

J Schootei merely premised a lemma and added an explanation by Erasmius Bartholin us. L. contingat." This enunciation is in part erroneous, for it does not follow, as is here affirmed, that the end of the staff at c must pass through the points A and B, because the end of the staff at A passes through B and c, and that of the staff at B through A and c: another circumstance must be given, namely, that the end of the staff at c passes through A, so that it is necessary to change "et ex consequent!, &c. into baculi c per punctum A, et ex consequent etiam baculi c per punctum B." In this manner it is enunciated by Schooten, with this difference only, that the consequence from the other part of the data the end of the staff at c's passing through B is demonstrated by him algebraically; and the same is done by Newton.

The following is a geometrical demonstration.

The end of the shadow of the staff at A describes a conic section, which let be Cedgb (Tig. 1.). Let A, B, C, be the places of the three staves, and let Ba, Ca be produced to meet the curve in n, G. Draw also Ef through A parallel to Bc, to meet the curve in E, F, and join De, Cf. Then when A casts the shadow Ad, B casts the shadow Ba; and when A casts Ae, B casts Bc. Therefore Ad is to Ba as Ae to Bc; but Ae is parallel to Bc by the construction, consequently De is parallel to Ac Now Bc being parallel to Ef, cc parallel to Ed, and c. E two points in the conic section, Gf is parallel to Bd, by Simson's Con. Sect, lib. iv. prop. 29. Hence Bc is to Af as Ca to Ag, and the end of the shadow of c therefore passes through the point B, whatever be the conic section described by the extremities of the shadows. Q. E. D.

This property in the ellipse may be still more easily demonstrated by first shewing its truth in the circle, and thence transferring it to the ellipse by cutting a cylinder obliquely.

We shall now proceed to point out our method of resolving the problem, for which purpose the following lemma is required., Lemma. If the altitudes of the sun be taken at the same place on the same day, when he is in two opposite directions, the sum of their tangents will be to the sum of their secants as the sine of the sun's declination to the sine of the latitude of the place.

Let z fig. 2.) be the zenith, p the pole, zp the co-latitude, Zq, zo the co-altitudes, and Pq or Po the complement of the sun's declination. Draw Pm perpendicular to zo, and Qm, Om will be equal to each other; therefore Om is equal $i(zo + Zq)$ and Zm equal to $j(zo — Zq)$ Then, by an elementary property of spherical triangles, cos Pq: cos Zp:: cos Om:cos Zm:: cos '(zo + Zq): cos (zo — Zq). But cos f (zo + Zq) ls to the cos (zo — Zq), as the cot zo + cot Zq to the cosec zo + cosec Zq; therefore cos Pq: cos zp:: cot zo + cot Zq: cosec zo + cosec Zq, that is, the sine of the lun's declination is to the sine of the latitude of the place as the sum, &c. *Q. E. D. Cor.* If two altitudes of the sun be taken on the same day, when he is in opposite directions, and other two altitudes when he is likewise in opposite directions, the sum of the tangents of the first two will be to the sum of the tangents of the second two, as the sum of the secants of the first two to the sum of the secants of the second two. This corollary follows directly from the lemma, as the latitude and declination remain the same.

Now as the heights of the two staves at A and B *(fig 3.)* are given, and the lengths of their respective shadows, when the sun is in opposite directions, the two altitudes are likewise given, and consequently the ratio of the sum of their tangents to the sum of their secants. Let Ad represent the staff at A, and Ce the staff at c. Take Cf on Ec produced equal to Ad, and join Ae, Af. Then will Ce and Cf represent the tangents, and Ae, Af the secants of the sun's altitudes, when in the opposite directions Ac, Ca; and therefore by the lemma the ratio Ef to Ae + Af is given; but Ef is given, consequently Ae + Af is given. Now, by an elementary proposition in plain trigonometry, Ae + Af is to Ef as the difference hetween Ce, Cf to the difference between Ae, Af; which difference is therefore given, and consequently Ae, Af. Hence Ac, the distance between the two staves A and c, becomes known.

In a manner exactly similar may the distance Bc, between the two staves B and c, be found, for the data are the same in both.

Then having given the three sides of the triangle Abc, the angle Bac may be determined; and as the heights of the staves at A and c are given, and their distance Ac, the sun's altitudes, when in the opposite directions Ca, Ac, are likewise given.

Now let z on the glube represent the zenith of the place, *(fig. 2.)* at which the observation is made, p the pole, Zp the co-latitude, Zq, zo the zenith distances of the sun, when in the opposite directions Ab, Ba, and zs, Zt the zenith distances of the sun, when in the opposite directions Ca, Ac. Draw the great circles Pq, Po, Ps, Pt, which will be all equal, being the co-declination of the sun: also Pm perpendicular to Oq, and Pn to St.

It is evident that Zm, which is equal to-§(zo — Zq), and Zn, which is equal to *(zs — Zt)*, are both given, but Nzm is equal to the angle Bac *(fig. 3.)*, being the difference of the sun's azimuths when in the directions Ab, Ac. Hence this construction.

Take Zm in zo equal to *(zo — Zq)*, and Zn in zs, whose position is given, equal to *(zs— Zt)*; draw the great circle Mp perpendicular to Oq, and Np perpendicular to St; the point p where they inter-, sect each other is the pole, which being determined the latitude and declination are given.

Wc shall now give the numerical calculation.

Let Ad *(fig. 3.)* perpendicular to Ab be equal to the staff at A, Eh perpendicular to Ab equal to the staff at B, and let Bo, Ah be dra . n. Then will Ad = 6, Bh — 18, Ce = 8, and Ab = 33. Hence Newton's *Solution being so very elegant and complete, the Editor has thought fit to insert it here for the sake of those who are not in possession of the Arithmetica Universalis. % Solution by Sir* Isaac Newton.

Because the shadow of each staff describes a conic section, or the section of a luminous cone, whose vertex is the top of the staff; I will feign Bcdef to be such a curve, (whether it be an hyperbola, parabola, or ellipse) as the shadow of the staff A describes that day, -*Jjks::!* by putting Ad, Ae, Af, to have been its shadows, when Bc, Ba, Ca, were respectively the shadows of the staves B and c. And besides I will suppose Paq to be the meridional line, or the axis of this curve, to which the perpendiculars Bm, Ch, Dk, En, and Fl, being let fall, are ordinates. And I will denote these ordinates indefinitely by the letter *y*, and" the intercepted parts of the axis Am, Ab, Ak, An, and Aj, by the letter *x*. I will suppose, lastly, the equation aa -L bx -L $cxx — yy$, to express the relation of a; and *y*, (*i. e.* the nature of the curve) assuming aa, *b* anoc, as known quantities, as they will be found to be from the analysis. Where I made the unknown quantities of two dimensions only because the equation is to express a conic section: and *I* omitted the odd dimensions of *y*, because it is an ordinate to the axis. And I denoted the signs of *b* and *c*, as being indeterminate by the note X, which I use indifferently for + or —, and its opposite T for the contrary. But I made the sign of the square aa affirmative, because the concave part of the curve necessarily contains the staff A, projecting its shadows to the opposite parts (c and r, D and E); and therefore if at the point A you erect the perpendicular A(3, this will somewhere meet the curve, suppose in g, that is, the ordinate *y*, where *x* is nothing, will still be real. From thence it follows that its squire, which in that case is aa, will be affirmative.

It is manifest therefore, that this fictitious equation aa X X $cxx — yy$, as it is not filled with superfluous terms, so neither is it more restrained than what is capable of satisfying all the conditions of this problem, and will denote the hyperbola, ellipse, or parabola, according as the values of aa, *b*, c, shall be determined, or perhaps found to be nothing. But what may be their values, and with what signs *b* and *c* are to be affected, and thence what sort of a curve this may be, will be manifest from the following analysis.

The former Part of the Analysis.
Since the shadows are as the altitudes of the Staves, you will have Bc: Ad:: Ab: Ae (:: 18: 6):: 3:1. Also Ca: Af (:: 8: 6):: 4: 3. Wherefore naming Am — *r*, Mb — *s*, Ah Z= *t*, and Hc = J.s. From the similitude of the triangles Amb, Ane,

and Ahc, Alf, An will be — — r. Ne — —-J-.?, Al — — t, and Lf = Tf w; whose signs I put contrary to the signs of Am, Mb, Ah, Hc, because they tend contrary ways with respect to the point A from which they are drawn, or to the axis Pq on which they stand. Now these being respectively written for x and y in the fictitious equation aa JL bx X cxx — yy r and s will give aa X br X err — ss.

— £r and — s will give aa T $-jbr$ X $icrr$ zz ss. t and X v will give aa X W X ctt zz vv.

— it and T f o "will give aa T bt JL dt —fvv.

Now, by exterminating ss from the first and second equations, in %aa order to obtain r, there comes out Tt = r. Whence it is manifest that-X b is affirmative. Also by exterminating ca from the third *Questions proposed in* 1744, *and answered in* 1745. I. Question 244, *by Mr.* John Turner. Suppose a heavy flexible chain 18 inches long, suspended at.it ends from two pins in the same horizontal line, 12 inches asunder; how far is the lowest point of the chain below the line of the pins: also required a general theorem expressing the area of the space included by the chain and the line joining the pins.

.... » *Answered by Mr.* N. Farrer.
Let a — the force which keeps the chain in its position at A, x zzt Ac, y — Bc, z Ab; draw the tangent Bs, and Bt — Ba perpendicular to the horizon, and Ts parallel thereto. Then will the line Ab be sustained by three forces; for its gravity acts In the direction Bt, it is drawn dt A in an horizontal direction by the force a, and it is sustained in B by the tension of the line Sb; which three forces are'consequently as Bt, Ts, and Bs; as Bt — z: Ts — a :: i: y. Take sr eb, and draw rn parallel to Bs, and an perpendicular thereto; then Bt is the perpendicular force or weight of the line at B, is. the fluxion of the tension at B, whose fluent (x) is the tension or force in the direction nr; but in A where a: — O, this tension zz a, ergo by correction the whole tension drawing in the direction ot the curve is $a + x;$ then Bs =: $a + x : z :s : i, .-. ai + xi$ zz. zi its fluent is $2ar + xx = zz$, therefore y zz j t i j, $a + x +$ /$(2az + xx)$,. . $a.ndy$ —: hyp. log. of — -';which hence yx the flux, of the variable area vmn is

————; r X + zz) — a) = oi 77-—7 r whose fluent is za— ax — the area, and when $z — c$ (x being then — 6) becomes (c — 6) X a the expression for the area Cde,.. the area of the curve is 50-1888, and Db the lowest descent of the chain zz 6-0317 inches.

11. Question 245, *by Mr.* John Landcn. I hare one hundred pieces of gold; some of which are pistoles, some guineas, and the rest moidores. Now if a pistole was worth 18s. 6d. a guinea worth II. 3s. and a moidore 11. 10s. my hundred pieces would be worth one hundred pounds. Quere, how many ha?a I of each sort? *Answered by Mr.* Heath.
Let x — the number of moidores, y — guineas; then $b — y — x$ — the pistoles (putting for 100 pieces); hence $60x$ $37b$ — $37y$

— 37,z 4-$46y$ zz 4000 the number of sixpences; whence x zz 300 — $9y$ 300 — 23x.,,..
or y — ;from whence x and y are determined in whole numbers 6 and 18, also $b — y — x$ zz. 76. *Remark.* This question may also be solved after the manner of several others of the same kind already given in this work. H.
Hi. Question 246, *by Mr.* Peter Kay.

To find the centre of oscillation of a pendulum, whose bob u composed of two equal and similar parabolical conoids, joined together at their bases; the thickness of the bob being three inches, the diameter of its greatest circle seven inches, and the distance of its centre from the point of suspension 395 inches?
Solution.
Let A represent the point of suspension. Now here is given A = 39-5 — d, Bo = 3-5 = m, and co = 1-5 — $n:$ Let y — Sf = Sg, ar=cs, and put c for the distance of the centre of oscillation from the point of suspension, nature of the centre) 2d x flu. of nxx $m'x$, «' + 3dlT $d + 3d$ (when = »$l0TX$ = ») m 3-59 + 3d = 39'5 + FJnSi = 39'5 +-103376 = 39-603376 the distance required, H.
Mr. *N. Farrer's* solution, being erroneous, is omitted,

iv. Question 247, *by Mr.* J. Bctts.

A set of men and women were drinking together, and their reckoning came to just six guineas; towards the discharging of which, each man agreed to pay a certain sum, and each woman the square root of the same: Now it was found, if the number of men and women were mutually changed the one for the other, the reckoning would have come to half a Portugal piece less, or only to 41. 10s. Again it was found, that each man paid as many shillings more than each woman, as there were women in company. It is required what number were of each, and what each paid? *Answered by Mr.* R. Gibbons.
Put m — the number of men, n — the number of women, and
— what each woman paid; then, per question, each man paid xx. Hence $mxx + nx — 126$, $nxx + mx = 90$, and $xx — x — n$. Now 126—nx by taking the value of m in the two first equations, we have ———
— 90 — nxx. From which and the third equation we get $x — x — a? + = 90 — 126$; whence $x = 3$ the shillings each woman paid, and =: 9 what each man paid; consequently there were 12 men and 6 women.
v. Question 248, *by Mr.* William Daniel.
In an oblique-angled triangle (egf) thero is given the difference of 2/(aa — 6 &eM) s '2y'(aa — 6/dd) ac a = the less, and,.-=-056033 = s. 3 12, so that the $y + b$ 25 greater angle is 36 54', and the less 30 29'.
Additional Solution.
With the centre F, and radius Fg, the shorter side, describe a circle cutting the base in B, and the longer side Ef in D: then Ed is — the difference of the sides, and Eb — the difference of the segments of the base. J oin Db, Gd; then the angle Bdg = half Bfg, and the angle Bgd =: half Bfd; therefore Ebd — Bdg + Ego — half Dfo — half the given vertical angle. Whence this construction.

Make Eb — the given difference of the segments of the base, and the angle Ebd — half the given vertical angle; from E to Br), apply Id the difference of the sides and produce Ed. Draw Bf to make the angle Dbf, — Bdf meeting Ed

VI. Question 249, *by Mr.* William Brown.

In the latitude 52 so7, on the 10th of June (supposing it the longest apparent day) I asked a mathematical friend, what o'clock it was? who made me this puzzling answer: Count (says he) the hours from the visible time of the rising of the sun's centre, and add their cube root to the square root of the hours to the apparent time of its setting; and it will give you the hour of the day. Quere, What o'clock was it?

Answered by Mr. Farrer.

Let y — the hours from sun-rising, n his true time of rising, and m the length of the day; then the time to his setting is $m - y$, and per question $/y + /(m - y) - n + y$ the hour of the day: Put $y = x'$, and we hare $x + V(m -) - n + ' m - x' = + x6 + x + 2/jx3 - 2nx - 2r$ which in numbers is $x6 - 2x4 + 8-4002x' + xs - 7-4022x = m! - ns = 2-8997$; hence $x = 1-0919$, and $x' - y - 1-3083$, aud $n + y - 5-0029 = s$ 5h 0ra 10-44' the time required.

Tii. Question 250, *by Mr.* John Hill.

There is a river, whose stream is divided into two parts; and after running some space the waters are united; between which it has inclosed an island in the form of a geometrical ellipsis, whose transr verse diameter is 40 chains (according to Gunter) and conjugate — 30 chains. Upon the transverse diameter is built a farm or cottage house, 132 yards from the centre; and as this piece of land is to be divided by straight hedges from the house to the water, one of them, which should be the shortest that can be made, is to convey the water from the river to fill a cistern by the cellar. It is required to find the shortest distance, and the position it will make with the transverse.

tt—cc -' 'tt — cc consequently Hw = 13-36 chains, making an angle with the trans, verse of 54 45'. *Answered by* Amicus.

Draw the lines Eh, *rg*, *Hg*, and Lc will represent the weights upon every particle of any curve: let Fm = *y*, Th — *x*, Cf — *a*, Am — a, and by similar triangles, we shall have $y : :: a : Lc$ —— whose fluxion is Lc — y ayx—axy,. ,,

———, a general expression for all yy curves. In the present case we have $ax = y$, whose fluxion is = Jo?' which substituting in the above equation (IX.

Lc ——, and taking its fluxion we shall have Lc — $lyyy$; and if $tt\ y$ expresses the weight that presses the particle M, we shall have $mi - lyyy$, or — $/aa + 16y) = lZyyy$, or as the cube of the ordinate directly and tangent inversely. Q. E. I. *Answered by Mr.* Farrer.

Draw the lines as per figure to the solution of question 244; and let a represent the tension in A, X — Ac, y — Cb, and z — curve Ab. Then we have, by the nature of the curve in the solution to question 214, zy—ax, $lax + xx =$ ss and a 4-x — the tension: Now per question $ax - y$, its fluxion $ax - 4y\ y,.: 4y'y - zy$, and $4y'$ = the gravity of the line or required law of the weights pressing every particle of the line; which is as the cubes of the ordinates.

ix. Question 252, *by Mr.* T. Sandatls.

In an oblique-angled plain triangle, there is given the difference of the sides which include the angle of 112 = 20, and the perpendicular let fall from the angle on the base = 60. Required a theorem to determine the base and sides of the triangle?

Answered by Mr. T. Atkinson.

Given Ef— Fg = 20 = *In* see the fig. to question 248J Fp Ss 60 = *m*, s. Zefg or 68 = *s*, its cosine = c j put %*y*= Ef +fg, e*JfL*±5ip :: i & = the lesser side, », — the greater, and their sum — -r- —*x*,.: *xx*— (-«" = SC (OCX " CLCl *j sc* W — ssd_ of — 2/k# _ Qyjj Jicy = 44. which reduced gives T±S(PP+ «M)= 180.m. whence _ / (dd + X Qjc + f(jMe + Mw))). — 2£ —L±i-H8-42 the greater side, or 98-42 the less.

Additional Solution.

Let Acb be the triangle required, draw Cp perpendicular to Ab and take co — Ca and make the triangle Cgd equal in all respects to Cap, viz. the angle Bcg — Acp and the angle Cdg = Apc = a right angle; then the angle Pcd is — the given angle Acb, Cd = the given perpendicular Cp, and Gb — the difference of the sides; and the lino Dh being perpendicular to Cd, it is given by position with respect to Ab; whence we have only to draw the line Cb through the given point c, which is equidistant?from the lines Dh, Ab, so that the part Gb intercepted by those lines may be of a given length, which is one of the problems of inclinations, and which is constructed in. th« additional solution to question 199, and in several other places.

If the nim of the sides were given instead of the difference, then If *eg* be taken equal to Cb, on Ac produced, and the triangle *cgd* be made equal in all respects to Bcp, namely, the. angle *cgd* — Cbp and the angle at *d* a right angle, then the angle pc/ will be the supplement of the given angle Acb, and the line *dg* will be given by position as before, and we shall have to draw Athrough the given point c, so as to be equal to the given sum of the sides. v

When the given angle is right, as in quest. 22, the lines Cd and cf coincide, and afe parallel to Ab, and consequently Dh and *dg* are then perpendicular to that line. L. x. Question 253, *by Mr.* J. Powle.

Granting the resistance, as the square of the celerity-; in what law of density will a heavy body moving describe a curve, whose equation is $ax = ys$?

Answered by Mr. N. Farrer.

Let Arc represent the curve described; draw the lines as in the figure, and let the velocity at *r* in the direction rc — *v*, Ah = *x*, rn— nr = *y*, mn — *y*, rm — *z*, the required density as D, C the celerity, and law of resis tance as ac''; theny : » r: a?: =: the velocity

"... '1 in the direction *nr*. its fluxion is — T — =: the in crease of velocity during the time of describing rm', y x x :: o: — the part arising from the resistance of the medium; therefore —— the part arising from the force of gravity. The resistance is to the c r VX VX VX VX ,, force of gravity as —— to —, or as to 1; but —, the ve y y vx y locity arising from gravity, being proportional to the time of describing *rm*, may be expressed thereby; hence —— l-or vvx zz. yy, in fluxions Zvvx + vvx — 0, or —, which substi 2x tuted in the foregoing proportion —:1, gives _: 1 the ratio $vx \over 2ss$ of the resistance to the gravity.

Again, since the absolute velocity is — the resistance by supposi *Ansicered by the Proposer.* Because the resistance is as the square of the celerity, — (Simpson's Essays, p. 60) will express the required density: But by the equation of the curve *(ax — y")* we have x — -j = = 3?C, and +y) = + 9/); therefore, by substi tutian, the required density becomes

—, -4x; or by a fartlicr reduction r:-7; ——T; i. e.
it is always as the tangent of the distance from the vertex to unity. xi. Question 254, *by* Diophantus.
Since the doctrine of triangles has an unbounded use and application in most parts of the mathematics, and the similarity of them generally had recourse to; let it be required to find eight right-angled plain triangles, whose hypothenuses are all equal; and shew a general method for determining the same?
Answered.
Let bb the square of the common hypothennse, and xx the square of one leg, then will $bb — xx$ be the square of the other leg. Suppose $b — nx$ — that leg whose square is $bb — xx$, then will $bb — xx — bb — 2bnx + nnxx$, which equation reduced gives $x — —n 1 + nn$ = to one leg, and if instead of x in $b — nx$ we take its value last found, we shall have ss the other leg; since n may be as $7 1 + nn'$ sumed at pleasure, not only eight, but any number of right-angled plain triangles-whatsoever may be found; which will also appear by making the common hypothenuse the diameter of a circle.

XII. Question 255.
Being at so large a distance from the dial-plate of a great clock, that I could not distinguish the figures; but as the hour and minute hands were very bright and glaring, I could perceive, that the minute hand pointed upwards to the right hand, at the same time the hour index pointed downwards to the left, so as both were in a right line, or diametrically opposite, and in such position, as that the elevation (I guessed) was some few degrees more than 50 above the horizon. Quere, The hour and minute of the day.
v *Answered by Mr.* J. Landcn.
By considering the question, I find that the first time the hands are diametrically opposite after 6 o'clock, is the time of the day sought. Let x hours be the time from 6: now the minute hand going round once in an hour, the rounds it will be carried in the time x, may be represented by x: and the hour hand going round once in 12 hours, the part of the circumference it will be carried in the same time by -jx. It is evideut that the index whose motion is swiftest, will outgo the slowest, one circumference in x hours; whence $x —$ iV: = 1, and x = therefore the time required is 5m 27' past 7.
Answered by Mr. James Terey.
By the data it appears to be somewhat past 7. Let $x —$ the number of minutes past 7; then will -fax be the distance of th« hour hand from 7, and 25 — -x the distance of the hour hand from 12; hence 25 + & — Tv — 30';.. $x—$ = 5 past 7, the time required.

The Prize Question, *by Mr.* J. May, *jun. of Amsterdam.*

An architect, or master carpenter, in Holland, had (from that slender knowledge which usually attends mechanics) conceit enough to fancy, he could find the dimensions of any piece of timber in a building, of which a design should be given: A burgo-master of the city of Amsterdam, intending to build a handsome house fronting the street, where his length was limited, because he would save the charges of double roof and gutter, and at the same time put his best side outward, gives the said architect these dimensions, *viz.* That the building should be forty feet wide, and the front waH twelve feet higher than the back wall: Also, because too much of a large roof should not appear in view of the street, he will have the length of the rafters, from wall to ridge, on the back side of his house, just 37 feet; but the rafters on the front side to be of such a length, as may form the pitch, or steepness of the roof, the same on each side. The owner being frugal (not to say wise) orders the builder to sit down and count up the cost: But although he was skilful in numbers, and pretty well versed in some parts of geometry, yet he found the first would be so much adfected, and the latter only an approximation, that he was not able to know how high the roof would rise, nor the length of the rafters in front, and therefore was incapable of computing the timber and roofing. The burgo-master surprized, probably thinking so famed an architect must be little less than a conjuror (when himself was none) resolves not to have his house begun until he can have the measures exact, and leaves him bare-breach'd, riding on the strange roof, although he is furnished with mathematical instruments, to describe curves and conic sections organically. But having heard of such things being effected by geometrical construction, he has, through the mediation of a friend, applied to the artists of Great Britain; and thinking the author of the Ladies' Diary deals in quibbles and quaint questions, hopes to see both methods in the next year's production. an angle of 14 29' with the horizon, fell at the feet of a person some distance ofl the very moment he heard the report of the piece. Quere, how far he was from the place of projection? numbers, x' —4482m + 107744 = 513375; whence x = 6-51224 &C. or $x — 2021768$ &c. either of which determines the length of the front rafters.
Geometrically thus: Let AG — 37 always pass through the point c, the point A sliding along the line Ab; then will G the point at the other, end of the line Ag describe the curve Cggl. On D as a centre with the radius — 37, describe a circle, and it will cut the said curve in, the points G, G, which determines the length and position of the front rafters, as is evident by inspection.

Or let Af — 2ag be moved as before, and it will cut the perpendicular Df in the points F and F, whence Cg, &c. is known as before.

N. B. If Af, Cb, ci, and Ih be called a, *b, x,* and *y* respectively; $xx(tCl$ then will——$xxzzyy$ express the nature of all such *xJC* -j-*Jlox J 00* curves. found. Prolong Bd and Ac to K. Put Iu or Ik —

x, and $Ai - y$; then is $Iik - 2jt$, from which subtract $Bd\ a$, and there will remain $Dk - 2r - a$. Now $Dk (2x - a)$: Dc (6):: $Ik\ (x)$: $Aifjy$),.-. $2xy - ay - bx$, an equation belonging to an hyperbola. Put x infinite, then is $y\ b$; and by putting y infinite, $x - ,a$. Hence, if Bd and Dc are bisected, and the lines Po, Pr drawn respectively parallel thereto, they will be two asymptotes to the said hyperbola. To find a point in the curve, put $x - a$ in the hyperbolic-equation, then is $y - b$. Consequently c will be a point in the curve, through which draw the hyperbola Aac

Per 47 Euc. I. $ar + Ai - Ab\ (= cc)$, or $xx = cc - yy$ (which is an equation belonging to a circle), therefore $x - /(cc-yy)$. Put the surd $- 0$, then $x\ zz\ 0$, whence the centre will be in B; whence also $y - c$, or $y -- c$, which determines the radius: Therefore, if on the centre B, with the radius Ab, be described the arc Aa, which cuts the above constructed hyperbola in the points A, a, and the lines Ab and Ac, or tra and ac, be drawn, they will be the sides of the f oof required.

This question admits likewise of a very easy and elegant solution, by the help of another curve, and is thus performed: Bd and Dc being drawn as before, and likewise on the centre B the arch a; lengthen the line Dc,. drawing cv parallel to Bd, and suppose an infinite number of radii drawn from the centre B, on which make Fg, &c. $= Fe$, &c. drawing through the points G, G, G, &c. the curve, whose equation is $+ xx\ j)\% + lyb - 4aay + lxxby + xxbb\ 0$, and it will cut the line $+ bb$

Dc in H and h. Lastly, draw Bh and Ba, which cut the above circle in A and », as before.

Questions proposed in 1745, *and answered in* 1746. i. Question 256, *by Mr.* J. Turner.

The inside dimensions of an, apothecary's mortar were found to be as follows: top diameter 12, bottom diameter 6, and depth 9 inches. The internal superficies of the mortar was formed by the revolution, of a conic parabola about an axis parallel to the principal diameter of the curve, the vertex being in the edge of the top diameter. Required the content in wine gallons?
Answered by Mr. J. Landen.

Let Abcd represent the mortar, generated by the revolution of the parabolic curve Bd, about the axis Ef, parallel to Bh. Call Eb, b; Bh, X; Gh,«/; and A Jj jg put 31416=p. Then will *pic (fib — 4by +yy) A* be. fluxion of the required solidity. which, Qi „ by putting for y and yy, their values xl and $x\ i\ /\ i$ (found by the equation of the curve) will be j: $\_J\ j\ pi\ (bb + x - ihtl/x)$ and its fluentssa $+ pxx\ Q\ \&\ J)$
$- pbx/x$; which, when $x = .9 - Ef$, will be 466-5276 inches = 2-0108, &c. wine gallons?

ii. Question 257, *by Mr.* T. Cowper.

On the 12th of February, 1744, in Jat. 52 20/, at 53 minutes past 5, apparent time, the altitude of the nucleus of a comet was observed to be 5-, and its distance from the planet Venus 56. Required the comet's place, allowing for refraction.' *Answered by* Bironnos.

The place of Venus at the given time is vf 20 50' 49// her latitude 1 22' 7' N. declinaf-on 20 27' south, and is 44 29' 45" short ot the meridian: Hence there is known z©, the comet's true zenith distance = 84 48' 35", Zp, the co-latitude of place, = 37 40', Zzpo = 44 29', 45", Op the distance of Venus from the pole = 110 27', and o0 the comet's distance from Venus — 56 36'. In Azpo is known Zp, Po, and /p: Find the Z Zop = 25 35' 49" and zo =82 25' 41". In the Azo©, are known the three sides: Find the Zzo© = 88 44' 54": From which *Answered by Mr.* N. Farrer.

Let Asd represent the path of the projectile, thrown from A, with a velocity that will carry it in a perpendicular ascent to K; or in the direction Al, to L; and let this celerity carry it through the distance d in the time u, and the distance run through by a falling body in that time $-w$. Put any distance Ab y, s and e the sine and cosine of the angle of direction $-L\ JSC\ D$

Lad, then will be the time in which '*de* the projectile runs through the curve xa, and $v6$ the dis tance descended by a heavy body in that time;.. Bo $= seddy - wuussyy\ ...,\ sedd\ ,,\ jr$ and when this — cs, then « = —-, and the *ddee to' scUsS* time of description =—-. Put 1142 the feet sound moves in 1 *1S3* second $- q$ j then $q : 1:::s$-, therefore $d - -$: conse $ww\ e\ sqauu$ quently zz the required distance. Now let $n\ X'''$, then $wza\ ew\ 7$ 16-feet; hence Ad $-$ 20895106 feet = *3* m. 7 f. 21 p. and 2 yards nearly, and the time of description $- = 1829$ seconds.
Mr. Tho. Cowper's *answer.*

Let Al be the line of direction, and Ad the distance of the person from the place of projection. Put t — tangent of the Zdal; d 16tj feet, the perpendicular descent of heavy bodies in 1 second; b 1142 feet, the velocity of sound in the same time; and x — the time the ball was in motion. Then bx — Ad, and dxx — Dl; but as 1: $t :: bx : tbx$ — Dl, .. x — tb -r-d; hence tbb-i-d Ad — 2094559 feet, the distance sought.

v. Question 260, *by Mr.* N, Farrer.

In an oblique-angled triangular grove, one of whose sides is 20 chains, and the'angle opposite thereto 78 45', if a perpendicular be let fall from each angle to its opposite side, they intersect at a fountain within the grove, whose nearest distance to the given side is 8-19 chains: Quere, its distance from each of the other sides, by a simple equation?
Answered by Mr. Heath.

It is evident by the data that the triangle must be isosceles. In the A Abc, the Za =: Zc, or the Z» must be the given angle; and either way the $S\ Z.Arn - ZcrB$, or Z Af.c is given =: 101 15' opposite to the side given — 20 chains, on which describing a segment of a circle to contain it, and drawing the parallel distance 8-19 (or rather 8-2 as it should be) chains $= cr$, and it will be found a maxi-A $c\ C$ mum (as is also proved by trigonometry), therefore the data are rc, Ac — cc, and Zb, Za =: Zc, and Zba6; whence follow by trigonometry $r - cr$ 12-925, ar $rb - 25215$ (ab= Bc r= 15.0 4) chains required.

Additional Solution.

The meaning of this prob. is thus: In a triangle we have given the base (ac), the vertical angle (abc), and the distance (cr) of the base from the common point of intersection of three lines drawn from the three angles perpendicular to the opposite sides ; to determine the triangle.

We are not at liberty to suppose the triangle isosceles, for that would be introducing a condition too much into the problem; and whether it be isosceles or of any other form, can only appear from the construction or calculation.

Construction. On the given base describe two segments of circles, the one Abc to contain the given vertical angle, and the other Arc to contain its supplement; parallel to Ac, and at the given distance of the point from it, draw a line to cut or touch Arc in *r*; then through *r* draw cr6 _L Ac, and B will be the vertex of Abc the triangle required.

For, through r drawing Ar6 and crc, since by the construction Ac is the given base, Aiic the given vertical angle, and *rc* the given distance, we have only to prove that the angles at *a* and *b* are right angles. Now by the construction it appears that Arc, Abc are segments of equal circles, and that the two segments together make up a whole circle; then the $\angle$ ABr or *anr* $==$ $\angle$ Acr as standing on equal segments Ar, and the opposite angles ros, crc are also equal;.. the third angles are equal, that is $\angle$«= Zc = a right angle. In the like manner *b* is proved to be a right angle. » *Scholium.* Another method of construction might be by first finding the point *r* as before, through which draw the indefinite lines *Arb, era,* and perpendicular to them the lines C6b, Aob. And then we should have to prove that these last two lines and er, produced, meet in the same point B, and that Abc is = the given angle.

Corollary. The equal opposite angles *kra, crb,* being the supplements of the $\angle$ Arc, are each — the Zabc, which is also the sup. plement of Arc by the construction. *Corollary 1.* Hence also the $\angle$ Ba/1 — Bc/-, and the four triangles Ba6, «Ar, Bc«, *bcr* are all similar. *The Method of Calculation* will be, first to calculate the angles rAc, rcA, of the $\triangle$ Arc, by prob. V. Simpson's Algebra, and then the segments Ac, Cc; then to each of these two angles adding the Zba6 or Bc«= the comp. of Zabc, there will be had the Zbac and Bca; from which, and the segments Ac, Cc, tfic two hypothenuscs Ab, Bc are easily got, and will come out

15-386 and 16-127, the angles at A and c being 52 16' and 48 59'. H. vr. Question 261, *by Mr.* C. Cockson.

There are two ponds of water of the same quality and depth, under the same meridian, one in the lat. of a — 166 north, and the other 86 r= 5125 miles due north from it. In the year 1743-4, the 16th of January, at three of the clock in the morning, the thickness of the ice in the southermost was 6 inches. Quere the latitude) and thickness of the ice of the nothermost pond at the same time? faaa + / aaa — *j aa* vn. Question 262, *by Mr.* Powle.

To determine the asymptotes of a curve whose equation is $xJ — y + axi/ =z 0$, Solution.

In the given equation $x — if + axy — 0$, supposing to be in, finite, the term *axy* will vanish in comparison of *x* or *y* and then $xh— y = 0$, and $x — y$; that is, at an infinite distance the abscissa is — the ordinate, and therefore the asymptote, or tangent at the infinite distance, must make an angle of 45 with the abscissa. Again the given equation in fluxions $5i/J — ax 1$ gives $x — . y y$, hence the subtangent *y*. sy — *axy*. is $5x + Aaxy$

Bt or-T-is =-,- (by expunging *y*) 4,-3 and *y* 5x + ay J r 9' 5x + ay 3axy ... consequently Vt Bt — x =: , — (when x = y — infinite) 5?, = 0, and therefore the asymptote passes through the vertex v and 5x makes an angle of 45 with Vb. And the form of the curve is as represented in the figure, where va is the asymptote, H, *Another Solution by Mr.* Landcn, *taken from the Appendix to Dr.* Huttou's *Edition of the Diaries.*

Of $x — ys + axy =. 0$, the equation of the curve, take the fluxions; and for and *y* put the invariable quantities *m* and » respectively: repeating the operation till you get an equation consisting only of invariable quantities. By so doing you will get $5m4 — bny + amy + anx = 0$, $10/nV — 10«y + amn = 0$, $m x — n y =0$, $m'x — n'y — 0V$ $ms — n — 0$: each of which equations, shewing the relation of *x* and «, will (as appears by chap. IX, of my *Resid. Anal.)* express a line which will be an asymptote to the curve expressed by the given equation, whefl — is determined by the final equation $ms —\%s = 0.$
n

Now by that final equation — is — 1: therefore each of the equations $5x" — 5y + ay + ax — 0$, $10x3 — 10y' + a = 0$, $xx —yy—0$, $x — y = 0$, is an asymptotic equation with respect to the proposed curve.

The 4th asymptotic equation corresponds to a right line, passing through the point where *x* begins, making an angle of 45 with the base on which *x* is measured. The 3d asymptotic equation corres. ponds to two right lines; one of which is the same as that expressed by the 4th asymptotic equation; and the other, expressed by $x + y =$; O, is (by what is said chap. X, of my *Resid. Anal.*) a diameter of the proposed curve; which diameter cuts the asymptote at right angles. The 2d asymptotic equation corresponds to a line of the 3d order (which is Sir Isaac Newton's 45th species) having the same asymptote as the proposed curve. The 1st asymptotic equation likewise appertains to a line of the the 3d order (of the species just now mentioned), having the same asymptote as the proposed curve, and to the right line which I have observed in the diameter of that curve. And the form of the proposed curve, with its rectilineal asymptote and diameter, is(bychap.VIII, IX, and X of my *Resid. Anal.)* as in the marginal figure; *x* being measured on Ab (a tangent at the node A) to which the ordinate Bc *(y* is perpendicular; AD the asymptote; Ae the diameter.

Mr. N. Farrer's solution being very erroneous is omitted.

Till. QUESTION 2S3.

Let Afk be the conchoid of Nicomedes, and Bc the asymptote whose length is 60, and P the pole'; a line drawn from p perpendicular to the asymptote, to the curve at A, is 40; also from the pole to the asymptote is 20. Required the length of the curve line Afk, witji the analytical investigation f *Answered by Mr.* Heath,

To rectify the conchoid of Nicomedes generally. Let $b = Pb$, fl Ba (— b — 20), y =; Ef any ordinate, and x — no — Be. 96c,w— 32yJ— 72cty,', y = 34-89 by a new method of solving equations, and consequently « = 35543 fere, and the area of the whole parabola formed thereby (which is now the greatest) 14474 fcre

In answer to the objections by *Amicus, a,* in the equation, is as much a variable quantity as x or?/, till it is determined. And in the equation —) — — — *c* (where $y - 27\ 4a/27$ v

«$(27c + 8«)"J - 1(7..,..,,...., 4. ---- =)$ it has a variable relation to *y,* when *y a* i or *y* -r-s to be determined a maximum; and substituting this i j way for the value of y,—i— —', or a$15\ (27c-f\ 8a)T$

— 4«J, will as properly express the maximum, as if it had been I denoted by relative *y's*; hence by making the fluxion of it = 0, we get by reduction *aa — — a —* where the value of $a = J\ 16\ 10$"
— — =35-5433 *Sic.* whence *y*— 34-8909 &c. and $6j/2$ -r-$5al$ — 1447-4001, the area of the greatest parabolic space, as before. Also whenc = 10, then x = 6-913, $y - 6\ 9787$ and $a - 7$-1087 &c. And when c = 1000, x = 691'3; $y - 697$-82, and $a - 710$-87; by which it is proved that when the figure is a maximum, the abscissa and ordinate will be nearly equal.

In the present case, where c n 50, let $x - y,$ then the equation oxx —,$y3$ becomes «xx xxy when the semi-parabola is nearly the greatest; and consequently $a - y - x,\ J.$ at that time = 27c + (1 3 T — 8) = 317292 &c. from' what is done above. Whence 1447 34 will be the 'V, area of the parabola very nearly a maximum. And -" ?dP therefore in all questions of this nature the area may be computed by taking the ordinates and abscissas equal; the error being inconsiderable in the maximum. Draw the parabola Aib'ca correct, and it will approach the form of a quadrant *aakcfa,* as near as the inequality of the curve B('c permits; and hs double will ever be inscribed in a segment of a circle something less than a semi-circle: but if tiie point c be made to pass through/, it will be inscribed exactly in a semi-circle, and the area of the semi-space Abj'ca will vary from the true maximum, but by an exceeding small quantity, as is evident from above. When Abaca is a maximum, the space Abca, or A Abc is a maximum, which is when $u - xc:$ for, by the equation $x - $—and$yx$; or — is a maximum tack describes 23-392 feet in one revolution,-whilst the nail describes 28. and the axis 21-9911485 &c. = 7 X 3-141592653 the wheel's circumference; by which the wheel will revolve 48019-31995 times as-proved before: but since the relation of *y* and *a* can be only had from the rectification of the curve Bzg, and its equation, with the length of curvature given, the inequality of the *(fiddlestick)* space B2cb, or unequal curvature of B£c, involves a necessity of some little inequality betwixt Ab and Ac, when Abz'ca is most capacious.

Remark. This question is the same as the 185th. the solution of which was not compleated. Both the above two methods of solution bring out true answers, but the latter is much the easier. By Mr, *Emerson's* method explained at the solution of the prize question for 1741 the same conclusions are also easily obtained. H. THE PRIZE QUESTIOW.

Suppose a cask composed of two equal conoids, formed by the reTolution, about its axis of a curve whose equation is $yv - 1000000 - 0$. Required the content of the cask if its length is 31-907 inches and bung diameter 14 inches?

Answered by Mr. R. Heath.

Projecting the curve *Amnc,* which is easily done by making $y - J,\ 2,\ 3,\ 4,\ 5,$ &c. and thence finding the a;'s by the equation $qqqqqq - x$» whence it will appear that when the semi-bung diameter $y - 7$ inches,, that *x* will be but-823543 which the halt length of the cask should $0\ 1\#$ be taken out of, and proves an answer to be impossible: but correcting the data, and making the semi-bung diameter $y - 8 = Bg,$ then $x = 16$-777216 = Ab; " vr whence taking 15-9535 (or 15-953673) the semi-length of the cask, and there remains-823543 =: Ao; whence $am - 7$ inches, or the head diameter:r 14, bung diameter — 16, and length 31907346 inches; and being near the form of a cylinder, the mean diameter — 15 inches, and content of the semi-cask by the rotation of *Boamna* about $aoB - 2819$-25 &c. or 10 ale gallons, and the wjhole cask 20 gallons.

Questions proposed in 1746, *and answered in* 1747. r. Question 265, *by Mr.* Heath.

If the hind wheel of a coach be seven feet in diameter, and a tack be driven into the middle of the spoke (or radius) standing next the ground, and a nail touch the ground at the end of the said spoke (or radius) when the coach sets out to travel: Quere how many miles will the tack and nail travel respectively in driving the coach from London to Exeter; allowing the distance between those two places to be 200 miles? What will be the nature of the curves they describe? And their position, or height of tack and nail from the ground, at the end of the journey.

consequently Nonnl — $4a = 28$ feet, the nail describes in one revolution of the wheel. The nature of the curve described by the tack is expressed by $cq - 2$ arch qt, which referred to the foregoing symbols will bey — $1z + v$, parts of the lesser circle. Consequently, by substitution in this case, the fluxion of the inner curve ctt will be $9aa - Sax$,',... , „ _. x : whose fluent, by series, is $y\ ax$ X: 3 +— $xx\ 7\ J\ 1S$« in travelling 200 miles. iiut 21'9911485: 2S:: 200: 254-648 miles, travelled by the nail. And 21-99U4S5: 23-392:: 200: 212-74 miles travelled by the tack pretty nearly; the small difference being only what En (-31905 part oi a revolution) differs in proportion with N, N, and *t, t,* part of curves described by n'utt and tack at the end of the journey, in the position of N, *t, r,* making an Znt-e = 31995 X 360 = 115 11', or Nro = 25 11' with the horizon. Whence *an zz* 4-988 feet, and *trn zz* 4-244 the height of nail and tack from the ground. N. B. The number of whole revolutions multiplied into the whole curves aforesaid, and the rectifications of the last parts being respectively added, will exactly shew the distances described by the nail and tack, very nearly as before. Or this question might be resolved by a curve described upon the curve of a great circle of the earth, which solution would come out not much different.

Surveying a triangular field Abc, and standing at the corner c, I took the angle included between the side Bc and a line drawn from the angle c, to a house situated within the field, and found it 78 10'. I then proceeded to measure the shortest distance to the oppo- site side Ab, and having measured 20 chains, I observed the house and the angle A in a right line; then measured on 10 chains to the side Ab: I likewise observed that the sides Ac and Bc were equal, and the house equally distant from the angles A and c. Quere the area of the field?

ii. Question 266, *by Mr.* Farrer. *Answered by Mr.* 1. Waine. 35m; whence $x - 43m \ 4-39 = 82$ or 39, $y = 60 — 35ot = 60$ or 35, $z=$. And thus by assuming $z = 1, 2, 3, 4$, &c. we obtain all the possible values of x, y, and «, viz. s admitting of 65 different' values, and x and y of 89.

iv. Question 268, *by* Fortunatus.

Let the sorts of faces to be thrown on seven dice by four persons, at a single throw each, be as follows, *viz.* by A, *a bed*; by B, *arbcdef*; by c,; by D, *a'bcd*: Quere their respective chances of-winning r And what throw as to sorts of faces, has the greatest number of chances for coming up, at a single throw, of all the sorts which can be thrown on the said number of dice?

N. B. The number of the same and different letters represent so many of the same and different sorts of faces, *viz.* so many aces, duces, trays, cators, &c. of the same and different sorts. *Ansezered by Mr.* Heath.

No solution has appeared in any author to questions of this nature, which will admit of several varieties still to be proposed. Mr. *Kay's* question was the first proposed, in a particular case, and the general method of solution is exhibited in the following examples, not hit upon before, that I have seen, by any.

No. of
Chances
6
150
300
1200
1800
3600
720
= 7776
6
180
450
1800
300
7200
7200
1800
16200
10800
720
= 46656

Hence the respective chances of A, B, C, and D winning are obvious, Bs 12600, 15120, 37800, and 75600, the same as 1, 12, 3, and 6 exactly. And *asbbcd* and *aabbcde* have equal, and the greatest number of chances for coming up, *viz.* 75600. Hence also is inferred that the best throw for winning will be when the sorts arf within a place or two of being all different.

v. Question 269, *by Mr.* J. Ash.

A gentleman has a piece of ground, ivhose three sides are an abscissa, semi-ordinate, and curve, the equation of which is *axzzy'*; he has taken from thence the biggest oblong garden which he could possibly enclose, whose area is 14184243 poles; and he finds the abscissa longer than the semi-ordinate by 5 poles. It is required from thence to find the area of the whole enclosure, its perimeter, and th» sides of the garden (taken out of it) separately?

To proceed, put $z — an, z — $ Hg, Z $— 5 — $ Da, $=:$ Gd, $m = r \ 141 \ 84243$; then Gf $— 1/ Qaz)$, Da $= 1/ az = z — 5$, $d = 1/4 = 1-5874$, and per quest. X $z — m$-Hence $lj \ az — 4dm \ \text{-}f\text{-}3z = z — 5$; $3zz—15z = 4dm$; here $z = 20$ exactly. And $a = 168\text{-}75$; also the length of the curve Hfa $= 27 \ 014$. So that the fences of the garden are Gf $= 9"4494$, and Gd $= 15$: Moreover Hd $=20$, Da $= 15$. And the area Hfadh $= £hd \ X \ Da = 225$ square poles, or 1 acre, 1 rood, 25 perches.

vi. Question 270, *by* Rhinoceros.

The perpendicular of a triangular field is 200 poles; the line equally bisecting the angle opposite to the base, drawn to the base, is 250 poles; and the distance from the said obtuse angle to the middle of the base is 295 poles: Quere the sides and area of that triangular field, with the geometrical construction of the same?

Answered by Mr. Farrer.

At the point D, on the line Ad raise the perp. Cd $= 200$ poles; make Ce $= 250$, and Cf $= 295$; produce Ce to cut the perp. Fg in G, draw Ch making the Zgch $=i$ Zcgh; then upon H, as a centre, with the rad. Hg describe the arch Cbga. Join c» and Ca, and the Aabc is that required.

Calculation. Having Cd, Ce, and Cf given, find Ed $= 150$, Fd $= 216\text{-}85$, and Ef $= 6615$. But Ed: Dc:: Ef: Fg $= 8914$;. -. Ge — $111\text{-}42$; and Gf: Ge:: Gi: OH — $225\text{-}89$; hence Ab $= 359\text{-}58$, Bc $= 203\text{-}41$, and Ac $= 441\text{-}21$. The area 31958 squar poles, or 224 acres 2 rood 38 perches..

Required the time of the year when there is the shortest twilight in lat. 50 46'?

Answered by Mr. J. Turner.

If N represent the north pole, z the zenith, H® an arch of tht horizon, Aqa a parallel of the sun's depression 18 below it; and ©Q a parallel of declination descended; then the angle Qnq will be a minimum: but 'tis also evident that when the crepusculum is the shortest, the distance © © descended in the parallel of declination will be a minimum: being the arch of a lesser circle cutting the same azimuth in the points of setting and end of twilight. And this will be when the motion of the sun is most perpendicular, and therefore descends the fastest to 18, or the parallel of A0a; which he does by touching at the points © and 0 in the same azimuth z@0 with his setting, instead of making an oblique angle with the setting azimuth, as in the position of 0mQ with za$. This being admitted, put $y — $ cos. N0 $— $N©; m and n sine and cos. $zQ — $ 108, or sines of 72 and 18; p and q sine and cos. Nz $= $ comp. lat. and rad. unity $— z@$.

Then per spherics $— = $ cos. Nz©, and also $— — $ cos. Nz0, $p \ mp$ which (for the above reasons) are to each other, i. e. y-r-p rz

$—$, therefore $y — —nl'$ which is a general theorem for all $mp' \ m + V$ s questions of this nature. And the sun's declination in the present case is found by it $— 7 \ 2' \ 42"$ southerly, answering to Feb. 19, or

Sept. 30;..»» + 1: $n :: q : y$. *N. B.* If

the lat. is north, the declination must be south, and vies versa.

Mr. Farrer *answers thus.*
Let 0 be the point in the circle bounding twilight 18 below the horizon, where the shortest twilight happens (without saying why the bounding point falls in the same azimuth circle with the sun's setting.) Then in the triangle Ac®, Z© = 90, Zc = co-lat. ©6 — 9, c© — era, whence rad.: tang. ©6:: sine lat.: sine arc — 7 fere, the sun's declination.

A construction to this question is given at question 564.

viii. Question 272, *by* F. R. S.
In what law of gravity will a projectile describe a curve expressed by the equation $ax\,zz\,y$ in a non-resisting medium?

Aiiszccrcd by Mr. Landen.
Let Arc represent the curvej AB the axis thereof; B»i and nr ordinates indefinitely near each other, ('all AH, x; nr, y; and the gravity G. Then since the velocity in the direction ur is always the same, that in the direction rn will be-, whose fluxion — (h being constant) will be as G X y; that is, as the force by which the body is accelerated at r drawn into the time of describing rm. Hence patting G X y — - we have $a - y$

A. In which expression if for jj we put its value ML found yy 4V« $fnJy$ by the equation of the curve $(axx - tf)$ we get G = g 5 e the gravity in this case must be in a sabduplicate ratio of the ordinates, or in a subquintuplicate ratio of x, the distance of the ordinate from the vertex.

ix. Question 273, *by Mr.* Farrer.
Quere the area of a right-angled triangle whose hypothenuse is and the two legs $x2x$ and x'''?

Answered by Mr. I. Ash.
Let $y - xx$, then (per 47 Euc. I. and per quest.) $y + y = y$

V = V'5-+-= 1-618034, y = 1-272019, and the area required z = 1-02908.

Remark. Of this triangle, the perpendicular from the right angle on the hypothenuse is zz 1. For it is — the double area divided by the hypothenuse = the product of the two legs divided by the hypo. x X x x thenuse = s = —= 1. H. x x x. Question 274, *by Mr.* Clarke.
The thickness of a Ting belonging to a ship's anchor is nine inch«e in circumference, and the outward circumference shewing the width of that ring is 50 inches? Quere the solid content, and weight thereof?

Solved by Mr. Landen. Put $d\,zz$ diff. of the given circumferences, $r\,zz$ rad. of the lesser circumference, and x — any abscissa of the circle whose radius is r. Then $dx\,2/(2ox - xx)\,x$ is the fluxion of half the required solidity.

But the fluent of $2(lax - xx)\,x$, when $x - r$, is the area of the semi-circle, whose radius is r; therefore the area of the circle shewin? the thickness of the ring, multiplied by rf, the dift". of the given circumferences, will give the solid content of the ring — 264 inches, fere. Whence the weight thereof, according to Dr. Wiberd, is nearly — 77 pounds avoirdupois.

XI. Question 275, *by* Filius Diophanti.
To find three numbers, that when each is subtracted from the cube of their sum, a cube number shall remain?

Answered by Mr. J. Hampson.
The numbers are,, and;these fractions are in lower terms than those given by Dr. Wallis from Dr. Pell, where the method of solution may be seen.

Mr. Turner *gives this Answer from Dr. Wallis"» Algebra.* ,. 4944?. a . 479696,, 44S00O, = S=£-The cube of their sum = L, from which numbers taking severally the values of a, 6, and c, there will remain v 17576 39304, 64000, these three cubes, *viz. f,* and j-, whose roots are SB 34 i 40 TSI' I8f aUU *Remark.* This is the same with question 51. xn. Question 276, *by Mr.* J. Landen.
It is required to find the periodic time of a pendulum describing a conical surface; the perpendicular height of the described cone being two hundred inches?

Answered by Mr. I. Ash.
Suppose the sine of the vertical angle of the cone-0507; then by trigonometry the side or length is found — 3944 77 inches or 32873 feet — length of the pendulum's string. Hence (per Keil's lntrod. Theor. 11, p. 302), tlie time of one revolution is equal to the time of the perpendicular fall of a heavy body from a height equal to the pendulum's length,.- . 16-: ":: 328-73: 20 439442" the square of the time, whose root — 4-521 seconds required.

Remark. The principle used in the above solution is not general for any angle at the vertex, but only for that one particular aagle there used, as may be seen in the Prop, of Keil there referred to. But the times of gyration do not depend on the length of the string but only on the altitude of the cone, they being universally as the square roots of the altitudes; and when the altitudes are equal, the times will be equal also, whatever the length of the pendulums may be.
By Prop. IX. Emerson's Centrip. Forces, the proportion is uniyersally thus, as $/6fo$ feet: $f400$ inches (twice the given J _):: / 400 62832 31416: 314161/ —-= 4-5228 seconds, the time required. H.

mi. Question 277, *by* Crocus Metallorum.
What annuity, to continue as many years as its pounds, can I purchase for the square root of its pounds ready money, allowing me 51. per cent, per ann. compound interest for my bargain?

Answered by Mr. Heath.
Put a the pounds of an annuity, r — 1-05 the amount of a pound and its interest for one year at 5 per cent, $t\,zz$ the year's .$a\,a$ continuance; then «, the present worth.

$r - 1\ r(y\_i)$

And if the conditions of the question be substituted therein, the equation becomes — $zz\,Ja$. Whence 1-05 a—1 $ra(r-l)\,zz$, $a\,nc$; here $a\,zz$ 1-034 fere zz 11. Os. 7d. the annuity re quired.

Xit. Question 278, *by* Hurlothrundro.
Required the ratio of the diameter of the bore to the length of a piece of cannon (or other fire arms) to make it capable of throwing a ball the farthest possible; supposing the diameter of the ball nearly equal to the diameter of the bore, with a proportionable weight of powder, and the metal of the piece formed sufficient to sustain the effect?

Observations on this Question by the Editor.
This question was proposed with an intent t6 improve gunnery, of which there are several things wanting. In particular, a treatise on the subject by an experienced hand: For to be treated on by any

other person, will only be compiling of matters already known. And in order for this improvement, and the solution of this question, experiments should be made in a general way, which we have net yet received.

Remark. The Editor observes above that this question was proposed with an intent to improve practical gunnery, though it does not appear from the nature of the science that it would at all have answered that purpose. It is well known that *short pieces* are requisite at *sea,* both for the convenience of working them in an engagement, and on account of the small space they must stand in when the ports are closed. The *land service,* on the contrary, requires *long pieces,* particularly in the attack of a place, in order to preserve the embrasures from the blast of the powder, which short pieces would soon destroy, besides the danger of setting fire to a fascine battery. Not only the *lengths* of pieces are *limited* by the nature of the service, but also the *diameters of the bores*; for pieces which carry balls from 24 to 42 pounds comprehend the limits of *battering* cannon and those from 3 to 12 pounds limit *field* pieces. Experience proves that balls of a less weight than 24 pounds are insufficient to make a moderate breach; and that pieces carrying 42 pound balls, or upwards, become unmanageable from their great weight; so that in general the 32 pounder is the most common battering piece. When the field piece exceeds 12 pounds, it, in like manner, becomes too unwieldy for *that* service.

Mr. *Robins* is the only author that I know of, who has solved a proposition exhibiting the relation between the *velocity* of the ball and the *dimensions* of the piece. Another author, who proceeds in a very different manner, makes the *velocity* always increase with the *length* of the piece.

If any person, however, think it worth his while to go through the calculation of this problem, he may easily do it, making the expression for the velocity found by prop. 7, of *Robins* Principles of Gunnery, a maximum, then its liuxion being taken, &c. there will be determined the relation between the diameter and length, H. *Additional Remarks.* What could not be accomplished, with respect to this question, by Mr. Heath in 1747, nor by Dr. Hutton in 1774, we are now happily enabled to do, by the aid of those very extensive and accurate gunnery experiments, lately published by the latter author, in the 2d and 3d vols, of his Tracts. We there find, particularly in the Tablet, p. 310, vol. 2, M hat are the quantities or the lengths of the charges, for all kind of guns, in terms of their calibers or diameters, to discharge their balls with the greatest velocity. This of course answers one part of the enquiry; for all guns, whether great or small, from the largest cannon to the musket, discharge their balls with equal velocity, when they are formed of similar dimensions, and similarly loaded, that is, the like parts measured by the same number of calibers. Thus then the greatest velocity is determined for any piece of ordnance, which is perhaps all that the proposer meant by his problem; for he does not appear to be aware that, with the same initial velocities, the ranges will be greater, as the ball is larger, without end, (when of the same kind of matter), nor even that these initial velocities are all equal, as above mentioned, L.

The Prize Question, *bg Mr. W. Chappie.*

A gentleman has a circular garden, whose diameter is 310 yards, in which is contained a circular pond, whose diameter is 100 yards, so situated in respect of each other, that their peripheries will inscribe and circumscribe an infinite number of triangles (i. e. whose sides shall be tangents to the pond, and angles in the fence of the garden.) He being disposed to make enclosures for different uses, and farther ornaments on his scheme begun, in order thereto applies himself to the artists of Great Britain for the dimensions of the greatest and least triangles that can be inscribed and circumscribed as aforesaid? and the nearest distance of the peripheries of the garden and pond.' and for a demonstration of the truth of the pond's situation? *Answered by Mr. R. Heath.*

The biggest two circles, within one another, admitting of an infinite number of triangles to be drawn with their angles and sides terminating in their outer, and touching their inner peripheries, are those which are concentric, and their diameters exactly as 2 to 1; in which case the triangles will be all equal and equilateral. This is so evident as to appear upon the slightest examination. And if the diameters be in proportion less than 2 to 1, then no triangle whatsoever can be drawn as aforesaid. Bat if the proportion be greater than 2 to 1 (as 310 to 100, or 3-1 to 1 as in the present case) their peripheries being eccentric and at a proper distance, will admit of an infinite variety of triangles to be drawn in and about them, from the isosceles A Acc to that of Bdd, which are the greatest and least triangles: Because the area of every triangle so drawn, being equal to the sum of all the sides into half the given radius of the inscribed circle, the more the sides of any triangle are situated about the centre, or diameter, or the farther removed from them, the greater or less will the periphery, and consequently area, of that triangle be: the sides of the triangles Acc and Bbd being the most near and remote to such a situation.

For the property of drawing triangles as aforesaid, in and about eccentric circles, there is this demonstration.

First to inscribe the isosceles, or one A, Acc in the greater circle, which at the same time shall circumscribe the lesser circle. Put m = rad. greater circle — *Act,* n — rad. lesser = o», and x — Ao; then $/(xx-nn)$ — Av; per sim.

$x + »$

As, *Av:* Ao:: *At* : Ac —

— *Imn)* — *ao,* shewing the distance of the centres to be least, or 0, when *In m;*

both circles being then concentric, and radius of the greater twice the radius of the less. Whence 12-268074 = itf the nearest distance of the peripheries. And area AACcz: 18242-89yards, the greatest;

and that of A Bed = 1G796-82, &c. the least.

The distance of thi-se centres of the

circles being known, as d—co capable of having one triangle drawn as aforesaid: Suppose any chord Ac = x touch the inner circle at v, then it is plain another chord can touch it somewhere at t, and if another can touch it at r, the property is proved. But, in general, the Zabc — Zadc Z«oc its sine —x lm; and Zbc = Zcb£ = Z«dc (per 33 and 20Euc. III. =-.— X, —1 re; the couip. or Zcb ; whence (i $V(mm — xx)$ — ")') » hence rc = $x + vn$, $Av = Ar — x$ —l and Ah and Bc, also /Lvcc = Zee/, and /.vet are expressed. Say x--$1m$ (s. Z Abc): x (Ac) or 1: $1m$ :: s. /.vet: Ab, which gives an equation shewing the general value of x, whilst two other chords are tangents likewise; and triangles ilk, gef, will revolve as in the 1st fig. Hence, if any chord or side of a triangle is given, the others follow by trigonometry; having first found the distance of the centres aforesaid. This property of drawing triangles about circles I discovered some years ago, as may be seen in the Monthly Oracle; though the proposer has greatly deserved in a long account of it from Scilly, printed in a book called the Quarterly Miscellanea Curiosa. Mr. Landen puts b — "rad. lesser circle, a — diam. greater, and $x = 207$-33 or 112-67 &c. Whence he infers this construction (see jig. 1.) From the centre of the garden, along the diameter, set off the diameter of the pond, find a centre (at n) betwixt that point and the other end, describing a circle Apq, draw pm parallel, and mo perpendicular to Ab, and the point o will be the centre of the pond.

Questions proposed in 1747, *and answered in* 1748.' 1. Question 279, *by Mr.* Landen. A charming brisk maid has assur'd me and said,

Since I'm such a tine mathematician,
(Laying puzzling aside, for the joys of a bride)
She will wed me but on this condition:
 That I first shall unfold what pieces of gold
Her father has for her in store:
And these I must find from the data subjoin'd,
And then I'm to puzzle no more.
The pieces are half guineas, guineas, moidores, and three pound twelves. The whole number is 4000. And if v, x, y, and z be put for the number of each sort respectively, $vx'yz$ is a maximum. Quere what is the lady's fortune?
Answered by Mr. J. Turner.

Let v — the half guineas, x — guineas, y moidores, and z — 31. 12s. By the question »-f Jc + $y + z$ — 4000 = b: JVow $v'x'y'z$ being a maximum, or (expunging z) $b — v — y — $, ,. In $v x y$ General Rule.

Make the sum of the exponents a denominator, and each particular exponent (of the quantities) the numerator of a fraction, these respectively multiplied into the whole number of pieces, will shew the particular number of pieces of each sort.

11. Question 280, *by Mr.* John Williams. Going along a river's side, on an even direct road ABC, I observed a tower on the other side of the river, whose angle of altitude at A was 5-24'; going farther on to B, 100 yards, the angle of altitude was 6 27'; and intending, again, to take an observation when directly opposite to the tower, but was prevented by an island in the river (over-grown with furz), I then came to c, 400 yards from B, where I found the angle of altitude was 8 36'. Quere the tower's height?
Answered by Mr. James Tercy.

Put x — tower's height, Ac — 500 zz b, Ab — 100 = d, Bc = 400 — a. Cosec. Za /, of $v zz v$, of c — y. Then (rad. v. — 1) tx zz At, vx Bt, and yx T/ zz Ct. Now (geometrically) making $t : v:: $ Ai: Ib:: Ak: $1S/I$;

Kb, and describing the semi-circle /vp J;'

Itk; alsot: y :: Bl: Lc:: $A1JS$-bCX M Bm: Mc, describing the semi-circle Ltm; the intersectionT, being the place of the tower, (forwhich see Universal Arith. prob. 26) let down TP-L Ac Per fig. b: $tx + yx$ $tlxx$ — $yyxx$ :: tx—yx: b — AF_FC" also Bt—Bf'= At' Afs; whence $atlxx + dyyxx — bvvxx = abd$, and x — V/ i "$att + dyy$—bxm zz 44-4609 &c. yards, the tower's height.

The same answered by Mr. J. Ash.

Call the co-secants of the three angles of altitude o, b, and c; AB, ; Bc, 4s; the tower's height, x. By trigon. (t being the top) At zz ax; Ht zz bx; Ct zz cx; cos. ZCbt =: $Ssbx$ equal, = / ss .— = 44-1557 yards, the tower's V cc — 566 + 4oo height required.

A Geometrical Solution, by Caput Mortuum, *taken from tlie London Magazine Improved,* 1784. *Analysis.* Let A, B, C, be the places of observation, D the foot f the tower; and suppose a circle to be described on the horizon with the radius »e, — the height of the tower. Make the angles Ade, Bdf, Cdg right angles, and draw Ae, Bf, Gc. Then because the angles Dae, Dbf, Dcg, are given by the question, the triangles Dae, Dbf, Dcg, are given in species; and, moreover, since the side De, (df, Dg) is common to all the triangles, the ratio of the sides Ad, Bd, Cd is given. Draw Dn, Ns, parallel to Cd, Bc respectively; then Ns = Bc, and Nb — sc; consequently, by similar triangles, Ab: Ns (bc):: NB (sc): Sd; and hence we have this *Construction.* Having on a base De assumed at pleasure, made three right-angled triangles (eda, Fdb, Gdc) So that the vertical angles (ead, Fbd, Gcd) are = 5 24', 6 27', and 8C 30', respectively; divide Da and Dc, in N and s, in the given ratio of Ab: Bc (1: 4). With Nd, Nb (sc) and Db constitute a triangle Dnb; join Ab and make the angle Dae — 5 24'; also draw Df perpendicular to Ad. Then it is evident from the analysis, that Ab: De:: 100: the height of the tower. *Calculation.* Suppose De — 1; then Da = 10'5789, Db = 8-833. »c — 6-6122 the natural cotangents of the angles Ead, Fbd, and Ggd. Consequently in the Abnd, there are given the three sides, Dn = 8-4631, Bn = 1-3224, and Bd = 8 833, from whence the Zbnij will be found = 101 59' 20", the supplement of which is 78 0' 40" = Z.bna. Then in the Abna there are given two sides and the included angle, from whence Ab will be found — 2-25. Therefore, 2-25 (ab): 1 (de):: 100: 44-41 &c. yards, the tower's height. in. Question 281, *by Mr.* J. May, *jun. of Amsterdam.*

It is required to find (by a general theorem) the number of fractions of different values, each less than unity so that the greatest denominator be less than 100?
Answered by Mr. Heath.

The number of fractions of different and like values, each being less than unity, and the greatest denominator being any number, (from 2 upwards) will appear by the following series, continued to

Here it is evident, that the J greatest numerator, or greatest TM denominator less unity, will be Jj the number of terms, which will alwaj s be equal to the last term;

§ therefore ———-X n = the sum of the series, or the number of different and like fractions in all cases. The fractions of like talue with some of the rest, are all those not in their lowest terms: As those of different value are all the incommensurable ones: For the more speedy determining of which, all the incommensurable denominators, from the least in the series to the greatest, must be taken, viz. 3, 5, 7, 11, 13, &c. to 97, which are 25; and the sum of their different fractions will be the series 2, 4, 6, 10, 12, &c. to 96; each row being one less than the dcnom. To these if the different fractions (in lowest terms) of the commensurable denominators 2, 4, 6, 8, 10, &c. to 99, be added, the sum will be all the different fractions. But a» there is more trouble than art to discover them, I shall ljeave it to persons of leisure to pursue the computation, the method being here planned out.

Mr. *Ash*, upon the same principles, computes the number of different fractions to be 3055; but doubts the truth.

N. B. By the above theorem, the whole number of fractions = 4851 (as Mr. Bam/Se//madeit) from which subducting those of like values, all the different fractions will remain. *A general method for Solving this Question from the Diary for* 1751, *by Mr.* Flitcon. + ++++++

I I *N. B.* P signifies each prime number in the second column in scheme 2, with a new nun;ber to each in the 3d column, deduced from the series in the first scheme, according to the general method: the ditto en t denominators being placed in the first column all along. *For the multipliers, or powers of each.* Against $ in the 1st column, stands 2 in the 3d column, each being drawn into 3 gives 6 to be set in the 3d column, against 9 in the first collection. Against 6 in the 1st col. is set 2-3 in the 2d col. whence (by 4th step) is found 2 for the 3d collection. Also for its multiples, into either, or both its parts, as 2 X 3 = 6, drawn into 6 and 2 gives 12 (by 6th step) to be set in the 3d col. against 36 in the first: dotting through all the second columns all such multiples, *by* which the fractions are found. Proceeding thus, the whole number of diU'erent fractions are. truly determined in a short time. iv. Question 282, *by the Rev.* Anth. Baker.

A gentleman would have a silver punchbowl made in the form of a parabolic conoid, containing exactly two gallons, but being frugally inclined, desires first to know what ought to be its inside dimensions so that, caeteris paribus, it may require the least quantity of silver possible?

Answered by Mr. J. Turner.

When the convex superficies is the least, the conoid must come nearest to the form of a semi-sphere (being under the least surface of all solids of given solidity formed by the rotation of a curved space about its axis) which is when the abscissa and semi-ordinate of the generated parabola are nearly equal: the conoid then being nearly most capacious. Putting b — 462 inches in two wine gallons, p — 31416, y — ordinate, x — abscissa of the parabola. Then the solidity of the conoid — b — $pyyx$ (when y — x) $py3$; where y — 6"65 inches. But accurately, £-$(aa + 4yv)$£— is the su

"6av " 6 perficial content of the same (see p. 202, of Mr. Emerson's Fluxions). Now if the value of yy be substituted therein, and the fluxion of it made = 0, then a — 6-l; y — 6-54: = 6-94; and the cunvex surface — 235-5 square inches.

The same answered by Mr. Ash.

The conoid's convex surface is — $(aa + 4yy)2$ — a mini mum $(p$ — 1 "5703);.- . aat + l£jt— aa is also a minimum. Put cc = double solidity = 4 wine gall, qq — area of a circle whose rad.

— 1. Then, by the curve, ax yy, and $qqyyx$ — cc, whence 4yy 4c /

— ———; and substituting for *4yy* in the minimum, it becomes

— 6-03; whence semi-axis — 6-98, and semi-ordinate — 649 maxime.

v. Question 283, *by Mr.* N. Farrer.

Quere the axis and parameter of a parabola and semi-ellipsis, when the latter is circumscribed by the former, whose ordinate is equal to the conjugate axis, and abscissa equal to the semi-transverse: both curves having the same focus, the difference of their parameter 2, and the length of the parabolic curve being 28" 68?

Anszsered by Mr. Ash.

'Tis inconsistent with the nature of the parabola and semi-ellipsis that the latter should be circumscribed by the former, when the ordinate — conjugate, and axis semi-transverse (which Mr. Turner also observes):.. semi-ellipsis must.be read for parabola, & contra. Then from the properties of the curve and conditions of the question, the parameter of the parabola is found.= 2. Suppose Ah = $ 12-5 the corresponding curve Ar — 13-90375 &c... the remaining part *rm* (= *z*) of the curve = 0 43625.

Put $y = nm$, $x =. nr$, and we shall have j ... . o andXi4+yT + /(4ac + *4axy* v v v *a* 1. *a* 1 *ax aax* -I *x* whose fluent is x + *Additional Solution.*

As the method of finding the parameter is not inserted, I shall here supply it, and at the same time give another very easy method of solving the latter part of the question.

Since then ax — yy by the nature of the parabola, putting y r: the ordinate, x — the abscissa, and a — the parameter of the parabola; and, by the nature of the ellipse, $x : y :: 1y: \%yy$ — $x\,z$: parameter of the ellipse = a + 2 by the question; or $ax + 2x =: lyy$; subtract the former equation from this, then $1x - yy - ax$, and therefore a — 2 the parameter of the parabola.

The parameter being thus found, by p. 309, of my Mensuration, the length of the double curve will *bey «/(+ yy)* + hyp. log. of $(y + V(l + yy))$ — 28-68, by the question, = c; call the hyp. log. of $(y + + yy))$, v; then $y + yy)$ — c — v Now it is easy to perceive that y — 5 nearly; then since a small difference in the value of y w ill make a still smaller and inconsiderable difference in the value of v, and when y is supposed 5 then v 2-312456, and then the equation $y + vy) — c — v$ becomes?/ + yy) — 26 367564 = d, and y-"dd +) 4-) = 5-08-With this value of y find a new value of $v — 2'328281$, and thence of $d = 26$-3513719; and this same theorem will give $y = 5$-08501, which is very exact.

Then $x = $ —— = = 12-92806. H. a 2 vr.

Question 284, *by Mr.* Cuth. Cockson.

Quere with what part of a cylindrical stick should a person strike, to give the greatest blow; the length of the arm being 20 inches, and that of the stick 50?

Answered by Mr. J. Turner.

Put $a = 70$, the length of the arm and stick; $6 = 20$ the length of the arm; then the distance of the centre of percussion of the stick from the upper end of the arm will be — 208 + $iao + 2$ _ $3a + 3b$ 49-63 inches, and from the farthest end of the stick = 20-37 inches (vide Stone's Flux. p. 177).

The same answered by Mr. J. Ash.

Let $20 = e$ represent the length of the arm, and put x — the distance of the centre of percussion from the hand. Then $(c + xx)$ X i = fluxion of the momentums; and $(c + x)$ X = that of the forces; the fluent of which divided by that of the momentums is s—r—s = the distance of the centre of percussion of the $6c+ 3x$ v part xp, from the point of suspension; which (when x zz 50) will be = 49-6296 &c. Consequently the part of the stick required is 20-37037 &c. inches from the top.

vn. **Question 285**, *by Mr.* Landen.

I am about building a house, the breadth whereof I design shall be 24 feet, and the perpendicular height from the ground to the ridge 42 feet. The ends, which arc to point directly east and west, will be sheltered by neighbouring tenements; but the sides will be exposed to the fury of the north and south winds. I therefore would be satisfied what the angle of the ridge must be, and how the side walls, that the wind blowing from either of those quarters shall have the least effect on the building?, *Answered by Mr.* Landen, *the Proposer.*

Put $a = 42$ the height of the building; $b — 12$, half the breadth; = perpendicular height of the roof. The force of all the particles of the air impinging against the wall, to blow upon the building, will be as $aa — lax + xx$. The effect of any particles striking against the roof (found by mechanics) is to the effect the same would have had, striking directly against an upright plane, as the square of the sine of the angle of incidence to the square of radius; therefore the force of all the particles against the roof, to blow down the building, will $2ar3 — x$ x. $2ax3 — x'$, be as Tt And by the question —; + $aa — 2ax + $ = 10-4076 feet: Whence the height of the sidewalls must be 31-5924 feet, and the ridge angle 98 7'. *Mr.* Jepson's *Solution is as follows.*

Let Br — 42= a, Ab = Cd S= 12 = b, Cr — y, Dh x, then Ac —bd =$a — x$. By p. 255 of Emerson's Fluxions, the resistance of the plane Dr, to the resistance of the plane Cr, is as yy to xx (supposing the wind to blow in a direction parallel to the plane of the horizon); but the resistance of the plane De is ss cx (putting c — the length of the building) and (per 47 Euc. I.) $yy = bb + xx$, therefore the re cx «istance of the plane Cr is = —-, and; that x' of the side wall Ac — $ca — ex..$: ——. + $a — x$ is a mini. 7 00 + xx mum; which in fluxions, &c. gives $bbxx — b — 0$, and = b zz. 12. Hence the height of the side walls = 30 feet, and ridge angle 90, which will always be the same, let the height and length of the building be what they will. Tin. **Question 286**, *by Mr.* 3. Ash.

If a parabolic conoid, whose altitude is 9, and base 6 inches be cut by a.right line at some distance from, but parallel to its axis, what is the solidity and convex surface of that segment, or part cut off, when the height of the plane of that section is 5 inches?

Answered by the Proposer Mr. Ash.

Let x = Fp, $n — 2$ Fe — 6. By the nature of the circle we get /$(nx — xx) — vm — /pa$ by the nature of the parabola (because 9 the altitude of the whole parabola — 3 the square of its senii-ordinate, and all the perpendicular sections are similar parabolas); and %$(nx — xx) —$ area $mA.ni;$ consequently (nir-$xx)2 x —$ flux. Qf 4f *TUC* of the solidity; whose fluent is-x: *O Lnx% 6x' 6x s*,,...

— $i4 + Wn$ solld content

Again, since $nx — xx — $p«i = Ap, whence the fluxion of the curve is x/nn— 4nx + 4xx + 1), or putting cc for $nn + 1$, $x(cc$—, 4$nx + 4xx);$ and because 2/$(nx — xx)$ — chord of the arch $mvtn$, and (nx) — chord of half that arch j therefore (by Huygen's Theor.) , %$A/ (nx) — 1(nx — xx)$ the arch $rnvm$ =- nearly. Consequently %%/$(nx) — 1/(nx — xx)$.

-X $xi/(cc — 4nx + 4xx)$ — fluxion of the surface. The fluent of which (when $x = 1$) is (if no mistake be made) — $16'34$ fere. *Remark.* It may also be observed that the solidity required in this question, may be found without an infinite series, by the rules at p. 335, &c. of my *Mensuration.* And using the numbers given in this question, the solidity by those rules will become = 6-48510957 very accurately, H. *Solution from the 5tk book of* Diophantus, Quest. 18. To find rational values of $x, y, 2, u, v, w$, such that put ar4-«/-t-s = «, = $7n3$, $y — 16n3$, a = $63n3$.

And it is plain that the cube of the sum increased by $x, y,$ or « will make a cube. It remains to make the sum of the three equal to n, or $96rc3 = n$, or $96re = 1$.

Now unity is a square number, and if 96 were also a square the problem would be solved. Now 96 is the sum of three numbers, any one of which increased by unity makes a cube. We are therefore to find three numbers, such that each increased by unity is a cube, and the sum of the three a square.

For the side of the first cube, put n' + 1, of the second 2 — of 1 the third 2. The first cube is n'J+ 3»/s+ 3n'+1, the second —$n'3$ + $6n"$ — $12re'$ + 8, the third 8. The numbers therefore are $n"$ + $3n"$ + $3re'$, — $n'3$ + $6ra/J$ — $12ra'$ + 7, and 7. And the sum of these 9$n/4$ — 9n' + 14, which therefore must be a square, suppose $(3«' — 4)$. Therefore $nf — j$&. The first sought number is therefore second j, third 7. Thus I arrive at what was at first proposed, 157464 v ' 3 X 183 , s s $sO3$ — 15s 23625 xi. **Question 289**, 6y ikfr. Heath.

On what days of the year do our shadows move slowest and fastest in London? And at what times do they move

slowest and fastest on any day?
Answered by Mr. Heath.
It is evident, that, when the sun's motion is most vertical, his increase of azimuth is least, and consequently of altitude greatest; and when his motion is most horizontal, his increase of azimuth greatest, and of altitude least.

At 12 each day, the sun's motion is parallel to the horizon, or least vertical, buing then perpendicular to the meridian, or vertical circle: therefore the circular motion of shadows, in general, is at noon the fastest.

To find when the increase of azimuth is least on any day, afid in any place.

Put/) — s. 0p, the sun's distance from the pole; d — its cos. or sine of declination; c s. Zp; b — its cos or s. of latitude; y s. azim. Qzp. Now if $rQom$ be the semi-diurnal arc of a lesser circle, it is evident that the sun's motion is most vertical when angle oQz is Kast, or its cos. Zqp greatest (the lesser circle coinciding, at the point 0, with a greater, at right angles with Qp); say, $p : y :: q: cy - p - a$ maximum, which is evidently when $y = 1$, the sine of 90. Whence, azimuth increases slowest and altitude fastest when the sun is due east, on all days, and in all places whatsoever; and therefore shadows in general move slowest when the sun is due east; or at sun-rise (the most easterly) in the southern declinations.

In the maximum cy-f-p, when p is least Cthe sine of 66 30' or 113 30') the azimuth on those days increases the slowest of all other days, and altitude fastest: Whence, our shadows move slowest of all on the longest and shortest days of the year: the sun due east, or at rising. But when/) — 1, the increase of azimuth, on that day, is least slow (at sun due E.) and the increase of altitude the least fast; and as the azimuth increases its swiftness till noon, therefore our shadows move fastest of all at noon, on the day of the year when the sun is in the equinoctial.

By ereciing a wire perpendicular to an horizontal plane,.and. marking the circular increase of the shadow at equal distances of time, the truth of the foregoing will appear by inspection. And by this circular motion, and the shortening'one of the shadow, or by the increase of azimuth and altitude together, the summit of it is made to describe a curve, whose nature is determinable according to the latitude of the place and sun's declination.

N. B. The increase of azimuth being always as the angle t0z, and the increase of altitude as its comp. the *£oQt,* the sum of both increases (viz. of aziin. and alt.) will be at all times and all places alike; *i.e.* the sum of the circular and shortening motions of shadows on a horizontal plane will be every where equal.

The increase of an azimuth is but the fluxion of it, and the slowest increase of an azimuth is but the least fluxion of that fluxion of azimuth; therefore if the angle of time be substituted for (which flows equally) and an expression be raised of the azimuth angle (by trigon. and series) the fluxion of that fluxion made = 0 will exhibit an equation, shewing the azimuth properties as aforesaid.

Otherwise by the Rev. Mr. Cha. Wildbore, *from Dr.* Hutton' *Edition of the Diaries.*

'Tis manifest from my solution to the 654th diary question, that at all places within the polar circles, the velocity of the shadow of the summit of an object, increases from passing due north (or south in the Antartic) till it attains the maximum there determined, after which the velocity continually decreases till noon, when it is the least possible. And with regard to the different greatest velocity on different days, 'tis evident that the expression for the maximum Fes X Pe X $rs + vb$ — rp X Pe x $rs - vb + rv$ will continually increase, by increasing rs or diminishing the declination; consequently the greatest velocity on the longest day will be less than the maximum on any other day: the said maximum increasing till its time and that of rising coincide, when it will be infinite

There is likewise a time in problems of this kind, when the velocity of the shadow, after being the greatest, decreases the fastest which may be found *by* taking the second fluxion of the above maximum =: 0. But in our latitude both these times coincide at sunrising, when the velocity being always infinite, decreases, and that more and more slowly till noon, when it is always the least possible. And the same may much more be said of the velocity with which the altitude alone increases. As to the velocity with which the azimuth alone increases, what Mr. Simpson has done upon the subject is right; for it must increase the slowest when the fluxion of the hour angle p bears the greatest ratio possible to that of the azimuth z, the reason for which is no more, than if any small distance i be divided by the time x -r v in which it is gone over, it will give v the velocity of uniform motion at that time. Therefore the fluxion of the azimuth, divided by that of the time, must give the velocity with which the azimuth increases at that time, or CS ® (vide my

's.z0' solution above referred to) P--5 — or (because ao — — J rs. Eo. ao Ep/ pft.PE5 — rp. Pe vb—rp.PE... TM..,... ; or s is a minimum. Which will evi Pe — 1 Pe" — 1 dently be less, the greater rp the sine of declination is taken; and therefore the longer the days are, the less will the slowest increase of azimuth be, and consequently it will be less on the longest day than on any other day. Moreover, when the sun is in the equinoc

"*vb* tial, the minimum becoming —*t* - will ba less as Pe is greater, and therefore will be the least possible when Pe is greatest, and the altitude 0, or at sunrising; therefore on the equinoctial days the azimuth will increase the slowest at rising due east. Consequently when the declination is south, the minimum will be before sun-rising, and therefore in that case the azimuth will increase faster and faster from sun-rising till noon,- when it will in all cases increase the fastest, but on the shortest day slower than on any other day, and on the longest faster.

Xii. Question 290, *by Mr.* Bulman.

Being at a town in Kent, I observed three objects on the other side of the river Medway, (a castle, wind-mill, and spire) whose distances from one another are known: From the castle (the nearest object seen) to the spire, is 10 furlongs; from the castle to the windmill 23 furlongs; and from the wind-mill to the spire is 25 furlongs. I also observed the town angle between the castle and spire zz 28 34', and the town angle between the castle and wind-mill = 57 45'. What distance did I stand from each of those objects? And give a geometrical construction of the same.

Answered by Mr. J. Ash.

The Acsw being formed, make Zwsd = 57" 45', and Zbws = 28 34'; then circumscribe A Swd with a circle: draw Dt through c, and the point T is the town's situation. From whence by trigonometry, Tc 0-65707, iw = 23-3439, and Ts = 10-5721 fere.

See also question 100.

Xiii. Question 291, *bij Mr.* J. Ash.

A lady of important speculation, Would gladly know her age from this equation.

1-05-. 1 —-05/ A xiv. Question 292, *by Mr. Heath.*

Suppose a person has a legacy left him, such, that the pounds power of Napier's logarithm thereof, is equal to the shillings in the legacy raised to the power denoted by Napier's logarithm of tha pounds: what is the amount of the legacy?

Answered by Mr. J. Turner.

Put a:=the pounds of the legacy; then (1. x)x — (20x)'' x per question; or putting b — 2-30258 kc. (b 1. xf — (20)1 x by common logarithms: And by a few trials x— 15-615 = 151. 12s. 3d. required.

xv. Question 293, *by Mr.* Bulman.

A spheroidal ullage lies upon the ground with the bung uppermost, from whence to the surface of the liquor (which is exactly the height of the upper ends of the cask) is 9 inches, and its diagonal either way from the bung to the lower ends — 55 inches, its ullage is a maximum: Qucre the content of the cask and ullage, brother gaugers?

Answered by Mr. Heath

As the contained liquor always bears a proportion considerably greater than the vacuity, in the several variations of the form of the cask (which supposing but 2 to 1) the greater the vacuity, the greater will be the quantity of liquor, and consequently the sum of both; therefore when the ullage is a maximum, the whole cask will be also a maximum.

First, *to find the content of spheroidal frustums.* Let t — Tt, the transverse; b— Bg, the conjugate of the generating ellipsis; and $x =$

Cl. By the property of the curve, $tt: bb :: — xx : —$ flux. frust. Bgdhb (n being XX; in which substitute 7854) whose fluent is nx x

., t $ibb + hh$

ing for tt, we have nx X 1 the content Bgdhb, which holds true when it is the segment or frustum of a sphere.

Theorem. Multiply the length of any spheroidal cask into the sum of twice the square of the bung diameter added to the square of the head diameter, and that product multiplied by-2618 will give the content in inches; or divided instead by 1077'! 58, or 8823529 will give the content in ale or wine gallons: or multiply instead by 00092837, or- 0011333, &c. proved also in Diary, p. 45, 1747). But, by above / =z /(bb—hh) — 874207; whence the content of the frustum or segment Hbh — 3499 gallons; consequently 384-322 ale gallons of liquor remain in the cask.

The principle of the above solution is not accurately true, but only an approximation, as will appear from the following *Solution by the Rev. Mr. Wildbore, taken from the Appendix to Dr. Hutton' Edition of the Diaries.*

In the original solution to this question, it is said that the greater the vacuity, the greater will be the quantity of liquor, and consequently the sum of both; therefore when the ullage is a max. the whole cask will be also a max. But this method of reasoning is not altogether to be depended on: for retaining the notation there given, viz. x Dm — Gt, d — Bd, and c — Bi; then the conjugate semiaxis of the surface of the liquor, being the semi-ordinate passing through t of the circle whose diam. is Bo, must be = $/cx$; whence, $(x—$ c being the head, $x + c$ the bung diam. Z/(dd— $xx)$ — the length of the cask, and/) =: 314159) by Button's Mensuration, pa. 278 and 287, we have p X $(3xx + 2cr +$ $3aa)$ /(dd — $xx)$ — the $3ccx$ 4-cs content of the whole cask, and £p X — $f(dd— xx)$ = that of the empty part; consequently the diff. of these two must be the ullage.

But these expressions are so very different, that it is evident at first sight that the one will not be a max. when the other is so; and consequently their diff. cannot be a max. when either of them is so. But the question expressly requires the ullage to be a max. and though this, by reason of the smallncss of the vacuity in this particular case, be nearly a max. when the cask is a max. it will not be exactly so; and cases may be put iu which they will be very different: and in tlie present, though there be but little difference in the content, the form of the cask will come out considerably different, when the ullage is a max. from what it does when the cask *'3v* is so. Thus, putting cx — vv, when the ullage is a max. then + 2bp + 3cc — $3cs$ — $f(dd$ — V is so; the fluxion, rc „. 9, 4cV eV-2d¥ — c4, cV 2fcV tluccd gives $v +$ —-— ;—v xvi. Question 294, *by Mr.* Chr. Mason.

In an evening lately, hearing the noise of guns at a small distance off at sea, I straight repaired to the strand, where I loomed a man of war's tender giving chace to a French privateer; I perceived a flash of a gun from the tender S.W. by S. at 33 half seconds of time heard the report: Eight minutes after T observed another flash at S.S.W. from the same, and at 25 half seconds heard the report. The chase kept her course, making equal way; in 35 minutes more was drove on shore, being but two minutes of time a-head of the tender. What was the bearing and distance between my station, the tender, and the pilfering poltroon when stranded?

Aimcered by Mr. T. Cowpcr.

Let D and T be the places of the tender at the first and second observations; t and p the places of the tender and privateer when the latter is Td stranded; and s the station of the ob. server. By the quest. £tsd = 11 15', and sound moving 1142 feet per second, Sd zz 18843 feet, and St = 14275; whence by trigon. Td Zz 5586, and £sto 3 41 £!'. Now the interval *jr* between the first and second flashes at

D, and T, being 8' 16//, and from the flash at T, till the privateer was drove ashore at p, by the tender at *t*, 35' 12 j"; by proportion of motion, *it* will be found 23767-22, and *to* = 1350-09 feet. Whence *£oU* — 80 31/, the bearing of the tender about E. by S. dist. *st* — 3-04061 miles; also the Zosp = 84 107, the privateer's bearing about E. S. dist. Sp — 3-2514 miles required.

The Prize Question, *by Mr.* Bamfield.

If the diameter of Sysiphus's cylindrical Stone be two feet, which he continually rolls upon the surface of a semiglobular mountain, half a mile high.- Quere what space will a spot on the convex surface of that stone travel through in rolling directly up and down the said mountain? And what will be the time of its descent from the top by the force of gravity?

Anszcered by Mr. J. Landen.

Let *yid* be perpendicular to the epicycloid *AMin*, and *md* another perpendicular supposed infinitely near the former; then the concentric arches *yib, mc*, being described from the centre r of the immovable circle; the chords *cb, cc* of the moyeable one will be respectively — *Mo, mn*.

From the centre *d* (the point where the perpendiculars -*yid*, *md* touch the evolute) describe the small arch *nv;* and the small right lines *be, ce*, being considered as small arches, described from their respective centres A and c; the small rightangled triangles *bee, vno*, will be similar and equal; *be* being = *no*, and *ce* — *no*; .-. cc: *dn*:: /.*ndv*: *cce*. But *ndv* — *nvo+cce. And* calling Ac, *a* — 2; Cd, *b* — 2640 feet; Ab, *x;* we get *nd* — a spot on the convex surface of the stone will go through in one revolution (when $x = a = 2$) = 4 001515, &c. Consequently 8-00303, &c. feet is the whole space described at each revolution; and the stone revolving exactly 1320 times, going up and down the mountain, the whole space gone through by the spot will be 10564 feet, or 2 00075 &c. miles.

Removing the stone to the next point from the vertex, the gravity will make it descend along the side of the mountain, till its velocity, in an horizontal direction, is the greatest it can acquire; when it will fly off, and descend to the bottom, in the curve of a parabola. Putting *a* — 2640 feet, the mountain's height, *x* — dist. perp. descended, s — feet, a space perp. descended in the 1st second of time, then /*s* : 2s:: /*x* : 2/*sx* the velocity in the curve, which is to the velocity in an horizontal direction, as the tan *a* 2/*s* gent is to the ordinate, i. e. —:1 :: *lsx*: *(aax— (l x u, luxx + x3)* the velocity in a direction parallel to the horizon, whose fluxion reduced is $xx - + - 0$, wliere $x - fyz$ the distance descended when the stone ceases to touch the mountain.

QX

The velocity-2/*sx* applied to —— r-, the fluxion of the arc, gives —— X —*rr*— r the fluxion of time, whose fluent

'6 2 2y'(2a '' *Ja,. Ja x 3x* ,S 5727 X l0§-*X* + iTii X ' 2X« + 2.2.4.2V + 32 46 2V &c = 31"Ohen $x = ia)$-If t0 which 6" 18'" the time of descending through the parabolical arch, be added, the sum is 37" 18"', the whole time of descent required j and the stone will fall 326 feet from the foot of the mountain.

Mr. Stone observes in his Mathematical Dictionary, that "as semidiam. resting circle: sum diameters of both circles:: double sine of half the arc, touching the circle at rest: length of the part of the epicycloid described by a point in the revolving circle; if upon the convexity of the resting circle. But if upon the concavity; as semi, diam. resting circle, to the difference of diameters of the touching circle."

In a semi-revolution, 180 of the moving circle touched the circle at rest; the double sine of its half arc = 2 (its rad. being unity); v 2640: 5282:: 2: 4-001515, &c. = half the epicycloidal curve, as before.

CPSIA information can be obtained at www.ICGtesting.com
Printed in the USA
BVOW03s0204100614

355830BV00028B/476/P